D1522620

SENSITIVE PERIODS IN DEVELOPMENT:
Interdisciplinary Perspectives

CROSSCURRENTS IN CONTEMPORARY PSYCHOLOGY

A series of volumes edited by Marc H. Bornstein
New York University

SENSITIVE PERIODS IN DEVELOPMENT:
Interdisciplinary Perspectives

Edited by

MARC H. BORNSTEIN
NEW YORK UNIVERSITY

LEA LAWRENCE ERLBAUM ASSOCIATES, PUBLISHERS
1987   Hillsdale, New Jersey   London

Lawrence Erlbaum Associates, Inc., Publishers
365 Broadway
Hillsdale, New Jersey 07642

Library of Congress Cataloging-in-Publication Data

Sensitive periods in development.

    (Crosscurrents in contemporaryy psychology)
    Includes bibliographies and index.
    1. Developmental psychobiology.   2. Critical periods
(Biology) I. Bornstein, Marc H.   II. Series. [DNLM:
1. Behavior, Animal.   2. Critical Period (Psychology).
3. Human Development.   4. Neurobiology. BF 713 S478]
QP360.S46   1987   155.2   86-29042
ISBN 0-89859-696-3

Printed in the United States of America
10 9 8 7 6 5 4 3 2 1

For Two Scientists

Anthony A. Wright
and
Charles G. Gross

Series Prologue

CROSSCURRENTS IN CONTEMPORARY PSYCHOLOGY

Contemporary psychology is increasingly diversified, pluralistic, and specialized, and most psychologists venture beyond the confines of their substantive specialty only rarely. Yet psychologists with different specialties encounter similar problems, ask similar questions, and share similar concerns. Unfortunately, there are very few arenas available for the expression or exploration of what is common across psychological subdisciplines. The *Crosscurrents in Contemporary Psychology* series is intended to serve as such a forum.

The chief aim of this series is to provide integrated perspectives on supradisciplinary themes in psychology. The first volume in the series was devoted to a consideration of *Psychological Development from Infancy;* the second volume to *Comparative Methods in Psychology;* volumes 3, 4, and 5 examined relations between *Psychology and Its Allied Disciplines* in the humanities, social sciences, and natural sciences. This volume concerns itself with sensitive periods. Future volumes in this series will focus on interaction as an independent variable in psychological research and on the segmentation of behavior. Thus, each volume in this series treats a different issue and is self-contained, yet the series as a whole endeavors to interrelate psychological subdisciplines by bringing shared perspectives to bear on a variety of concerns common to psychological theory and research. As a consequence of this structure and the flexibility and scope it affords, volumes in the *Crosscurrents in Contemporary Psychology* series will appeal, individually or as a group, to psychologists with widely diverse interests. Reflecting the nature and intent of this series, contributing authors are drawn from a broad spectrum of humanities and sciences — anthropology to zoology — but representational emphasis is placed on active contributing authorities to the contemporary psychological literature.

Crosscurrents in Contemporary Psychology is a series whose explicit intent is to explore a broad range of crossdisciplinary concerns. In its focus on such issues, the series is devoted to promoting interest in the interconnectedness of research and theory in psychological study.

Marc H. Bornstein
Editor

Contributors to This Volume

C. Robert Almli, *Departments of Anatomy and Neurobiology, Washington University School of Medicine, St. Louis, Missouri 63110*

Charles Annecillo, *Departments of Psychiatry and Pediatrics, The Johns Hopkins University and Hospital, Baltimore, Maryland 21205*

Patrick Bateson, *Department of Zoology, Cambridge University, Cambridge CB3 8AA, England*

Benjamin Beit-Hallahmi, *Department of Psychology, University of Haifa, Haifa 31999, Israel*

Elliott M. Blass, *Department of Psychology, The Johns Hopkins University, Baltimore, Maryland 21218*

Marc H. Bornstein, *Department of Psychology, New York University, New York, New York 10003*

Stanley Finger, *Department of Psychology, Washington University, St. Louis, Missouri 63130*

Robert A. Hinde, *MRC Unit on the Development and Integration of Behaviour, Cambridge University, Madingley, Cambridge CB3 8AA, England*

Helmut V. B. Hirsch, *Department of Biology, State University of New York, Albany, New York 12222*

Howard S. Hoffman, *Department of Psychology, Bryn Mawr College, Bryn Mawr, Pennsylvania 19010*

John Money, *Departments of Psychiatry and Pediatrics, The Johns Hopkins University and Hospital, Baltimore, Maryland 21205*

Barbara J. Myers, *Department of Psychology, Virginia Commonwealth University Richmond, Virginia 23284*

J. P. Scott, *Department of Psychology, Tufts University, Medford Massachusetts 02155*

Catherine Snow, *Graduate School of Education, Harvard University, Cambridge, Massachusetts 02138*

Catherine Tamis-LeMonda, *Department of Psychology, New York University, New York, New York 10003*

Suzannah Bliss Tieman, *Department of Biology, State University of New York, Albany, New York 12222*

Contents

AND HUMAN NEUROPSYCHOLOGY

3. Perceptual Development and Experience-Dependent
    Changes in Cat Visual Cortex
    Helmut V.B. Hirsch and Suzannah Bliss Tieman...................... **39**

      Introduction   39
      Visual Development in the Cat   40
      Activity-Dependent Development in Area 17   49
      Behavioral Significance of Experience-Dependent Brain
        Development   58
      Conclusions   70
      References   70

4. Critical Events During Sensitive Periods of Social
    Development in Rats
    Elliott M. Blass.. **81**

      Introduction   81
      The Setting   85
      Suckling   85
      Huddling Behavior   88
      Home Orientation   89
      Sexual Behavior   90
      Conclusions   92
      References   95

5. Imprinting and the Critical Period for Social Attachments:
    Some Laboratory Investigations
    Howard S. Hoffman.. **99**

      Introduction   99
      Laboratory Investigations of Imprinting   100
      The Motivational Substrate for Imprinting   114
      Conclusions   118
      References   119

6. Neural Insult and Critical Period Concepts
    C. Robert Almli and Stanley Finger.. **123**

      Introduction   123
      Conceptions and Definitions of Critical Periods   124
      Neural Maturation and Optimal/Sensitve Periods   127
      Recovery From Acute Brain Lesions   128
      Effects of Early Undernutrition   134
      Conclusions and Implications   138
      References   139

Preface

Despite its contemporary diversity and high degree of specialization, psychology embraces many phenomena that are of interest across subdisciplines largely because of the generality and ubiquity of those phenomena. The *sensitive period* is one. Sensitivity to different kinds of experience varies over the life cycle of an organism. It has been found time and again and in widely different structural and functional systems that the presence or absence of certain experiences at particular times in the life span influences that system well beyond the time that they first occur. Examples of sensitive period effects may be found in neurobiology, animal behavior, and human development. Monocular deprivation during a sensitive period in the development of vision in the kitten results in anatomical degeneration of visual pathways innervated by the deprived eye and a concomitant domination of cortical physiology by the nondeprived eye. Likewise, deprivation of "contact comfort" during a sensitive period in the first year of life in rhesus monkey results in maladjustment of normal mature social behaviors. Similarly, inculcation of a "sense of trust" in the sensitive infancy period of human development is theorized to be critical to the differentiation of a healthy adult personality.

This range of application notwithstanding, several common issues about sensitive periods arise across subfields, as sensitive periods have been found to share several characteristics. They include: (a) the need for operationalization of parameters and the dissociation of sensitive periods from other continuous developmental sequences; (b) genetic preparation and constraints versus environmental controls over sensitive periods; (c) temporal features of sensitive periods, including age of onset and offset, duration, and frequency over the life span; (d) the necessary and sufficient conditions that give rise to sensitive periods; (e) the enduring quality and reversibility of sensitive period effects; and (f) the meaning and function of sensitive periods for development.

Can the principles of sensitive periods clarified by students of one system be useful to students of other systems? An important lesson of modern science is that the coordination of different disciplines over a given phenomenon usually contributes toward the comprehensive understanding of that phenomenon. Thus, the purposes of this volume of interdisciplinary perspectives on *Sensitive Periods in Development* are to bring together contributions in neurobiology, animal behavior, and human development and to take advantage of the variety of perspectives that result from such a convergence to achieve greater insight into this special and ubiquitous developmental event. *Sensitive Periods in Development* makes available to the psychological community essays that examine the expression, investigation, and meaningfulness of this widespread psychological phenomenon. The chapters in this collection introduce students of psychology to sensitive periods from the perspectives of prominent contributors and are intended to promote mutual discussion among investigators in different subfields of psychology concerned with issues and principles common to as well as varying across different domains in which sensitive periods recur. These essays focus on an individual author's own work, but also enlarge in scope to encompass sensitive periods in the systems with which each contributor is intimately specialist. The value of this volume rests on the assumption that our understanding of sensitive periods per se can advance from thoroughgoing assessment of the phenomenon at different levels of analysis.

No volume could be comprehensive in its coverage of sensitive periods in development. Unhappily, some well-known examples of the phenomenon had to be omitted from this collection, among them perception and production in song bird and the influence of exogenous stimulation on physical growth. The inevitable result is a less rich and textured treatment. Nevertheless, the essays presented here go far to summarize, examine, interpret, and evaluate a sufficiently wide and representative variety of instances of sensitive periods to satisfy specialist and generalist alike.

The chapters in *Sensitive Periods in Development: Interdisciplinary Perspectives* are organized into three sections. Part I makes introductory observations and systematically sketches topics that need to be considered in first broaching and evaluating sensitive periods. Part II, on Sensitive Periods in Infrahuman Psychobiology and Human Neuropsychology, includes perspectives from visual system neurobiology, affiliation and attachment, and recovery from brain insult as well as the dynamics of psychoendocrinological function. Part III, on Sensitive Periods in Human Psychology, includes perspectives from the development of thinking, language, personality, bonding, and social organization. As a whole, this collection fits the theme of its parent series, *Crosscurrents in Contemporary Psychology,* in that it is devoted to intensive and comprehensive examination of an issue that crosses traditionally separate psychological subdisciplines.

Several individuals aided in the preparation of this volume. Among them I would like especially to thank H. G. Bornstein, E. Fields, D. Morris, and I. Seguí.

Marc H. Bornstein

SENSITIVE PERIODS IN DEVELOPMENT: INTERDISCIPLINARY PERSPECTIVES

1 Sensitive Periods in Development: Definition, Existence, Utility, and Meaning

Marc H. Bornstein
New York University

INTRODUCTION

Scientists who study psychological structures or functions from all but an entirely static perspective, and in particular those who are interested in origins and development, inevitably confront the truism that their phenomena are shaped by both endogenous and exogenous forces interacting through time. Moreover, it is now commonplace to find phases in the development of many different psychological structures and functions that are unique in the evolving transaction between these two life forces. At certain times in their life cycles, many structures and functions become particularly susceptible to specific experience (or to the absence of that experience) in a way that then alters some future instantiation of that structure or function. So, during such *sensitive periods in development* specific experiences dramatically influence eventual outcomes.

   Sensitive periods are meaningful across many subdisciplines of psychology, but particularly to developmental psychology, for several reasons. First, sensitive periods evidence the extraordinary influence of experience in development and on the mature psychological nature of an organism. Second, the fact that sensitivity to experience waxes and wanes through the life span gives clear evidence of the interactional nature of development. Third, the demonstration of sensitive periods in the life course evinces discrete stages in development. Fourth, the fact that specifiable early experiences may have far-reaching consequences in the life span renders the sensitive period of potentially great practicable significance. For these reasons, sensitive periods have been the subject of intensive empirical and theoretical scrutiny since their earliest discovery.

3

Sensitive periods were identified first in experimental embryology: certain cell masses were found to be affected by intruding chemicals during a particular stage in their ontogeny but not earlier or later, and certain cells transplanted at a particular time in ontogeny were found to assume the characteristics of host location cells and thrive, but wither if transplanted at times preceding and following. Soon, however, sensitive periods came to be implicated in a plethora of fields central to psychological inquiry: Sensitive periods have been uncovered in studies of brain and bodily growth and function across the phylogenetic series as well as in studies of survival and social behavior in animals and of cognitive and social competence amongst human beings.

In this volume, specialists from several fields of psychology whose work has led them to an interest in sensitive periods contribute essays that define and explain the psychological nature of the sensitive periods they study and how those sensitive periods relate to larger psychological concerns. The contributions collected herein are noteworthy for many reasons, not the least significant of which is their demonstration of the range of psychological phenomena that profitably submit to a sensitive period conceptualization. Given so broad a sweep of theoretical interest and scope of experimental investigation, it would be natural to expect a certain heterogeneity of focus and perhaps of definition about the sensitive period, as previous reviewers of the event have astutely noted (e.g., Bateson, 1979; Colombo, 1982; Immelmann & Suomi, 1981; Oyama, 1979; Scott, 1978). In fact, the typical style of investigators of sensitive periods historically has been to devote attention to the intersection of a particular species and a particular topic — cocoon preference in ant, aggression in mouse, imprinting in duck, cortical specificity in cat, sociability in dog, emotionality in monkey, language acquisition in human being — resulting inevitably in a remarkably diverse and daunting literature. A conclusion of this intensive study is that sensitive periods reflect idiosyncratic multifaceted phenomena.

Moreover, a concomitant of life and work in a field as conceptually deep and empirically broad as the sensitive period is inevitable misattribution, misconstrual, and misconception — even of first principles. For example, what shall the thing be called? The term "critical" has clear historical precedent, but derives from an early time when an absolutist and doctrinaire set of values defined the most important parameters of the phenomenon. Later, "critical" was replaced by the relative, less constraining and dogmatic term "sensitive." Some theorists along the way have attempted to retain the two terms, reserving critical to timed experiential interactions necessary for normal development of a system or to experiential interactions that stimulate normal development, and applying sensitive to timed experiential interactions in which the organism displays especial susceptibility generally or particular vulnerability to noxious stimuli. Others have invoked contrasting terms like "optimal" and "vulnerable." Such distinctions have proven troubled (and troublesome), however, and are not altogether straightforward. In actuality, no investigator today subscribes to the strong form, and the terms critical and sensitive are used universally, interchangeably, and generically.

The astonishing diversity and disparateness of substantive content areas that typifies sensitive period study notwithstanding, the psychological and biological investigators who contribute to this volume acknowledge a common set of characteristics that define the structure of the sensitive period they study as well as a common set of causal interpretations that guide thinking about the nature of their sensitive period. To be sure, these and other investigators of sensitive periods often treat both structural characteristics and causal interpretations implicitly. In some sense, the pluralistic organization of sensitive period research, usually designed around the close specification of selected examples or features, has unfolded so as to obscure an underlying unified framework common among approaches to the sensitive period. However, sensitive periods reflect a developmental event impressive for its supradisciplinary unity and coherence just because of this identifiable set of meta-issues of structure and interpretation that transcend individual variations.

The sensitive period as a psychological and biological concept initially underwent detailed description in widely diverse systems, followed immediately by intensive experimentation; both efforts were organized to quantify parameters of its various manifestations. The concept failed to reach the next-expected high level of theoretical development, however, perhaps on account of the rich variety of individual types and scattered literatures in which they appeared. Alternatively, perhaps, descriptions of sensitive periods, however detailed, and experiments on sensitive periods, however defining, have insufficiently framed overarching issues of structural character and causal interpretation. It is possible, however, to build a framework that makes explicit common structural characteristics definitive of sensitive periods and common causal interpretations integral to an understanding of the deeper nature of this significant developmental event.

STRUCTURAL CHARACTERISTICS

Among the first questions that arises about a sensitive period is *what* are its particular structural characteristics. Early theoretical overviews identified and discussed five parameters of its structure, viz. onset, terminus, intrinsic and extrinsic factors that specify, respectively, the triggering maturational event in the organism and the influential experiential event outside the organism, and the organismic system that is affected by stimulation during the sensitive period. In actuality, however, the sensitive period is described by at least seventeen operationally definable characteristics. These seventeen may be categorized into two sets: twelve distinguish the sensitive period at the time that it occurs, plus five distinguish the sensitive period in terms of its consequences. Thus, a sensitive period at a given point in the life cycle is demarcated by contours of its actual appearance as well as by reference to an outcome. As is clear in the chapters that follow, the empirical operationalization of both sets of parameters is requisite to a comprehensive and systematic understanding of any particular sensitive period, and perhaps of sensitive periods generally.

Consider a "system" to specify the organismic structure or function that is the subject of a sensitive period. The first set of characteristics defines the sensitive period when it occurs, and each individual characteristic must be specified with several values.

(1) *Onset,* i.e., the rise time of sensitivity. What is the growth slope of the sensitivity function? Is it a step function or gradual, and is it linear? How do rise times vary among systems? How ought onset best be characterized, qualitatively or quantitatively? In terms of absolute time, or developmental time as a proportion of the life cycle of the system? Is the system sensitive during the onset, or only after it achieves an asymptote of maximal sensitivity?

(2) *Asymptote,* i.e., the degree and direction of change and uniformity of system sensitivity during the sensitive period relative to system sensitivity outside the sensitive period. By how much is the sensitivity of the system reset during this period? Is the sensitivity threshold always lowered during this period, or can it also be raised? Is the maximum of sensitivity constant, or does it fluctuate during this period?

(3) *Duration,* i.e., the temporal phase of altered sensitivity. How long does the system remain at its asymptote of maximal sensitivity? How ought duration best be characterized, qualitatively or quantitatively? In terms of absolute time, or developmental time as a proportion of the life cycle of the system? Does duration begin at the onset and end at the offset of the sensitive period, or is duration confined to a time of maximal sensitivity?

(4) *Offset,* i.e., the decay time of sensitivity. What is the slope of decline of the sensitivity function? Is it a step function or gradual, and is it linear? How do declines vary among systems? How ought offset best be characterized, qualitatively or quantitatively? In terms of absolute time, or developmental time as a proportion of the life cycle of the system? Is the system sensitive during the offset, or only until the end of an asymptote of maximal sensitivity?

(5) *Developmental timing,* i.e., the point in the life cycle of the system when the sensitive period occurs and the frequency of such occurrences in the life span. When in the developmental life course of the system does the sensitive period occur? How frequently does it recur? How shall developmental

timing be specified, qualitatively or quantitatively? In terms of absolute time or developmental time? Shall it be specified in conceptional age or in postnatal age?

(6) *System,* i.e., the organismic structure or function that is the subject of the sensitive period, and specification as to whether it is directly observable or only inferrable. What system is directly affected during the sensitive period? Is whatever is affected itself measurable, or must it be inferred from change that is observed later?

(7) *Mechanism,* i.e., the process that regulates the sensitive period and (presumably) determines parameters of onset, asymptote, duration, and offset of sensitivity of a particular system with respect to a particular experience. By what action(s) does the sensitive period arise, endure, and decay? Is this action monistic, or does it vary vis-à-vis onset, outcome, etc. Is it endogenously or exogenously driven?

(8) *Experience,* i.e., the effective stimulus event (or nonevent) in the sensitive period, its specific or nonspecific nature, its duration and intensity, and its exogenous or endogenous origin. What features of the stimulus are effective in a sensitive period; that is, what stimulus matters in the phenomenology of the system, as opposed to that of the experimenter? Are the presence and absence of the stimulus equally meaningful? To what degree is the effective stimulus particular, or will any stimulus bring about an equivalent outcome? How long must the stimulus be present (or absent), and if present how intense must it be to be effective? What proportion of the duration of sensitivity is the duration of experience effectiveness? From where does the experience arise, outside the system or within the system itself?

(9) *Pathway,* i.e., the means by which experience affects the system. By what chemical, neural, or sensory channels does experience connect with the system during the sensitive period?

(10) *Specialty,* i.e., the uniqueness of processes functioning and effects obtained during the sensitive period in contrast with identical processes and effects occurring outside the sensitive period. In the development of a system, how exclusive is the sensitive period "interaction" in terms of the actions and outcomes of system and experience?

(11) *Variability,* i.e., the range of intraspecific individual differences and the degree of interspecies variance in onset, asymptote, duration, offset, developmental timing, system, mechanism, experience, pathway, and specialty for a given sensitive period. What are the species-modal values for the several parameters of the sensitive period? How do values for individual members of a species compare to population central tendencies? Since it may occur that individuals each gives a discrete value for a parameter but at different times, over ages is the group function for the parameter abrupt and representative of individuals or continuous and unrepresentative? Is the distribution of individual differences meaningful?

Finally,

(12) *Modifiability,* i.e., the degree to which onset, asymptote, duration, offset, developmental timing, system, mechanism, experience, pathway, and specialty of a sensitive period may be altered, and the age-graded nature of that flexibility. How modifiable is each of the parameters of a system's sensitive period? Does that modifiability vary at different developmental points in the life course of the system? Is the modifiability natural, must it be induced, or is it an epiphenomenon of testing procedures?

The second set of parameters provides evidence that a sensitive period has occurred by its effects. It includes:

(1) *Locus,* i.e., the later developing structure or function affected by experience sustained during the sensitive period. What molecular, physiological, or behavioral aspect of the system is influenced by experience during the sensitive period? Is the result anomalous, or is it typical of the species?

(2) *Outcome,* i.e., the eventual result of alteration in the affected system. How does the influence of experience during the sensitive period manifest itself? Is the experiential effect induced (stimulating emergence of the outcome), attuned (altering ongoing function or structure of the system), or maintained (continuing the status quo of the system)?

(3) *Outcome timing,* i.e., the temporal emergence of the effect following onsets of the sensitive period and of the critical experience. When in later development does the influence of experience manifest itself relative to the onset of the sensitive period and relative to the onset of the experience itself? Is the effect immediate, or is it a "sleeper?"

(4) *Duration,* i.e., the temporal nature of the sensitive period effect. How enduring is the outcome based on experience sustained during the sensitive period relative to an effect of the same experience sustained outside the sensitive period? What factors influence the longevity of the sensitive period effect?

Finally,

(5) *Reversibility,* i.e., the fixed quality of the sensitive period effect. How modifiable is the outcome based on experience sustained during the sensitive period relative to an effect of the same experience sustained outside the sensitive period? What factors influence the resistance of the sensitive period effect?

However diverse and idiosyncratic their subject matter, investigators of reliable sensitive periods like the ones collected here agree, first, on the existence, function, and importance of all of these parameters and, second, on the requisiteness of specifying them quantitatively. Essentially, therefore, a comprehensive statement about a sensitive period ought reasonably to include information about (1) how long it took to develop, (2) how sensitivity changed and whether the change was stable, (3) how long the sensitive period lasted, (4) how long it took to decay, (5) when and how often in the life cycle it occurred, (6) what was changed, (7) what process regulated the change, (8) what the effective stimulus was, (9) how that stimulus affected whatever changed, (10) whether the change was unique, (11) individual and species variation in the change, and (12) how fixed the sensitive period is. Moreover, such a statement ought to indicate (1) what in later development showed a change, (2) what the change was, (3) when it occurred, (4) how long it lasted, and (5) how fixed it was. In discussing their particular phenomena, all of the contributors to this volume in one way or another consider most, if not all, of these parameters.

This descriptive framework has several strict implications for research and theory in the sensitive period, beginning with the raison d'être of experimental contrasts. The research designs that dominate investigations of sensitive periods independent of content area are uniformly geared to specify one or more of these several characteristics. The literature abounds with specific examples of experimental and observational investigations of each. In typical experimental designs, investigators manipulate values of a given parameter, holding other parameters constant (to the degree possible), in order to determine the meaningful range of values for the parameter of interest. So, for example, in an experimental series a neuropsychologist might first expose several groups of animals to the same visual experience at random times in their ontogeny, later to assess the interaction of experience and developmental time on physiology and behavior in order to evaluate the nature of the developmental timing parameter of the sensitive period. In the next experiment, the neuropsychologist might then expose several groups of animals to different visual experiences at the same time in their ontogeny in order to evaluate the nature of the experience parameter in the sensitive period. And so forth. In the traditional observational approach, investigators evaluate the effects of conditions of rearing that naturally vary in onset time among different individuals, as for example when a neuropsychologist assesses the effects on language acquisition of cerebral insults sustained at different points in childhood. In so far as examining each parameter may require a separate group or treatment, not all might be deemed meritorious of so extensive a study. Further, parameter values are known to vary on account of different experimental designs and to reflect different empirical indexes: The fine-grainedness of analysis places limits on specifying developmental timing of visual system sensitivity; behavioral data suggest one parameter value for offset of the sensitive period in language deprivation, whereas physiological data suggest another; and, isolation versus communal rearing differentially alter variability in imprinting.

Despite impressive variation among individual cases, this framework of research has been used profitably to establish common quantitative values for different parameters of sensitive periods. In turn, this agreement has had nontrivial implications for making sense of the sensitive period. Developmental timing exemplifies one parameter about which many investigators in different substantive areas such as those reviewed in this volume have converged in assigning a value. Specifically, it has been found that sensitive periods tend to occur early in the ontogenetic history of many systems across many species, during prenatal development or in infancy in the life course of human beings for example. The value of cross-disciplinary use of the framework and agreement about particular parameter values cannot be overestimated in planning and evaluating research in sensitive periods. As noted, general experience indicates that sensitive periods tend to occur early in the life cycle of systems; this result in turn suggests that it is strategically efficient to search for sensitive periods in any new system by initially focussing on the infancy of that system. Such an approach essentially reduces the risk of missing and enhances the likelihood of payoff in finding a sensitive period.

Reciprocally, results that contradict general experience based on this research framework flag the need for close scrutiny. The question of a sensitive period for maternal bonding provides an illustration. In spite of how extraordinary and powerful an experience the birth of a child may be, claims for a systemic sensitive period for maternal bonding at parturition ought to have been greeted with reserve simply on the argument that the timing of sensitive periods has more often been localized to the infancy of a system than to its maturity. A priori, therefore, a sensitive period for mother-to-infant bonding constitutes a low probability event, and claims and desires to the contrary, contemporary research has largely failed to substantiate the existence of such a sensitive period. This conclusion does not mean that parameter characteristics outside general norms are unobtainable or even unheard of, but rather that investigators can and ought to avail themselves of common parameter values growing out of the research framework to predict and to evaluate new findings. Of course, such strategizing cannot be relied on exclusively as it may prove overly conservative; for example, wholly depending on general experience risks losing the potential reward to be reaped, say, from discovering a sensitive period in mature phases of the life cycle of a system.

As our contributors show, each sensitive period is constrained to a particular system sui generis. On this ground sensitive periods in different systems may behave differently, and systems vary in values assigned to defining parameters. Systematicity and accuracy, therefore, require working out of the research framework proposed. Thus, the possibility of interspecies comparison and concomitant understanding of cause only come into consideration as a result of exhaustive specification of these parameters. Sensitive periods for different systems extend for different durations: For example, hours for ducklings to imprint, days for birds to learn a song, weeks for canine socialization, months to ensure sexual normalcy in monkeys, and years in the case of human language learning. Likewise, sensitive periods for similar systems have been found to extend for different durations depending on the species: The sensitive period for visual binocularity endures weeks in cats, months in monkeys, and years in humans.

These kinds of variation may have been principally responsible historically for obfuscating a unified perspective on the sensitive period; however, that unified *perspective* to some degree depends on investigators' delimiting a unified *framework* for studying sensitive periods. Clearly, not all parameters of every sensitive period warrant investigation, nor do all research investigators meet the challenge of specifying parameter values for all characteristics of their sensitive period. However, investigators' witting or unwitting failure to explore parameter values comprehensively with such a framework in mind has time and again provoked consequential differences of opinion or of fact. For example, on account of the speed, rapidity, and permanence of the social attachments precocial ducklings were observed to form, Konrad Lorenz identified and described imprinting as a "critical period." Systematic investigation subsequent to Lorenz led to quantitative modification of his qualitative attributions about several aspects of the nature of imprinting — not insignificantly to reversals of his pronouncements on the abruptness, uniqueness, and modifiability of these time-bound attachments. Similarly, research reliance on correlational techniques and natural experiments in human sensitive period effects has often lacked proper experimental control at the expense of accuracy. For example, Eric Lenneberg speculated that the effects of language deprivation between 2 and 12 years would reverberate immutably in the child's inability to acquire and use language with facility later in life. But Lenneberg failed exhaustively to examine cases that would test his speculation about the duration parameter; such examples emerged later, as in the celebrated study of Genie, that undermined strong claims for the sensitive period in human language acquisition.

A framework of seventeen separate structural characteristics indigenous to sensitive periods can be identified. Implicitly or explicitly, all researchers confront the task of defining all of these characteristics; indeed, many researchers view the quantitative description of these parameters as a primary goal of studying sensitive periods. The specification of sensitive period characteristics is important in itself, as well as for understanding the origins of the phenomenon.

CAUSAL INTERPRETATIONS

Next to quantifying characteristics that define its structure, that aspect of the sensitive period that confronts, tantalizes, and mystifies investigators is identifying underlying causes. Questions of cause are of two types: One is *why* do sensitive periods arise in the first place, and the second is *how* specifically are they instigated. The sensitive period challenges researchers and theoreticians working in different systems with a conceptually complex and evolutionally rich phenomenon to explain, and one in which the significance of factors like nature, nurture, and their transaction are clearly at issue. Major points of contention and confusion reign with respect to varying interpretations of their evolutionary meaning (the "why" question) as well as varying attributions about the level at which sensitive periods obtain (the "how" question). As indicated, a complete treatment of the sensitive period at the descriptive level (the "what" question) is requisite to addressing each type of causal interpretation. The two causal questions are taken up in seriatim.

Ultimate Cause

From early experience, the sensitive period forecasts mature structure or function and thereby operates to buffer a system against later change in the self or in the environment. Clearly, such a powerful and pervasive developmental mechanism reflects an important adaptation in the evolutionary programme of an organism. Indeed, comprehensibility of the sensitive period improves when it is viewed as a successful form of adaptation: As has been pointed out after all, this phenomenon reflects a developmental phase of built-in competence for specific exchange between organism and environment. Like all adaptations, even homologous sensitive periods can be expected to vary among species with respect to their particular manifestations on account of different histories of natural selection of those species in their environments. Of course, sensitive periods are expected to be universal within a species, again because of their (partial) dependence on species-specific intrinsic maturational timetables.

Ethologists have been most concerned with addressing the why question, and they have been want to speculate upon so-called "ultimate causes," viz. those factors that affect survival and reproductive success of organisms which inhabit different niches. Presumably, ultimate causes are selected for in the natural history of the organism and eventuate in specific adaptations. Immelmann and Suomi (1981) viewed the sensitive period out of this evolutionary perspective, accounting thereby for species variation in parameter values of many structural characteristics of the sensitive period. Consider, for example, the duration parameter. Young animals must acquire critical social knowledge from conspecifics before leaving the family, and therefore sensitive periods for learning social behaviors must fall within the bounds of chronological times that the young are still with their mothers: Avian species spend considerably less time with their parents than do mammals, and therefore it is predictable that avian sensitive periods are shorter-lived than mammalian ones and that individual variation among birds is narrower than among mammals. As Immelmann and Soumi (1981) point out,

> . . . [I]n many species and for different functional systems, strong selection pressures that favor great sensitivity to certain environmental stimuli and a maximum of learning during early stages of life may well exist. They may also favor great stability of the results of such early experience, providing some kind of degree of protection against some later possible influences on the individual. *In addition, it becomes apparent that differences in such specific needs and demands between species are almost certainly responsible in large part for the enormous diversity in the degree of stability and in the duration and characteristics of sensitive phases.* (emphasis added) (p. 399)

On this account, it behooves researchers of sensitive periods to consider their phenomenon out of an evolutionary perspective, since taking such a stand may well enrich the researcher's understanding of individual structural characteristics as well as the greater meaningfulness of the sensitive period for the species in question.

Proximate Cause

Adaptive significance defines the ultimate cause of the sensitive period for a species generally. There also must exist corresponding "proximate causes" that regulate sensitivity to meet the aim of natural selection for sensitive periods. Examination of proximate cause addresses the "how" question.

It is understandable that pinpointing the mechanism of a natural interaction, such as the sensitive period is, challenges many investigators conceptually. It is not uncommon today to find that a simplistic reductionism permeates proximate cause theorizing about sensitive periods, so that (as can be seen in the chapters to follow) behavioral forms often immediately invoke explanations in terms of physiological substrates — language development is reducible to progressive hemispheric lateralization — just as physiological forms immediately invoke explanations in terms of molecular substrates — cortical plasticity is reducible to the presence or absence of neurohormones. Only systematic treatment can clarify the nature of cause and bring explicitness to deductions so common and seemingly necessary to theorizing about the sensitive period.

In Chapter 2, Patrick Bateson and Robert Hinde provide an all-important orientation to first principles of such theory about sensitive periods. Invoking a wide range of examples — physiological and behavioral, infrahuman and human — Bateson and Hinde distinguish and discuss two pertinent perspectives on sensitive periods. First, they delineate clearly the signal confounds of empirical designs typical of research in sensitive periods, and they point out the problems of proper inference that derive from stumbling into such pitfalls. Second, they take up the issue of causal ascription in sensitive period research, providing the important service of both classifying types of explanation and arguing the permissible limits of causal ascription bound up in each. Logically, sensitive period changes in the individual may be regulated by alterations at the molecular, the organismic, or the behavioral levels, operating alone or in concert.

Two caveats obtain in determining proximate cause for a sensitive period as given by change at one or more of these levels. First, although these explanations are operationalized distinctively, the attribution of causality is (somewhat) arbitrary, since as Bateson and Hinde point out, the levels of cause they imply are not (necessarily) mutually exclusive. Clearly, molecular change in the system can be a first cause for physiological change that effects the sensitive period, just as physiological change can induce molecular change that effects the sensitive period. The second caveat is that an explanation may apply at the time the sensitive period actually arises, or it may apply at an earlier time. For example, physiological change in a system could engender a sensitive period immediately, or physiological change could prepare a system for later provocation of the sensitive period. Some ambiguity must be expected in distinguishing an immediate cause from one displaced in the past. As a consequence of these two considerations, assigning monistic proximate cause in the domain of the sensitive period is hazardous. Theoretically, it ought to be possible to do so, however, even if these various explanations are hardly incompatible. Thus, it may be both desirable and feasible to contrast explanations at different levels experimentally to achieve insight into the greater aptness of one or the other. If, for example, programmed molecular change excites a sensitive period the system ought to display altered responsiveness independent of any behavioral expression.

In their overview of issues and methodology intrinsic to the identification of sensitive periods, Bateson and Hinde provide generalist guidelines that reader and researcher, novice and expert alike will do well to heed in approaching the phenomenon of the sensitive period. Their systematic treatment of types and levels of explanation succeeds admirably in bringing explicitness to implicit assumptions so common in theorizing in this field.

Altogether, causal classification calls for an investigator of a sensitive period to specify both the level and temporal characteristics of explanations believed best to apply in an instance case. Insight into proximate cause, along with some indication of ultimate cause will go far toward enlarging the scope of the investigator's understanding of the sensitive period of interest. Unfortunately, even these types of information are not complete. Even where there may be widespread empirical agreement about the value of a sensitive period characteristic and some indication of ultimate and proximate cause, there may still be no theoretical convergence about its conceptual source. To return to the example of developmental timing, different theoretical traditions propose different reasons why sensitive periods tend particularly to recur early in ontogeny. Maturational theory argues that the period of greatest susceptibility, vulnerability, or responsivity to stimulation in a system coincides with its period of most rapid growth, usually early in the life cycle; information theory posits that systems in a state of developmental flux, as is usually true early in ontogeny, are more open to influence than are fixed and organized systems; learning theory suggests that acquisition proceeds most efficaciously when there are no extant competing responses, the situation that necessarily characterizes the early life history of a system; and, cognitive developmental theory proposes that mature and complex capacities are constructed of simple elements that themselves first develop in infancy. Complete interpretation of cause in sensitive periods is a complicated and multifaceted issue.

CONCLUSIONS

Despite its contemporary diversity and high degree of specialization, psychology embraces many phenomena that are of interest across subdisciplines largely because of the generality and ubiquity of those phenomena. The *sensitive period in development* is one. Sensitivity to certain kinds of experience vacillates over the life cycle of an organism, and many examples have emerged in widely different structural or functional systems that the presence or absence of certain experiences at particular times in the life span may influence that system well beyond the time of the experience. Examples of sensitive periods may be found in animal and in human neurobiology and behavior. Proof of the extraordinary potential of the concept of the sensitive period is that it has been applied profitably, as evinced in this volume, to cells, to human beings, and to institutions.

Whatever their subfield, investigators of sensitive periods confront similar challenges, because all sensitive periods are described by a common set of characteristics and provoke the need for explanation. On these bases, a consensual system of overarching considerations about the sensitive period has developed. Clearly, the principles of sensitive periods clarified by students of one system can be useful to students of other systems. Yet, many investigators seem genuinely unaware of the relevance to their own work of sensitive periods unearthed in allied fields; indeed, some research and write as though oblivious to other manifestations of the phenomenon.

No sensitive period in one system has to be like that in any other, and no one sensitive period need serve as a model for others. There is no all-encompassing theory of *the* sensitive period. Many investigators and theoreticians have spent themselves in an elusive search for such a theory. It is possible, however, to derive a framework of structural characteristics and causal interpretations out of which to consider sensitive periods generally. In turn, that framework can prove valuable toward redefining theory and experiment in sensitive period research. Elucidating that framework is the subject of this introduction. A conceptual analysis of the sensitive period suggests that researchers actually need to specify seventeen different parameters of their particular sensitive period *and* to discuss both ultimate cause in terms of the evolutionary history of their system as well as proximate cause in terms of the level at which change in that system is believed to obtain. Perhaps no existing report of a sensitive period — the undeniable popularity of this phenomenon in many areas of biological and social science notwithstanding — meets the task of specifying all structural characteristics and causal interpretations.

Sections II and III of this volume examine substantive topics and applications of sensitive periods. Section II, on Sensitive Periods in Infrahuman Psychobiology and Human Neuropsychology, presents chapters by Helmut V. B. Hirsch and Suzannah Bliss Tieman on visual system development, Elliott Blass on suckling and affiliation, Howard Hoffman on imprinting and attachment, C. Robert Almli and Stanley Finger on brain insult, malnutrition, and recovery of function, and finally John Money and Charles Annecillo on psychoendocrinological function. Section III, on Sensitive Periods in Human Psychology, presents chapters by Catherine Tamis-LeMonda and Marc Bornstein on mental development, Catherine Snow on language development, Benjamin Beit-Hallahmi on personality development, Barbara Myers on mother-infant bonding, and J. P. Scott on social organization. Each section is introduced with a brief summary of chapters and a forecast of common themes that emerge in considering these different perspectives on the sensitive period.

The contributors to *Sensitive Periods in Development: Interdisciplinary Perspectives* were asked to place their own systematic lines of research at the center of broader thought pieces, bringing into their discussions background materials and other relevant studies, and relating their work to sensitive period research generally. What emerges is an intriguing and novel, sometimes counterintuitive, but comprehensive treatment of what is for psychology a familiar though fragmented phenomenon.

The demonstration of a sensitive period should not focus developmentalists' attention singlemindedly on one point in the life span either because of the attraction of what has been referred to as the "pleasing dactylic rhythm" of the term itself or its "exciting connotation of developmental brinksmanship." The notion of the sensitive period minimally implies that a certain experience at a certain time in the life cycle of a system may exert a dramatic effect on the future developmental course of that system. Research shows, however, that events subsequent to the sensitive period may intervene to modify or undo earlier effects or it may be in the character of the system itself to change at later points in development. As is widely recognized, every time period in the life course is somehow critical; nevertheless, theory and data indicate that some periods in life may be more critical than others. Those periods constitute our subject of study.

ACKNOWLEDGMENTS

M.H.B. was supported by research grants (HD20559 and HD20807) and by a Research Career Development Award (HD00521) from the National Institute of Child Health and Human Development. Preparation of this chapter was also supported by a grant from the Center of Developmental Education and Research, Tokyo. I thank the Faculty of Education of the University of Tokyo for gracious hospitality during my stay as Visiting Professor. Request reprints from M.H.B., Infancy Studies Program, Department of Psychology, New York University, 6 Washington Place, Room 1065, New York, New York 10003.

REFERENCES

Bateson, P. How do sensitive periods arise and what are they for? *Animal Behaviour,* 1979, *27,* 470–486.

Colombo, J. The critical period hypothesis: Research, methodology, and theoretical issues. *Psychological Bulletin,* 1982, *91,* 260–275.

Immelmann, K., & Soumi, S. J. Sensitive phases in development. In K. Immelmann, G. Barlow, L. Petrinovich, & M. Main (Eds.), *Behavioral development.* New York: Cambridge University Press, 1981.

Oyama, S. The concept of the sensitive period in developmental studies. *Merrill-Palmer Quarterly of Behavior and Development,* 1979, *25,* 83–103.

Scott, J. P. (Ed.). *Critical periods.* Stroudsburg, PA: Dowden, Hutchinson & Ross, 1978.

2 Developmental Changes in Sensitivity to Experience

Patrick Bateson
Robert A. Hinde
Sub-Department of Animal Behaviour and
MRC Unit on the Development and Integration of Behaviour,
University of Cambridge, England

INTRODUCTION

Sensitivity to certain types of experience changes throughout life. It is not surprising, then, that particular experiences should sometimes produce long-term effects on behavior more readily at certain stages of the life-cycle than at others. A classical example is imprinting in birds; a young duckling quickly learns to direct its filial behavior toward a particular moving object when it is exposed to that object within a period of time that starts soon after hatching and finishes some days later (Lorenz, 1935; see also Hoffman, this volume). Another good example is provided by the song-learning of many birds; details of the species-characteristic song are acquired by example only if the male Chaffinch has heard that song during an early period in its life (Thorpe, 1961). Similar examples occur in human development. Learning a language and, particularly, learning to articulate its distinctive sounds is much easier in childhood than in later life (Lenneberg, 1967; see also Snow, this volume). Such phenomena are clearly important for those interested in the study of behavioral development. However, they have been undervalued in recent years as a consequence of the wide-ranging attacks on the notion of continuity and connectedness in development and the suggestions that the effects of early experience are obliterated later in life (e.g., Clarke & Clarke, 1976; Kagan, 1984; see also Hinde & Bateson, 1984, for further discussion of the issue).

This controversy should be seen in historical perspective. Periods of susceptibility to long-term effects of current experience were originally termed "critical periods" by ethologists. This term, previously used in embryological studies, was first applied in the English language to behavioral examples by Lorenz (1937) when he published a translation of his famous Kumpan paper. "Critical period" implies a sharply defined phase of susceptibility preceded and followed by lack of susceptibility; if the relevant experience is provided before or after the period, no long-term effects are supposedly detectable. Experimental work on imprinting in the 1950s and 1960s showed, however, that the period was not so sharply defined as had been previously supposed and the term "sensitive period" was substituted by many ethologists (e.g., Hinde, 1961; see also Bateson, 1979, and Immelmann & Suomi, 1981, for discussions of terminology). The sensitive period concept implies a phase of greater susceptibility preceded and followed by lower sensitivity, with relatively gradual transitions.

Despite this revision by the ethologists, the earlier concept of "critical period" persisted, particularly in the secondary literature, and was generalized to studies of human children. Clarke and Clarke (1976) sharply attacked the critical period concept, largely on the basis of evidence that children reared under conditions of extreme social deprivation could be rehabilitated later in life. Rutter (1980) agreed that the notion of fixed and absolute critical periods no longer warranted serious consideration with respect to human behavioral development. However, he also pointed out that periods of heightened resonsiveness during development had obvious validity in certain cases. If a child is too old, rehabilitation of certain deficits could be difficult. Rutter's position was, therefore, substantially the same as that of those ethologists who had used the less rigid notion of sensitive period. Nonetheless, differences of opinion remained between the biologists and those developmental psychologists who were sceptical about the importance of early experience.

In this chapter we therefore begin by stressing the nature of the evidence for sensitive periods. How is the evidence collected? What operations are required to demonstrate the existence of a sensitive period? After dealing with these questions we go on to consider how the evidence is interpreted. We argue that different explanations for a particular case may refer to different levels of analysis or to events occurring at different moments back in time from the observed alteration in sensitivity; therefore, they need not be mutually exclusive. We classify these explanations according to whether behavioral, physiological, or molecular events are postulated as the cause of the change in sensitivity and whether or not they are supposed to occur immediately before the change.

However, some explanations are at the same level and refer to events that are believed to occur at the same time with respect to the change in sensitivity. Such rival interpretations are mutually exclusive and it may be possible to distinguish between them. As an example, we consider the relative merits of a clock model and a competitive exclusion model both of which have been used as physiological explanations for what happens prior to a reduction in sensitivity. In the final part of the chapter we emphasize that, even when variability in behavior can normally be attributed to differences in experience within a finite part of the life-cycle, it does not follow that such differences remain stable under all conditions. Indeed, some evidence suggests that, in special circumstances, a seemingly unmodifiable preference arising from early experience may be changed in adulthood. When this is realized, it becomes possible to perceive how the concept of the sensitive period remains valid within limits but how, under particular conditions, the long-term effects of early experience may be overlain or modified by the effects of events occurring later in life. Therefore, the view that the characteristics of certain forms of behavior are *normally* dependent on experience obtained early in life can be reconciled with the view that *sometimes* they can be changed later.

THE NATURE OF THE EVIDENCE

Even though the attacks on the "myth" of early experience were in our view somewhat misplaced (see Hinde & Bateson, 1984), it remains true that if the concept of sensitive period is to be useful, it is necessary to be precise about what has to be done in order to demonstrate that a particular aspect of behavior is more strongly affected by an experience at one stage of development than at others. The operations needed to establish the existence of a sensitive period are shown in Figure 1. The time when exposure to a given agent takes place is shown by the heavy lines. If the duration of exposure is merely started at different times and ended at the same time, then the evidence that is taken to support an age-specific effect is ambiguous; it could arise because the individuals that were exposed at an earlier age were also exposed for longer. Similarly, if the time from the end of exposure to testing is not kept constant, differences between the groups could arise because the effects of exposure could have attenuated more in Group 1 than in Group 5. A more subtle point is that, if the length of time from exposure to testing is kept constant (as shown by the arrows), the age of onset of exposure is confounded with the age of testing; but if the age of testing is kept constant, then the age of onset of exposure is confounded with the time from exposure to testing. Strictly, the only way to be sure that neither of the confounded variables is responsible for the differences between the groups is to run two separate experiments. In one experiment the time from the end of exposure to testing is kept constant and in the other the age of testing is kept constant. However, in many cases the plausibility of one or other of the alternative explanations for the results would be low and the extra work unjustified.

Groups

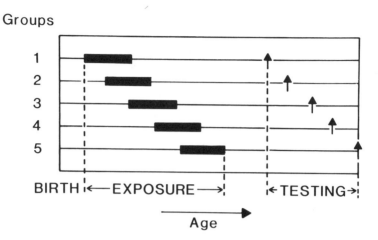

FIG. 1.   The operations required to demonstrate the existence of a sensitive period in development. Exposure is denoted by the thick bars. The number of groups is obviously arbitrary. Note that if the length of time from exposure to testing is kept constant (as shown by the arrows), the age of onset of exposure is confounded with the age of testing; but if the age of testing is kept constant, then the age of onset of exposure is confounded with the time from exposure to testing.

These points about the ambiguity of findings that purport to have demonstrated a sensitive period are not hypothetical. In some well-known studies of sexual imprinting in zebra finches, Immelmann (1969) fostered the nestlings with another species, the Bengalese finch. When adult, the zebra finch males fostered in this way preferred to court Bengalese finch females to females of their own species. Immelmann started the fostering at different ages and found that when the nestlings were above a certain age at the onset of fostering, their subsequent sexual preferences were for members of their own species. He attributed the lack of effectiveness of exposure to the Bengalese finches in the older birds to the existence of a sensitive period (Immelmann, 1972). However, an alternative explanation was not excluded. The birds first exposed to Bengalese finches at a later age also received less exposure overall. So the differences in outcome could have been ascribed to differences in length of exposure to the Bengalese finch foster parents.

Another example of potentially misleading conclusions being drawn from an inadequate demonstration of a sensitive period was Shepher's (1971) famous study of Israeli kibbutzniks. Most preferred not to marry a person they had known from early life. However, a few did and these people had usually entered the kibbutz after their sixth birthday. On the basis of this evidence, Shepher (1971) suggested that humans have a sensitive period for "negative imprinting" which ends by the age of 6 years. However, the people concerned did not withdraw from the kibbutz at a fixed period of time after entry, so age of entry into the kibbutz is confounded with length of exposure to class mates. Possibly the process that eventually influences mate choice has to be initiated before the age of 6, but even this conclusion is equivocal since many other variables might have been confounded with late entry into the kibbutz. Such difficulties can be overcome by properly controlled experiments, although these are admittedly much easier to do with animals than with people. A good example of an animal study is Landsberg's (1976) work on the sensitive period for imprinting in ducklings.

The influence of initial contact with her new born on the human mother's subsequent affection for her child provides yet another area of research where the claims for a sharply defined sensitive period have far outrun the evidence. In an excellent and well-balanced review, Goldberg (1983) notes that, among other shortcomings, the majority of the studies confound timing with amount of contact — the mothers having contact with their babies closer to birth also have more exposure to them. She also notes that even the relatively unambiguous evidence suggests that the contact is mildly beneficial rather than essential. Its effects can easily be over-ridden by subsequent experience. These points draw attention to the general limitations of much of the evidence for sensitive periods. Nonetheless, experimental demonstration of a sensitive period for a given type of stimulation can (and should) involve adequate controls for the length of exposure and the length of the interval between the stimulation and testing.

LIMITATIONS OF THE EVIDENCE

Even when the evidence for a sensitive period satisfies the requirements which we have outlined above, the conclusions that can be drawn from the findings are often limited in extent. It is well worth bearing in mind the following cautions before generalizing too widely:

(1) Even the most perfect demonstration of a sensitive period does not mean that the length of the period will be constant when the conditions are altered. In the case of filial imprinting in birds, social isolation lengthens the period (see Bateson, 1979).

(2) Sensitive periods relate to specific types of input; other types of experience may exert effects at quite different times in the life-cycle. While several types of behavior may be affected by experience during a given period of development, it does not follow this is the only sensitive period in the life-cycle (contrast this view with Scott, 1962).

(3) Evidence for the existence of a sensitive period is not an explanation for the ineffectiveness of stimulation outside that period. Nothing new is added by stating that something has to occur "within the sensitive period" in

order to be effective, since the operations used to define the period are precisely those that generate the evidence to be explained.

(4) The explanation for the onset of sensitivity need not necessarily be the same as the explanation for the end. The end of the sensitive period for filial imprinting is almost certainly brought about by different processes from those responsible for the onset, a point we consider in greater detail later.

(5) The grouping of phenomena under the descriptive heading of "sensitive periods" does not imply that they can all be explained in the same way. For instance, processes that regulate the stage in childhood when language development can begin must surely be different from those controlling when an attachment is most readily formed to an adult.

(6) Many descriptively defined sensitive periods may have no biological function whatsoever. They may merely represent a time of rapid reorganization when a given system is more easily disrupted by deprivation or insult. Even the implication that filial and sexual imprinting in a given individual have the same biological function is probably false (see Bateson, 1979).

TYPES AND LEVELS OF EXPLANATION

Distinct types of explanations for sensitive periods are easily confused. This is partly because the difference between an immediate cause and one that operated further back in time is, as always, a matter of degree and, therefore, not always obvious. The problem is compounded because explanations are offered at a number of distinct levels of analysis ranging from the organismic to the molecular. In an attempt to bring some order into the tangle, we have classified six types of explanation in Table 1. Our aim is both to distinguish between these separate types of explanation for the sake of clarity and also to relate them. The classification arbitrarily separates explanations in terms of events that accompany or immediately precede a change in sensitivity from those that postulate causes that lie further back in time. It also only considers three of the levels at which the change might be explained.

(1) *Immediate organismic.* A striking correlate of the end of the sensitive period for imprinting in birds is the increase in avoidance of novel objects. The end of sensitivity was therefore attributed to neophobia or the fear of novelty (Hess, 1959; Hinde, Thorpe, & Vince, 1956).

(2) *Preceding organismic.* One commonly invoked explanation for the growth of avoidance of novel objects was that prior experience with another object had led to the establishment of a preference for the familiar and rejection of anything that the animal could detect as being different (Bateson,

TABLE 1
The Variety of Ways in Which Evidence for a
Sensitive Period Might Be Explained

Level	Immediate	Preceding
Organismic	Type 1	Type 2
Physiological	Type 3	Type 4
Molecular	Type 5	Type 6

1979; Bindra, 1959). As another example, in the cognitive development of the child, Vygotsky (1962) pointed out that experiences influencing a child's cognitive development must lie within the "zone of proximal development." Many kinds of information processing are only possible when they have been preceded by experiences that set up the necessary cognitive capacities.

(3) *Immediate physiological.* Irrespective of how they are generated, alterations in the abilities to perceive and deal with the external world could play an important role in determining when a sensitive period starts. In the case of filial imprinting some evidence suggests that the onset of the sensitive period is associated with an increase in visual efficiency (Paulson, 1965) and an increase in motor ability (Hess, 1959). In birds that are hatched naked and helpless, the onset occurs much later than in precocious birds such as Mallard and domestic chicks (e.g., Burtt, 1977). In addition, an increase in the state of general "arousal" has often been thought to be important in imprinting (e.g., Kovach, 1970; Martin & Schutz, 1974; Rajecki, 1973).

Some sensitive periods can be fruitfully explained in terms of increased vulnerability to external influences at times of rapid change, as Bloom (1964) and Scott (1978) have argued. This usage seems particularly apt in the case of physical growth. Starvation or illness reduce rates of growth but the individual can subsequently catch up if it has not been held back too much. The physiological threshold for less than full recovery is much more likely to be exceeded during the stages of development when growth is normally rapid (see Bateson, 1976).

(4) *Preceding physiological.* Onsets and ends of sensitivity have often been explained in terms of changes governed by a postulated physiological clock. Alternatively, when prior experience prevents or permits sensitivity to the long-term effects of novel input, it may pre-empt other types of experience from having the same impact (e.g., Sluckin & Salzen, 1961). The phenomenon may then be explained in terms of competitive exclusion (e.g., Bateson, 1981). The essence of this view is that a particular member of a class of inputs from the environment gains access to the systems responsible for executing the relevant behavior and thereby excludes access to others.

(5) *Immediate molecular.*   Some changes in sensitivity to experience may spring from gene expression at that particular moment in development. Although no clear examples are well known to us, we presume that when the onset or end of a sensitive period is attributed to "genetic programming" (e.g., Hess, 1973), the author of such an explanation believes that activation of particular genes exerts an immediate influence on sensitivity at the behavioral level.

(6) *Preceding molecular.*   Gene expression, if involved in the onset of a sensitive period, will usually precede it, since many intermediate steps will probably intervene before sensitivity is altered. It seems likely for instance that the onset of sexual maturity in humans involves expression of genes that were previously latent, since many structural changes requiring protein synthesis occur at the time. Furthermore, it is probable that many stable preferences and habits are established when sexual behavior is first performed. Inasmuch as both these possibilities are real, gene expression at an earlier moment in time is responsible for the onset of some sensitive periods.

It must be stressed that a link between a behaviorally defined sensitive period and preceding gene expression would not imply that further explanation at higher levels was no longer required. Apart from the need to know the processes that mediate between molecules and behaviour, gene expression is itself regulated and dependent on the characteristics of larger systems. Both the individual's state and its social environment can be important factors in influencing the onset of sexual maturity in mice (e.g., Drickhamer, 1982). In Western countries the age of puberty in humans has been dropping steadily in recent decades and, even though the extent of the change may have been exaggerated (see Bullough, 1981), considerable evidence suggests that the prior nutritional plane of the individual is important in the timing of puberty (e.g., Frisch, 1978). So descending to Type 6 explanations in our Table 1 might well be followed by ascent to Type 2 explanations.

In summary, our major point here is that the various types of explanation listed in Table 1 are not necessarily incompatible with each other. However, we believe it is essential to be clear about the type of explanation under discussion.

DISTINGUISHING BETWEEN
EXPLANATIONS OF THE SAME TYPE

While the various types of explanation listed in Table 1 need not be incompatible, two explanations of the same type for the same phenomenon may well be in competition with each other. Particularly clear examples of opposed explanations are the two of Type 4 (i.e., Preceding Physiological) mentioned above as being used to account for the end of the sensitive period for imprinting. The first suggests that an internal clock determines when sensitivity declines, as well as when it initially increases. The second suggests that, while the onset of sensitivity is dependent on developmental state (and in that sense is determined by an internal time-keeper), the end is a result of competitive exclusion, resulting from induced neural growth.

Support for a clock model was provided by data which seemed to show that the sensitive period for filial imprinting is better calculated in terms of age from the beginning of embryonic development rather than in terms of age from hatching (Gottlieb, 1961; but see Landsberg, 1976). Although preceding events at the behavioral level might influence a clock in non-specific ways (see Aslin, 1981), the postulation of such mechanisms implies the proposal of a strong degree of autonomy from preceding external experience.

A number of possible physiological mechanisms could be suggested for the alternative model of competitive exclusion. For instance, suppose that gaining access involves growth of neural connections and that the area available for connections has finite size. When growth has proceeded beyond the halfway point and cannot be reversed easily, the input experienced first will be better able to control the behavior than other forms of input. The outcome of such a process is illustrated in Figure 2, which shows the proportion of access captured by first one (A) and then a second stimulus (B), assuming that the growth curves have an exponential character. This view of what happens was initially developed by Bateson (1981). It was dubbed the "capacity model" by Boakes and Panter (1985) and underlies the modeling attempts of Bischof (1985).

On the model of neural growth, an influence of the input on the rate of growth will also affect whether or not the input experienced first is subsequently more or less effective than input experienced later. For instance, a weak and impoverished stimulus might be reasonably expected to promote much slower growth than a strong and rich one. This point is illustrated in Fig. 2. When birds such as mallard ducklings or domestic chicks are reared in the dark or have their visual experience attenuated by being reared in patternless environments, the sensitive period for filial imprinting can be extended (e.g., Moltz & Stettner, 1961). This result is readily explained by the competitive exclusion model on the hypothesis that the rate of growth is slower when the intensity and quality of the input is low. However, the result can also be explained by the clock model if the supposition is that the running speed of the clock is partly dependent on external stimulation. Does this mean that no evidence can help us to distinguish between the two rival explanations? Not quite, since the experience is portrayed as having a non-specific stimulatory effect in the clock model, whereas it is thought to have a specific pre-emptive effect in the competitive exclusion model. In the second case some specific memory of the experience is required, otherwise it cannot have a pre-emptive effect.

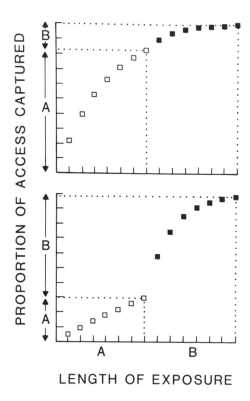

FIG. 2.   Results of a simple competitive exclusion model when access to an executive system is captured at a particular stage in development. The amount of access captured by a stimulus equals $1 - e^{-K.t.r}$ where e is the base of the natural logarithm, K is a constant set at 0.5 in these simulations, t is the length of exposure to the stimulus and r is the initial responsiveness to the stimulus. In the top simulation the initial responsiveness (r) is 0.25 to stimulus A and 0.5 to stimulus B. In the bottom simulation the values of r are 0.05 to A and 0.5 to B.

When domestic chicks or mallard ducklings are reared in isolation in a static but patterned environment, the sensitive period for imprinting is extended (e.g., Bateson, 1964). However, when the sensitive period comes to an end, it can be shown that the birds have a memory for the environment which they had experienced. The birds are more likely to respond socially to a moving object if it bears the same pattern as the walls of the cages in which they were previously isolated. This means that it would be incorrect to argue that rearing the animals in isolation merely delays a postulated clock bringing the sensitive period to a close. So, at least in the case of the end of the sensitive period for filial imprinting, the competitive exclusion model seems preferable to the clock one.

RECOVERING THE CAPACITY FOR CHANGE

The concept of sensitive period implies sensitivity of a particular type of behavior to a given form of stimulation during a limited phase in development. The concept does not necessarily imply that the behavior patterns in question cannot be influenced later in life under any circumstances. However, some proponents of the "critical period" concept believed that, at crucial moments in development "decisions" are made and cannot be repeated or reversed later in development (e.g., Scott, 1978, p. 5). Sometimes a decisive event early in development can indeed set in train a set of changes that are so great and inter-related that virtually nothing can be done to alter the outcome later in life. The determination of gender by ambient temperature early in the development of turtles is a striking example (Bull, 1980).

Furthermore, at the purely behavioral level, a biologist would expect adaptations that protect certain well-developed preferences and habits from alteration. If knowledge of kin acquired in early life plays an important role in mate choice, as seems to be the case in many species (see Bateson, 1983a), such knowledge ought not to be easily disrupted by later experience, since opportunities for encountering kin will be limited in later-life. Immelmann (1984) gives many other cases where preservation of information acquired early in life is likely to be of great importance to the animal.

However, Clarke and Clarke (1976), taking such claims for immutability to be the major proposition about "critical periods," attacked it vigorously. At the end of their book devoted to examining the available evidence, they claimed that virtually no behavioral deficit induced by early experience was irreversible. They overstated their case. Forms of behaviour that are normally well buffered from change later in life may, nevertheless, be altered under special conditions.

Sargant (1957), drawing on a wide variety of examples ranging from military "brain-washing" and police interrogation to religious conversions and psychotherapy, noted that attempts to change adult minds were especially likely to be successful if the person had been made extremely frightened or upset. Once such a state of stress has been induced, Sargant argued, humans are enormously suggestible. The common element in the various military, political, religious, and therapeutic attempts to change the way human adults think and behave is a *combination* of stress and suggestion. Similarly, cases where trauma has renewed the plasticity of behavior have been observed in animals (see Bateson, 1983b).

High levels of stress are associated with rapid synthesis and turnover of noradrenalin (see Anisman, 1978; Ursin et al., 1978). Strikingly, noradrenalin (or norepinephrine) is implicated as a factor by the neurophysiological work on brain plasticity (see Pettigrew, 1982). These studies are especially relevant because they were carried out on a form of neural plasticity that characteristically occurs at a particular stage early in the life-cycle.

The influence of early experience on the development of human binocular vision is well known (see Banks et al., 1975; Hohmann & Creutzfeldt, 1975). The physiology of what probably happens is now largely understood from studies of the domestic cat's visual system (e.g., Horn, 1985, Rauschecker,

1984). The capacity of an eye to drive neurones in the cat's visual cortex depends on whether that eye received visual input from about 1 to 3 months after birth (e.g., Hubel & Wiesel, 1970; Rauschecker & Singer, 1981). If an eye is visually deprived during this period, it virtually loses its capacity subsequently to excite cortical neurones. Once established, it is exceedingly difficult, on the one hand, to reverse the dominance of one eye over the other or, on the other hand, to impair binocular vision in normally reared subjects. The phenomenon looks like and, indeed, has become one of the classic examples of sensitive periods in development. Even so, infusion of noradrenalin into the visual cortex of older cats can re-establish plasticity (reviewed in Pettigrew, 1982). If normally reared animals are monocularly deprived during the period of noradrenalin infusion, binocular control of the neurones is lost in the visual cortex of the hemisphere that was infused. No such change occurs in the visual cortex of the other hemisphere. The neural sites that are known to be affected by monocular deprivation are innervated by the diffuse projections of the locus coeruleus, a structure in the mid-brain that actively synthesises noradrenalin (e.g., Amaral & Sinnamon, 1977; Redmond & Huang, 1979).

It would be wrong to suppose that noradrenalin is a sufficient condition for all forms of neural plasticity and it may well be too simple an idea to suppose that this neurotransmitter alone puts a particular set of neuronal connections in a state where they can be changed by a new input. Sites of neural plasticity in the visual cortex of the cat are innervated by many different fibres coming from other parts of the brain. The enabling condition for change could, therefore, be a particular cocktail of neurotransmitters rather than the presence of just one. The attraction of this possibility is that a particular site could be differentially prepared for change, giving much greater specificity to the influence of afferent input at a particular stage in development. Although a lot remains to be done, the work pioneered by Pettigrew and his colleagues starts to point to neural mechanisms by which behavioral systems, normally stable once formed, can be changed again later in life.

CONCLUSIONS

It is clear that sensitivity to those types of stimulation that influence the development of behavior can change with time. In this chapter we have been concerned with what generalizations may be drawn from such examples. We noted that the processes that augment the sensitivity of particular systems to particular events at particular stages are not necessarily the same as those that subsequently reduce the sensitivity. Nor are the sets of processes that give rise to one sensitive period necessarily the same as those that give rise to another. This lack of generality raises a difficulty for the use of a common term, like "sensitive period," which can easily be taken to imply a common underlying mechanism. If the term has little explanatory power, why use it? The answer, we believe is simply that it draws attention to the fact that all forms of stimulation are not equally important at all stages in development. Descriptions of sensitive periods are an important first step towards understanding an aspect of development. The description of regularity invites analysis of the *processes* that generate such regularity. Such analysis is the kind of research which will eventually unlock the mysteries of neural and behavioral development.

We suggest that much of the argument over sensitive periods has been at cross-purposes. In part, confusion has arisen because different types of explanation have been treated as though they were the same. In order to bring some sharpness of focus to the debate, we have suggested a classification that draws attention to the ways in which they differ and, having made the distinctions, shows how the explanations may then be related. It also enables the relative merits of genuinely rival explanations, such as the physiological clock and competitive exclusion models, to be examined more closely.

Another difficulty about the way in which the concept of sensitive periods has been used was that the greater effectiveness of a stimulus at a particular stage in development was taken to mean irreversibility of its effects. Admittedly, in some cases the presence (or absence) of the appropriate form of stimulation within a sensitive period sets in train changes in structure that are so great that virtually nothing can be done to alter them later in life. However, many behaviorally outcomes of early experience can be changed, even though sometimes only under rather special conditions. When that point is appreciated, the views of the enthusiastic proponents of the sensitive period concept and those of their critics can be reconciled.

In summary, we consider the operations required to demonstrate the existence of a sensitive period in development. However, we emphasize that in many cases the times of onset and ending of sensitivity are dependent on conditions. Having noted that the causal and functional explanations for sensitive periods vary widely from case to case, we then classify the varieties of levels and moments back in time at which explanations may be offered. Once distinguished, many of these may be usefully related to each other. Two rival explanations of the same type for the end of the sensitive period for imprinting are considered: a physiological clock and competitive exclusion resulting from induced neural growth. The competitive exclusion model seems the more satisfactory of the two. Finally, we discuss how, under certain conditions such as those that generate high stress, behavior that is influenced by early experience in early life can sometimes be changed once again in adulthood.

REFERENCES

Amaral, D. G., & Sinnamon, H. M. The locus coeruleus: Neurobiology of a central noradren-ergic nucleus. *Progress in Neurobiology,* 1977, *9,* 147–196.

Anisman, H. Neurochemical changes elicited by stress: behavioral correlates. In H. Anisman & G. Bignami (Eds.), *Psychopharmacology of aversively motivated behavior.* Plenum: New York, 1978.

Aslin, R. N. Experiential influences and sensitive periods in perceptual development: A unified model. In R. N. Aslin, J. R. Alberts & M. R. Petersen (Eds.), *Development of Perception: Psychobiological Perspectives* (Vol. 2). *The Visual System.* New York: Academic Press, 1981.

Banks, M. S., Aslin, R. N., & Letson, R. D. Sensitive period for the development of human binocular vision. *Science,* 1975, *190,* 675–677.

Bateson, P. P. G. Effect of similarity between rearing and testing conditions on chicks' following and avoidance responses. *Journal of Comparative and Physiological Psychology,* 1964, *57,* 100–103.

Bateson, P. P. G. Rules and reciprocity in behavioural development. In P. P. G. Bateson & R. A. Hinde (Eds.), *Growing points in ethology.* Cambridge: Cambridge University Press, 1976.

Bateson, P. [P. G.] How do sensitive periods arise and what are they for? *Animal Behaviour,* 1979, *27,* 470–486.

Bateson, P. [P. G.] Control of sensitivity to the environment during development. In K. Immelmann, G. W. Barlow, L. Petrinovich & M. Main (Eds.), *Behavioral development.* Cambridge: Cambridge University Press, 1981.

Bateson, P. [P. G.] (Ed.), *Mate choice.* Cambridge: Cambridge University Press, 1983. (a)

Bateson, P. [P. G.] The interpretation of sensitive periods. In A. Oliverio & M. Zappella (Eds.), *The Behavior of human infants.* Plenum: New York, 1983. (b)

Bindra, D. *Motivation: A systematic reinterpretation.* New York: Ronald Press, 1959.

Bischof, H. J. Environmental influences on early development: A comparison of imprinting and cortical plasticity. In P. P. G. Bateson & P. H. Klopfer (Eds.), *Perspectives in ethology (Vol. 6) Mechanisms.* New York: Plenum, 1985.

Bloom, B. S. *Stability and change in human characteristics.* New York: Wiley, 1964.

Boakes, R., & Panter, D. Secondary imprinting in the domestic chick blocked by previous exposure to a live hen. *Animal Behaviour,* 1985, *33,* 353–365.

Bull, J. J. Sex determination in reptiles. *Quarterly Review of Biology,* 1980, *55,* 3–21.

Bullough, V. L. Age at menarche: A misunderstanding. *Science,* 1981, *213,* 365–366.

Burtt, E. H. Some factors in the timing of parent-chick recognition in swallows. *Animal Behaviour,* 1977, *25,* 231–239.

Clarke, A. M., & Clarke, A. D. B. *Early experience: myth and evidence.* London: Open books, 1976.

Drickhamer, L. C. Delay and acceleration of puberty in female mice by urinary chemosignals from other females. *Developmental Psychobiology,* 1982, *15,* 433–445.

Frisch, R. E. Population, food intake and fertility. *Science,* 1978, *199,* 22–30.

Goldberg, S. Parent-infant bonding: another look. *Child Development,* 1983, *54,* 1355–1382.

Gottlieb, G. Developmental age as a baseline for determination of the critical period in imprinting. *Journal of Comparative and Physiological Psychology,* 1961, *54,* 422–427.

Hess, E. H. Two conditions limiting critical age for imprinting. *Journal of Comparative and Physiological Psychology,* 1959, *52,* 513–518.

Hess, E. H. *Imprinting.* New York: Van Nostrand Reinhold, 1973.

Hinde, R. A. The establishment of the parent-offspring relation in birds with some mammalian analogies. In W. H. Thorpe & O. L. Zangwill (Eds.), *Current problems in animal behaviour.* Cambridge: Cambridge University Press, 1961.

Hinde, R. A., & Bateson, P. Discontinuities versus continuities in behavioral development and the neglect of process. *International Journal of Behavioral Development,* 1984, *7,* 129–143.

Hinde, R. A., Thorpe, W. H., & Vince, M. A. The following response of young Coots and Moorhens. *Behaviour,* 1956, *9,* 214–242.

Hohmann, A., & Creutzfeldt, O. D. Squint and the development of bincoularity in humans. *Nature,* 1975, *254,* 613–614.

Horn, G. *Memory, imprinting, and the brain.* Oxford: Oxford University Press, 1985.

Hubel, D. H., & Wiesel, T. N. The period of susceptibility to the physiological effects of unilateral eye closure in kittens. *Journal of Physiology,* 1970, *206,* 419–436.

Immelmann, K. Über den Einfluss frühkindlicher Erfahrungen auf die geschlechtliche Objektfixierung bei Estrildiden. *Zeitschrift für Tierpsychologie,* 1969, *26,* 677–691.

Immelmann, K. Sexual and other long-term aspects of imprinting in birds and other species. *Advances in the Study of Behavior,* 1972, *4,* 147–174.

Immelmann, K. The natural history of bird learning. In P. Marler & H. S. Terrace (Eds.), *The biology of learning.* Berlin: Springer-Verlag, 1984.

Immelmann, K., & Suomi, S. J. Sensitive phases in development. In K. Immelmann, G. W. Barlow, L. Petrinovich & M. Main (Eds.), *Behavioral development.* Cambridge: Cambridge University Press, 1981.

Kagan, J. *The nature of the child.* New York: Basic Books, 1984.

Kovach, J. K. Critical period or optimal arousal? Early approach behavior as a function of stimulus, age and breed variables. *Developmental Psychology,* 1970, *3,* 73–77.

Landsberg, J. W. Posthatch age and developmental age as a baseline for determination of the sensitive period for imprinting. *Journal of Comparative and Physiological Psychology,* 1976, *90,* 47–52.

Lenneberg, E. H. *Biological foundations of language.* New York: Wiley, 1967.

Lorenz, K. Der Kumpan in der Umwelt des Vogels. *Journal für Ornithologie,* 1935, *83,* 137–213, 289–413.

Lorenz, K. The companion in the bird's world. *Auk,* 1937, *54,* 245–273.

Martin, J. T., & Schutz, F. Arousal and temporal factors in imprinting in Mallards. *Developmental Psychobiology,* 1974, *7,* 69–78.

Moltz, H., & Stettner, L. J. The influence of patterned light deprivation on the critical period for imprinting. *Journal of Comparative and Physiological Psychology,* 1961, *54,* 279–283.

Paulson, G. W. Maturation of evoked responses in the duckling. *Experimental Neurology,* 1965, *11,* 324–333.

Pettigrew, J. D. Pharmacologic control of cortical plasticity. *Retina,* 1982, *2,* 360–372.

Rajecki, D. W. Imprinting in precocial birds: interpretation, evidence and evaluation. *Psychological Bulletin,* 1973, *79,* 48–58.

Rauschecker, J. Neuronal mechanisms of developmental plasticity in the cat's visual system. *Human Neurobiology,* 1984, *3,* 109–114.

Rauschecker, J. P., & Singer, W. The effects of early visual experience on the cat's visual cortex and their possible explanation by Hebb synapses. *Journal of Physiology,* 1981, *310,* 215–239.

Redmond, D. E., & Huang, Y. H. Current concepts II. New evidence for a locus coeruleus-norepinephrine connection with anxiety. *Life Sciences,* 1979, *25,* 2149–2162.

Rutter, M. The long-term effects of early experience. *Developmental Medicine and Child Neurology,* 1980, *22,* 800–815.

Sargant, W. *Battle for the mind.* London: Heinemann, 1957.

Scott, J. P. Critical periods in behavioral development. *Science,* 1962, *138,* 949–958.

Scott, J. P. *Critical periods.* Stroudsberg, Pa.: Dowden, Hutchinson & Ross, 1978.

Shepher, J. Mate selection among second generation kibbutz adolescents and adults: incest avoidance and negative imprinting. *Archives of Sexual Behavior,* 1971, *1,* 293–307.

Sluckin, W., & Salzen, E. A. Imprinting and perceptual learning. *Quarterly Journal of Experimental Psychology,* 1961, *13,* 65–77.

Thorpe, W. H. *Bird-song.* London: Cambridge University Press, 1961.

Ursin, H., Baade, E., & Levine, S. (Eds.). *Psychology of stress.* New York: Academic Press, 1978.

Vygotsky, L. S. *Thought and language.* Cambridge, Mass.: M.I.T. Press, 1962.

II

SENSITIVE PERIODS IN INFRAHUMAN PSYCHOBIOLOGY AND HUMAN NEUROPSYCHOLOGY

The first appearance of sensitive periods in anatomical study seems to have lent the phenomenon credibility in psychology and may even have motivated psychological research. Section II of *Sensitive Periods in Development* surveys sensitive periods in physiological systems in infrahumans and humans and in the behavior of infrahuman organisms. Sensitive periods in visual system sensitivity, social attachment, recovery from brain insult, and psychoendocrine function are all represented.

Chapters 3, 4, and 5 review classic instances of sensitive periods in brain-behavior relations in three lower organisms, cat, rat, and duck. In Chapter 3, Helmut V. B. Hirsch and Suzannah Bliss Tieman examine sensitive periods in mammalian visual development referring to physiological and behavioral ontogeny in the cat to illustrate how exogenous as well as endogenous experiences function at the neuronal level to influence perceptual development. Through close analysis of developmental stages of the feline visual system, Hirsch and Tieman show how at particular times the visual system expresses sensitivity to particular experiences and how they in turn influence subsequent differentiation of physiology and behavior. Beyond the role of endogenous experiences in sensitive period phenomena, an important lesson that the study of neurobehavioral development in the cat affords is that experiences during the sensitive period may have differential long-term effects. Hirsch and Tieman's treatment is exemplary of that requisite to our understanding of the development of the brain-perception-behavior nexus.

In Chapter 4, Elliott Blass focuses on influences of the experience of social interaction during the period of nursing-suckling in the rat pup's expression of social behavior in maturity. Partitioning the early maturation of the rat into phases of suckling, huddling, and budding sexual activity, Blass provides a careful examination of the long-term consequences of particular experiences sustained during each of these formative stages. At one point, for example, the motor act of suckling comes under the control of stimuli that seem in turn literally to define "mother." Further, Blass demonstrates that specifiable effects of infantile experiences endure, manifesting themselves in mature sexual behavior.

One of the first behavioral examples of a "critical period" was demonstrated by Konrad Lorenz in his reports of ducklings' imprinting on objects in view soon after hatching. Lorenz's vivid demonstration that he himself could substitute as one of those objects of attachment caused palpable and widespread recognition of this phenomenon among both lay and academic audiences. In Chapter 5, Howard Hoffman explores in substantial experimental detail parameters of the imprinting process, which has become one of the paradigmatic examples of a sensitive period. Through a systematic examination of the many facets of imprinting, Hoffman reports the findings of experimental procedures designed to probe the nature of this attachment, its developmental timing, and its relevant exposure stimuli. Hoffman's interpretations of sensitive periods are revisionist on two counts, leading him to a third significant conclusion. First, Hoffman argues that the sensitive period for attachment submits to a kind of learning analysis akin to classical conditioning and, second, Hoffman shows that imprinted attachments are less special than heretofore regarded since an animal's imprinting on one object does not preclude its later imprinting on another. Sensitive periods for attachment in animals, Hoffman therefore concludes, are not so fixed as they once appeared, but rather are flexible and so may be even more robust than previously thought.

Chapters 6 and 7 begin to bridge from infrahuman to human applications of the sensitive period notion, remaining still within the realm of neuropsychological study. In Chapter 6, C. Robert Almli and Stanley Finger examine mammalian neurobehavioral development from the viewpoint of sensitive periods. In particular, they take up two separate but interrelated sensitive period effects in human beings, those that stem from injuries to the central nervous system and those produced by malnutrition. Their investigations ask whether each insult has consequences for mature function contingent on the developmental timing. In the case of CNS damage, the authors conclude that the picture that emerges from extant data is enormously complicated and can only be evaluated on a case by case basis taking into account the kind of lesion, its severity, and its location, as well as the outcome it is thought to affect. On the basis of numerous exceptions, they therefore question the specialty of infancy in this regard. Almli and Finger argue that the picture with respect to undernutrition effects is much clearer, perhaps because the consequences of nutrition deprivation are more thoroughgoing.

In Chapter 7, the final contribution to Part II, John Money and Charles Annecillo take up the issue of how particular early experiences in humans might affect physiological functioning as well as physical growth. Money and Annecillo invoke case studies of abuse dwarfism and female hermaphroditism to demonstrate how early experiences may have penetrating ramifications in the mature psychological life of the human. These two case studies do not parallel one another, however, but diverge in many ways. For example, in the instance of sexual dimorphism, prenatal exposure to circulating hormones is shown to have rather fixed and long-term effects on sexual selection even into adulthood. In the instance of psychological dwarfism, by contrast, remediation of neglect can constitute rescue.

In overview, the chapters in Part II, on Sensitive Periods in Infrahuman Psychobiology and Human Neuropsychology, illustrate a broad range of applications of the sensitive period conceptualization in psychological thinking, they raise considerations of universal import in this field of inquiry, and they document known conclusions as well as provide some counterintuitive insights into the nature of sensitive periods generally.

3 Perceptual Development and Experience-Dependent Changes in Cat Visual Cortex

Helmut V.B. Hirsch
Suzannah Bliss Tieman
Neurobiology Research Center
State University of New York at Albany

INTRODUCTION

Neuronal activity is necessary for the normal development of mammalian sensory systems; sensory stimulation appears to be an important source of this activity. For example, the cat's visual system, which has been very extensively studied, is immature at birth and undergoes substantial postnatal development. The course of this development is affected by neuronal activity. For more peripheral structures (e.g., the visual thalamus), the necessary neuronal activity is generated mainly by spontaneous firing of nerve cells in the retina, but for more central structures (e.g., the primary visual cortex), much of the necessary activity results from patterned visual stimulation. The developmental impact of neuronal activity in visual cortex is greatest during a brief *critical period,* at a time when large numbers of synaptic contacts are being formed within this structure.

Nervous system changes produced by neuronal activity during the critical period can influence behavior well after this period has ended. We refer to such changes in behavior as *second order effects.* By studying these effects we can further our understanding of the role of neuronal activity in behavioral development. With this in mind, we describe two paradigms (stripe-rearing and unequal alternating monocular exposure) for providing controlled visual stimulation during the critical period; each paradigm enables quantitative manipulation of *one* aspect of an animal's visual exposure. Using these paradigms it is possible to determine the relation between specific aspects of visual experience during the critical period and the resulting second order effects of that experience and thereby gradually build up some understanding of how experience-dependent neuronal activity affects behavioral development.

VISUAL DEVELOPMENT IN THE CAT

The Cat As Model System

The cat has been studied so extensively that we use this species to show in detail how experience-dependent activity can influence development of brain and behavior. Although neuronal activity can affect development at several points within the visual system (for reviews see Fregnac & Imbert, 1984; Hirsch, 1985a,b; Mitchell & Timney, 1984; Movshon & Van Sluyters, 1981; Sherman & Spear, 1982), experience-dependent changes have been most clearly demonstrated for the primary visual cortex, area 17. Area 17 is thus the focus of this review.

In describing effects of neuronal activity on development of vision in the cat, it is convenient to divide postnatal development into three stages (Hirsch, 1985a): (1) the first three weeks, during which kittens make relatively little use of vision, and activity-dependent developmental changes in the visual system are influenced mainly by activity generated by the spontaneous firing of retinal ganglion cells; (2) the second three weeks, during which kittens develop many visually guided skills, and activity-dependent developmental changes require exposure to patterned visual stimulation; and (3) the next 6–10 weeks, during which kittens begin to actively seek visual stimulation, and experience-dependent development of the visual system continues, although probably at a reduced rate. The second and third stages together comprise the classical "critical period" for area 17 in the cat (e.g., Hubel & Wiesel, 1970; Olson & Freeman, 1980).

Development of Visual Behavior in the Kitten

Stage one. A kitten makes little use of vision during the first weeks of postnatal life. The eyes, which are closed at birth, open around the end of the first postnatal week (e.g., Braastad & Heggelund, 1984). By the end of the first postnatal week a kitten removed from the nest will use olfactory and thermal stimuli to guide its return to the nest (Freeman & Rosenblatt, 1978); it will not use visual stimuli to do this until the beginning of the third postnatal week (Rosenblatt, Turkewitz, & Schneirla, 1964).

Stage two. There is a profound increase in visually guided behaviors during the second postnatal stage. Kittens start to use vision to avoid obstacles (Norton, 1974; Van Hof-Van Duin, 1976) and to avoid the deep side of a visual cliff (Karmel, Miller, Dettweiler, & Anderson, 1970; Norton, 1974; Van Hof-Van Duin, 1976; Villablanca & Olmstead, 1979; Walk, 1968; Warkentin & Smith, 1937; but cf. Fox, 1970, who reports that reaction to the visual cliff develops near the end of the third postnatal week). They will also use vision to guide placement of the paws to meet an edge when lowered towards it (Fox, 1970; Karmel et al., 1970; Norton, 1974; Sherman, 1972; Van Hof-Van Duin, 1976; Villablanca & Olmstead, 1979; Warkentin & Smith, 1937). Their ability to resolve spatial details begins to improve (Giffin & Mitchell, 1978; Mitchell, Giffin, Wilkinson, Anderson, & Smith, 1976); see Figure 1. They also begin to show a marked binocular superiority when tested for their ability to discriminate small differences in depth, suggesting they are beginning to develop stereopsis (Timney, 1981). Near the end of the second postnatal stage kittens can learn to discriminate between complex visual patterns (Wilkinson & Dodwell, 1980). As kittens develop these visual capabilities, they become more active (Frederickson & Frederickson, 1979; Levine, Hull, & Buchwald, 1980) and they begin to leave their nest (Rosenblatt et al., 1964).

There are important changes in the kitten's lifestyle during the second postnatal stage. Around the beginning of this stage kittens begin to engage in *social play,* including stalking, chasing, and pouncing on either their siblings or their mother (Martin, 1982; Moelk, 1979; Rosenblatt & Schneirla, 1962; West, 1974); social play increases in frequency throughout the second stage (Baerends-van Roon & Baerends, 1979; Barrett & Bateson, 1978; Kolb & Nonneman, 1975; Martin, 1982; Villablanca & Olmstead, 1979; West, 1974, 1979). In addition, the mother cat begins to wean her kittens (Martin, 1982).

Stage three.   During the third postnatal stage the ability of kittens to resolve spatial details continues to improve but does not reach adult levels until later (Figure 1; Giffin & Mitchell, 1978; Mitchell et al., 1976). Binocular depth perception also improves, reaching adult levels by 15 weeks (Figure 1; Timney, 1981). Furthermore, during this stage behaviors emerge that suggest the kitten is now beginning to seek interactions with stimuli outside the nest.

A very dramatic example of the latter is that around the eighth or ninth postnatal week kittens begin to make active efforts to obtain visual stimulation (Dodwell, Timney, & Emerson, 1976; Timney, Emerson, & Dodwell, 1979). When kittens are given access to a lever which when depressed gives them an opportunity to view a visual stimulus, younger kittens can perform this task, but do so very infrequently. Suddenly, at 8 or 9 weeks postnatal, the frequency and duration of lever pressing to obtain visual stimulation increases dramatically (Figure 1). This increase occurs in kittens that have been dark-reared from 1 month of age or from birth (Timney et al., 1979). In short, if visual stimulation is not provided automatically by the environment, an 8 or 9 week old kitten will work to obtain it.

During the third postnatal stage the kitten's behavior also changes in other ways. Between postnatal week 7 and 8, *object play* increases sharply, including mouthing, patting, poking, and batting almost any suitable object (Barrett & Bateson, 1978). Locomotor activity in an open field also increases

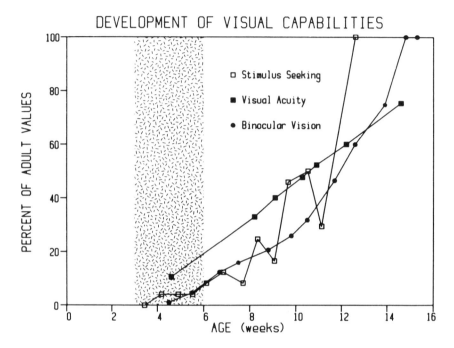

FIG. 1.   Postnatal development of three visual behaviors, stimulus seeking, visual acuity and binocular vision. Each measure has been converted to percent of adult value and plotted as a function of animal age. In this and the next five figures, the shading indicates the time interval corresponding to the second stage of development (3–6 weeks). Stimulus seeking was measured as duration of self-produced exposure to light averaged for one kitten over five days (two 1-hr sessions per day). Since no adult values were given, data are plotted as percent of the value for the oldest age available. Note that the kitten actively seeks visual stimulation starting at about 8 weeks postnatal. (Replotted from Dodwell et al., 1976.) Visual acuity was tested using a jumping stand: kittens were trained to jump to one of two stimuli mounted on adjacent platforms. The positive stimulus was a grating of parallel bars; the negative stimulus was a uniform gray. Acuity was defined as the number of cycles per degree in the finest grating that could be discriminated from gray. (Replotted from Giffin & Mitchell, 1978.) Binocular vision was also tested with a jumping stand. In this case, the landing surface had two transparent windows that permitted the kitten to see two other surfaces positioned at different depths. The kittens were trained to jump toward the nearer surface. Timney (1981) computed a threshold retinal disparity corresponding to the smallest discriminable separation in depth. This threshold decreases with age. To make the data more comparable to those for visual acuity, the inverse of retinal disparity, which increases with age, is plotted as a percent of adult value. (Replotted from Timney, 1981.)

(Levine et al., 1980). Finally, the kitten must learn to kill prey effectively; if the mother cat does not bring her kittens live prey between about the sixth and twentieth postnatal weeks, they do not learn to kill or do so only in slow and laborious ways (Leyhausen, 1979).

Development of Area 17

Area 17 is relatively immature in the newborn kitten, and undergoes substantial postnatal changes. Some of these changes reflect maturation in the retina and visual thalamus, but others result from extensive maturation within the cortex (for reviews see Fregnac & Imbert, 1984; Hirsch, 1985a; Mitchell & Timney, 1984; Movshon & Van Sluyters, 1981; Sherman & Spear, 1982). Neuronal activity, generated either spontaneously or as a result of sensory stimulation, affects the course of postnatal development in area 17. Non-retinal afferents associated with arousal and attention appear to modulate this dependence on activity (e.g., Kety, 1970; Pettigrew, 1978; Singer, 1979).

Stage one.   Retinal afferents, relayed by way of the visual thalamus (dorsal lateral geniculate nucleus or dLGN), reach area 17 before birth (Anker, 1977), but their initial distribution is different from that in the adult. During the first postnatal week thalamic afferents project more heavily to the upper layers of area 17 (especially layer I) than in adult cats (Anker, 1977; Anker & Cragg, 1974; Laemle, Benhamida, & Purpura, 1972; LeVay, Stryker, & Shatz, 1978; Kato, Kawaguchi, Yamamoto, Samejima, & Miyata, 1983; Kato, Kawaguchi, & Miyata, 1984). Also, at this stage the projection to layer IV spills over into layer V (LeVay et al., 1978). In addition, during the first two postnatal weeks afferents from the two eyes have extensive overlap in layer IV (LeVay et al., 1978). The adult distribution of thalamic afferents, in which terminals from the two eyes are segregated into ocular dominance patches, appears by the end of the third postnatal week (Kato et al., 1983, 1984; Laemle et al., 1972; LeVay et al., 1978).

During the time that thalamic afferents to area 17 are being elaborated, there is a pronounced increase in the density of synaptic connections between nerve cells in area 17. A few synapses are present in area 17 as early as 3 weeks before birth, but at birth fewer than 1% of the adult number of synapses are found on an average neuron (Cragg, 1972, 1975). Synaptic density increases during postnatal life, especially during the first 40 days; see Figure 2 (Cragg, 1972, 1975; Winfield, 1981).

As synapses develop in area 17, response properties of the cells start to mature. Cells in area 17 may be activated by light as early as postnatal day 6 (Huttenlocher, 1967), but, unlike the cells in adult cats (e.g., Barlow, Blakemore, & Pettigrew, 1967; Hubel & Wiesel, 1959, 1962; Maffei &

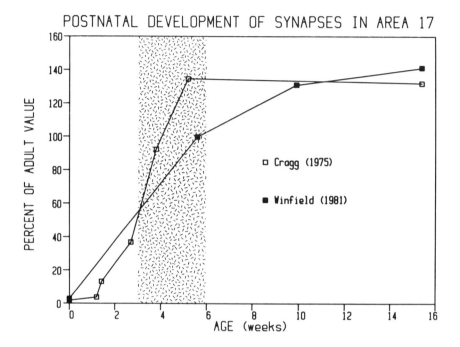

FIG. 2.   Postnatal development of synapses in area 17. The average number of synapses per neuron in area 17 as a percent of adult value is plotted for kittens of different ages. The number of synapses per neuron increases very rapidly between 3 and 6 weeks postnatal and stays above adult levels until at least 16 weeks postnatal. The number of synapses per neuron subsequently declines to adult levels, suggesting that there is a "pruning out" of synapses, perhaps as a result of experience-dependent changes. (Replotted from Cragg, 1975, and Winfield, 1981.)

Fiorentini, 1973) most do not vary their response as a function of stimulus orientation, spatial frequency, or disparity (Fregnac & Imbert, 1978; Pettigrew, 1974; but see Beckmann & Albus, 1982; Braastad & Heggelund, 1985; Hubel & Wiesel, 1963). During the remainder of the first stage there is an increase in the proportion of area 17 cells selective for stimulus orientation and spatial frequency; see Figure 3 (Albus & Wolf, 1984; Beckmann & Albus, 1982; Blakemore & Van Sluyters, 1975; Bonds, 1979; Braastad & Heggelund, 1985; Buisseret & Imbert, 1976; Derrington & Fuchs, 1981; Fregnac & Imbert, 1978; Hubel & Wiesel, 1963; McCall, 1983; Tsumoto & Suda, 1982). Many of the remaining cells are responsive to visual stimulation, but are not selective (Blakemore & Van Sluyters, 1975; Braastad & Heggelund, 1985; Buisseret & Imbert, 1976; Fregnac & Imbert, 1978; Pettigrew, 1974; Tsumoto & Suda, 1982). The great variability in the percent of cells that are reported to be selective at 3 weeks (see Figure 3) may be due to differences in the criteria for what constitutes orientation selectivity. Nevertheless, virtually all studies agree that some but not all of the cells in area 17 are selective by the end of the first stage.

The early maturing cells have several distinctive characteristics. First, they are likely to be first order neurons and are concentrated in layers IV and VI where most thalamic afferents terminate (Beckmann & Albus, 1982; Blakemore & Van Sluyters, 1975; but see also Tsumoto & Suda, 1982, who claim that the first cells to display orientation selectivity are in layer V). Second, they receive inhibitory inputs from other area 17 cells, whereas most immature cells do not (Sato & Tsumoto, 1984). Iontophoretic application of N-methyl-bicuculline, an antagonist of the inhibitory neurotransmitter gamma-aminobutyric acid (GABA), temporarily reduces the sharpness of tuning of the early maturing orientation selective cells, but has little or no effect on the immature cells. Third, the distribution of the orientation preferences of the early maturing cells is not uniform (as it is in the adult cat, e.g.,

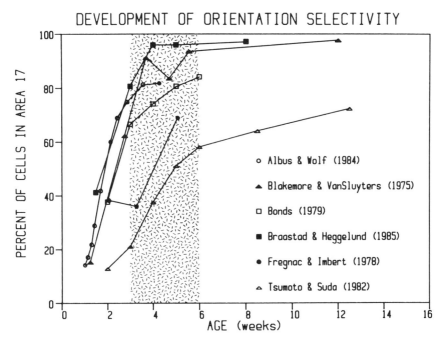

FIG. 3.   Development of orientation selectivity. The percent of cells in area 17 that are selective for orientation are plotted as a function of animal age. Because researchers differ in how they define orientation selective cells, very different values have been reported for any given age. In general, however, the percentage of area 17 cells classified as orientation selective increases rapidly between the end of the first postnatal week and the end of the sixth postnatal week. (Replotted from Albus & Wolf, 1984; Blakemore & Van Sluyters, 1975; Bonds, 1979; Braastad & Heggelund, 1985; Fregnac & Imbert, 1978; and Tsumoto & Suda, 1982.)

Hubel & Wiesel, 1962; Leventhal & Hirsch, 1980), but shows a bias towards horizontal and vertical (Fregnac & Imbert, 1978; McCall, 1983; but see also Albus & Wolf, 1984, who do not find such a bias). Fourth, although most area 17 cells in the adult are binocular, that is they respond to stimulation of either eye (e.g., Hubel & Wiesel, 1962), the early maturing cells are monocular, that is they respond only to stimulation of one eye (Blakemore & Van Sluyters, 1975; Fregnac & Imbert, 1978; McCall, 1983), usually the contralateral eye (Fregnac & Imbert, 1978; but see Blakemore & Van Sluyters, 1975; McCall, 1983). In contrast, the later maturing cells tend to be binocular (Blakemore & Van Sluyters, 1975; Fregnac & Imbert, 1978; McCall, 1983). The distinctive characteristics of the early maturing cells may make it possible to identify them in mature animals (e.g., Hirsch, Leventhal, McCall, & Tieman, 1983; Leventhal & Hirsch, 1977, 1980).

The visual cortex also receives non-retinal afferents from a variety of sources. Of particular importance are the monoaminergic and cholinergic afferents, which appear to be involved in attention and arousal (e.g., Moore & Bloom, 1978, 1979; Shute & Lewis, 1963). Monoaminergic neurons arise early during ontogeny and are the earliest afferents to invade the neocortex (for review, see Schlumpf, Lichtensteiger, Shoemaker, & Bloom, 1980). Measurable amounts of endogenous monoamines, noradrenalin (NA), dopamine (DA) and serotonin (5-HT), are present in area 17 at birth, and their levels rise during the first postnatal stage (Jonsson & Kasamatsu, 1983). Postsynaptic receptors for the monoamines also increase throughout this stage; see Figure 4 (Jonsson & Kasamatsu, 1983). The ß-adrenergic receptors for NA are densest in layer IV (Shaw, Needler, & Cynader, 1984b).

According to Bear, Carnes, and Ebner (1985), cholinergic inputs are present in area 17 at birth. During the first postnatal stage the density of cholinergic axons is greatest in the lower layers (IVc-VI). By the end of this stage, a distinct horizontal plexus of cholinergic axons has appeared in the bottom of layer III. Postsynaptic receptors for acetylcholine (ACh) increase throughout the first postnatal stage (Shaw, Needler, & Cynader, 1984a). Like the ß-adrenergic receptors, the muscarinic ACh receptors are concentrated in layer IV (Shaw et al., 1984a,b). Acetylcholinesterase (AChE), the major degradative enzymne for ACh, is present at fairly high levels at end of the first postnatal week; these levels drop by the end of the second postnatal week and remain low (Potempska, Skangiel-Kramska, & Kossut, 1979).

Stage two.   During the second postnatal stage there is a large increase in the number of synapses in area 17 so that the number reaches or exceeds adult levels; see Figure 2 (Cragg, 1975; Winfield, 1981). In addition, the cells in area 17 continue to develop selectivity for stimulus orientation; see Figure 3 (Albus & Wolf, 1984; Blakemore & Van Sluyters, 1975; Bonds, 1979; Braastad & Heggelund, 1985; Fregnac & Imbert, 1978; McCall, 1983;

Pettigrew, 1974). Many area 17 cells also develop selectivity for disparity (Pettigrew, 1974) and spatial frequency (Derrington, 1984). There is some evidence (Tsumoto & Suda, 1982) that maturation of orientation selectivity of cells in layers II/III and lower VI lags behind that of cells in other layers. Many of the cells that mature during this stage are likely to be higher order cells that receive significant excitatory input from other cells in area 17.

During the second postnatal stage development of the aminergic and cholinergic inputs to area 17 continues. Endogenous levels of NA, DA, and 5-HT continue to rise, as do the binding levels of the postsynaptic mono-amine receptors; see Figure 4 (Jonsson & Kasamatsu, 1983). There is, how-

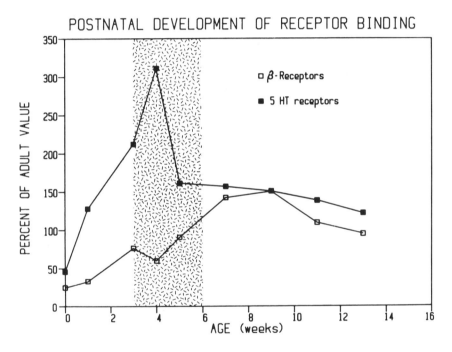

FIG. 4.   Postnatal development of receptor binding. Developmental changes in specific H³-DHA (H³-dihydroalprenolol) binding were used as an assay for development of postsynaptic ß-adrenergic receptor binding sites. Developmental changes in specific H³-5-HT binding were used as an assay for development of postsynaptic serotonin recep-tor binding sites. The data are represented as a percentage of the adult value for the re-spective parameter measured (calculated per gm wet weight of tissue). Note that the peak for serotonin binding sites occurs as early as 3–5 weeks postnatal, whereas the peak for ß-adrenergic receptor binding sites occurs at 7–9 weeks postnatal. If the serotonin system plays a role in regulating the critical period, then it must be to induce or trigger the onset of sensitivity. On the other hand, the noradrenalin system, especially the ß-adrenergic re-ceptors, may be involved in facilitating experience-dependent changes during the critical period. (Replotted from Jonsson & Kasamatsu, 1983.)

ever, a significant difference between the NA and the 5-HT systems; the level of endogenous 5-HT and the binding of 5-HT receptors peak during the second postnatal stage (Jonsson & Kasamatsu, 1983), whereas endogenous NA levels and binding of ß-adrenergic receptors continue to increase throughout this stage (Jonsson & Kasamatsu, 1983; Wilkinson, Shaw, Kahn, & Cynader, 1983).

The density of cholinergic axons remains above adult levels in layers IVc-VI throughout the second postnatal stage. By the end of this stage the density of cholinergic axons increases to adult levels in layers II and III but remains below adult levels in layer I (Bear et al., 1985). There are also laminar changes in the binding of muscarinic ACh receptors, which increases in layers I-III (and to a lesser degree in layers V-VI) and decreases in layer IV during this stage (Shaw et al., 1984a). Overall binding levels of muscarinic ACh receptors reach a peak at about five weeks (Shaw et al., 1984a). Finally, AChE activity remains depressed throughout the second postnatal stage (Potempska et al., 1979).

Stage three. During the third postnatal stage the number of synapses per neuron shows little change, remaining above adult levels throughout; see Figure 2 (Cragg, 1975; Winfield, 1981). There is thus an overproduction of synapses, many of which may later be "pruned away" as a result of neuronal activity. There is some evidence that there is an increase in the numbers of inhibitory synapses during the third postnatal stage (Winfield, 1981).

Synapse elimination between postnatal days 70 and 220 occurs mainly in the upper layers (I-III) of area 17, and is greater near the cortical projection of the center of gaze than in regions subserving the peripheral part of the visual field (O'Kusky, 1985). There is physiological evidence (Tsumoto & Suda, 1982) that cells in the upper layers (II-III), many of which project out of area 17 to other cortical visual areas (Gilbert & Kelly, 1975; for reviews see Gilbert, 1983; Swadlow, 1983) do not develop adult levels of orientation selectivity until the third postnatal stage (Figure 3).

During the third postnatal stage endogenous levels of NA and DA continue to increase (Jonsson & Kasamatsu, 1983). ß-adrenergic receptor binding is reported either to peak at 9 weeks postnatal (Figure 4; Jonsson & Kasamatsu, 1983) or to rise to adult levels at about 12 weeks postnatal and remain there (Wilkinson et al., 1983). ß-adrenergic receptor binding decreases in layer IV and increases in other layers, so that by 12 weeks postnatal, binding is greatest outside layer IV (Shaw et al., 1984b). Endogenous levels of 5-HT do not show dramatic changes duing this stage; there is a slight decrease in 5-HT binding (Jonsson & Kasamatsu, 1983).

The distribution of cholinergic axons takes on the adult pattern during the third postnatal stage; their density continues to decrease in layers IVc-VI and increase in layer I (Bear et al., 1985). The density of muscarinic ACh receptors becomes greatest in layers I-III and VI (Shaw et al., 1984a). Finally, AChE activity rises to reach adult levels by the end of the third stage (Potempska et al., 1979).

In summary, area 17 is immature when the kitten is born and undergoes substantial postnatal development. Among the most dramatic changes are (1) the re-distribution of both retinal and extra-retinal afferents to area 17, (2) the proliferation of synaptic contacts in area 17, and (3) the development of orientation, spatial frequency, and disparity selectivity of area 17 cells. Maturation of the ability of kittens to resolve spatial details and to discriminate depth follows the development of selectivity for orientation, spatial frequency, and disparity of area 17 cells. In the following section we discuss evidence that neuronal activity plays an important role in many of these postnatal developmental changes.

ACTIVITY-DEPENDENT DEVELOPMENT IN AREA 17

Role of Activity During the Three Stages

Stage one.   Activity plays a limited role during the first postnatal stage. The normal segregation of dLGN afferent terminals from the two eyes into ocular dominance patches can be prevented by blocking all retinal ganglion cell activity by repeatedly injecting tetrodotoxin (TTX) into both eyes (Stryker & Harris, 1986). Further, recordings in layer IV of area 17 show that cells in TTX-treated cats are activated equally by both eyes. Blocking only experience-dependent activity by rearing cats in darkness decreases, but does not totally abolish, segregation of thalamic afferents from the two eyes (Swindale, 1981; Swindale & Cynader, 1986). In these experiments cats are usually dark-reared for long periods of time; it may be that segregation is simply slower in the dark. Thus, spontaneous and perhaps to a lesser degree experience-dependent firing of retinal ganglion cells is necessary for development of the segregation of afferents from the two eyes during this stage.

Manipulations that enhance differences in their activity can enhance segregation of the inputs from the two eyes. After alternating electrical stimulation of the two optic nerves in kittens that had both eyes blocked with TTX, most area 17 cells are monocular (Stryker & Strickland, 1984). Furthermore, when kittens are reared under conditions in which the two eyes receive very different stimulation, such as results when the lids of one eye are sutured closed (monocular lid-suture) or the eyes are misaligned by cutting the eye muscles, the ocular dominance distribution, that is the proportion of cells activated by either eye, may be altered as early as the end of the second postnatal week; see Figure 5 (Freeman, 1978; Levitt & Van Sluyters, 1982; Olson & Freeman, 1980).

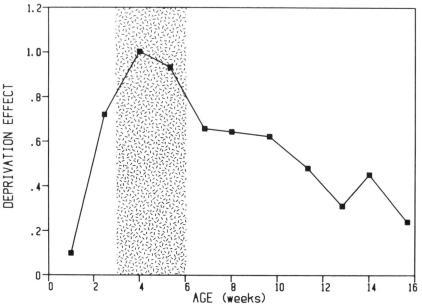

FIG. 5.   Effects of short (10–12 days) periods of monocular lid-suture, starting at different ages, on ocular dominance of area 17 cells. Recordings were made ipsilateral to the
non-deprived eye. The abscissa gives animal age at the onset of the period of deprivation.
Deprivation effect was computed as follows: for each cat the proportion of cells dominated by the non-deprived eye was computed ([(% cells in OD groups 5–7)-N]/[100%-N])
where N = 36%, the average proportion of cells activated by the ipsilateral eye for four
normal kittens. Vulnerability to monocular lid-suture is greatest during the second postnatal stage and trails off gradually during the third postnatal stage. (Replotted from
Olson & Freeman, 1980.)

Bilateral lid suture, which reduces but does not abolish patterned stimulation, slows the rate of synaptogenesis in area 17 (Winfield, 1981). As a result, synaptic development in bilaterally lid-sutured animals lags behind that
seen in normally reared animals.

It is not known whether spontaneous firing of retinal ganglion cells is necessary for development and/or maintenance of orientation selectivity of
early maturing cells in area 17; experience-dependent activity is not. The
early maturing cells develop orientation selectivity in kittens reared in darkness from birth (Bonds, 1979; Fregnac & Imbert, 1978). Furthermore, they
are likely to maintain their orientation selectivity even if experience-dependent activity is withheld; in area 17 of cats raised in darkness from birth for
7–10 months there are orientation selective cells that have the same characteristics as the early maturing cells (Leventhal & Hirsch, 1977, 1980). These cells

are not as finely tuned for orientation as in normal adults (Leventhal & Hirsch, 1980), and there is some evidence that their morphology is abnormal (Coleman & Riesen, 1968). Development of selectivity for spatial frequency is also not affected by dark-rearing during the first stage (Derrington, 1984).

Stage two. Activity plays its greatest role during the second stage. Effects of an imbalance in stimulation of the two eyes are maximal during this stage; see Figure 5 (Olson & Freeman, 1980). Perceptible shifts in the ocular dominance distribution are seen after as little as one day of monocular lid suture (Movshon & Dürsteler, 1977). During this stage alternating monocular exposure (AME), in which kittens are allowed one hour of monocular visual exposure per day and the two eyes are exposed on alternate days, results in a sharp decline in the proportion of binocular cells in area 17 (Presson & Gordon, 1979).

Visual stimulation continues to be important for synaptic development during this stage; synaptic development in area 17 is delayed in bilaterally lid-sutured cats (Winfield, 1981).

Exposure to patterned visual stimulation during the second postnatal stage is necessary for most cells in area 17 to develop orientation and spatial-frequency selectivity. If kittens are kept in darkness beyond the third postnatal week, the proportion of orientation selective cells remains at (Bonds, 1979), or possibly drops below (Blakemore & Van Sluyters, 1975; Buisseret & Imbert, 1976; Fregnac & Imbert, 1978), the 3-week level; see Figure 6. (Braastad & Heggelund, 1985, however, report that dark rearing does not affect development of orientation selectivity during the first postnatal month). Some of the variability in the results of studies of dark-reared cats may reflect differences in the criteria for what constitutes orientation-selectivity; some of it may reflect differences in the rearing. In some studies cats received limited exposure to light during the dark-rearing (e.g., Buisseret, Gary-Bobo, & Imbert, 1982), and this may have made the cells more vulnerable to dark-rearing (see Mower & Christen, 1985; Mower, Christen, & Caplan, 1983). If animals are dark-reared after the third postnatal week the normal increase in selectivity for spatial frequency does not take place (Derrington, 1984).

Stage three. The role of activity decreases gradually during the third stage. Susceptibility to monocular lid-suture declines; see Figure 5 (Olson & Freeman, 1980). Susceptibility to alternating monocular exposure (Presson & Gordon, 1979) and misalignment of the eyes (Levitt & Van Sluyters, 1982) also declines. By 16 to 20 weeks postnatal, none of these manipulations is very effective.

Bilateral lid-suture, which reduces but does not abolish patterned visual stimulation, delays until 110 days postnatal the peak in synaptic density that normally occurs at 70 days postnatal; subsequently, synaptic density declines

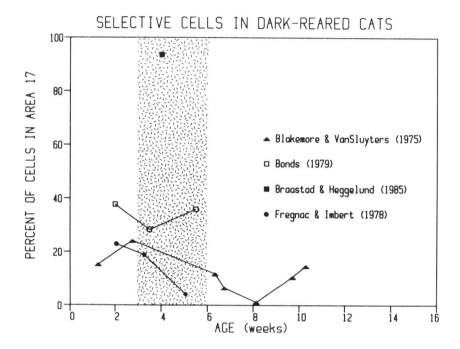

FIG. 6.   Development of orientation selectivity in area 17 of dark-reared cats. The percent of cells that are orientation selective in area 17 of dark-reared cats is plotted as a function of age. In the studies of Blakemore & Van Sluyters and Fregnac & Imbert, some cats
had very limited exposure to light during the rearing, whereas in the study by Bonds, none
did. Although there is considerable variability in the data from these studies, all but those
of Braastad & Heggelund suggest that many area 17 cells fail to develop normal orientation selectivity in dark-reared cats. One reason for the discrepancy in results may be that
Braastad & Heggelund's orientation selective cells included cells that others would call
orientation-biased. (Replotted from Braastad & Heggelund, 1985; Blakemore & Van
Sluyters, 1975; Bonds, 1975; and Fregnac & Imbert, 1978.)

to reach adult levels (Winfield, 1981). The relative proportion of different
types of synapses remains abnormal in bilaterally lid-sutured cats; there are
fewer symmetric synapses, which are thought to represent inhibitory contacts, and this may offer the anatomical basis for reduced levels of intracortical inhibition found in physiological recordings from area 17 of bilaterally lid-sutured animals (e.g., Singer & Tretter, 1976; Watkins, Wilson, &
Sherman, 1978).

If cats are reared in a normal environment until postnatal day 70, and are
then dark-reared to postnatal day 220, synapse elimination is enhanced in regions of area 17 that get input from peripheral retina, but not in those with input from the vicinity of the area centralis (O'Kusky, 1985). Since there is evidence that many cells in the upper cortical layers (and in lower layer VI) do

not develop orientation selectivity until this stage (Tsumoto & Suda, 1982), it would be important to know how physiological development of cells in these layers is affected by dark-rearing during this stage.

In summary, segregation of thalamic afferents from the two eyes during the first postnatal stage depends on neuronal activity; most of the necessary activity seems to be produced by spontaneous firing of retinal ganglion cells. An imbalance in stimulation of the two eyes, such as is produced by monocular lid suture, has some effects on ocular dominance near the end of the first stage, but is most effective in altering ocular dominance during the second stage. Susceptibility to monocular lid suture declines during the third postnatal stage.

The early maturing, first order cells in area 17 have robust orientation preferences which they develop during the first postnatal stage, and then maintain in the absence of experience-dependent neuronal activity. The late maturing cells, which normally develop orientation selectivity and spatial frequency selectivity during the second postnatal stage, require visual stimulation to develop and maintain their selectivity. This experience-dependent development may involve changes in synaptic connections within area 17. As we see below, it may also involve changes in dendritic morphology of cells that develop orientation selectivity only if visual stimulation is provided.

Structural Basis of Experience-Dependent Changes

Evidence from very different species suggests that the critical period for activity-dependent changes in sensory systems coincides with the time that afferents make synaptic contacts. For example, in the cricket, competitive interactions between sensory afferents have the largest effects during the time these afferents form synaptic contacts with their target cells (Murphey, 1986). Similarly, in the goldfish, activity has the greatest effect on the distribution of retinal ganglion cell afferents within their target zone, the optic tectum, during the period of greatest synaptogenesis (Schmidt, 1985). Finally, in the cat, activity-dependent changes in area 17 are most pronounced during the period of greatest synaptic proliferation. These results suggest that developmental plasticity may involve changes in the number and/or position of synaptic contacts. Several lines of evidence provide support for this hypothesis (for review see Greenough, 1984).

First, decreased visual stimulation resulting from dark-rearing or binocular lid-suture can reduce the frequency of dendritic spines (presumably the site of synaptic contacts) in the rat (Fifková, 1970; Rothblat & Schwartz, 1979; Valverde, 1971) and decrease dendritic field size of some area 17 neurons in the cat (Coleman & Riesen, 1968). Second, increased stimulation, achieved by rearing rats in "enriched environments," results in small increases in the frequency of dendritic spines (Globus, Rosenzweig, Bennett, & Diamond, 1973) and increases in the amount of dendrite per neuron (Greenough & Volkmar, 1973; Greenough, Volkmar, & Juraska, 1973; Holloway, 1966; Pysh & Weiss, 1979). Third, in the cat, monocular deprivation decreases the proportion of layer IV over which the deprived geniculocortical afferents terminate (Shatz & Stryker, 1978), and it both reduces the number of synaptic contacts from the deprived afferents and alters their morphology (Tieman, 1984, 1985). Fourth, exposure to patterned stimuli can affect dendritic morphology of some cells in area 17; the resulting changes reflect the specific characteristics of the stimulus presented to the growing animal (Tieman & Hirsch, 1982; Zec, Tieman, & Hirsch, 1985).

Thus, synaptic plasticity probably provides a structural basis for at least some of the activity-dependent changes that are a part of normal development of many sensory systems. There is increasing evidence that this plasticity is dependent on neuromodulators released by extra-retinal afferents to area 17 (e.g., Kety, 1970; Pettigrew, 1978; Singer, 1979).

Role of Extra-Retinal
Afferents in Experience-Dependent Changes

In adult cats the transmitters released by extra-retinal afferents to area 17, such as NA and ACh, can help regulate synaptic transmission within area 17 (e.g., Kasamatsu & Heggelund, 1982; Sillito & Kemp, 1983; Videen, Daw, & Rader, 1984). Several lines of evidence suggest that in the kitten these same neurotransmitters may help to determine whether activity-dependent changes in synaptic efficacy occur.

Changing sites of developmental plasticity.   Over the course of the three postnatal stages, the site of activity-dependent changes shifts from one layer of area 17 to another; for each postnatal stage there is a corresponding shift in the cortical distribution of monoaminergic and/or cholinergic afferents to area 17. During the first stage there are developmental changes in the lower layers of Area 17; cells in layers IV and VI (and possibly, layer V) are developing orientation selectivity, and there is segregation of thalamic afferents from the two eyes in layer IV. Cholinergic axons are most common in the lower layers (IVc–VI), and muscarinic receptor binding is highest in layer IV. Similarly, ß-adrenergic binding is highest in layer IV. It is not known whether neuronal activity plays a role in development of the early maturing cells; it is involved in the segregation of afferents from the two eyes. During the second stage cells outside layer IV, that is, those in the extragranular layers, acquire orientation selectivity; this process requires visual stimulation. At this time, the density both of cholinergic axons and of muscarinic receptors increases in the extragranular layers. During the third stage experience-dependent development of orientation selectivity may continue in layers II/III and in the bottom of layer VI. The highest density of cholinergic axons is now in the upper layers (I-III), and muscarinic ACh receptor binding is also highest in layers II/III. During this stage, binding of ß-adrenergic receptors decreases in layer IV and increases outside layer IV so that by 12 weeks the binding is higher outside than inside layer IV. Thus, during each postnatal stage aminergic and cholinergic afferents and their respective receptor binding is highest in those layers of area 17 that are the site of activity-dependent developmental changes; these extra-retinal afferents are thus in a position to control experience-dependent developmental changes. There is direct evidence that they do so.

Effects of first exposure to light.   Sensitivity to the effects of early visual experience is to some extent determined by the early experience itself. On the one hand, the decrease in sensitivity to monocular lid-suture that normally occurs during stage three can be prevented, or at least greatly delayed, by keeping animals in darkness (e.g., Cynader, Berman, & Hein, 1976; Cynader & Mitchell, 1980; Mower, Burchfiel, & Duffy, 1981a; Mower, Berry, Burchfiel, & Duffy, 1981b; Timney, Mitchell, & Cynader, 1980). Similarly, the period during which stimulation-dependent development of orientation selectivity can occur is also extended by dark-rearing (Cynader et al., 1976). On the other hand, brief exposure to a lighted environment appears to start the decline in plasticity, and once started the process continues in the absence of any further visual stimulation (Mower et al., 1983; Mower & Christen, 1985). These effects of visual stimulation in regulating experience-sensitivity may, in part, reflect effects of the first exposure to light on extra-retinal afferents to area 17. First exposure to light affects the levels of enzymes and receptors for at least one of these systems: there is a transient increase in muscarinic ACh receptors in visual but not motor cortex of dark-reared rats on first exposure to light (Rose & Stewart, 1978). There are also transient increases in the synthesizing and degradative enzymes for ACh, choline acetyltransferase and AChE (Rose & Stewart, 1978; Sinha & Rose, 1976).

Regulation of neuronal plasticity by neuromodulators.   Once sensitivity to monocular lid-suture has declined after the end of the third postnatal stage, it can be restored by perfusing NA into area 17 (Kasamatsu, 1983; Kasamatsu, Pettigrew, & Ary, 1979) or by electrically stimulating the locus coeruleus, which is the source of most of the noradrenergic input to area 17 (Kasamatsu, Watabe, Heggelund, & Scholler, 1985). Furthermore, administration of NA facilitates the rate of recovery from the effects of monocular lid-suture (Kasamatsu, Pettigrew, & Ary, 1981).

Developmental plasticity during the critical period can be reduced, or possibly even abolished, by some procedures that deplete neurotransmitters released by extra-retinal afferents to area 17. For example, depleting NA by administering the specific neurotoxin 6-hydroxydopamine (6-OHDA) directly into area 17 prevents the shift in ocular dominance that normally results from monocular lid-suture during the critical period (Bear, Paradiso, Schwartz, Nelson, Carnes, & Daniels, 1983; Daw, Rader, Robertson, & Ariel, 1983; Kasamatsu et al., 1979; Paradiso, Bear, & Daniels, 1983). Injecting NA directly into area 17 can counteract the effects of administering 6-OHDA (Kasamatsu et al., 1979; Pettigrew & Kasamatsu, 1978).

The effects of other approaches to depleting NA, such as intraventricular administration of 6–OHDA, are somewhat controversial: although some authors report that intraventricular 6–OHDA reduces the ocular dominance shift produced by monocular lid-suture (Kasamatsu & Pettigrew, 1976, 1979; Trombley, Allen, Soyke, Blaha, Lane, & Gordon, 1986) others do not (Adrien, Blanc, Buisseret, Fregnac, Gary-Bobo, Imbert, Tassin, & Trotter, 1985; Daw, Robertson, Rader, Videen, & Coscia, 1984; Daw, Videen, Robertson, & Rader, 1985a; Daw, Videen, Rader, Robertson, & Coscia, 1985c). Trombley et al. (1986) point out that the data from all these studies agree in that the proportion of cells activated by the deprived eye is consistently higher in treated cats than in untreated cats, but that the number of animals is often too low for this difference to be statistically significant. Thus, intracranial administration of 6–OHDA affects developmental plasticity, suggesting that cortical levels of NA play an important role in regulating experience-sensitivity; other neurotransmitters, especially ACh, may also have a part to play in this regulation.

Indirect evidence that NA levels are not the sole determinant of developmental plasticity comes from the observation that cortical levels of NA do not correlate well with sensitivity to monocular lid suture. First, Trombley et al. (1986) found that the dose of 6–OHDA needed to reduce the shift in ocular dominance was more than 30 times that needed to deplete NA in the cortex. Second, several procedures that deplete cortical NA but do not involve intracranial administration of 6–OHDA are ineffective in blocking sensitivity to monocular lid-suture. Destruction of the noradrenergic afferent pathway fails to protect the kitten from the effects of monocular lid suture (Bear & Daniels, 1983; Bear et al., 1983; Daw et al., 1984; Daw, Videen, Parkinson, & Rader, 1985b). Thus, while NA levels do affect developmental plasticity, depletion of NA does not appear to be sufficient to abolish plasticity during the critical period. This suggests that, in addition to depleting cortical NA, 6–OHDA has some other effect, which, alone or in combination with the decreased NA, is responsible for its ability to reduce sensitivity to monocular deprivation.

Bear and Singer (1986) provide evidence that another transmitter of extra-retinal afferents, ACh, is also important in regulating experience-sensitivity. They report that 6–OHDA antagonizes the effects of ACh on cortical neurons at concentrations similar to those required to prevent plasticity in kittens, suggesting that cortical administration of 6–OHDA is effective in disrupting plasticity because it interferes with both the noradrenergic and cholinergic afferent pathways. Using a variety of methods Bear and Singer (1986) showed that lesions of both aminergic and cholinergic pathways effectively reduce sensitivity to monocular lid suture in kittens, whereas lesions of either pathway alone do not. Thus, both the cholinergic and noradrenergic projections to area 17 may be involved in the regulation of experience-dependent changes.

A Cellular Basis for Experience-Dependent Development

Results of a recent study by Aoki and Siekevitz (1985) provide an indication of the cellular mechanisms by which NA may influence experience-dependent development of area 17 cells. Because NA stimulates adenylate cyclase, thereby increasing the production of cyclic adenosine monophosphate (cAMP), Aoki and Siekevitz (1985) examined the ontogeny of cAMP-dependent phosphorylation of certain proteins in area 17 and its modification by changes in visual exposure. Specifically, they examined changes in the phosphorylation of proteins associated with synaptic function (e.g. Synapsin I) or with intracellular structures in dendrites (e.g., microtubule associated protein 2, or MAP2).

Dark rearing during the critical period appeared to decrease the *in vitro* cAMP-dependent phosphorylation of MAP2, and exposing dark-reared cats to light increased it (Aoki & Siekevitz, 1985). In contrast, when normally reared adult animals were dark-reared for comparable periods and then exposed to a lighted environment, there was no consistent change in phosphorylation of MAP2. The phosphorylation of other proteins, such as Synapsin I, which is associated with synapses, did not show comparable sensitivity to the animals' visual exposure history.

An experience-dependent increase in the *in vitro* cAMP-dependent phosphorylation of MAP2 suggests that, in the animal, first exposure to light causes *de*phosphorylation of MAP2, which would increase its association with microtubules, and so increase the rigidity of dendrites in area 17 as synapses are forming during the critical period. In contrast, the modifiable state maintained by dark rearing would be associated with relatively more flexible or malleable dendrites (Aoki & Siekevitz, 1985). This interpretation is consistent with the report of Spinelli, Jensen, and Standish (1979) that administration of colchicine, which disrupts microtubules, can lead to a re-instatement of some degree of developmental plasticity in adult cats; perhaps the plasticity occurs as the microtubules reform. This interpretation is also consistent with findings that dark rearing suppresses the synthesis of tubulin in the visual but not motor cortex of rats (Cronly-Dillon & Perry, 1979) and that first exposure to light stimulates it (Cronly-Dillon & Perry, 1979; Rose, Sinha, & Jones-Lecointe, 1976). Although Cronly-Dillon and Perry report that light will stimulate tubulin synthesis only during a relatively brief critical period that is not prolonged by dark rearing, Rose et al. observe a light-stimulated increase well after that time. The reason for this discrepancy is not clear.

In summary, experience-dependent changes in the synthesis of tubulin and cAMP-dependent phosphorylation of MAP2 may be involved in synaptic plasticity. NA, by increasing c-AMP, should stimulate the phosphorylation of MAP2 and make the dendrites flexible. First exposure to light, which increases choline acetyltransferase and muscarinic ACh receptors, thus enhancing effectiveness of cholinergic extra-retinal afferents, also stimulates tubulin synthesis and dephosphorylation of MAP2, thereby making the dendrites less flexible. This suggests that NA and ACh play rather different roles in modulating plasticity: NA may permit changes by making things flexible, and ACh may help solidify the changes as they occur.

BEHAVIORAL SIGNIFICANCE OF
EXPERIENCE-DEPENDENT BRAIN DEVELOPMENT

In order to understand the functional significance of experience-dependent development it is necessary to examine how it affects behavioral development after the critical period. This requires the use of paradigms that can produce selective changes in visual system development by controlling an animal's exposure history, a procedure referred to as *environmental surgery* (Hirsch, 1972). We describe two such procedures, one for studying the functional significance of experience-dependent development of orientation selectivity of cells in area 17, the second for studying functional effects of an imbalance in stimulation of the two eyes during the critical period.

The Function of Experience-Dependent
Development of Orientation Selectivity

Effects of selective exposure to lines of one or two orientations during the critical period. Stimulation-dependent activity has both non-specific and specific effects on development. For example, exposure to small spots enhances the responsiveness of cells in area 17 (Blakemore & Van Sluyters, 1975; Pettigrew & Freeman, 1973; Van Sluyters & Blakemore, 1973), whereas exposure to elongated contours is necessary to increase the proportion of cells that are orientation selective (Blakemore & Van Sluyters, 1975). Among the most dramatic and well-documented of these specific changes occurs in kittens exposed to lines of one orientation, a procedure referred to as stripe-rearing.

Kittens were housed in darkness from birth. Beginning at 28 days of age the kittens were brought out into a lighted environment for daily exposure periods wearing masks within which each eye could view a field of three parallel black lines (Figure 7). Some animals viewed lines of the same orientation with both eyes (horizontal or vertical); other animals viewed horizontal lines with one eye and, simultaneously, vertical lines with the other eye. A third group of animals viewed 45 degree lines with one eye and 135 degree lines with the other eye. The masks were put on and taken off while animals were in the darkroom and thus provided the only patterned visual stimulation these cats received. Once animals had been given between 150 and 650 hours of exposure the response properties of cells in area 17 were studied.

In stripe-reared cats exposed to one (or two) orientation(s), the distribution of orientation preferences of area 17 cells reflects the orientation of the lines presented during rearing: (1) in cats exposed to horizontal lines, the distribution of preferred orientations was shifted towards horizontal (Figure 8); (2) in cats exposed to vertical lines, it was shifted towards vertical (Figure 8); (3) in cats exposed to horizontal lines with one eye and vertical lines with the other eye, for each eye the distribution of cells activated by that eye was shifted towards the exposed orientation; and (4) in cats exposed to diagonal lines, the distribution of preferred orientations was shifted towards diagonal (Hirsch et al., 1983; Hirsch & Spinelli, 1970, 1971; Leventhal & Hirsch, 1975; Pettigrew, Olson, & Hirsch, 1973; Tieman & Hirsch, 1982). (Although

FIG. 7. One technique used for providing controlled visual stimulation. Kittens wear these goggles whenever they are in a lighted environment. Stimulus patterns are mounted on the inside surface of the plastic sheet at the front of the goggles: one pattern is in front of the left eye; a second in front of the right eye. A lens is mounted in the mask in front of each eye so that the patterns are at the focal plane of the lens. Light enters at the side through diffusing plastic and illuminates the pattern. (Reprinted with permission from Hirsch, 1985b.)

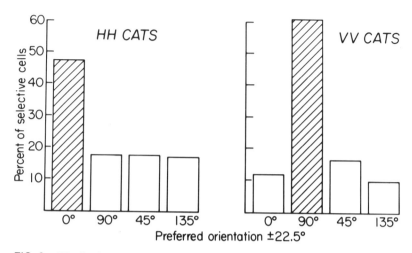

FIG. 8.   Distribution of preferred orientations of orientation-selective cells recorded from area 17 of (A) six cats exposed to horizontal lines and (B) six cats exposed to vertical lines. Note that for each group the distribution peaks at the exposed orientation. (Reprinted with permission from Hirsch, 1985b.)

Stryker & Sherk, 1975, suggested that effects of stripe-rearing might be an artifact of sampling biases, there is now substantial agreement that stripe-rearing alters the distribution of preferred orientations, at least when goggles are used to restrict the exposure; see Blakemore, 1976; Blasdel, Mitchell, Muir, & Pettigrew, 1977; Gordon & Presson, 1982; Hirsch et al., 1983; Leventhal & Hirsch, 1975; Stryker & Sherk, 1975; Stryker, Sherk, Leventhal, & Hirsch, 1978; Rauschecker & Singer, 1981; Tieman & Hirsch, 1982.)

Visual exposure does not affect physiological and morphological development of all area 17 cells equally. It is possible to use physiological measures to identify, in stripe-reared cats, cells that are comparable to those that develop and maintain orientation selectivity in cats dark-reared from birth for 7 to 10 months (Leventhal & Hirsch, 1977, 1980). Stripe rearing does not affect the distribution of the preferred orientations of these cells, as shown in Figure 9A; it does produce a bias in the distribution of the preferred orientations of the other cells, as is shown in Figure 9B (Hirsch et al., 1983). Thus, physiologically identified cell groups in area 17 differ in experience-sensitivity.

Stripe rearing affects dendritic orientation for some, but not all, cells in area 17 (Tieman & Hirsch, 1982; Zec et al., 1985). The visual cortex of stripe-reared cats and normal cats was impregnated by the Golgi-Kopsch method and the dendritic morphology of individual neurons was examined in the plane of the visual map. The dendritic fields of stellate cells in layer IV and of the basal dendrites of pyramidal cells in layers III and V were elongated in both normal and stripe-reared cats. For the pyramidal cells in layers III and

V, but not for the stellate cells in layer IV, the distribution of the long axis of these dendritic fields is altered in a specific fashion by stripe rearing (Figure 10). Thus, morphologically identified cell groups in area 17 also differ in their experience-sensitivity. For cats exposed only to vertical lines, most layer III pyramidal cells have dendritic fields oriented orthogonal to the cortical representation of the vertical meridian; for cats exposed only to horizontal lines, most layer III pyramidal cells have dendritic fields oriented parallel to the vertical meridian.

Although stripe-rearing does not affect the orientations of the dendritic fields of the layer IV stellate cells, it does affect them in other ways (Tieman and Hirsch, unpublished observations). The dendritic fields of the layer IV stellate cells were both less extensive and more elongated in stripe-reared cats. Similar effects are seen in layer V pyramidal cells (Zec et al., 1985). Since

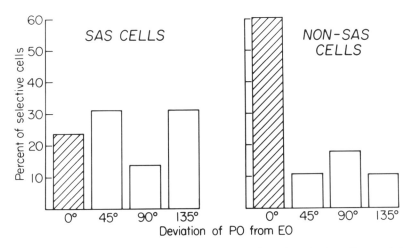

FIG. 9.   Distribution of preferred orientations of orientation-selective cells recorded from area 17 of stripe-reared cats. Data for cells with a small receptive field and a low cutoff velocity, SAS cells, are shown in A; data for all other cells are shown in B. For these histograms, preferred orientations are computed as deviations from the exposed orientation as follows: Cells in bins labeled 0 degrees have a preferred orientation within 22.5 degrees of the exposed orientation; cells in bins labeled 45 degrees have a preferred orientation within 22.5 degrees of the exposed orientation + 45 degrees; cells in bins labeled 90 degrees have a preferred orientation within 22.5 degrees of the exposed orientation + 90 degrees; cells in bins labeled 135 degrees have a preferred orientation within 22.5 degrees of the exposed orientation + 135 degrees. For non-SAS cells (B), the largest bin consists of cells within 22.5 degrees of the exposed orientation. The distribution of preferred orientations of non-SAS cells is thus biased significantly toward the exposed orientation. For SAS cells (A), there is no such relation between the number of cells in a bin and the differences between preferred and exposed orientation. Thus, the distribution of preferred orientations of cells with response properties matching cells that remain orientation selective in long-term dark-reared cats is not altered by stripe-rearing. (Reprinted with permission from Hirsch, 1985b.)

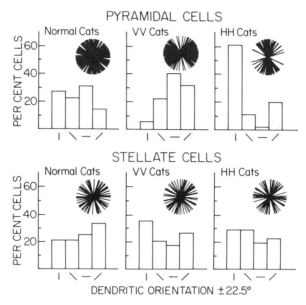

FIG. 10.   Dendritic-field orientations of layer III pyramidal cells and layer IV stellate cells from area 17 of normal cats, cats exposed to vertical lines (VV cats), and cats exposed to horizontal lines (HH cats). The data from all the cats in each condition are grouped together. The dendritic fields were examined in a plane parallel to the surface of the brain, i.e., in the same plane as the map of the visual field. Dendritic fields were elongated in this plane, and the major axis of this elongation was determined for each cell. This dendritic-field orientation could then be related to the representation of horizontal and vertical within the cortical map of the visual field. The histograms plot the percentage of cells having dendritic-field orientations within 22.5 degrees of 90 degrees (|), 135 degrees (\), 0 degrees (−), or 45 degrees (/). The inserts are the polar plots for these distributions. The dendritic fields of the pyramidal cells from the normally reared cats were uniformly distributed, whereas most of the pyramidal cells from VV cats had dendritic field orientations within 22.5 degrees of the cortical representation of horizontal, and most of the pyramidal cells from HH cats had dendritic field orientations within 22.5 degrees of the cortical representation of vertical. In contrast the dendritic fields of layer IV stellate cells were uniformly distributed in all three groups. (Reprinted with permission from Tieman & Hirsch, 1982.)

these changes are not specifically related to the orientation of the lines viewed during rearing they may be non-specific effects of restricting visual experience. Coleman and Riesen (1968) examined visual cortex of dark-reared cats and found a decrease in total dendritic length for layer IV stellate cells, but not layer V pyramidal cells. Greenough and Volkmar (1973) found an increase in total dendritic length for all cells examined (including both layer IV stellate cells and layer V pyramidal cells) in the visual cortex of rats reared in enriched environments. Thus, the total dendritic length of cells in visual cortex may simply reflect the complexity and variety of visual stimulation received during development.

In summary, visual exposure has both specific and non-specific effects on physiology and morphology of cells in area 17. Layer III pyramidal cells show the largest specific morphological effects, whereas layer IV stellate cells show the largest non-specific morphological effects; layer V pyramidal cells show a blend of specific and non-specific morphological effects (Zec et al., 1985). Laminar differences in physiological effects of stripe-rearing have been determined to only a limited degree; results of studies using C^{14}-2-deoxyglucose to map the distribution of cells responding to stimuli of a particular orientation suggest that the orientation preferences of cells in layer IV are less affected by stripe-rearing than are those of cells in other layers (Singer, Freeman, & Rauschecker, 1981).

Second order effects of exposure to lines of one or two orientations. The behavioral effects of stripe-rearing are related in a systematic and specific fashion to the stimulus orientations presented during the rearing. They include deficits in sensori-motor coordination (Blakemore & Cooper, 1970; Muir & Mitchell, 1975), orientation-specific reductions in visual acuity (Blasdel et al., 1977; Fiorentini & Maffei, 1978; Muir & Mitchell 1973, 1975; Thibos & Levick, 1982; but see also Wark & Peck, 1982), and orientation-specific deficits in the ability to discriminate differences in stimulus orientation (Hirsch, 1972; Wark & Peck, 1982).

Stripe-rearing may also influence which cues the animal will attend to after the rearing has ended (Hirsch, 1972, 1985a). Stripe-reared cats exposed to vertical lines with one eye and horizontal lines with the other eye were trained to select a black outline square. They were then given a series of equivalence trials to determine which portion of the stimulus they were attending to. One cat chose the vertical sides of the stimulus with the vertically exposed eye, and the horizontal sides with the horizontally-exposed eye (Hirsch, 1972); other cats performed at chance levels on the equivalence trials and so did not provide any information. These results suggest that early visual experience may influence the stimuli to which a cat will attend.

Studies of rats raised in controlled visual environments (Tees, Midgley, & Bruinsma, 1980) provide additional evidence for experience-dependent changes in attention; stimulus choices were affected by a bias in the animals' early visual exposure. Deprivation had relatively limited effects on rats' capacity to discriminate even very small differences between stimuli (e.g., Tees, 1968, 1979), but early visual experience affected preferences among stimuli (Tees et al., 1980). Thus, stimulation that affects development of the orientation-selectivity of cells in area 17 may also affect the development of attentional processes. The effects of a biased early visual environment would thus be exacerbated by an enduring experience-dependent bias in visual attention. As described below, such a process is seen even more clearly in cats reared with unequal AME and then given binocular visual exposure.

Functional Significance of an
Imbalance in Stimulation of the Two Eyes

Advantages of the paradigm of unequal alternating monocular exposure.
The most common method of producing an imbalance in stimulation of the
two eyes has been monocular lid-suture, but this method has the disadvantage that the difference in stimulation is qualitative as well as quantitative.
One eye is deprived of almost all patterned visual stimulation. Some consequences of monocular lid suture result from the imbalance in stimulation;
they affect the outcome of binocular competition, a struggle between afferents from the two eyes for control of cells in area 17 (Guillery, 1972; Wiesel &
Hubel, 1965). Other consequences, however, result from the deprivation of
patterned visual stimulation. The confounding of these two variables makes
it difficult to sort out how they each affect subsequent behavioral development. For these reasons, we have developed a technique, unequal alternating
monocular exposure, or unequal AME (Tumosa, Tieman, & Hirsch, 1980a;
Tumosa, Tieman, & Hirsch, 1982), that produces an imbalance in stimulation of the two eyes without continuous pattern deprivation of one eye and
permits systematic variation of the magnitude of the imbalance in stimulation.

In unequal AME, kittens receive patterned visual stimulation with each
eye, but on alternate days and for different periods of time. To vary the magnitude of the imbalance, the duration of exposure is changed: the more experienced eye receives 8 hours of exposure every other day, and the less experienced eye receives 1 hour (AME 8/1), 4 hours (AME 8/4), or 7 hours (AME
8/7) of exposure on the intervening days. As controls, animals receive equal
periods of exposure with each eye, again on alternate days (1 hour/day,
AME 1/1; 8 hours/day, AME 8/8; or 24 hours/day, AME 24/24). The
rearing procedures are described in detail in Tumosa et al. (1982).

Effects of unequal AME during the critical period.   The behavioral, anatomical and physiological effects of unequal AME show that it affects the
outcome of the competition between afferents from the two eyes (for a review see Hirsch, Tieman, Tieman, & Tumosa, 1986). Although the critical
period for these effects has not been determined, it is likely to be similar to
those for monocular lid-suture, equal AME, and strabismus, all of which are
very similar (Ikeda, Tremain, & Einon, 1978; Levitt & Van Sluyters, 1982;
Presson & Gordon, 1979; Yinon, 1976).

Rearing cats with unequal AME produces changes in their visual fields. A
normal cat, when tested monocularly for its ability to orient to targets in
space as in Figure 11A, responds to stimuli between 30 degrees nasal and 90
degrees temporal; thus the central 60 degrees can be seen with either eye, as
shown in Figure 11B (Sherman, 1973; Tumosa et al., 1980a, 1982). A cat

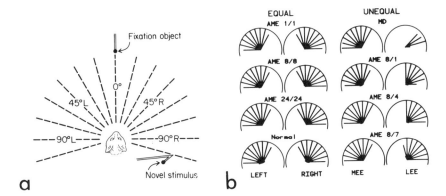

a   b

FIG. 11.   (A) Method for testing visual fields. The cat was restrained with its lateral can-
thi aligned along the 90 degree guidelines and its nose pointed along the 0 degree guideline
toward the fixation object (a piece of food on a wire). A novel stimulus (a piece of food on
another wire) was then introduced along one of the guidelines. A positive response was recorded when, upon being released, the cat turned and immediately approached the novel
stimulus. A negative response was recorded if the cat approached the fixation object or if
it scanned the field before approaching the novel stimulus. If the animal turned toward
the novel stimulus but then turned back toward and approached the fixation object, the
response was recorded as plus/minus since the animal apparently saw the novel stimulus
but chose not to respond normally to it. (Reprinted with permission from Tumosa et al.,
1982.) (B) Visual fields for each eye of cats reared with equal (left) or unequal (right) exposure to the two eyes. The fields are represented by polar plots showing the responses to
stimuli presented at every 15 degrees of the visual field. The semicircle represents a level of
12 positive responses in 12 trials. Averaged data are shown for 5 normal cats, one AME
24/24 cat, 4 AME 8/8 cats, 9 AME 1/1 cats, 2 monocularly deprived cats, 20 AME 8/1
cats, 14 AME 8/4 cats, and 5 AME 8/7 cats (tested at 10 weeks). The data are plotted as if
the less experienced eye were always the right eye, although for many animals it was the
left. For all the cats reared with equal exposure, the fields of the two eyes are normal. For
all cats reared with unequal exposure, the field of the more experienced eye is normal, but
the field of the less experienced eye is restricted, and the degree of this restriction is a function of the size of the imbalance in exposure. (Reprinted with permission from Hirsch et
al., 1986.)

reared with equal AME, no matter what the duration of the daily periods of
exposure (24 hours, 8 hours, or 1 hour) has normal visual fields, as shown in
Figure 11B (Tumosa et al., 1980a, 1982). A cat reared with an imbalance in
stimulation, however, shows visual field deficits when tested with its less experienced eye: the greatest deficits are within the binocular portion of the visual field, and the size of the deficit is related to the degree of the imbalance in
exposure; see Figure 11B. The deficit in animals reared with a large or moderate imbalance in stimulation, AME 8/1 or AME 8/4, encompasses the entire
nasal field. A smaller imbalance, AME 8/7, results in an initally incomplete,
but progressive loss of responsiveness in the nasal hemifield (Tumosa et al.,
1982; Tumosa, Nunberg, Hirsch, & Tieman, 1983). Thus, the effects of une-

qual AME appear to be cumulative, and at least in AME 8/7 the nasal-field deficit appears to involve something more than a simple failure of development, probably reflecting the results of competition. The fact that the deficits are restricted to the nasal portion of the binocular visual field suggests that the ipsilateral pathway from retina to visual cortex, which subserves the nasal visual field, is at a competitive disadvantage.

Unequal AME also produces changes in area 17. Although the cells have relatively normal selectivity for stimulus orientation (Smith, Reeves, & Holdefer, 1982; Tieman, McCall, & Hirsch, 1979; Tieman, McCall, & Hirsch, 1983), most can be activated by stimulation of only one eye, usually the more experienced one. The AME 8/1 cats show a greater shift in ocular dominance than the AME 8/4 cats; see Figure 12 (Smith et al., 1982; Tieman et al., 1979, 1983; Tumosa & Tieman, 1981). Consistent with the physiologically measured ocular dominance changes, ocular dominance patches for the less experienced eye (as demonstrated by transneuronal transport after intraocular injection of H^3-proline) are smaller than those for the more experienced eye (Tumosa, 1982; Tumosa, Tieman, & Hirsch, 1980b). Furthermore, the effects of unequal AME are more apparent ipsilateral to the less experienced eye than contralateral to it, suggesting, as did the behavioral results and changes in the dLGN (Tieman, Nickla, Gross, Hickey, & Tumosa, 1984), that the contralateral pathway from retina to visual cortex has some advantage in the competition for access to cortical cells; this advantage is sufficiently strong to overcome a moderate, but not a large imbalance in stimulation.

Second order effects of unequal AME.   Although the effects of unequal AME during the critical period are comparatively mild, once both eyes are stimulated simultaneously, the effects of the imbalance in stimulation are exacerbated. Thus, the pattern of visual stimulation received during the second and third postnatal stages can have severe consequences on visual system development long after the end of the classical critical period.

Animals were reared with AME, either equal or unequal, until they were between 3 and 9 months of age, at which time they were allowed unrestricted binocular exposure. Visual fields of these animals were determined at regular intervals throughout the period of binocular visual exposure (Tumosa et al., 1983). For cats reared with little or no imbalance (AME 1/1 and AME 8/7), subsequent binocular exposure had no effect on the visual fields: Both the binocular and monocular fields remained unchanged throughout 4 months of binocular exposure; see Figure 13.

The results were very different for animals that received a larger imbalance in stimulation of the two eyes during the critical period (i.e., AME 8/4 and AME 8/1). At the end of the alternating monocular exposure the visual field of the less-experienced eye was restricted to the temporal hemifield, and as a

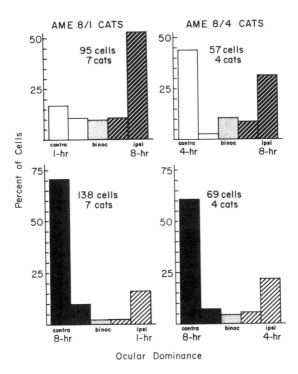

FIG. 12.   Histograms showing the percent of cells in area 17 activated by each eye of AME 8/1 cats and AME 8/4 cats. Cells in the bin labeled contra were activated only by the contralateral eye; cells in the bin labeled ipsi were activated only by the ipsilateral eye; cells in the bin labeled binoc were activated equally by both eyes; cells in the remaining two bins were activated by both eyes, but in one case the contralateral eye was dominant and in the other case the ipsilateral eye was dominant. Cells recorded from the cortical hemisphere contralateral to the less experienced eye are above, and those from the hemisphere ipsilateral to the less experienced eye below. Darker bars represent cells dominated by the 8-hour eye and lighter bars represent cells dominated by the 1-hour eye. Solid bars represent cells driven predominantly by the contralateral pathway and striped bars represent cells driven predominantly by the ipsilateral pathway. In both hemispheres of the AME 8/1 cats and in the hemisphere ipsilateral to the 4-hour eye of the AME 8/4 cats, most cells are dominated by the 8-hour eye. (Reprinted with permission from D. Tieman et al., 1983.)

result of subsequent binocular exposure there was a further restriction of both the binocular field and the monocular field of the less experienced eye. This is illustrated in Figure 13 for one AME 8/1 cat that was reared with unequal AME for 12 weeks and one AME 8/4 cat that was reared with unequal AME for 9 months. After 26 weeks of subsequent binocular exposure, the binocular visual field of the AME 8/1 cat became equivalent to the monocular field of the 8-hour eye, suggesting that, when both eyes were open, this an-

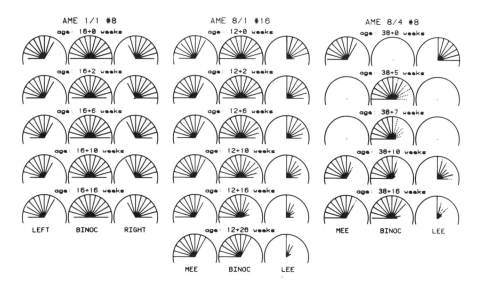

FIG. 13. Effects of subsequent binocular exposure on the visual fields of an AME 1/1 cat, an AME 8/1 cat, and an AME 8/4 cat. The exposure history of the animal is indicated above each visual field plot. The first number gives the animal's age in weeks at the end of AME, and the second number indicates the length of binocular exposure, also in weeks. Plus/minus responses are plotted as dashed lines. For the AME 1/1 cat, the fields are normal both immediately after the alternating exposure and throughout the 4 months of binocular exposure. For the AME 8/1 cat, both the binocular field and the monocular field of the 8-hour eye were normal in extent at the onset of binocular exposure, whereas that of the 1-hour eye was restricted to the temporal hemifield. With continued binocular exposure, both the binocular field and the field of the 1-hour eye became more restricted until eventually the binocular field was equivalent to the monocular field of the 8-hour eye, and the field of the 1-hour eye was restricted to the central 30 degrees of the hemifield. Similar changes occurred in the fields of the AME 8/4 cat, whose binocular exposure did not start until the animal was 9 months old. The monocular fields of this cat were not tested at 5 and 7 weeks of binocular exposure, nor was the binocular field tested at 0 weeks. (Reprinted with permission from Tumosa et al., 1983.)

imal was not using its 1-hour eye at all. Furthermore, even when the animal was tested with the 1-hour alone, there was evidence of suppression: The field was restricted to the central 30 degrees of the temporal hemifield. Similar, though slightly less dramatic, results were observed for the AME 8/4 cat after 16 weeks of binocular exposure. Thus, binocular exposure created an almost complete suppression of the less-experienced eye, even when the onset of binocular exposure was delayed until the cat was 9 months old, well after the end of the classical critical period.

The amount of suppression seen after binocular exposure is positively correlated with the imbalance imposed during rearing (Figure 14). The AME 8/1 cats show the greatest suppression, the AME 8/4 cats show intermediate levels of suppression, and the AME 8/7 and AME 1/1 cats show none.

Although it is clear that the effects of unequal AME during the critical period involve competitive changes in the geniculocortical pathway, it is not clear in what part of the visual pathway the supression occurs (see Hirsch et al., 1986). Unequal AME during the first months of postnatal life must create a condition that is unstable once the animal receives binocular visual exposure. As a result, there is suppression of the less experienced eye, at least for tasks in which the animal must respond to a new stimulus presented while the animal is maintaining fixation on another stimulus. The resulting changes in visuomotor behavior occur well after the end of the critical period during which the effects of an imbalance in stimulation of the two eyes have previously been demonstrated. Thus, a bias in early experience can produce cascading effects even after the experimentally induced initial bias in early experience has ended.

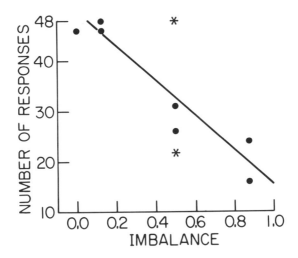

FIG. 14.   Suppression as a function of imbalance. The number of responses to targets presented 45, 60, 75, and 90 degrees ipsilateral to the less experienced eye, with plus/minus responses given half weight, is plotted as a function of the imbalance imposed during rearing. Imbalance is defined as the difference in the duration of stimulation of the two eyes divided by the longer of the two durations. That is, I = (A-B)/A, where A is the longer duration (usually 8 hours) an B is the shorter (7, 4, or 1 hours). The data were obtained under binocular testing conditions after 16 weeks of binocular exposure. The data for the two late-exposed cats are plotted as asterisks. The line shown is the best-fitting straight line through all 9 data points. (Reprinted with permission from Tumosa et al., 1983.)

CONCLUSIONS

Exposure during the critical period can have dramatic effects on physiology and morphology of cells in the visual system. An imbalance in stimulation of the two eyes can affect the outcome of competitive interactions between afferents from the two eyes, and visual experience can affect the development of orientation selectivity of some cells in area 17. Experience-dependent changes may include long-lasting changes in attention; stripe rearing may affect which cues the animal attends to as it learns to respond in a discriminative fashion to its visual environment. Furthermore, when both eyes receive some normal patterned visual stimulation, an imbalance in exposure times of the two eyes during the critical period can create stimulation-dependent vulnerability that extends past the end of the classical critical period; subsequent binocular exposure results in suppression of the less experienced eye. Thus, experience-dependent changes during the critical period can have far-reaching consequences, affecting the animal's later interactions with its environment. If these developmental principles can be applied to primates, the implications for human development are apparent; limitations in early environment may bias the young child's behavior even if these limitations are subsequently removed. Critical period studies show that a long shadow can be cast by an impoverished early environment.

ACKNOWLEDGMENTS

We thank H. Ghiradella, R. K. Murphey, J. Schmidt, D. G. Tieman, B. Timney, and N. Tumosa for critical comments and helpful suggestions; A. Appleby helped in the preparation of the manuscript.

REFERENCES

Adrien, J., Blanc, G., Buisseret, P., Fregnac, Y., Gary-Bobo, E., Imbert, M., Tassin, J. P., & Trotter, Y. Noradrenaline and functional plasticity in kitten visual cortex: A re-examination. *Journal of Physiology (London)*, 1985, *367*, 73–98.

Albus, K., & Wolf, W. Early post-natal development of neuronal function in the kitten's visual cortex: A laminar analysis. *Journal of Physiology (London)*, 1984, *348*, 153–185.

Anker, R. L. The prenatal development of some of the visual pathways in the cat. *Journal of Comparative Neurology*, 1977, *173*, 185–204.

Anker, R. L., & Cragg, B. G. Development of the extrinsic connections of the visual cortex in the cat. *Journal of Comparative Neurology*, 1974, *154*, 29–42.

Aoki, C., & Siekevitz, P. Ontogenetic changes in the cyclic adenosine 3', 5'-mono-phosphate-stimulatable phosphorylation of cat visual cortex proteins, particularly of microtubule-associated protein 2 (MAP 2): Effects of normal and dark rearing and of the exposure to light. *Journal of Neuroscience*, 1985, *5*, 2465–2483.

Baerends-van Roon, J. M., & Baerends, G. P. *The morphogenesis of the behaviour of the domestic cat.* Amsterdam: North-Holland, 1979.

Barlow, H. B., Blakemore, C., & Pettigrew, J. D. The neural mechanism of binocular depth discrimination. *Journal of Physiology (London),* 1967, *193,* 327–342.

Barrett, P., Bateson, P. The development of play in cats. *Behaviour,* 1978, *66,* 106–120.

Bear, M. F., Carnes, K. M., & Ebner, F. F. Postnatal changes in the distribution of acetyl-choline-esterase in kitten striate cortex. *Journal of Comparative Neurology,* 1985, *237,* 519–532.

Bear, M. F., & Daniels, J. D. The plastic response to monocular deprivation persists in kitten visual cortex after chronic depletion of norepinephrine. *Journal of Neuroscience,* 1983, *3,* 407–416.

Bear, M. F., Paradiso, M. A., Schwartz, M., Nelson, S. B., Carnes, K. M., & Daniels, J. D. Two methods of catecholamine depletion in kitten visual cortex yield different effects on plasticity. *Nature (London),* 1983, *302,* 245–247.

Bear, M. F., & Singer, W. Modulation of visual cortical plasticity by acetylcholine and noradrenaline. *Nature (London),* 1986, *320,* 172–176.

Beckmann, R., & Albus, K. The geniculocortical system in the early postnatal kitten: An electrophysiological investigation. *Experimental Brain Research,* 1982, *47,* 49–56.

Blakemore, C. The conditions required for the maintenance of binocularity in the kitten's visual cortex. *Journal of Physiology (London),* 1976, *261,* 423–444.

Blakemore, C., & Cooper, G. F. Development of the brain depends on the visual environment. *Nature (London),* 1970, *228,* 477–478.

Blakemore, C., & Van Sluyters, R. C. Innate and environmental factors in the development of the kitten's visual cortex. *Journal of Physiology (London),* 1975, *248,* 663–716.

Blasdel, G. G., Mitchell, D. E., Muir, D. W., & Pettigrew, J. D. A physiological and behavioural study in cats of the effect of early visual experience with contours of a single orientation. *Journal of Physiology (London),* 1977, *265,* 615–636.

Bonds, A. B. Development of orientation tuning in the visual cortex of kittens. In R. D. Freeman (Ed.), *Developmental neurobiology of vision.* New York: Plenum Press, 1979.

Braastad, B. O., & Heggelund, P. Eye-opening in kittens: Effects of light and some biological factors. *Developmental Psychobiology,* 1984, *17,* 675–681.

Braastad, B. O., & Heggelund, P. Development of spatial receptive-field organization and orientation selectivity in kitten striate cortex. *Journal of Neurophysiology,* 1985, *53,* 1158–1178.

Buisseret, P., Gary-Bobo, E., & Imbert, M. Plasticity in the kitten's visual cortex: Effects of the suppression of visual experience upon the orientational properties of visual cortical cells. *Developmental Brain Research,* 1982, *4,* 417–426.

Buisseret, P., & Imbert, M. Visual cortical cells: Their developmental properties in normal and dark reared kittens. *Journal of Physiology (London),* 1976, *255,* 511–525.

Coleman, P. D., & Riesen, A. H. Environmental effects on cortical dendritic fields: I. Rearing in the dark. *Journal of Anatomy,* 1968, *102,* 363–374.

Cragg, B. G. The development of synapses in cat visual cortex. *Investigative Ophthalmology,* 1972, *11,* 377–385.

Cragg, B. G. The development of synapses in the visual system of the cat. *Journal of Comparative Neurology,* 1975, *160,* 147–166.

Cronly-Dillon, J., & Perry, G. W. Effect of visual experience on tubulin synthesis during a critical period of visual cortex development in the hooded rat. *Journal of Physiology (London),* 1979, *293,* 469–484.

Cynader, M., Berman, N., & Hein, A. Recovery of function in cat visual cortex following prolonged deprivation. *Experimental Brain Research,* 1976, *25,* 139–156.

Cynader, M., & Mitchell, D. E. Prolonged sensitivity to monocular deprivation in dark-reared cats. *Journal of Neurophysiology,* 1980, *43,* 1026–1040.

Daw, N. W., Rader, R. K., Robertson, T. W., & Ariel, M. Effects of 6-hydroxydopamine on visual deprivation in the kitten striate cortex. *Journal of Neuroscience,* 1983, *3,* 907–914.

Daw, N. W., Robertson, T. W., Rader, R. K., Videen, T. O., & Coscia, C. J. Substantial reduction of cortical noradrenaline by lesions of adrenergic pathway does not prevent effects of monocular deprivation. *Journal of Neuroscience,* 1984, *4,* 1354–1360.

Daw, N. W., Videen, T. O., Robertson, T., & Rader, R. K. An evaluation of the hypothesis that noradrenaline affects plasticity in the developing visual cortex. In A. Fein & J. S. Levine (Eds.), *The visual system.* New York: Allen R. Liss, 1985. (a)

Daw, N. W., Videen, T. O. Parkinson, D., & Rader, R. K. DSP-4 (N-(2-Chloroethyl)-N-ethyl-2-bromobenzylamine) depletes noradrenaline in kitten visual cortex without altering the effects of monocular deprivation. *Journal of Neuroscience,* 1985, *5,* 1925–1933. (b)

Daw, N. W., Videen, T. O., Rader, R. K., Robertson, T. W., & Coscia, C. J. Substantial reduction of noradrenaline in kitten visual cortex by intraventricular injections of 6-hydroxydopamine does not always prevent ocular dominance shifts after monocular deprivation. *Experimental Brain Research,* 1985, *59,* 30–35. (c)

Derrington, A. M. Development of spatial frequency selectivity in striate cortex of vision-deprived cats. *Experimental Brain Research.* 1984, *55,* 431–437.

Derrington, A. M., & Fuchs, A. F. Development of spatial-frequency selectivity in kitten striate cortex. *Journal of Physiology (London),* 1981, *316,* 1–10.

Dodwell, P. C., Timney, B. N., & Emerson, V. F. Development of visual stimulus-seeking in dark-reared kittens. *Nature (London),* 1976, *260,* 777–778.

Fifková, E. The effect of unilateral deprivation on visual centers in rats. *Journal of Comparative Neurology,* 1970, *140,* 431–438.

Fiorentini, A., & Maffei, L. Selective impairment of contrast sensitivity in kittens exposed to periodic gratings. *Journal of Physiology (London),* 1978, *277,* 455–466.

Fox, M. W. Reflex development and behavioral organization. In W. A. Himwich (Ed.), *Developmental neurobiology.* Springfield, IL: Thomas, 1970.

Frederickson, C. J., & Frederickson, M. H. Developmental changes in open-field behavior in the kitten. *Developmental Psychobiology,* 1979, *12,* 623–628.

Freeman, N. C. G., & Rosenblatt, J. S. The interrelationship between thermal and olfactory stimulation in the development of home orientation in newborn kittens. *Developmental Psychobiology,* 1978, *11,* 437–457.

Fregnac, Y., & Imbert, M. Early development of visual cortical cells in normal and dark-reared kittens: Relationship between orientation selectivity and ocular dominance. *Journal of Physiology (London),* 1978, *278,* 27–44.

Fregnac, Y., & Imbert, M. Development of neuronal selectivity in primary visual cortex of cat. *Physiological Reviews,* 1984, *64,* 325–434.

Giffin, F., & Mitchell, D. E. The rate of recovery of vision after early monocular deprivation in kittens. *Journal of Physiology (London),* 1978, *274,* 511–537.

Gilbert, C. D. Microcircuitry of the visual cortex. *Annual Review of Neuroscience.* 1983, *6,* 217–247.

Gilbert, C. D., & Kelly, J. P. The projections of cells in different layers of the cat's visual cortex. *Journal of Comparative Neurology,* 1975, *163,* 81–106.

Globus, A., Rosenzweig, M. R., Bennett, E. L., & Diamond, M. C. Effects of differential experience on dendritic spine counts in rat cerebral cortex. *Journal of Comparative and Physiological Psychology,* 1973, *82,* 175–181.

Gordon, B., & Presson, J. Orientation deprivation in cat: What produces the abnormal cells? *Experimental Brain Research,* 1982, *46,* 144–146.

Greenough, W. T. Structural correlates of information storage in the mammalian brain: A review and hypothesis. *Trends in Neurosciences,* 1984, *7,* 229–233.

Greenough, W. T., & Volkmar, F. R. Pattern of dendritic branching in occipital cortex of rats reared in complex environments. *Experimental Neurology,* 1973, *40,* 491–504.

Greenough, W. T., Volkmar, F. R., & Juraska, J. M. Effects of rearing complexity on dendritic branching in frontolateral and temporal cortex of the rat. *Experimental Neurology,* 1973, *41,* 371–378.

Guillery, R. W. Binocular competition in the control of geniculate cell growth. *Journal of Comparative Neurology,* 1972, *144,* 117–130.

Hirsch, H. V. B. Visual perception in cats after environmental surgery. *Experimental Brain Research,* 1972, *15,* 405–423.

Hirsch, H. V. B. The tunable seer: Activity-dependent development of vision. In E. M. Blass (Ed.), *Handbook of behavioral neurobiology.* New York: Plenum 1985. (a)

Hirsch, H. V. B. The role of visual experience in the development of cat striate cortex. *Cellular and Molecular Neurobiology,* 1985, *5,* 103–121. (b).

Hirsch, H. V. B., Leventhal, A. G., McCall, M. A., & Tieman, D. G. Effects of exposure to lines of one or two orientations on different cell types in striate cortex of cat. *Journal of Physiology (London),* 1983, *337,* 241–255.

Hirsch, H. V. B., & Spinelli, D. N. Visual experience modifies distribution of horizontally and vertically oriented receptive fields in cats. *Science,* 1970, *168,* 869–871.

Hirsch, H. V. B., & Spinelli, D. N. Modification of the distribution of receptive field orientation in cats by selective visual exposure during development. *Experimental Brain Research,* 1971, *12,* 509–527.

Hirsch, H. V. B., Tieman, D. G., Tieman, S. B., & Tumosa, N. Unequal alternating exposure: Effects during and after the classical critical period. In J. P. Rauschecker & P. Marler (Eds.), *Imprinting and cortical plasticity.* New York: Wiley, 1986.

Holloway, R. L. Dendritic branching: Some preliminary results of training and complexity in rat visual cortex. *Brain Research,* 1966, *2,* 393–396.

Hubel, D. H., & Wiesel, T. N. Receptive fields of single neurones in the cat's striate cortex. *Journal of Physiology (London),* 1959, *148,* 574–591.

Hubel, D. H., & Wiesel, T. N. Receptive fields, binocular interaction and functional architecture in the cat's visual cortex. *Journal of Physiology (London),* 1962, *160,* 106–154.

Hubel, D. H., & Wiesel, T. N. Receptive fields of cells in striate cortex of very young, visually inexperienced kittens. *Journal of Neurophysiology,* 1963, *26,* 994–1002.

Hubel, D. H., & Wiesel, T. N. The period of susceptibility to the physiological effects of unilateral eye closure in kittens. *Journal of Physiology (London),* 1970, *206,* 419–436.

Huttenlocher, P. R. Development of cortical neuronal activity in the neonatal cat. *Experimental Neurology,* 1967, *17,* 247–262.

Ikeda, H., Tremain, K. E., & Einon, G. Loss of spatial resolution of lateral geniculate nucleus neurones in kittens raised with convergent squint produced at different stages in development. *Experimental Brain Research,* 1978, *31,* 207–220.

Jonsson, G., & Kasamatsu, T. Maturation of monoamine neurotransmitters and receptors in cat occipital cortex during postnatal critical period. *Experimental Brain Research,* 1983, *50,* 449–458.

Karmel, B. Z., Miller, P. N., Dettweiler, L., & Anderson, G. Texture density and normal development of visual depth avoidance. *Developmental Psychobiology,* 1970, *3,* 73–90.

Kasamatsu, T., & Heggelund, P. Single cell responses in cat visual cortex to visual stimulation during iontophoresis of noradrenaline. *Experimental Brain Research,* 1982, *45,* 317–327.

Kasamatsu, T., & Pettigrew, J. D. Depletion of brain catecholamines: Failure of ocular dominance shift after monocular occlusion in kittens. *Science,* 1976, *194,* 206–209.

Kasamatsu, T., & Pettigrew, J. D. Preservation of binocularity after monocular deprivation in the striate cortex of kittens treated with 6-hydroxydopamine. *Journal of Comparative Neurology,* 1979, *185,* 139–161.

Kasamatsu, T. Neuronal plasticity maintained by the central norepinephrine system in the cat visual cortex. In J. M. Sprague & A. N. Epstein, (Eds.), *Progress in psychobiology and physiological psychology*. New York: Academic Press, 1983.

Kasamatsu, T., Pettigrew, J. D., & Ary, M. Restoration of visual cortical plasticity by local microperfusion of norepinephrine. *Journal of Comparative Neurology*, 1979, *185*, 163-182.

Kasamatsu, T., Pettigrew, J. D., & Ary, M. Cortical recovery from effects of monocular deprivation: Acceleration with norepinephrine and suppression with 6-hydroxydopamine. *Journal of Neurophysiology*, 1981, *45*, 254-266.

Kasamatsu, T., Watabe, K., Heggelund, P., & Scholler, E. Plasticity in cat visual cortex restored by electrical stimulation of the locus coeruleus. *Neuroscience Research*, 1985, *2*, 365-386.

Kato, N., Kawaguchi, S., & Miyata, H. Geniculocortical projection to layer I of Area 17 in kittens: Orthograde and retrograde HRP studies. *Journal of Comparative Neurology*, 1984, *225*, 441-447.

Kato, N., Kawaguchi, S., Yamamoto, T., Samejima, A., & Miyata, H. Postnatal development of the geniculocortical projection in the cat; electrophysiological and morphological studies. *Experimental Brain Research*, 1983, *51*, 65-72.

Kety, S. S. The biogenic amines in the central nervous system: Their possible roles in arousal, emotion, and learning. In F. O. Schmitt (Ed.), *The neurosciences: Second study program*. New York: Rockefeller University Press, 1970.

Kolb, B., & Nonneman, A. J. The development of social responsiveness in kittens. *Animal Behaviour*, 1975, *23*, 368-374.

Laemle, L., Benhamida, C. & Purpura, D. P. Laminar distribution of geniculocortical afferents in visual cortex of the postnatal kitten. *Brain Research*, 1972, *41*, 25-37.

LeVay, S., Stryker, M. P., & Shatz, C. J. Ocular dominance columns and their development in layer IV of the cat's visual cortex: A quantitative study. *Journal of Comparative Neurology*, 1978, *179*, 223-244.

Leventhal, A. G., & Hirsch, H. V. B. Cortical effect of early selective exposure to diagonal lines. *Science*, 1975, *190*, 902-904.

Leventhal, A. G., & Hirsch, H. V. B. Effects of early experience upon orientation sensitivity and binocularity of neurons in visual cortex of cats. *Proceedings of the National Academy of Sciences (USA)*, 1977, *74*, 1272-1276.

Leventhal, A. G., & Hirsch, H. V. B. Receptive-field properties of different classes of neurons in visual cortex of normal and dark-reared cats. *Journal of Neurophysiology*, 1980, *43*, 1111-1132.

Levine, M. S., Hull, C. D., & Buchwald, N. A. Development of motor activity in kittens. *Developmental Psychobiology*, 1980, *13*, 357-371.

Levitt, F. B., & Van Sluyters, R. C. The sensitive period for strabismus in the kitten. *Developmental Brain Research*, 1982, *3*, 323-327.

Leyhausen, P. *Cat behavior*. New York: Garland Press, 1979.

Maffei, L., & Fiorentini, A. The visual cortex as a spatial frequency analyzer. *Vision Research*, 1973, *13*, 1255-1267.

Martin, P. H. *Weaning and behavioural development in the cat*. Ph.D. Thesis, Cambridge, England: Christ's College, 1982.

McCall, M. A. *The relationship between ocular dominance and other response properties of cortical cells in normal kittens and in monocularly deprived kittens*. Ph.D. Thesis, Albany, New York: State University of New York, 1983.

Mitchell, D. E., Giffin, F., Wilkinson, F., Anderson, P. & Smith, M. L. Visual resolution in young kittens. *Vision Research*, 1976, *16*, 363-366.

Mitchell, D. E., & Timney, B. Postnatal development of function in the mammalian visual system. In *Handbook of Physiology-The Nervous System III*. Bethesda, MD: American Physiological Society, 1984.

Moelk, M. The development of friendly approach behavior in the cat: A study of kitten-mother relations and the cognitive development of the kitten from birth to eight weeks. *Advances in the Study of Behaviour*, 1979, *10*, 163-224.

Moore, R. Y., & Bloom, F. E. Central catecholamine neuron systems: Anatomy and physiology of the dopamine systems. *Annual Review of Neuroscience*, 1978, *1*, 129-169.

Moore, R. Y., & Bloom, F. E. Central catecholamine neuron systems: Anatomy and physiology of the norephinephrine and epinephrine systems. *Annual Review of Neuroscience*, 1979, *2*, 113-168.

Movshon, J. A., & Dürsteler, M. R. Effects of brief periods of unilateral eye closure on the kitten's visual system. *Journal of Neurophysiology*, 1977, *40*, 1255-1265.

Movshon, J. A., & Van Sluyters, R. C. Visual neural development. *Annual Review of Psychology*, 1981, *32*, 477-522.

Mower, G. D., & Christen, W. G. Role of visual experience in activating critical period in cat visual cortex. *Journal of Neurophysiology*, 1985, *53*, 572-589.

Mower, G. D., Burchfiel, J. L., & Duffy, F. H. The effects of dark-rearing on the development and plasticity of the Lateral Geniculate Nucleus. *Developmental Brain Research*, 1981, *1*, 418-424. (a)

Mower, G. D., Berry, D., Burchfiel, J. L., & Duffy, F. H. Comparison of the effects of dark rearing and binocular suture on development and plasticity of cat visual cortex. *Brain Research*, 1981, *220*, 255-267. (b)

Mower, G. D., Christen, W. G., & Caplan, C. J. Very brief visual experience eliminates plasticity in the cat visual cortex. *Science*, 1983, *221*, 178-180.

Muir, D. W., & Mitchell, D. E. Visual resolution and experience: Acuity deficits in cats following early selective visual deprivation. *Science*, 1973, *180*, 420-422.

Muir, D. W., & Mitchell, D. E. Behavioral deficits in cats following early selected visual exposure to contours of a single orientation. *Brain Research*, 1975, *85*, 459-477.

Murphey, R. K. Competition and the dynamics of axon arbor growth in the cricket. *Journal of Comparative Neurology*, 1986, *251*, 100-110.

Norton, T. T. Receptive-field properties of superior colliculus cells and development of visual behavior in kittens. *Journal of Neurophysiology*, 1974, *37*, 674-690.

O'Kusky, J. R. Synapse elimination in the developing visual cortex: A morphometric analysis in normal and dark-reared cats. *Developmental Brain Research*, 1985, *22*, 81-91.

Olson, C. R., & Freeman, R. D. Profile of the sensitive period for monocular deprivation in kittens. *Experimental Brain Research*, 1980, *39*, 17-21.

Paradiso, M. A., Bear, M. F., & Daniels, J. D. Effects of intracortical infusion of 6-hydroxy-dopamine on the response of kitten visual cortex to monocular deprivation. *Experimental Brain Research*, 1983, *51*, 413-422.

Pettigrew, J. D. The effect of visual experience on the development of stimulus specificity by kitten cortical neurones. *Journal of Physiology (London)*, 1974, *237*, 49-74.

Pettigrew, J. D. The paradox of the critical period for striate cortex. In C. W. Cotman (Ed.), *Neuronal plasticity*. New York: Raven Press, 1978.

Pettigrew, J. D., & Freeman, R. D. Visual experience without lines: Effect on developing cortical neurons. *Science*, 1973, *182*, 599-601.

Pettigrew, J. D., & Kasamatsu, T. Local perfusion of noradrenaline maintains visual cortical plasticity. *Nature (London)*, 1978, *271*, 761-763.

Pettigrew, J. D., Olson, C., & Hirsch, H. V. B. Cortical effect of selective visual experience: degeneration or reorganization? *Brain Research*, 1973, *51*, 345-351.

Potempska, A., Skangiel-Kramska, J., & Kossut, M. Development of cholinergic enzymes and adenosine-triphosphatase activity of optic system of cats in normal and restricted visual input conditions. *Developmental Neuroscience*, 1979, *2*, 38-45.

Presson, J., & Gordon, B. Critical period and minimum exposure required for the effects of alternating monocular occlusion in cat visual cortex. *Vision Research*, 1979, *19*, 807-811.

Pysh, J. J., & Weiss, G. M. Exercise during development induces an increase in Purkinje cell dendritic tree size. *Science*, 1979, *206*, 230–232.

Rauschecker, J. P., & Singer, W. The effects of early visual experience on the cat's visual cortex and their possible explanation by Hebb synapses. *Journal of Physiology (London)*, 1981, *310*, 215–239.

Rose, S. P. R., Sinha, A. K., & Jones-Lecointe, A. Synthesis of tubulin-enriched fraction in rat visual cortex is modulated by dark-rearing and light exposure. *FEBS Letters*, 1976, *65*, 135–139.

Rose, S. P. R., & Stewart, M. G. Transient increase in muscarinic acetylcholine receptor and acetylcholinesterase in visual cortex on first exposure of dark-reared rats to light. *Nature (London)*, 1978, *271*, 169–170.

Rosenblatt, J. S., & Schneirla, T. C. The behaviour of cats. In E. S. E. Hafez (Ed.), *The behaviour of domestic animals*. London: Bailliere, Tindall and Cox, 1962.

Rosenblatt, J. S., Turkewitz, G., & Schneirla, T. C. Development of home orientation in newly born kittens. *Transactions of New York Academy of Sciences*. 1964, *31*, 231–250.

Rothblat, L. A., & Schwartz, M. L. The effect of monocular deprivation on dendritic spines in visual cortex of young and adult albino rats: Evidence for a sensitive period. *Brain Research*, 1979, *161*, 156–161.

Sato, H., & Tsumoto, T. GABAergic inhibition already operates on a group of neurons in the kitten visual cortex at the time of eye opening. *Developmental Brain Research*, 1984, *12*, 311–315.

Schlumpf, M., Lichtensteiger, W., Shoemaker, W. J., & Bloom, F. E. Fetal monoamine systems: Early stages and cortical projections. In H. Parvez & S. Parvez (Eds.), *Biogenic amines in development*. Elsevier/North-Holland: Biomedical Press, 1980.

Schmidt, J. T. Factors involved in retinotopic map formation: Complementary roles for membrane recognition and activity-dependent synaptic stabilization. In G. M. Edelman, W. E. Gall, & W. M. Cowan (Eds.), *Molecular basis of neural development*. Neurosciences Research Foundation, 1985.

Shatz, C. J., & Stryker, M. P. Ocular dominance in layer IV of the cat's visual cortex and the effects of monocular deprivation. *Journal of Physiology (London)*, 1978, *281*, 267–283.

Shaw, C., Needler, M. C., Cynader, M. Ontogenesis of muscarinic acetylcholine binding sites in cat visual cortex: reversal of specific laminar distribution during the critical period. *Developmental Brain Research*, 1984, *14*, 295–299. (a)

Shaw, C., Needler, M. C., & Cynader, M. Laminar reversals of receptor binding patterns in cat visual cortex during the critical period. *Society for Neuroscience Abstracts*, 1984, *10*, 1038. (b)

Sherman, S. M., & Spear, P. D. Organization of visual pathways in normal and visually deprived cats. *Physiological Reviews*, 1982, *62*, 738–855.

Sherman, S. M. Development of interocular alignment in cats. *Brain Research*, 1972, *37*, 187–203.

Sherman, S. M. Visual field defects in monocularly and binocularly deprived cats. *Brain Research*, 1973, *49*, 25–45.

Shute, C. C. D., & Lewis, P. R. Cholinesterase containing systems of the brain of the rat. *Nature (London)*, 1963, *199*, 1160–1164.

Sillito, A. M., & Kemp, J. A. Cholinergic modulation of the functional organization of the cat visual cortex. *Brain Research*, 1983, *289*, 143–155.

Singer, W. Central-core control of visual-cortex functions. In F. O. Schmitt & F. G. Worden (Eds.), *The neurosciences fourth study program*. Cambridge: MIT Press, 1979.

Singer, W., & Tretter, F. Receptive-field properties and neuronal connectivity in striate and parastriate cortex of contour-deprived cats. *Journal of Neurophysiology*, 1976, *39*, 613–630.

Singer, W., Freeman, B., & Rauschecker, J. Restriction of visual experience to a single orientation affects the organization of orientation columns in cat visual cortex. *Experimental Brain Research,* 1981, *41,* 199–215.

Sinha, A. K. L., & Rose, S. P. R. Dark rearing and visual stimulation in the rat: Effect on brain enzymes. *Journal of Neurochemistry,* 1976, *27,* 921–927.

Smith, D. C., Reeves, T. M., & Holdefer, R. N. Unmasking silent synapses in cats reared with unequal alternating monocular deprivation. *Society for Neuroscience Abstracts,* 1982, *8,* 298.

Spinelli, D. N., Jensen, F. E., & Standish, L. Induced plasticity in visual cortex of adult cats. *Society for Neuroscience Abstracts.* 1979, *5,* 684.

Stryker, M. P., & Harris, W. A. Binocular impulse blockade prevents the formation of ocular dominance columns in cat visual cortex. *Journal of Neuroscience.* 1986, *6,* 2117–2133.

Stryker, M. P., & Sherk, H. Modification of cortical orientation selectivity in the cat by restricted visual experience: A reexamination. *Science,* 1975, *190,* 904–906.

Stryker, M. P., Sherk, H., Leventhal, A. G., & Hirsch, H. V. B. Physiological consequences for the cat's visual cortex of effectively restricting early visual experience with oriented contours. *Journal of Neurophysiology.* 1978, *41,* 896–909.

Stryker, M. P., & Strickland, S. L. Physiological segregation of ocular dominance columns depends on the pattern of afferent electrical activity. *Investigative Ophthalmology & Visual Science (Supplement),* 1984, *25,* 278.

Swadlow, H. A. Efferent systems of primary visual cortex: A review of structure and function. *Brain Research Reviews,* 1983, *6,* 1–24.

Swindale, N. V. Absence of ocular dominance patches in dark-reared cats. *Nature (London),* 1981, *290,* 332–333.

Swindale, N. V., & Cynader, M. S. Physiological segregation of geniculo-cortical afferents in the visual cortex of dark-reared cats. *Brain Research,* 1986, *362,* 281–286.

Tees, R. C. Effect of early restriction on later form discrimination in the rat. *Canadian Journal of Psychology,* 1968, *22,* 294–300.

Tees, R. C. The effect of visual deprivation on pattern recognition in the rat. *Developmental Psychobiology,* 1979, *12,* 485–497.

Tees, R. C., Midgley, G., & Bruinsma, Y. Effect of controlled rearing on the development of stimulus-seeking behavior in rats. *Journal of Comparative and Physiological Psychology,* 1980, *94,* 1003–1018.

Thibos, L. N., & Levick, W. R. Astigmatic visual deprivation in cat: Behavioral, optical and retino-physiological consequences. *Vision Research,* 1982, *22,* 43–53.

Tieman, S. B. Effects of monocular deprivation on geniculocortical synapses in the cat. *Journal of Comparative Neurology,* 1984, *222,* 166–176.

Tieman, S. B. The anatomy of geniculocortical connections in monocularly deprived cats. *Cellular and Molecular Neurobiology,* 1985, *5,* 35–45.

Tieman, S. B., & Hirsch, H. V. B. Exposure to lines of only one orientation modifies dendritic morphology of cells in the visual cortex of the cat. *Journal of Comparative Neurology,* 1982, *211,* 353–362.

Tieman, D. G., McCall, M. A., & Hirsch, H. V. B. Physiological effects of unequal alternating monocular deprivation. *Society for Neurosciences Abstracts,* 1979, *5,* 631.

Tieman, D. G., McCall, M. A., & Hirsch, H. V. B. Physiological effects of unequal alternating monocular exposure. *Journal of Neurophysiology,* 1983, *49,* 804–818.

Tieman, S. B., Nickla, D. L., Gross, K., Hickey, T. L., & Tumosa, N. Effects of unequal alternating monocular exposure on the sizes of cells in the cat's lateral geniculate nucleus. *Journal of Comparative Neurology,* 1984, *225,* 119–128.

Timney, B. N. Development of binocular depth perception in kittens. *Investigative Ophthalmology & Visual Science,* 1981, *21,* 493–496.

Timney, B. N., Emerson, V. F., & Dodwell, P. C. Development of visual stimulus-seeking in kittens. *Quarterly Journal of Experimental Psychology,* 1979, *31,* 63–81.

Timney, B. N., Mitchell, D. E., & Cynader, M. Behavioral evidence for prolonged sensitivity to effects of monocular deprivation in dark-reared cats. *Journal of Neurophysiology,* 1980, *43,* 1041–1054.

Trombley, P., Allen, E. E., Soyke, J., Blaha, C. D., Lane, R. F., & Gordon, B. Doses of 6-hydroxydopamine sufficient to deplete norepinephrine are not sufficient to decrease plasticity in the visual cortex. *Journal of Neuroscience,* 1986, *6,* 266–273.

Tsumoto, T., & Suda, K. Laminar differences in development of afferent innervation to striate cortex neurones in kittens. *Experimental Brain Research,* 1982, *45,* 433–446.

Tumosa, N. *Binocular competition affects the development of the visual system in the cat.* Ph.D. Thesis, Albany: State University of New York, 1982.

Tumosa, N., Nunberg, S. Hirsch, H. V. B., & Tieman, S. B. Binocular exposure causes suppression of the less experienced eye in cats previously reared with unequal alternating monocular exposure. *Investigative Ophthalmology & Visual Science,* 1983, *24,* 496–506.

Tumosa, N., & Tieman, S. B. Binocular competition determines the size and shape of ocular dominance columns in cats. *Society for Neurosciences Abstracts,* 1981, *7,* 674.

Tumosa, N., Tieman, S. B., & Hirsch, H. V. B. Unequal alternating monocular deprivation causes asymmetric visual fields in cats. *Science,* 1980, *208,* 421–423. (a)

Tumosa, N., Tieman, S. B. & Hirsch, H. V. B. Anatomical effect of unequal alternate monocular deprivation. *Investigative Ophthalmology & Visual Science (Supplement).* 1980, *19,* 59. (b)

Tumosa, N., Tieman, S. B., & Hirsch, H. V. B. Visual field deficits in cats reared with unequal alternating monocular exposure. *Experimental Brain Research,* 1982, *47,* 119–129.

Valverde, F. Rate and extent of recovery from dark rearing in the visual cortex of the mouse. *Brain Research,* 1971, *33,* 1–11.

Van Hof-Van Duin, J. Development of visuomotor behavior in normal and dark-reared cats. *Brain Research,* 1976, *104,* 233–241.

Van Sluyters, R. C., & Blakemore, C. Experimental creation of unusual neuronal properties in visual cortex of kitten. *Nature (London),* 1973, *246,* 506–508.

Videen, T. O., Daw, N. W., & Rader, R. K. The effect of norepinephrine on visual cortical neurons in kittens and adult cats. *Journal of Neuroscience,* 1984, *4,* 1607–1617.

Villablanca, J. R., & Olmstead, C. E. Neurological development of kittens. *Developmental Psychobiology,* 1979, *12,* 101–127.

Walk, R. D. The influence of level of illumination and size of pattern on the depth perception of the kitten and the puppy. *Psychonomic Science,* 1968, *12,* 199–200.

Wark, R. C., & Peck, C. K. Behavioral consequences of early visual exposure to contours of a single orientation. *Developmental Brain Research,* 1982, *5,* 218–221.

Warkentin, J., & Smith, K. U. The development of visual acuity in the cat. *Journal of Genetic Psychology,* 1937, *50,* 371–399.

Watkins, D. W., Wilson, J. R., & Sherman, S. M. Receptive-field properties of neurons in binocular and monocular segments of striate cortex in cats raised with binocular lid suture. *Journal of Neurophysiology,* 1978, *41,* 322–337.

West, M. J. Social play in the domestic cat. *American Zoologist,* 1974, *14,* 427–436.

West, M. J. Play in domestic kittens. In R. B. Cairns (Ed.), *The analysis of social interactions.* Hillsdale NJ: Lawrence Erlbaum Associates, 1979.

Wiesel, T. N., & Hubel, D. H. Comparison of the effects of unilateral and bilateral eye closure on cortical unit responses in kittens. *Journal of Neurophysiology,* 1965, *28,* 1029–1040.

Wilkinson, F. E., & Dodwell, P. C. Young kittens can learn complex visual pattern discriminations. *Nature (London),* 1980, *284,* 258–259.

Wilkinson, M., Shaw, C., Kahn, I., & Cynader, M. Ontogenesis of β-adrenergic binding sites in kitten visual cortex and the effects of visual deprivation. *Developmental Brain Research,* 1983, *7,* 349–352.

Winfield, D. A. The postnatal development of synapses in the visual cortex of the cat and the effects of eyelid closure. *Brain Research,* 1981, *206,* 166–171.

Yinon, U. Age dependence of the effect of squint on cells in kittens' visual cortex. *Experimental Brain Research,* 1976, *26,* 151–157.

Zec, N., Tieman, S. B., & Hirsch, H. V. B. Stripe rearing alters basal dendrites of layer V pyramidal cells. *Investigative Ophthalmology & Visual Science Supplement,* 1985, *26,* 165.

4 Critical Events During Sensitive Periods of Social Development in Rats

Elliott M. Blass
Johns Hopkins University

INTRODUCTION

The concept of a critical period was introduced into the embryological and biological literatures some 8 decades ago when Hans Spemann (1901), studying amphibia, demonstrated that grafts from one portion of the egg developed the characteristics of the host tissue. Tissue, that if left alone, would have developed into ventral surface, for example, developed into an eye cup when grafted to that designated area of the host. The reverse, of course, also held. When these surgical manipulations were undertaken sometime later in development, the donor tissue grew into the designated donor organ, regardless of where on the host's body the donor tissue was grafted (Mangold & Spemann, 1927).

The critical period of time during which a structure (system) was specified had passed. The interactions between a group of cells and its surrounding tissue (the environment) that determined structure, and presumably function, of those cells later on in development, occurred in a relatively short period of time (on a human scale at least) and could thus be analyzed experimentally. Moreover, the abstraction of time could be biologically defined by the preceding and contemporary anatomical and biochemical events that distinguished one developmental epoch from another (Vogt, 1925). These biological definitions broke the logical circularity that a period was critical for development of a feature because interference during this period altered normal development. Events could be defined biochemically. Consequently, considerable progress has been realized in the neuroembryology of development.

The concept of a critical period for the specification of behavioral phenotype contributed to Lorenz's (1935) compelling studies of imprinting in birds and to Scott's (1962) studies of social behavior in dogs. Lorenz demonstrated that the *following* response of precocial birds was not limited to the mother, but during the critical period could be directed towards other moving objects, including Lorenz himself. Scott's influential studies, conducted over the course of almost two decades, demonstrated clearly that dogs raised under extreme social conditions were behaviorally abnormal. This of course was very much in keeping with Harlow's (1962) reports on aberrant social and sexual development in isolated Rhesus monkeys.

Despite the acknowledged importance of the Lorenz and Scott studies, they were soon surrounded by controversy. Lorenz defined his terms and processes of the critical period far too narrowly and couched his theoretical position in a very strong genetic determinism. This gave rise to the famous controversies between Lorenz (1950) and Lehrman (1956). (For a cogent discussion of this issue, see Hinde, 1972.) Scott, on the other hand, defined his critical period far too broadly so that in the end, all of learning reflected events during lifetime critical periods (Scott, Stewart, & DeGhett, 1974). Under this theoretical umbrella, all forms of learning could find shelter so that the idea of a critical period lost the uniqueness and power that distinguished it in the hands of the embryologists. In addition, the presentations by both Scott and Lorenz precluded a more complete evaluation of development. They forced development into a very discontinuous mode, whereas continuity in certain systems was the rule rather than the exception (see Rosenblatt, 1983, and Schneirla & Rosenblatt, 1963, for discussions of this issue).

In response to controversies surrounding the term "critical period," "sensitive-period" has become the expression of currency. It refers to the optimal time for influencing a biological-behavioral process during development. In keeping with the embryological formulations, the sensitive period has generally referred to a developmental frame in which a later morphological or behavioral system is influenced, as for example, sexual differentiation or acquisition of bird song. The sensitive period can, however, also refer to processes that are expressed even while being formulated, as for example, "following behavior" of certain altricial birds.

In using the expression sensitive period, I make explicit the fuzzy time boundaries of optimality. This fuzziness is important because it reminds us that, generally, we do not know the biochemical (timing) characteristics of the developing system that determine when it will be receptive to biological or other influences of form or function. Further, I make explicit that a number of paths can specify a behavioral process. These avenues may be taken at different periods during development and they traverse different landscapes. Thus, isolate-reared rhesus monkeys made socially and sexually inept by their remarkable history can be rehabilitated by living with infant monkeys for relatively brief periods; even a few weeks suffice. The effects of the sensitive period therefore are not necessarily irreversible. Moreover, the rules governing acquisition and retention of information during the sensitive period and the expression of such information are not obviously different from those identified with general learning processes (Hoffmann, 1978; this volume). Learning occurs most readily and naturally in a social context and memory and performance are apparently sharpened by rehearsal and practice.

Figure 1 incorporates these ideas by demonstrating: (1) Multiplicity of pathways that can be taken at different times to specify sensory control over a behavioral process. (2) The temporal overlap of these pathways indicating opportunities for modifying initial influences. (3) Continuous influences of sensation, perception and "general-learning" processes (and also genetic dispositions towards individual differences) that influence the probability of whether a "determining" experience during the sensitive period will influence the process. (4) Implicit in the figure is the range of events in a given pathway that can determine the behavioral course taken. Thus, in the restricted time period for crystallizing "following" behavior in ducklings, the number of acceptable objects is seemingly unlimited — ranging from boxes to humans. This does *not* imply equipotentiality among detectable stimuli — it refers to potential for being followed. This scheme takes into consideration deter-

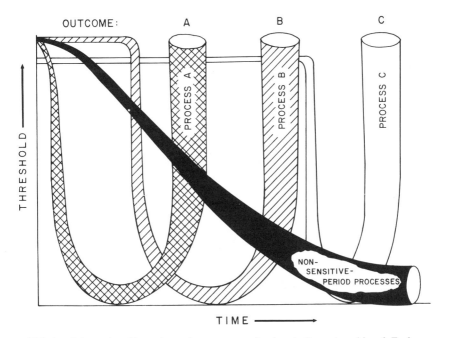

FIG. 1.   Schematics of how alternative outcomes of a given trait may be achieved. Each process has a different threshold over time. Outcomes are influenced by general learning and other capacities.

mining and interactive influences of earlier events, therefore, and makes explicit the idea that the sensitive period may serve to reduce the domain of biological and behavioral outcomes that may have previously been available to the developing infant.

Experiences can influence the formulation and expression of behaviors in different ways. They may simply maintain an act; or they may facilitate its occurrence as opposed to determining its form or circumstances of occurrence (Gottlieb, 1973, 1976). Gottlieb's formulation has it that experience may influence the frequency with which an act appears or the final asymptote of performance. Thus raising animals in large or small litters influences rate and frequency of feeding, metabolic rate and body weight but does not determine the feeding process itself. The nursing-suckling period is thus sensitive for ingestive facilitation and the effects are long-lasting, enduring after weaning when food is available ad-libitum.

Experience can also maintain behavior — and this may also work within a sensitive period. For example, suckling abstinence during the third through sixth days postpartum in rats, which are sustained by intragastric feeding, eliminates future suckling. When this restriction is imposed later in development, suckling is normal (Stoloff, Kenny, Blass, & Hall, 1980). As indicated, suckling is not necessary for the expression of normal adult feeding and drinking (Hall, 1975), but influences the types of foods selected by rats (Galef, 1977, provides a review).

Determinism is the most impressive influence of early experience. Behaviorally, it is the most scarce, and the most difficult to identify empirically. The clearest examples of specific behavioral determinism have come from the bird-song literature. Compelling examples for mammalian behavior are rare. Although the neurophysiology and morphology of kitten visual systems have been altered by extreme behavioral manipulations, the only report of behavioral change has been relatively poor depth perception in cats raised in a highly structured, unyielding visual space (Blake & Hirsch, 1975).

The present chapter deals with events during sensitive periods that seem to influence the expression of various social behaviors. It identifies in albino rats certain social interactions during the nest period that help direct early affiliative behaviors, including suckling and huddling. The influence of the nest experience on males responding to sexually receptive females at weaning, during the juvenile period, and in adult sexual behavior will be discussed. Some of the morphological and functional alterations that accrue in the olfactory bulb as a result of specific experiences are also considered. Studies of central structure and function within the context of behavioral modification as it may naturally occur provide considerable hope for a neurobiology of experience and individual differences.

This chapter also focuses on the circumstances under which information concerning certain stimuli is acquired. This includes changes in infant state as well as in maternal behaviors, and infant rewards that a stimulus predicts. The linkage of state and accurate predictions lead to changes in infantile affect that allow the predictive information to control infantile and, later, adult behavior.

THE SETTING

Rats give birth in large, well-maintained, well-insulated nests. After delivery, the mother deftly strips the amniotic sac from her newborns, ingests the sac and its attached placenta, vigorously licks her pup's anogenital area, and then grooms herself, especially her nipple region (Rosenblatt & Lehrman, 1963; Roth & Rosenblatt, 1967). After delivering her entire litter, the dam gathers individual pups into the nest and settles to nurse. The pups, for their part, locate and suckle her nipples and continue to do so as their sole source of nutrition and hydration for about 2 weeks. Then, for the next 2 weeks, they feed and drink in addition to suckle, with the former behaviors gaining ascendancy culminating with weaning at about 30 days in the absence of a new litter, or 26–27 days if a new litter is born (Gilbert, Burgoon, Sullivan, & Adler, 1983).

Three lines of research have been addressed to experiential factors that influence the social behaviors of suckling, huddling and nest orientation and occupancy. Early influences on adult sexual behavior will also be discussed.

SUCKLING

The mechanisms underlying nipple attachment and suckling behavior have been recently reviewed (Blass, 1986; Hall & Williams, 1983; Pedersen & Blass, 1981). To the present point, two sequences of experiences determine the chemical stimuli that elicit nipple attachment. The first precedes the rat's initial attachment; the second reflects mother-infant interactions that herald suckling during the first 5 days. As to the former, Teicher and Blass (1977) demonstrated that the amniotic fluid deposited by the mother on her nipples during parturition elicited the initial nipple attachment. Pedersen and Blass (1982) then found that amniotic fluid was effective because the fetus sampled it during the last days of gestation *and* the newborn smelled it during the period of licking by the mother. The former sampling appears to be detected through the vomeronasal organ (VMN) situated above the soft palate (Pedersen, Stewart, Greer, & Shepherd, 1983). It seems that some amniotic fluid swallowed by the fetus is captured by pumping action. According to Pedersen et al. (1983), information from VMN is processed centrally to the cortical medial amygdala. Suckling itself is apparently mediated by the primary olfactory system with its major projection to the lateral amygdala (Greer, Stewart, Teicher, & Shepherd, 1983). How the two systems communicate to assure symmetry between pre- and postnatal determinants is not known. Its resolution will shed light on how the nervous system is organized functionally by related prenatal and postnatal events and how, in turn, the CNS controls infantile behavior.

A second transitional period in determining nipple attachment occurs during postnatal days 1–5 when suckling shifts from amniotic fluid control to control by rat pup saliva. A possible basis of this transition has been identified by Pedersen, Williams and Blass (1983), who experimentally mimicked the key events that naturally predict suckling. The mother, upon returning to her nest, vigorously stimulates her young, especially by licking their anogenital area (Rosenblatt & Lehrman, 1963). This is done by holding the infant upside down with its snout opposed to the mother's ventral surface. Having so activated her sleeping pups the mother settles to nurse. The pups excitedly scurry about, scanning and probing her ventrum until a nipple is contacted, erected and grasped. According to Shair, Brake, and Hofer (1984) who measured pup EEG, infant rats are awake only when seeking a nipple or withdrawing milk from it. This is when learning must occur naturally. Pedersen, Williams, and Blass (1983) mimicked the activation sequence by stimulating the pup's anogenital area with a soft brush while the rats were in the presence of citral or benzaldehyde (a cherry-almond scent). The stimulation was mimicked neurochemically by amphetamine injection in the presence of the odors. Rats were then presented with washed females bearing one or the other scent.

Rats that were stimulated, mechanically or neurochemically, in citral for example suckled washed nipples presented in citral. The same holds for benzaldehyde. Animals either simply exposed to an odor without stimulation or stimulated without a new odor failed to suckle such nipples. They suckled unwashed nipples normally, however, demonstrating their general competence. Thus, in regard to the transitional period, we believe that pup saliva gains control over nipple attachment because when coupled with excitation (probably catacholaminergically mediated), it predicts the opportunity to suckle a nipple coated with saliva. In this regard, Blass, Ganchrow, and Steiner (1984) have shown that human infants at 2 hours of age can also learn predictive relationships between tactile information and suckling.

The rodent experiments have identified a period during which the organization of suckling undergoes two phases leading to final olfactory control. The specification process appears complete by 5 days of age. The Pedersen, Williams, and Blass (1983) findings have been replicated in 3-day-old rat pups but, during the same experimental session, not in 5-day-olds. These studies imply a period of fluidity in the organization of suckling behavior. There is additional evidence to this point. According to Teicher, Flaum,

Williams, Eckhert, and Lumia (1978), anosmia (inability to smell) is fatal to infant rats between 5 and 12 days of age. Older rats survive because they eat. Younger rats, because the suckling system has apparently not been fully specified (Stoloff et al., 1980), also survive anosmia. Presumably tactile information that triggers mouth-opening and tongue extension is available to the animal despite lack of olfactory stimulation. Such information normally elicits suckling only when detected in the ambiance of nipple odor. The olfactory system concerning suckling appears to have crystallized by 5–7 days of age because tactile information alone is ineffectual in eliciting suckling.

Tactile control over suckling appears to follow a similar time course in its fluidity. Hofer, Fisher, and Shair (1981) severed the trigeminal nerve in rats of various ages. Rats that received this insult at 14 days of age or older survived in apparent good health, presumably because they ate. Figure 2 demonstrates the fate of preweanling rats. The survival rate of Day 7 rats was rather low, whereas that of younger rats was very high. Careful functional neurological assessment confirmed surgical completeness. It seems that the earlier lesions were placed at a time of suckling organization, that is, when other oral afferents were sufficiently unspecified to be brought into play for nipple detection and grasping. In short, both olfactory and tactile aspects of suckling can at birth gain control over the motor patterns that lead to nipple

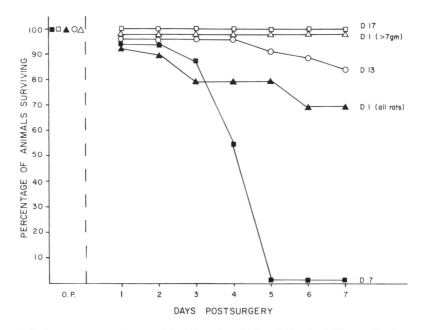

FIG. 2.   Percentage of rats surviving bilateral sectioning of trigeminal afferents. Day indicates time of surgery (from Hofer et. al., 1981).

grasping. These systems are not fully specified at first regarding either the effective olfactory stimulus or the tactile field that will elicit the behavior. With time and maternal prediction (Pedersen, Williams, & Blass, 1983), specification occurs.

Stoloff et al. (1980) used an entirely different approach to support this point. Rats separated from their dam on Days 3 and 4 and raised in the absence of suckling by continuous intragastric gavage were not able to locate the nipple of an anesthetized dam on Day 5 (almost all normal rats suckle under these circumstances). The deficit was prevented by allowing suckling-deprived pups 6–12 opportunities to suckle briefly a nonlactating nipple during each of the two days of abstinence. Suckling abstinence from 5–10 days of age did not affect subsequent nipple attachment.

These four interdependent lines of evidence concerning suckling behavior have revealed that the motor act, which is available to infant rats at birth, comes under the control of stimuli that define the mother. In this regard, the suckling system parallels other systems of sensory-motor coordination. It retains flexibility during the period of crystallization. Specifically, the necessity of olfactory stimulation permitting tactile control can be averted if anosmia is induced sufficiently early. In addition, there is substitutability among eliciting stimuli during the formative period. Under certain circumstances, even botanical stimuli elicit suckling behavior. Not engaging in suckling during its formative period makes this behavior essentially unavailable. This restriction may be limited to well-defined behaviors that, when crystallized, are under tight sensory control. It does not apply to more complex and subtle social behaviors, at least in primates and carnivors. Isolation-reared animals will form apparently normal social-sexual affiliations if allowed to interact with infant animals of the same species or friendly and playful animals of other species (Mason & Kenney, 1974).

HUDDLING BEHAVIOR

One function of the huddle in altricial mammals is thermo-regulation (Alberts, 1978a, 1978b). Through sibling contact an animal can significantly reduce its surface:mass ratio, thereby markedly reducing radiant and conductive heat loss. The huddle is actively maintained (Alberts, 1978b). While fulfilling its physiological function, huddling also helps prepare rats older than 2 weeks of age to engage in social affiliation. Until then, huddling is determined by thermal factors; a warm plastic tube is preferred to a cooled sibling. After 2 weeks, however, scent familiarity determines which object will be contacted (Alberts, 1981; Alberts & Brunjes, 1978).

Alberts and his colleagues have revealed the etiology of this preference by allowing rat pups raised by different types of scented females to choose among scents. They demonstrated that the sufficient reinforcing mechanism for contact preference was simply contact with an anesthetized female. The infants did not have to suckle from her — contact alone was sufficient (Alberts, 1981). The sensitive period for olfactory determination apparently starts after the period of thermoregulatory control has terminated. These periods may be related; development of filial behaviors takes place after the infant has used olfaction (i.e., during suckling) to help learn about certain consequences of its own actions. That is, the infant may associate siblings' odors with its own actions of moving deeper into the huddle thereby gaining additional contact and warmth, or associating these odors with movement towards the periphery of the huddle and thereby gaining relief from hyperthermia. The infant learns about the consequences of its own behavior within the context of olfactory and tactile changes. Thermotactile changes related to olfaction presumably complement information learned vis-á-vis the dam in regards to suckling. That is, by 10 days of age infant rats have learned that certain odors are associated with suckling, and other odors with pup contact. Infant rats can appreciate the consequences of their actions concerning these stimuli. They learn a spatial pattern to suckle, even at Day 7 (Kenny & Blass, 1977) and adjust their running speeds in a straight alley commensurate with the "saliency" of social reward (Amsel, Burdette, & Letz, 1976).

HOME ORIENTATION

At 15–16 days of age the rat's environment drastically expands as it starts, however tentatively, to explore its neighborhood. The rat, now sighted, must strike a delicate balance: On the one hand, it must ultimately abandon the nest (it slowly does this through longer forays). On the other hand, to leave precipitously invites certain predation and probably starvation in rats younger than 18 days of age. Balance is achieved in rats by an olfactory "tether," caecotroph, that is synthesized in the cecum by the hyperphagic mother and deposited in the nest area during the 14th–28th days after delivery. Leon and his colleagues demonstrated the time-linked receptivity of infant rats to the cecal odor (Leon, 1974, 1975; Leon & Moltz, 1972). The olfactory tether may be formed in rats by simple exposure to the odor. According to Leon, Galef, and Behse (1977), 14-day-old rats preferred an odor in which they were isolated for 2 hours.

It is of interest that simple exposure to an odor is sufficient to establish an olfactory preference in 14-day-old rats. Days 14–15 may be pivotal. Under normal circumstances rats may have learned by that time about the consequences of their own actions and about their surrounding stimuli in a positive ambience of warmth, suckling, contact, and a full stomach. These states are occasionally punctuated by the excitement of the mother visiting the nest and stimulating the infants anogenitally. Thus, under nest conditions, infant rats have probably not experienced pain or discomfort during these initial 2 weeks and, may not be neophobic. Days 14–15 are probably transitional because life will no longer be so amicable. The mother will be less available; infants will soon be leaving the nest area alone; and, there will soon be considerable rough and tumble behavior. Accordingly, it would be important to determine if olfactory exposure alone would continue to be effective in slightly older rats which have experienced some of the hardships of their station, or in younger rats that had been discomfitted experimentally.

According to Coopersmith and Leon (1984), there is apparently a hierarchy of reinforcers for this affiliation. Exposure and anogenital stroking, with a concomitant rise in brain temperature, is a more potent treatment than is exposure alone. Leon, Coopersmith, Lee, Sullivan, Wilson, and Woo (1986) have presented evidence for morphological and neurophysiological alterations in the olfactory bulb as possibly mediating these behaviors. It is of interest that these morphological alterations were obtained only in rats aroused in the presence of an odor. Simple exposure and also toxicity, while causing behavioral alterations, did not lead to functional or morphological changes.

SEXUAL BEHAVIOR

Fillion and Blass (1986) have investigated the long-term sexual consequences of exposure to particular odors. The impetus for these studies was the confluence of the following facts: (1) a component of rat pup saliva, dimethyldisulfide (DMDS), is a powerful stimulus for nipple attachment in rats (Pedersen & Blass, 1981), (2) DMDS is secreted vaginally by sexually receptive rodents (Gawienowski et al., 1978), and (3) the attributes of saliva as a stimulus eliciting nipple attachment are apparently acquired by specific experiences. From this it followed that DMDS, as a sexual attractant, might owe its biological effectiveness to events of the suckling period.

For this notion to be valid, we first had to demonstrate differential sensitivity to estrous odors during development and, second, that this sensitivity could be brought under experimental control. Accordingly, Fillion and Blass (1985a) presented infant rats 3, 7, and 10 days of age to females identified as in the estrous or diestrous portion of their cycles. Figure 3 demonstrates the probing response into diestrous or estrous females by rats of different ages. By 10 days of age, the effect was specific; the likelihood of probing estrous females was high and probing was largely directed at nipple and perivaginal areas.

Fillion and Blass (1986) treated females during the last 2 days of timed

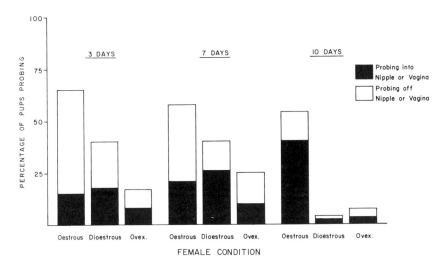

FIG. 3.   Percentage of pups 3, 7, and 10 days of age that probed into anesthetized females that were in behavioral estrous or diestrous or were ovariectomized. Filled portion
of the histogram indicates percentage that was directed at the nipple and vaginal areas.
Open portion indicates percentage directed at rest of body (from Fillion & Blass, 1985a).

pregnancies and daily during the entire 28-day nursing period by painting
their nipple and vaginal regions with citral. Control rats had isotonic saline
applied. Another group of rats received citral daily on their backs. Male offspring were separated from the mother when 28 days old and did not experience either citral or female contact until mating at about 100 days of age, that
is, when sexually mature. Each male was presented with either a normal sexually receptive female, or one that had citral painted perivaginally just minutes
prior to the mating test. A standard catalogue of measures was used to score
sexual performance.

Figure 4 demonstrates that latency to ejaculate was shortest when rats
mated with females bearing scents "familiar" to those on the mother's nipples
during suckling. This speaks to the memory of the suckling experience and to
the specificity of effect. "Back-Citral" rats mated quickly with both scented
and nonscented females suggesting that the familiar citral scent did not inter-
fere with mating that was elicited by females emitting normal estrous odors.
Taken together, the studies on sexual behavior demonstrate that through certain events during suckling, domesticated rats become differentially responsive to estrous odors. This line of analysis has just begun and the impact of
these early experiences on mating as it occurs more naturally, i.e. in groups
(McClintock & Anisko, 1982; McClintock, Anisko, & Adler, 1982), is currently being determined.

92   BLASS

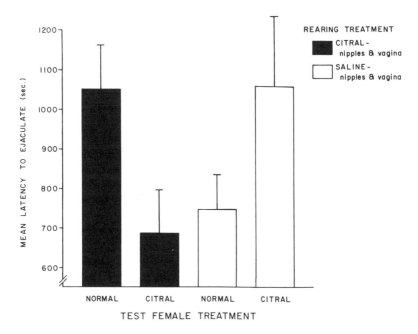

FIG. 4.   Mean latency to ejaculate of males mating with normal or citral scented, sexually receptive females. Males had been raised with mothers that were painted daily in the
nipple and perivaginal areas with either citral (filled histograms) or isotonic saline (open
histograms) (from Fillion & Blass, 1986).

CONCLUSIONS

The sensitive period concept has provided a useful framework for organizing several classes of social behavior in rats and their experiential determinants. Figure 5 reflects the sequence of developing social attachments during
the nursing period in rats. For ease of presentation, the figure consists of four
domains that probably reflect four interdependent processes. With time, the
demands for forming an olfactory social bond in rats appear to relax. At
first, for suckling, a bond is formed through experiencing odor when excited
(possibly catacholaminergic), predicting the occurrence of suckling. Next,
for huddling, the bond depends upon contact with a warm body. For nest orientation, exposure alone will do. Thus, specifiable multiple sensitive periods
exist for olfactory social bonding. The periods occur at different points in development, and govern different behaviors that apparently follow different
rules in forming their respective affiliations.

Suckling appears open-ended till about 5 days of age. Attraction by
caecotroph is limited to rats 14–28 days of age. Rats do not appear to be at-
tracted to it thereafter, although its consequences on later behaviors is not

known. In both cases the animal grows out of suckling and nesting behaviors. Huddling and sexual behaviors are essentially lifetime activities. As such, they are influenced by events beyond the early developmental period. Identifying the interactions among infantile, juvenile, and adult behaviors, their continuities and discontinuities, may provide insights into the organization of biosocial behaviors. Thus Fillion and Blass (1985a) have shown that estrous odors elicit probing of anesthetized females in Day 10 rats, wholebody exploration at weaning, self grooming in juveniles, and vaginal sniffing in adults (Fillion & Blass, 1985b). Sensory control is apparently continuous but the motor patterns elicited by the estrous stimulus differ markedly.

A psychological issue that surrounds these social behaviors concerns animals appreciating the consequences of their actions and their ability to modify behavior accordingly. It is of interest that by 2 weeks of age the infant has interacted with and become differentiated from its mother, siblings, and environment. That the demands are more modest for huddling than for suckling and more modest yet for nest affiliation may reflect the relative motor demands of each task. Alternatively, the huddling demand may be more relaxed than that for suckling because the animal has already learned about the consequences of its own actions and of external predicting stimuli through suckling. Nest-seeking development may be simpler yet for the animal that has learned about control in the huddle. These and other hypotheses de-

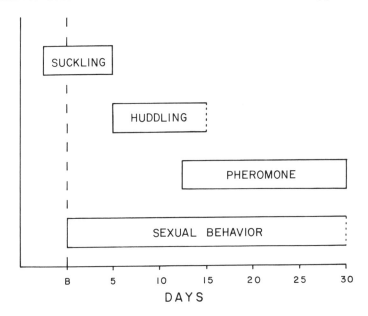

FIG. 5.   Schematic of when particular behaviors start to be channeled by environmental contingencies and when the influence wanes. Huddling and sexual behavior are left open ended as these processes continue beyond the point of demarcation.

signed to shed light on determining events during a sensitive period and the influence of processes and outcomes from one epoch to another constitutes an important chapter in development.

Ontogenetic narrowing of sensory control over social and affiliative behaviors and its empirical specification by natural stimuli invites linking developmental neurobiological and developmental psychobiological approaches. Developmental neurobiologists armed with new techniques to indicate functional characteristics of the central nervous system can seek a neural basis for behaviors governed by particular olfactory stimuli or by the confluence of sensory and motivational events that impart control to an otherwise neutral stimulus. Shepherd and his colleagues, using 14C 2DG autoradiography, have undertaken such an anlysis for the determination of nipple attachment in rats. Guided by the findings of Teicher and Blass (1977) and Pedersen and Blass (1982), Greer et al. (1983) demonstrated enhanced 2DG uptake in a specific macroglomerular complex of the olfactory bulb in 3-day-old suckling infant rats. This area had not been identified previously. It appears to be activated only during normal suckling. Infants exposed to citral odors by the procedures of Pedersen et al. (1983) and suckling a washed female annointed with citral did not show enhanced activity in this macroglomerular complex. Stated differently, this complex appears to be specifically activated by substances that normally appear on the nipple. It is clear, however, that this macroglomerular complex is not the only sensory afferent that can gain control over the motor act culminating in nipple attachment: there must be at least one other system in the olfactory bulb that has this property.

More recently, Pedersen et al. (1983) have demonstrated that the vomeronasal organ is involved in prenatal olfactory specification of the suckling odor. It is of considerable interest that the vomeronasal complex which projects through the accessory olfactory bulb to the medial amygdala, and the primary olfactory bulb which projects into the lateral amygdala, appear to be anatomically and functionally independent except for their amygdalar interface. These studies, rooted in behavior, point to a natural anatomical locus to explore. It is exactly this type of exploration geared to reveal potential changes in central structure that provides neural and behavioral linkages during the earliest developmental postnatal period.

The Pedersen et al. (1983) work is illuminating regarding sensitive periods because they have "isolated" spatially a specific portion (module) of the olfactory system. We can also apply this modular system to temporal isolation. That is, there are classes or systems of neurons that are available to the animal for a restricted period of time in the service of motor and affectional systems. We infer this from the observations that failure of these behavioral systems to become activated in a particular time frame generally leads to later unavailability. Potential connections of motor patterns with sensory information have not been formed so that integrated behaviors, a *following* pattern, for example, are not available to the animals.

This integrative response holds considerable potential for synthesizing a functional neurology with behavior. Behavioral narrowing, with its putative concomitant synaptic narrowing and long term maintenance of behavioral and anatomical change, encourages us to seek identification of small neural networks that are involved in the metamorphosis of biologically relevant behaviors.

The critical period concept in behavior had a stormy history, having been caught up in the debate between ethologists and psychobiologists during the 1950s and 1960s. The concept had difficulties in its own right until definitions either too rigorous or not sufficiently so fell by the way. Current ideas of sensitive periods fit into a broader biological perspective acknowledging (and assessing) behavioral continuities and discontinuities and the influence of previous periods on successive ones.

We may now try to link the particulars of early development with evolutionarily stable strategies of social and sexual behaviors that rely upon small but telling differences among individuals to identify optimal mates or kin (Bateson, 1983). There is reason to believe that prenatal and/or early postnatal events often coalesce to provide animals with such information (Bekoff, 1981; Holmes, 1986; Holmes & Sherman, 1982).

Finally, the major issues of proximal determination are starting to be addressed in a number of species at different ages. This strikes a fundamental chord for psychologists in general and for students of development in particular. Specifically, what are the properties of a reinforcing agent or event, and how is behavior altered? Developing infants, with time-limited opportunities of specification and restricted behavioral repertoires which rely upon complex events for expression, provide ideal subjects for the tasks of specifying informational and motivational ontogeny. That human distress and psychopathology often have identifiable developmental histories makes our undertakings the more worthwhile.

ACKNOWLEDGMENTS

Research supported by grant in aid of research AM 18560 from the National Institute of Arthritis, Metabolism, and Digestive Diseases; E. M. B. is also the beneficiary of a Research Scientist Award MH 00524. I thank Marybeth Baylin for her excellence in manuscript and graphics preparation.

REFERENCES

Alberts, J. R. Huddling by rat pups: Multisensory control of contact behavior. *Journal of Comparative and Physiological Psychology*, 1978, *92*, 220–230. (a)
Alberts, J. R. Huddling by rat pups: Group behavioral mechanisms of temperature regulation and energy. *Journal of Comparative and Physiological Psychology*, 1978, *92*, 231–245. (b)

Alberts, J. R. Ontogeny of olfaction: Reciprocal roles of sensation and behavior in the development of perception. In R. N. Aslin, J. R. Alberts, & M. R. Petersen (Eds.), *Development of perception: Audition, somatic perception, and the chemical senses.* New York: Academic Press, 1981.

Alberts, J. R., & Brunjes, P. C. Ontogeny of thermal and olfactory determinants of huddling in rat pups. *Journal of Comparative and Physiological Psychology*, 1978, *92*, 897–906.

Amsel, A., Burdette, D. R., & Letz, R. Appetitive learning, patterned alternation, and extinction in 10-day-old rats with non-lactating suckling as reward. *Nature*, 1976, *262*, 816–818.

Bateson, P. Optimal outbreeding. In P. Bateson (Ed.), *Mate choice*. Cambridge: Cambridge University Press, 1983.

Bekoff, M. Mammalian sibling interactions: Genes, facilitative environments, and the coefficient of familiarity. In D. J. Gubernick & P. H. Klopfer (Eds.), *Parental care in mammals.* New York: Plenum Publishing Corporation, 1981.

Blake, R., & Hirsch, H. V. B. Defects in binocular depth perception in cats after alternating monocular deprivation. *Science*, 1975, *190*, 1114–1116.

Blass, E. M. The development of olfactory control over behavior. In W. T. Greenough & J. M. Juraska (Eds.), *Developmental neuropsychobiology*. California: Academic Press, 1986.

Blass, E. M., Ganchrow, J. R., & Steiner, J. E. Classical conditioning in newborn humans 2–48 hours of age. *Infant Behavior and Development,* 1984, *7*, 223–235.

Coopersmith, R., & Leon, M. Enhanced neural response to familiar olfactory cues. *Science,* 1984, *225*, 849–851.

Fillion, T. J. & Blass, E. M. Infantile behavioural reactivity to oestrus chemostimuli in Norway rats. *Animal Behavior,* 1985, *34,* 123–133. (a)

Fillion, T. J. & Blass, E. M. Responsiveness to estrous chemostimuli in male rats (*Rattus Norvegicus*) of different ages. *Journal of Comparative Psychology*, 1985, *99*, 328–335. (b)

Fillion, T. J., & Blass, E. M. Infantile experience determines adult sexual behavior in male rats. *Science,* 1986, *231,* 729–731.

Galef, B. G. Mechanisms for the social transmission of food preferences from adult to weanling rats. In L. M. Barker, M. Best, & M. Domjan (Eds.), *Learning mechanisms in food selection.* Texas: Baylor University Press, 1977.

Gawienowski, A. M., & Stacewicz-Sapuntzakis, M. Attraction of rats to sulfur compounds. *Behavioral Biology*, 1978, *23*, 267–270.

Gilbert, A. N., Burgoon, D. A., Sullivan, K. A., & Adler, N. Mother-weanling interactions in Norway rats in the presence of a successive litter produced by postpartum estrous. *Physiology and Behavior*, 1983, *30*, 267–271.

Gottlieb, G. Introduction to behavioral embryology. In G. Gottlieb (Ed.), *Studies on the development of behavior and the nervous system: Behavioral embryology.* (Vol. 1). New York: Academic Press, 1973.

Gottlieb, G. Conceptions of prenatal development: Behavioral embryology. *Psychological Review*, 1976, *83,* 215–234.

Greer, C. A., Stewart, W. B., Teicher, M. H., & Shepherd, G. M. Functional development of the olfactory bulb and a unique glomerular complex in the neonatal rat. *Journal of Neurosciences*, 1983, *2*, 1744–1759.

Hall, W. G. Weaning and growth of artificially reared rats. *Science*, 1975, *190*, 1313–1315.

Hall, W. G. & Williams, C. L. Suckling isn't feeding, or is it? A search for developmental continuities. *Advances in the Study of Behavior*, 1983, *13*, 219–254.

Harlow, H. F. The heterosexual affectional system in monkeys. *American Psychologist*, 1962, *17*, 1–9.

Hinde, R. A. *Animal behavior: A synthesis of ethology and comparative psychology.* New York: McGraw-Hill, Inc., 1972.

Hofer, M. A., Fisher, A., & Shair, H. Effects of infraorbital nerve section on survival, growth and suckling behaviors of developing rats. *Journal of Comparative and Physiological Psychology,* 1981, *95,* 123-133.

Hoffman, H. S. Laboratory investigations of imprinting. In G. M. Burghardt & M. Bekoff (Eds.), *The development of behavior: Comparative and evolutionary aspects.* New York: Garland Press, 1978.

Holmes, W. G. Kin recognition by phenotype matching in female Belding's ground squirrels. *Animal Behaviour,* 1986, in press.

Holmes, W. G., & Sherman, P. W. The ontogeny of kin recognition in two species of ground squirrels. *American Zoologist, 22,* 1982, 491-517.

Kenny, J. T., & Blass, E. M. Suckling as incentive to instrumental learning in preweanling rats. *Science,* 1977, *196,* 898-899.

Lehrman, D. S. On the organization of maternal behavior and the problem of instinct. In Masson et Cie (Eds.), *L'instinct dans le comportment des animaux et de L'homme.* France: Masson et Cie, 1956.

Leon, M. Maternal pheromone. *Physiology and Behavior,* 1974, *13,* 441-453.

Leon, M. Dietary control of maternal pheromone in the lactating rat. *Physiology and Behavior,* 1975, *14,* 311-319.

Leon, M., Coopersmith, R. Lee, S., Sullivan, R. M., Wilson, D. A., & Woo, C. Neural and behavioral plasticity induced by early olfactory experience. In E. M. Blass, M. A. Hofer, N. Krasnegor, & W. Smotherman (Eds.), *Psychobiological aspects of behavioral development.* New York: Academic Press, 1986.

Leon, M., Galef, B. G., & Behse, J. H. Establishment of pheromonal bonds and diet choice in young rats by odor pre-exposure. *Physiology and Behavior,* 1977, *18,* 387-391.

Leon, M., & Moltz, H. The development of the pheromonal bond in the albino rat. *Physiology and Behavior,* 1972, *8,* 683-686.

Lorenz, K. Der Kumpan un der Umwelt des Vogels. *Journal of Ornithology,* 1935, *80,* 50-98.

Lorenz, K. The comparative method in studying innate behavior patterns. *Symposium, Society for Experimental Biology,* 1950, *4,* 221-268.

McClintock, M. K., & Anisko, J. J. Group mating among Norway rats. I. Sex differences in the pattern and neuroendocrine consequences of copulation. *Animal Behavior,* 1982, *30,* 398-409.

McClintock, M. K., Anisko, J. J., & Adler, N. T. Group mating among Norway rats. II. The social dynamics of copulation: competition, cooperation, and mate choice. *Animal Behavior,* 1982, *30,* 410-425.

Mangold, A., & Spemann, H. Homoplastische und heteroplastiche Verschnelzung ganzer Tritoheime. *Roux's Archives,* 1927, *3,* 494-665.

Mason, W. A., & Kenney, M. D. Redirection of filial attachments in rhesus monkeys: Dogs as mother surrogates. *Science,* 1974, *183,* 1209-1211.

Pedersen, P. E., & Blass, E. M. Olfactory control over suckling in albino rats. In R. N. Aslin, J. R. Alberts, & M. R. Petersen (Eds.), *The development of perception: Psychobiological perspectives.* New York: Academic Press, 1981.

Pedersen, P. E. & Blass, E. M. Prenatal and postnatal determinants of the first suckling episode in albino rats. *Developmental Psychobiology,* 1982, *15,* 349-355.

Pedersen, P. E., Stewart, W. B., Greer, C. A., & Shepherd, G. M. Evidence for olfactory function in utero. *Science,* 1983, *221,* 478-480.

Pedersen, P. E., Williams, C. L., & Blass, E. M. Activation and odor conditioning of suckling behavior in three day old albino rats. *Journal of Experimental Psychology, Animal Behavior Processes,* 1983, *8,* 329-341.

Rosenblatt, J. S. Olfaction mediates developmental transition in the altricial newborn of selected species of mammals. *Developmental Psychobiology,* 1983, *16,* 347-375.

Rosenblatt, J. S., & Lehrman, D. S. Maternal behavior of the laboratory rat. In H. L. Rheingold

(Ed.), *Maternal behavior in mammals.* New York: Wiley, 1963.

Roth, L. L., & Rosenblatt, J. S. Changes in self-licking during pregnancy in the rat. *Journal of Comparative and Physiological Psychology,* 1967, *63,* 397–400.

Schneirla, T. C., & Rosenblatt, J. S. "Critical periods" in the development of behavior. *Science,* 1963, *139,* 1110–1115.

Scott, J. P. Critical periods in behavioral development. *Science,* 1962, *138,* 949–958.

Scott, J. P., Stewart, J. M., & DeGhett, V. J. Critical periods in the organization of systems. *Developmental Psychobiology,* 1974, *7,* 489–513.

Shair, H., Brake, S., & Hofer, M. A. Suckling in the rat: Evidence for patterned behavior during sleep. *Behavioral Neuroscience,* 1984, *98,* 366–370.

Spemann, H. Entwicklungsphysiologische studien am tritonei I.*Arch. f. Entw. Mech.,* 1901, *12,* 224–264.

Stoloff, M. L., Kenny, J. T., Blass, E. M., & Hall, W. G. The role of experience in suckling maintenance in albino rats. *Journal of Comparative and Physiological Psychology,* 1980, *94,* 847–856.

Teicher, M. H., & Blass, E. M. First suckling response of the newborn albino rat: The roles of olfaction and amniotic fluid. *Science,* 1977, *198,* 635–636.

Teicher, M. H., Flaum, L. E., Williams, M., Eckhert, S. J., & Lumia, A. R. Survival, growth, and suckling behavior of neonatally bulbectomized rats. *Physiology and Behavior,* 1978, *21,* 553–561.

Vogt, W. Gestaltungsanalyse am Amphibienkiemit ortlicher vitalfarbung. Vorwort uber Wege und Ziele. I. Methodik u. wirungsweise der ortlichen Vitalfarbung mit Agar als Farbtragen. *Roux's Archives,* 1925, *106,* 542–610.

5
Imprinting and the Critical Period for Social Attachments: Some Laboratory Investigations

Howard S. Hoffman
Bryn Mawr College

INTRODUCTION

There are few concepts in the literature of developmental psychology that have commanded as much attention as the idea that the formation of primary social attachments must take place during a brief critical period if socialization is to proceed normally. The notion that there might be a critical period for social attachments was first brought to the attention of the scientific community and the general public when Konrad Lorenz described the process by which gray lag goslings come to follow and become socially bonded to whatever moving object they first encounter (Lorenz, 1935). Lorenz observed that if exposed to a human being during the first few hours after hatching, the goslings became socially attached to the human in much the same fashion as they would ordinarily become socially attached to their natural mother, and he illustrated the strength of these attachments with a now classic photograph of a half dozen or so goslings following him in a line.

Lorenz used the term "imprinting" to describe this attachment process and to emphasize its speed and permanence. It was as if, during imprinting, the image of the first moving object encountered, whether the goslings' natural mother or Lorenz himself, was somehow permanently and exclusively stamped (i.e., imprinted) on the goslings' nervous system. Thereafter the goslings directed their social behavior to the object and avoided or fled from others. Lorenz used the term "critical period" to describe the limited time span within which imprinting could occur. He reported that with goslings, if exposure to the moving object was delayed by as little as 48 hours, the resulting attachment was either weak or failed to develop at all.

In discussing these effects Lorenz indicated that he did not wish to infer that the imprinting process itself applied directly to humans or indeed to any mammals. But he noted certain analogies to pathological fixations of the drive object in human psychology, and his readers found themselves making similar analogies.

The idea that there might be a critical period for social attachment was especially compelling, and in the decades following World War II, when the "baby boom" was in full swing, much speculation ensued as to whether there might also be unique critical periods for all sorts of human attributes. Critical periods were proposed for the development of dependency and aggressiveness (Bloom, 1964) and for the development of linguistic skills (Scott, 1968; see Snow, this volume). It was even proposed that infantile autism might reflect an abnormality in the timing of an infant's critical period for social attachment (Moore & Sheik, 1971). Some infants, it was suggested, born either too late or with more highly developed nervous systems than most, might pass through their critical period while still in the womb. This would explain why these infants seemed to remain attached to and seek the stimulation provided by their own bodies and to avoid or withdraw from normal social interactions.

The pronouncements stimulated by these speculations were often considered infallible, and they exerted a powerful influence on social thought. If a child was to be healthy, he or she had to experience an intimate, early relationship with the mother. Any interruption in this relationship, even for a brief period, might result in the appearance of problem behaviors later. Because a child raised in an institution was almost certain to be permanently disadvantaged, late adoption was considered to be ill advised. It is difficult to ignore the self-fulfilling effects these pronouncements might have had on the way children were treated, but they serve to emphasize the potency of the concept of a critical period for attachment, once it was articulated.

In this chapter, I evaluate the concept of a critical period for attachment in the light of several experiments that my colleagues and I designed to examine imprinting in a direct empirical fashion.

LABORATORY INVESTIGATIONS OF IMPRINTING

Figure 1 shows the apparatus used in our laboratory. It consisted of a large wooden box divided into two compartments of approximately equal size by a fine-mesh stainless-steel screen: one compartment for the duckling and one for the imprinting object. The imprinting object was a rectangular block of foam rubber mounted over an electric train engine that could move back and forth along the length of its compartment. Since the stainless-steel screen separating the two compartments provided a one-way vision effect, the im-

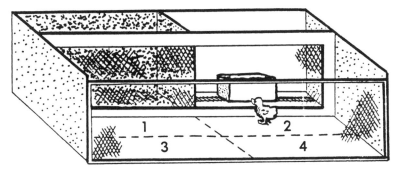

FIG. 1.   Apparatus used to study imprinting. The numbers on the floor of the subject compartment correspond to the four quadrants. The imprinting object consisted of a block of foam rubber mounted over the engine of an HO gauge model train. The screen between the subject and the object provided a one-way vision effect so that the object was only visible when its compartment was illuminated.

printing object was visible only when the lamps in its compartment were illuminated, and it would move only when power was supplied to its engine.

For many of our studies with this apparatus we allowed the imprinting object to move back and forth along the full length of its compartment, but in a study of the critical period for imprinting (Ratner & Hoffman, 1974), we inserted a vertical panel to divide the stimulus compartment in half, and we removed the lamps from the empty side. We then arranged that the other half of the stimulus compartment (which contained the imprinting object) would be illuminated only when the duckling was nearby. This was accomplished by using a set of infrared photo cells to divide the duckling's side of the apparatus (i.e., the subject compartment) into four equal quadrants and arranging to automatically illuminate the imprinting object and supply power to its engine whenever the subject entered Quadrant 2 (the quadrant immediately adjacent to the object) and to automatically turn off the lamps and terminate power to the engine whenever the subject left that quadrant. With this arrangement the object was visible and moving whenever the duckling was in Quadrant 2, and it immediately disappeared whenever the duckling moved out of this quadrant.

In this experiment, a number of ducklings were hatched in isolation and thereafter were maintained in individual housing units. Each duckling received two 30-minute test sessions on each of three successive days. In a given session, the duckling was gently lifted from its housing unit and quickly placed in the apparatus in Quadrant 2. For the next 30 minutes it was left alone and its movements into and out of the various quadrants were automatically recorded.

For some of the ducklings the initial test session occurred on Day 1, approximately 12 hours after the bird was free of its shell. For the others the first test session occurred on Day 5 post-hatch. For most of the ducklings tested on Day 1 as for most of the ducklings tested on Day 5 the imprinting object was visible and moving when the bird was placed in the apparatus, and the object would disappear whenever the duckling was out of Quadrant 2. For the rest, the object was withdrawn when the bird was placed in Quadrant 2 and it was never presented at any time. These birds served as controls for any differences in locomotor ability that might exist between 1- and 5-day old birds.

Figure 2 shows the results of these procedures. More specifically, it shows the percent of time in six successive 30-minute sessions that the birds in the experimental and control conditions spent in Quadrant 2. As indicated in Figure 2, ducklings that never saw the imprinting object (i.e., subjects in the control condition) spent about a quarter of their time in Quadrant 2, and this tendency did not change appreciably across sessions. More importantly for present purposes is that there are no appreciable differences in this respect between the young 12-hour-old and the more mature 5-day-old control birds. Clearly, in the absense of an imprinting object, younger and older birds display approximately equal locomotor activities in the apparatus used here.

As also indicated in Figure 2, ducklings exposed to the imprinting object

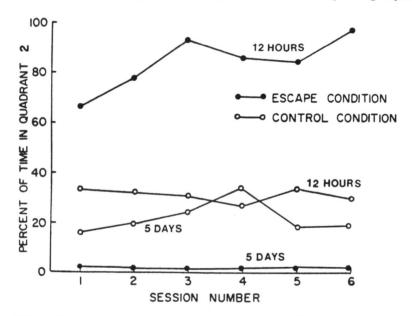

FIG. 2.   The mean percent of time spent in quadrant 2 by ducklings initially tested at 12-hours posthatch, and by ducklings initially tested at 5-days posthatch. Whenever a subject in the escape condition was in quadrant 2 the imprinting object was visible and moving and it disappeared when the subject left that quadrant. The object was never presented to subjects in the control condition regardless of their location.

during the test sessions behaved in opposite ways, depending on their ages at the time of their first exposure to it. Birds that were 12 hours old at this time tended to stay in Quadrant 2 near the imprinting object and as sessions accumulated they spent increasing amounts of time in that quadrant. Ducklings that were 5 days old during their initial exposure to the imprinting object immediately fled from it. Moreover, whenever they wandered back into Quadrant 2 and the object again appeared, they again fled. This pattern of behavior persisted throughout the six test sessions. Since the imprinting object was automatically withdrawn when the birds left Quadrant 2, these birds had very little exposure to the object in the course of these sessions.

Figure 3 portrays another aspect of the behavior of the 5-day-old ducklings. It shows the mean number of entries into Quadrant 2 as sessions progressed. For birds in the control condition, entries into Quadrant 2 had no experimental consequences. These birds tended to enter Quadrant 2 about five times per session. On the other hand, birds that saw the imprinting object whenever they were in Quadrant 2, quickly came to avoid entering that quadrant.

These data provide a dramatic demonstration of the critical period for imprinting as described by Lorenz. Even though afforded the opportunity to es-

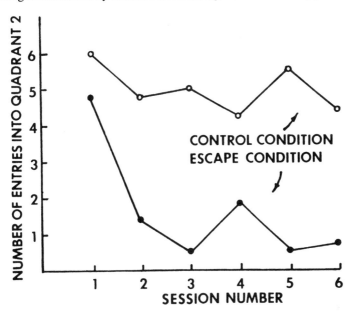

FIG. 3.   The mean number of entries into quadrant 2 made by ducklings first tested on Day 5 posthatch. For subjects in the escape condition each entry produced a presentation of the imprinting object. For these subjects departures from quadrant 2 produced withdrawal of the imprinting object; the control subjects were never exposed to the object regardless of their location.

cape from the imprinting object, the day-old ducklings approached it and in this sense exhibited filial behavior. Moreover, they continued to do so in successive sessions. Five-day-old ducklings with the same opportunity to escape did so persistently and even came to avoid the region of the apparatus where the object would appear. Clearly the timing of our duckling's initial exposure to the imprinting object was of the utmost importance. We wondered if the critical nature of this timing might have something to do with the stage of a bird's neuronal development when it was first exposed to the imprinting object. For many organisms, including man, the nervous system is incompletely formed at birth and, as maturation proceeds, there is a variety of orderly changes in the structure, organization, and metabolism of various brain systems.

More importantly for present purposes, depending on the system and the functions it mediates, the course of these changes is determined in part by the kinds of input the system receives. If, for example, kittens are deprived of visual experience with moving stimuli by rearing them under stroboscopic illumination, the proportion of direction selective neurons in the visual cortex is greatly reduced (Cynader & Chernenko, 1976). If kittens are raised in an environment of either horizontal or vertical stripes, the proportions of cortical cells responsive to vertical stripes in the former case, and horizontal stripes in the later case are greatly reduced (Blakemore & Cooper, 1970). The time span during development in which the nervous system is susceptible to these environmental manipulations is described as a critical — or sensitive — period. For the cat's visual system this period extends from approximately 2 to 14 weeks of age (Hubel & Weisel, 1970). In humans this period extends to about 2 years of age (Hickey, 1977). Adults with a history of severe early astigmatism (a condition that blurs the retinal image of lines or stripes in a particular orientation) exhibit lower acuity for lines in that orientation even though the astigmatic error had been corrected with lenses for many years. Apparently unless the lenses are applied during infancy when orientation-specific cortical cells are developing, the retinal input to certain of these cells is inadequate, and their full functional development is prevented. This would explain why the later application of corrective lenses could correct the image on the retina but still leave an orientation-specific loss of acuity (Freeman, Mitchell, & Millodot, 1972; Mitchell et al., 1973).

It seemed possible that a similar disruption of neural function or organization had occurred in our older ducklings. This would be expected if the critical period for imprinting is a period during maturation when an appropriate sensory input is needed if neuronal growth and organization is to proceed properly. Presumably by failing to receive this input at the appropriate time, some aspect of neuronal development was permanently arrested in our older birds. Of course this seemed an extreme possibility and we speculated that there might be other ways to account for the effects we had obtained.

Indeed, several investigators had previously suggested that the factor which underlies the critical period for imprinting is an age-related emergence of fear to novel stimulation (e.g., Candland & Campbell, 1962; Hersher, Richmond, & Moore, 1963; Hess, 1957, 1959a, b, 1962; Hinde, 1955; Hinde et al., 1956; Waller & Waller, 1963). Moreover, there were many data to support this proposition (Gray & Howard, 1957; Hess, 1959a; Jaynes, 1957; Ratner & Thompson, 1960). Furthermore, there had been a number of studies (Bateson, 1964; Hoffman, Ratner, & Eiserer, 1972; Slukin & Salzen, 1961) that indicated that new social alliances could in fact be formed by older subjects. Bateson (1964), for example, noted that, while older birds initially display a strong tendency to flee from an unfamiliar moving object with continued exposure to it, they gradually begin to emit the positive reactions characteristic of younger subjects. Similarly, Jaynes (1957), citing unpublished studies, noted that while older birds flee from a novel object when exposed to it for a 30-minute session, after several such sessions they begin to approach the object. Jaynes referred to this effect as "latent imprinting" and suggested that the tendency of an older bird to form a social attachment to an unfamiliar object depends on the duration of the bird's exposure to that object.

Was it possible, we wondered, that the fear exhibited by our older birds was masking an innate tendency to react affirmatively to the imprinting object. If such were the case, the older birds' failure to display filial behavior would not necessarily be permanent as implied if some aspect of neuronal development had been arrested. In order to examine this possibility in a direct quantitative way we arranged to continue testing the older birds. For half of these birds the conditions were identical to those that had prevailed during their previous six sessions. Twice every day the bird was placed in Quadrant 2 with the imprinting object visible and moving. If the bird left Quadrant 2 the object would immediately disappear, and it would not reappear until Quadrant 2 was again entered. The rest of the birds were treated similarly with a single exception. We arranged that the imprinting object would continue to move and be visible, regardless of the bird's location in the subject compartment. Thus, while a bird might put as much distance between itself and the imprinting object as possible, it could not completely escape from the sensory input provided by the object. Under these circumstances the object should eventually become familiar and hence be incapable of eliciting novelty induced fear. But what would happen when this fear no longer existed? If, a neuronal system responsible for attachment had in fact failed to develop properly, an older bird should be indifferent to the object. If, however, the tendency to form social attachments had merely been suppressed by a competing fear response, then instead of reacting with indifference and spending about 25% of its time in Quadrant 2, an older bird should begin to exhibit filial behavior. It should eventually approach and stay near the object and this tendency should increase as sessions progress.

Figure 4 shows what, in fact, happened in these circumstances. As sessions continued to accumulate, birds permitted to escape completely from the im-

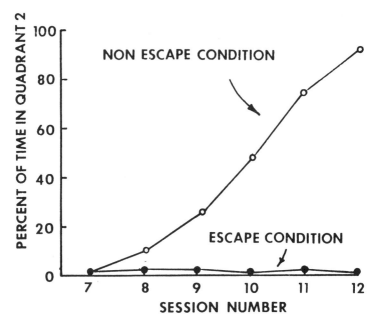

FIG. 4.   The mean percent of time spent in quadrant 2 when ducklings initially exposed to the imprinting object at 5 days posthatch were afforded six sessions of additional exposure. Whenever a subject in the escape condition left quadrant 2, the imprinting object was withdrawn. The object was never withdrawn from the subjects in the nonescape condition regardless of their location.

printing object persisted in doing so. Birds that could not completely escape also fled from Quadrant 2 initially. But as sessions accumulated, and the imprinting object became more and more familiar, rather than reacting with indifference, these birds spent more and more time in Quadrant 2. Eventually, by the sixth session (i.e., on Day 11 post-hatch), these birds spent almost all of their time near the object, just as the young birds had.

It is difficult to reconcile this behavior with the concept that the formation of social attachments is necessarily restricted to some brief "critical" period that ends a few hours after hatching. This is not to say that the notion of a critical period for attachment is totally without merit. On the contrary, it accurately describes the behavior that occurs in circumstances where escape is possible, as is usually the case in the natural settings where Lorenz made his observations. But the notion of a "critical period for imprinting," like the term "imprinting" itself carries with it a variety of surplus meanings, and these can be quite misleading. Clearly, the data obtained here run counter to the natural assumption that the critical period for imprinting might be analogous to a critical period for neuronal development.

The fact that, given appropriate circumstances, an older bird can form so-cial attachments and that once this occurs its behavior is quite similar to that of younger birds led both Bateson (1969, p. 113) and Hinde (1970) to ques-tion the utility and accuracy of Lorenz's notion of a "critical period", since it wrongfully implies an all-or-nothing effect, regardless of the circumstance. They proposed that the term "sensitive" period be used in its place to empha-size that the temporal boundaries of this period are not immutably fixed. As noted by Hinde (1983, p. 41), and as the title of this volume implies, it is now more popular to speak of a sensitive period for attachment.

A number of the experiments in my laboratory were designed to try to iden-tify what occurs during the critical or sensitive period. Though not men-tioned earlier, an important part of our apparatus to study imprinting was that it included an electronic system to detect and record distress calls. These consist of a sequence of intense peep-like sounds that are emitted when a duckling becomes separated from its natural mother, or from an imprinting object. Because these calls also occur when a duckling is deprived of nourish-ment, exposed to reductions in body temperature, or subjected to painful stimulation, they are thought to reflect an automatic response to aversive conditions (Hafez, 1962).

In one study (Hoffman, Stratton, Newby, & Barrett, 1970), we asked when during a duckling's exposure to an imprinting object does the object begin to exert control over distress vocalization. For that study the imprinting object moved back and forth along the entire length of its compartment during stim-ulus presentation. During stimulus withdrawal the object's motion ceased, and the lights in its compartment were turned off. From the duckling's point of view it ceased to exist.

We carefully monitored the incubation process, and when inspection of a given egg first revealed pip marks, it was placed in a small cardboard box. The duckling left its shell while in the box, and it remained in the box undisturbed until the tests began.

Approximately 17 hours after a given duckling was free of its shell, we quickly transferred the previously unopened box (containing the duckling and the remnants of its shell) from the incubator to the center of the subject compartment and, using a long string and a pulley system, remotely lifted the box from its detachable floor. Thus, except for its experience within the box, the duckling's initial visual stimulation occurred when the box was lifted.

For all ducklings the imprinting object had been withdrawn prior to placing the box in the apparatus. For several of the ducklings the imprinting object was presented a few seconds before the box was lifted and remained present for 1 minute. For the other ducklings the imprinting object was with-held until 1 minute had elapsed after the box was lifted. Thereafter, stimulus presentations and withdrawals occurred at 20-second intervals. With this ar-rangement the basic difference between the conditions for the two groups of ducklings was whether or not the imprinting object was visible at the time the box was lifted.

The upper portion of Figure 5 shows the distress vocalizations for several of the ducklings that saw only the subject compartment when the box was lifted. The birds in this condition began to emit distress calls when first exposed to the apparatus — i.e., when the box was lifted — but in most cases stopped almost immediately when the imprinting object appeared for the first time. The distress calls that occurred with subsequent withdrawals of the object typically had a latency of 2 to 5 seconds. In general, however, cessation of distress vocalization with presentation of the imprinting object continued to occur with very short (less than 1 second) latency.

The bottom portion of Figure 5 shows the records obtained when the imprinting object was presented just prior to lifting the hatch box. For these ducklings, distress calls did not occur until the object was first withdrawn; thereafter, however, the birds exhibited the same pattern of distress calling as was seen in the top portion of Figure 5.

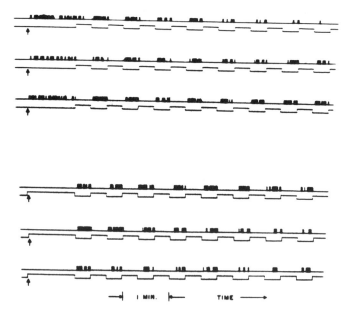

FIG. 5.   The initial control of distress vocalization by the presentation and withdrawal of an imprinting object. The records begin immediately following the placement of the hatching box in the apparatus (20 seconds prior to the lifting of the box). In each record the vertical arrow indicates the lifting of the hatching box. For the top three records the imprinting object was withdrawn at the time the box was lifted. For the bottom three records the imprinting object was visible and moving when the box was lifted. An upward deflection of the top of the two lines in each record indicate a distress call. An upward deflection of the bottom of the two lines indicates a presentation of the imprinting object.

Observation of the ducklings during the two test procedures made it clear that the cessation of distress calls with the first presentation of the object could not be ascribed to a fear or freezing response. The ducklings were very attentive to the object and frequently attempted to approach and/or to follow it. Occasional "contentment cheeps" also were emitted during stimulus presence.

These findings provide an answer to the question: "When in the imprinting process does the object begin to control filial behavior"? It does so immediately; hence, the data indicate that the initial phase of imprinting involves an innate rather than a learned reaction. Moreover, since the initial presentation of the stimulus consistently yielded a decrease in distress vocalization, it can also be concluded that the first contact with the imprinting stimulus reduces arousal.

In one sense, that finding in itself constitutes strong evidence that the filial response to an imprinting object is innate. Under most circumstances, the expected effect of increased stimulation is an increase in arousal (Schneirla, 1959). Indeed, most subjects began to emit distress calls as soon as the lifted box exposed them to the increased stimulation provided by the empty experimental chamber. When, however, the moving object was added to that stimulus complex, distress calls terminated abruptly. It seems apparent that the ducklings were differentially responsive to the kinds of stimulation arising from the static environment versus a moving object. Moreover, since nothing in the duckling's pretest experience (within the hatching box) would be expected to produce this kind of differential responsiveness, it seems safe to conclude that the initial imprinting reaction was based on a predisposition to exhibit filial behavior when exposed to the kind of stimulation provided by the moving object.

At this point in the research we had uncovered three important facts: (1) a newly-hatched duckling will immediately respond affirmatively when it encounters an appropriate moving object; (2) an older (5-day-old) duckling with no history of prior imprinting will also react affirmatively to the same moving object, but its positive reaction is initially inhibited by its fear of the object; and (3) once a duckling has been imprinted to a given object, it continues to react affirmatively rather than fearfully when that object is again encountered.

When we considered these facts it seemed apparent that imprinting must be the process by which a newly hatched duckling becomes familiar with, and in this sense learns to recognize, an object that itself innately evokes filial behavior. Such learning would ensure that during later encounters with the object the innate filial reaction would not be precluded by novelty-induced fear. There was, however, one problem with this deceptively simple conception: we did not know what kind of learning process might be involved. This problem had puzzled other investigators as well (e.g., Rajecki, 1973).

Our first breakthrough came when we began to consider an earlier observation that if our foam rubber object was stationary during its initial presentation to a 17-hour-old duckling it did not suppress ongoing distress vocalizations. As we pondered this observation we soon realized its implication: to a newly hatched duckling the static features of our imprinting object were initially neutral in the sense that they did not innately evoke a filial response. But if the color, shape, size, and other static features of our foam rubber object were neutral, it must be that the stimulation arising from visual movement itself was the feature of our imprinting object that evoked the filial reaction. We reasoned that if this were the case it should be possible, through a kind of classical conditioning process, for the static features themselves to acquire the capacity to evoke filial reactions — much like the sound of a bell comes to evoke salivation when it is paired with the delivery of food. When transposed to the context of imprinting, a classical conditioning process might be expected to operate if (1) visual movement itself functions as a Pavlovian unconditioned stimulus for the ducklings, (2) the static features of the imprinting object are initially neutral, but can become conditioned stimuli, and (3) the static features are, in effect, paired with visual movement while the object is seen in motion.

Under these circumstances, the imprinting object's static features themselves would be expected gradually to acquire the capacity to evoke conditioned filial reactions. Presumably, once this occurs the object will have been rendered familiar and, hence, it will be incapable of subsequently evoking the fear reaction that is induced by novel objects in older ducklings.

In an experiment designed to track the course of such learning (Hoffman, Eiserer, & Singer, 1972), previously isolated 17-hour-old ducklings were individually exposed to an extended session in which the object was repeatedly presented and withdrawn in cycles of 1 minute present and 1 minute absent. For subjects in the experimental condition, the object was stationary during the first stimulus presentation. It moved during the next, was stationary during the third, and so on. For subjects in the control condition, the object was always stationary during stimulus presentation.

As shown in Figure 6, the object in motion suppressed distress calling whenever it was presented, but the stationary object, when first presented, did not affect the rate of distress calling. Over the course of the session, however, the stationary object gradually came to suppress distress calling for the subjects that also saw the object in motion. The flat function for the control subjects indicates that mere exposure to the stationary object alone did not result in the development of suppressive properties.

It seems clear to us that the learning process elucidated in this experiment is the heart of imprinting. When the distinctive static features of the object have acquired the capacity to evoke the conditioned filial reaction, the object has

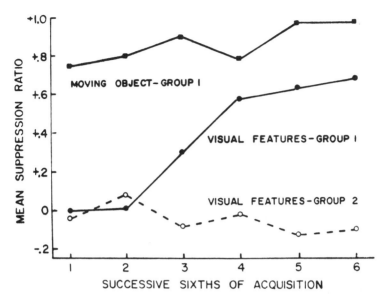

FIG. 6.   The control of distress calls by an imprinting object when that object was repeatedly presented and withdrawn in cycles of 1-minute each. For ducklings in group 1
the object moved during alternate presentations and was stationary during the rest. For
ducklings in group 2 the object was stationary during all presentations. With the index of
suppression used here, a ratio of 1.0 indicates that distress calls during stimulus absence
were completely suppressed during presentation of the object, and a ratio of zero indicates that distress calling continued unabated when the object was presented; a negative
ratio indicates that more distress calls occurred in the presence of the object than in its absence. The top function shows the suppression of distress calls afforded by presenting the
moving object to subjects in group 1. The middle function shows how presentation of the
stationary object (i.e., visual features only) gradually came to suppress distress calls for
these same subjects. The dashed line shows how presentation of the stationary object
failed to acquire the capacity to suppress distress calls for subjects in group 2 who never
saw the object move.

become familiar and will not later evoke the fear reactions to novel stimuli
that otherwise occur in older ducklings.

Although we have not here considered why ducklings might exhibit an innate positive reaction to visual movement, Sackett (1963) has offered a
neurophysiological explanation, and Hoffman and Ratner (1973) have examined the issue in some detail. Also, we have not yet considered why, as
ducklings grow older, they react fearfully during their first encounter with a
novel object. Both Cairns (1966) and Bateson (1966), however, have offered
interesting theoretical interpretations. These investigators suggest that the
fearful reactions result from perceptual and other incongruities that occur
when the subject is first exposed to unfamiliar stimulation. For present pur-

poses, it is sufficient to note that the concept of incongruity seems necessarily to imply the existence of contrasting familiar stimulation and it further implies that some form of learning (or classical conditioning) has occurred. More than 20 years ago, Fabricius (1962) suggested that classical conditioning is probably central to the imprinting phenomenon, and the data in Figure 6 are consistent with this suggestion.

It is easy to conceive of the same classical conditioning process occurring when a newly hatched duckling becomes attached to its biological parent in its natural environment. Like our imprinting object, the mother moves and thus provides at least one form of stimulation that innately invokes filial behavior. It is also likely that some of the static features of a mother duck possess such innate capacities, as some reports have indicated (Hess, 1973, p. 119; Ramsay & Hess, 1954). We also know that certain of her calls can innately evoke filial reactions (Gottlieb, 1965). Such redundancy would function to make it all the more certain that the duckling will stay near and become attached to the mother. In addition, it is likely to be the case that other static features of the mother duck are initially neutral but come to evoke conditioned filial reactions as a result of their temporal and spatial relationship with the features that innately evoke the filial response.

In retrospect, it was very fortunate that none of the static features of our imprinting object were innate elicitors of filial behavior. Had some static feature(s) of our object (e.g., its shape or color) possessed a strong innate capacity to control filial reactions (as might have been the case if we used a duck decoy instead of the block of foam rubber), then the object presented stationary might have suppressed the distress calling of a newly hatched duckling that had never seen it in motion. Had this happened, we might never have identified the learning process which seems to be the mechanism for the formation of specific filial bonds.

Once imprinting is viewed as an exemplar of learning, numerous questions come to mind. Among the most interesting is whether a duckling that has been imprinted to one object can subsequently become imprinted to a new object. According to traditional conceptions, the imprinting attachment that is established during the first few days of a duckling's life prevents the duckling from subsequently forming new attachments (Lorenz, 1935). If, however, imprinting is merely the process by which the young organism learns the features of stimuli that innately evoke filial behavior, imprinting to one object ought not necessarily prevent imprinting to another object. Indeed, there might even be some circumstances where imprinting to one object would facilitate the development of a subsequent social attachment.

In order to examine this possibility it was first necessay to find a second quite different imprinting object. A series of pilot studies suggested that a rotating amber-colored lamp, of the type used on many police vehicles, was likely to be an effective imprinting object for our birds and that subjects imprinted to it would not react affirmatively to the foam rubber object and vice versa. In one experiment using this object (Hoffman, Ratner, & Eiserer, 1972), we employed three conditions. Ducklings in the first condition were individually imprinted to either the moving block of foam rubber or the rotating amber lamp by giving them lengthy exposure to it during the first 2 days after hatching. Ducklings in the second condition were not exposed to either stimulus during this period. Ducklings in the third condition were individually exposed to both stimuli simultaneously.

When we tested each of the ducklings on Day 5 (by repeatedly presenting and withdrawing each of the stimuli for a short period), the distress calls of birds imprinted to one stimulus were suppressed by that stimulus but not by the other. For ducklings not imprinted to either stimulus, neither stimulus suppressed distress calls. For ducklings exposed to both stimuli during imprinting, only one of the stimuli suppressed distress calls — three of the five subjects in this condition apparently had imprinted to the rotating light, and the other two had apparently imprinted to the moving object. These findings made it quite clear that by Day 5 (when strong fear of novelty would have developed) ducklings imprinted to one stimulus did not respond to the other and that ducklings that had been imprinted to neither would respond to neither.

At the completion of this test, each subject was given extended exposure to one of the stimuli: a duckling that had been imprinted to only one stimulus was exposed to the other stimulus; a duckling that had been exposed to both stimuli during Days 1 and 2 was not required to remain in the presence of the less effective (presumably nonimprinted) of the two stimuli; and a duckling that had previously been imprinted to neither stimulus was now exposed to one or the other of the two stimuli. (Half the birds were exposed to one and the rest were exposed to the other.) Figure 7 shows the gradual development of control over distress calls when the stimulus was periodically presented and withdrawn in a series of brief tests administered every 20 minutes as exposure proceeded. At zero hours exposure (i.e., during the first test), the stimulus exhibited very little control over the distress calls of any bird. As exposure proceeded, however, the distress vocalization of all the ducklings began to come under the control of the stimulus, but it occurred most rapidly for birds that had been exposed to both stimuli during imprinting. Ducklings without prior imprinting did not come under very strong control during the 120-minute exposure period depicted in Figure 7, but when they were given 2 hours of additional exposure, their distress calls came under the control of the stimulus approximately to the extent exhibited by the others.

This configuration of results makes it quite clear that imprinting to one stimulus neither prevents nor retards the development of control by a second stimulus. Instead, it can facilitate this development. We do not at this time know the precise mechanisms responsible for this facilitory effect. It may re-

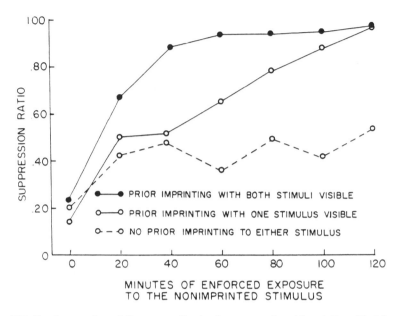

FIG. 7.   Suppression of distress vocalization by a nonpreferred imprinting object for ducklings that had previously been given imprinting sessions with both a moving foam rubber object and the rotating lamp visible, for ducklings previously given imprinting sessions with only one of the two objects visible, and for ducklings previously given imprinting sessions with neither object visible. The ordinate at 0 hours shows the suppression of distress calls during an initial test on Day 5. The other ordinates show the levels of suppression in subsequent tests following increasing amounts of enforced exposure to the nonpreferred stimulus. The suppression ratio is described in the caption for Figure 6.

flect some kind of stimulus generalization, or it may reflect a kind of learning to learn. Whatever its nature, its occurrence is consistent with the view of imprinting that our experiments have elaborated, and it is inconsistent with the early view that imprinting to a given object necessarily precludes imprinting to a subsequent object.

THE MOTIVATIONAL SUBSTRATE FOR IMPRINTING

The work described thus far was focused on identifying the nature of the imprinting process and the behavioral effects it might engender. One segment of our work focused on the motivational substrate for these effects.

In view of the immediacy of a duckling's filial reaction to the presentation of an imprinting object, one might suppose that this reaction reflects some form of intrinsic need for the kind of stimulation the object provides. Indeed, Bateson (1971) has reported that before it has ever seen an imprinting object, a newly hatched duckling often emits what seems to be "appetitive behavior" that terminates only when the bird makes visual contact with the object. Since this behavior includes the emission of distress calls, it might be taken to reflect an intrinsic need which is aversive. There is a problem, however, with this inference. The difficulty is that one cannot know if the ducklings' distress calls prior to seeing the stimulus reflected an intrinsic need for that stimulus, or if they were a reaction to circumstances that were aversive and hence would have themselves induced distress calls. What would happen, we wondered, if we were to arrange to expose ducklings to an imprinting object in a setting that was completely comfortable and hence would not itself induce distress calling? In an experiment designed to examine this issue (Hoffman, Eiserer, Ratner, & Pickering, 1974), the hatching process was monitored and as soon as a given duckling was free of its shell, the bird was quickly transferred to the illuminated subject compartment of the imprinting apparatus, where it remained, isolated and undisturbed with the imprinting stimulus withdrawn. At the end of its 17th hour in the apparatus, the stimulus compartment was illuminated and power was transmitted to the engine. In short, the moving imprinting object was presented for the first time. After 1 minute the stimulus was withdrawn and subsequent stimulus presentations occurred every other minute.

Figure 8 shows the pattern of distress calling that this procedure engendered. No distress calls occurred in the minute prior to the initial stimulus

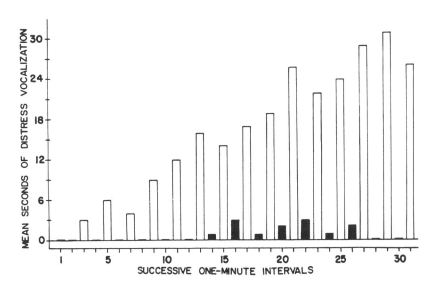

FIG. 8.   Mean number of seconds of distress vocalization during alternate 1-minute periods of stimulus presentation (solid bars) and withdrawal (open bars). Ducklings in this study were placed in the apparatus when they were first free of their shell and remained there undisturbed with the stimulus withdrawn until testing began (17 hours later).

presentation; but as the stimulus was repeatedly presented and withdrawn, the ducklings exhibited an increasing tendency to emit distress calls in the 1-minute periods of stimulus absence. Since most birds gave no distress calls whatsoever during the initial 17-hour period, it is apparent that the setting in which stimulus presentation first occurred was not itself aversive. Moreover since stimulus presentation invariably suppressed (rather than induced) distress calls and since most birds attended to and approached the stimulus during each of its presentations, it is also apparent that the stimulus was not merely adding increments in arousal. On this basis, one can conclude that the distress vocalization that ensues when an imprinting object is withdrawn is, in part, a product of the stimulus presentation itself and that the effects of repeated presentations are in some measure cumulative. This conclusion has important implications for an understanding of the attachment that imprinting ultimately entails. In particular, it implies that independent of any extrinsically determined needs, exposing a duckling to an imprinting stimulus serves to create its own need.

It is of special interest that empirical support for this interpretation of attachment behavior has been obtained from pharmacological studies. Panksepp and his associates (Herman & Panksepp, 1978; Panksepp et al., 1978) found that in newly hatched chicks separation-induced distress calling could be alleviated by intraventricular injections of minute quantities of either morphine or endorphins. Moreover, separation-induced distress vocalization could be enhanced by injections of a morphine-antagonist (naloxone). It is of interest that other work in Panksepp's laboratory indicated that even in large doses neither the tranquilizers, the barbiturates nor the amphetamines were able to alleviate separation-induced distress calling. This evidence points to the concept that attachment behavior is mediated by the production of opiate-like peptides. If one adds to this concept the idea that the stimulation provided by certain features of an appropriate attachment object is sufficient to initiate the production of these substances, it would explain why newly hatched ducklings immediately react affirmatively to the stimulation provided by a moving object.

The idea that an appropriate imprinting object stimulates the production of opiate-like peptides can also explain why an object for attachment can calm a frightened subject and why its withdrawal is so aversive. This idea also explains why, as was seen in Figure 8, ducklings that were otherwise comfortable began to emit distress calls after they had some exposure to the imprinting object and then it was withdrawn.

These considerations point to the conclusion that in the domain of social attachments there is much to be gained by viewing the behavior it entails as exemplifying a kind of addiction. Clearly, if social attachments are mediated by the production of endorphins, and if endorphins have addictive effects, one should expect to find many parallels between attachment behavior and addictive behavior. As noted by Hoffman and Solomon (1974), this seems to be the case. Furthermore, if social attachments in primates and man, like social attachments in birds, are also mediated by the production of endorphins, then one ought to be able to find parallels between the attachment behaviors of primates (including man) and the attachment behavior of ducklings. As it turns out, there are many such parallels and they are striking.

Just as 1-day-old ducklings will immediately exhibit filial reactions toward an appropriate imprinting object, immature monkeys exhibit immediate filial reactions toward objects with certain tactile properties (i.e., soft objects to which they can cling), indicating that for monkeys, as for ducklings, certain classes of stimulation innately elicit filial behavior, presumably by stimulating the production of endorphins (Harlow, 1961).

The learning processes examined above in the context of imprinting also have a striking parallel in primate attachment. Just as a duckling's distress reactions are not alleviated by a stationary object until the duckling has viewed the object in motion (Hoffman, Eiserer, & Singer, 1972), a monkey's distress reactions are not alleviated by the sight of a soft surrogate object encased in clear plastic (to prevent tactile contact) until the monkey has been raised with the claspable surrogate for several weeks (Mason, Hill, & Thompson, 1971). Likewise, for human infants, one might suppose that certain distinctive features of the mother (e.g., her particular face, voice, etc. that distinguish her from other people) are initially neutral and do not evoke positive reactions until they are paired during the first several months of the infant's life with those aspects of the mother that innately elicit pleasurable responses (i.e., responses that may be mediated by the production of endorphins).

The fear of strangers exhibited by human infants after eight months of age is obviously similar to the novelty-induced fear that prevents an older duckling from initially showing filial reactions toward a novel imprinting object. Schaffer (1966) has shown that the onset of the infant's fear reactions to strangers does not coincide with the point at which the infant begins to recognize strangers. He provided evidence that younger infants can readily discriminate their parents from strangers and yet not be fearful of the strangers. Similarly, we have found that the 1-day-old duckling that reacts affirmatively to either of two different imprinting stimuli can discriminate between them (Hoffman & Ratner, 1973). In the duckling, as in the human, the capacity to discriminate may be a necessary condition for fear of strangers to emerge, but it is not a sufficient condition — some maturation is also required.

These comparisons can help us place imprinting into evolutionary perspective. As noted by Jacob (1977, p. 1164), "Evolution does not produce novelties from scratch. It works on what already exists, either transforming a system to give it new functions or combining several systems to produce a more elaborate one." Our findings imply that imprinting is no exception to this principle. They reveal that most, if not all, of the seemingly distinctive features of imprinting are in fact the product of a limited number of well-known, if not yet thoroughly understood, behavioral processes. This in turn implies that the essential features of imprinting should be seen in any organism whose behavior is based on those processes.

In addition to providing a more nearly unified picture of attachment, the view of imprinting elaborated by our work can explain why attachment behavior exhibits such wide variations across species and among individuals within a given species. According to this view some aspect of an appropriate attachment object provides stimulation that innately elicits filial behavior. It does so by stimulating the production of endorphins. When a young organism has extended exposure to such an object the initially neutral features of the object come to elicit filial behavior through a classical conditioning process. While this is happening, the object is rendered familiar, and this serves to maintain the subject's tendency to respond filially after the tendency to respond fearfully to unfamiliar stimuli emerges. When viewed in this way, attachment is seen to encompass a number of basic and in some respects independent behavioral processes that interact in a variety of complex ways. Certain of these processes, such as those responsible for the innate tendency to respond filially, must ultimately depend upon the presence or absence of appropriate genetic factors. Others, such as those responsible for the development of familiarity, must depend primarily on experience. Still other processes, such as the emergence of novelty-induced fear, are undoubtedly based on an interaction between maturational and experiential factors.

Considering the variety of processes that contribute to attachment, it is no wonder that the attachment phenomenon should exhibit so many complex ramifications. Certainly the possibilities for variations across species and for individual differences are enormous. For example, a given organism might be more or less sensitive to a given form of eliciting stimulation. There must be individual as well as cross-species differences in rate of learning, just as there must be differences in the maturational factors that contribute to novelty-induced fear.

CONCLUSIONS

When viewed in their entirety our findings point to the conclusion that in the domain of social attachments nature is so designed as to make the notion of immediate irreversible environmental effects a concept of extremely narrow application – if it has any application at all. Our work indicates that social alliances are a product of learning and thus these alliances must be much more flexible than is usually supposed. As noted earlier, Lorenz's original concept was that imprinting is an immediate, irreversible phenomenon with ominous consequences to the organism should it fail to occur within a defined "critical period." This concept has been used to justify the notion that failure to be exposed to all sorts of environmental stimuli at an appropriate time dooms an organism to be permanently disadvantaged. Our findings would seem to indicate that this is not necessarily the case. Nature can in fact repair some of the unfortunate vagaries of environmental experience. Apparently it does so through the continually expanding and adjusting effects of learning.

ACKNOWLEDGMENTS

Throughout this chapter the term "we" refers to the author and to his former students who over the years participated in the research and made substantial contributions to the concepts presented here. The research on which this chapter is based was supported by NIMH Research Grant MH-19715.

REFERENCES

Bateson, P. P. G. Changes in chicks' responses to novel moving objects over the sensitive period for imprinting. *Animal Behavior*, 1964, *12*, 479–489.

Bateson, P. P. G. Imprinting. In H. Noltz (Ed.), *The ontogeny of vertebrate behavior*. New York: Academic Press, 1971.

Bateson, P. P. G. Mother-infant interaction: Effects and biological functions. In J. A. Ambrose (Ed.), *Stimulation in early infancy*. London: Academic Press, 1969.

Bateson, P. P. G. The characteristics and context of imprinting. *Biological Review of the Cambridge Philosophical Society*, 1966, *41*, 177–220.

Blakemore, C., & Cooper, G. F. Development of the brain depends on the visual environment. *Nature*, 1970, *228*, 477–478.

Bloom, B. S. *Stability and Change in Human Characteristics*. London: Wiley, 1964.

Cairns, R. B. Attachment behavior of mammals. *Physiological Review*, 1966, *73*, 409–426.

Candland, D. K., & Campbell, B. A. Development of fear in the rat as measured by behavior in the open field. *Journal of Comparative and Physiological Psychology*, 1962, *55*, 593–596.

Cyander, M., & Chernenko, G. Abolition of directional selectivity in the visual cortex of the cat. *Science*, 1976, *193*, 504–505.

Fabricius, E. Some aspects of imprinting in birds. *Symposium of the Zoological Society of London*, 1962, *8*, 139–148.

Freeman, R. D., Mitchell, D. E., & Millodot, M. A. Neural effect of partial visual deprivation in humans. *Science*, 1972, *175*, 1384–1386.

Gottlieb, G. Imprinting in relation to parental and species identification by avian neonates. *Journal of Comparative and Physiological Psychology*, 1965, *59*, 345–356.

Gray, P. H., & Howard, K. I. Specific recognition of humans in imprinted chicks. *Perception & Motor Skills*, 1957, *7*, 301–304.

Hafez, E. S. E. *The Behavior of Domestic Animals*. London: Bailliere, 1962.

Harlow, H. F. The development of affectional patterns in infant monkeys. In B. M. Foss (Ed.), *Determinants of infant behavior*. New York: Wiley, 1961.

Herman, B. H., & Panksepp, J. Evidence for opiate mediation of social affect. *Pharmacology, Biochemistry & Behavior*, 1978, *9*, 213–220.

Hersher, L., Richmond, J. B., & Moore, A. V. Modifiability of the critical period for the development of maternal behavior in sheep and goats. *Behavior,* 1963, 311–320.

Hess, E. H. Effects of meprobamate on imprinting in water fowl. *Annals of New York Academy of Science,* 1957, *67,* 724–732.

Hess, E. H. Two conditions limiting critical age of imprinting. *Journal of Comparative and Physiological Psychology,* 1959, *52,* 515–518. (a)

Hess, E. H. Imprinting. *Science,* 1959, *130,* 133–141. (b)

Hess, E. H. Imprinting and the 'critical period' concept. In E. L. Bliss (Ed.), *Roots of Behavior.* New York: Hoeber, 1962.

Hess, E. H. *Imprinting: Early experience and the developmental psychology of attachment.* New York: Van Nostrand Reinhold, 1973.

Hickey, T. L. Postnatal development of the human lateral geniculate nucleus: relationship to a critical period for the visual system. *Science,* 1977, *198,* 836–838.

Hinde, R. A. *Animal behaviour.* New York: McGraw Hill, 1970.

Hinde, R. A. Ethology and child development. In P. H. Mussen (Ed.) *Handbook of child psychology.* New York: Wiley, 1983.

Hinde, R. A. The following response of moor-hens and coots. *British Journal of Animal Behaviour,* 1955, *3,* 121–122.

Hinde, R. A., Thorpe, W. H., & Vince, M. A. The following response of young coots and moor-hens. *Behaviour,* 1956, *11,* 214–242.

Hoffman, H. S., Eiserer, L. A., Ratner, A. M., & Pickering, V. L. Development of distress vocalization during withdrawal of an imprinting stimulus. *Journal of Comparative and Physiological Psychology,* 1974, *86,* 563–568.

Hoffman, H. S., Eiserer, L. A., & Singer, D. Acquisition of behavioral control by a stationary imprinting stimulus. *Psychonomic Science,* 1972, *26,* 146–148.

Hoffman, H. S., & Ratner, A. M. A reinforcement model of imprinting: Implications for socialization in monkeys and men. *Psychological Review,* 1973, *80,* 527–544.

Hoffman, H. S., Ratner, A. M., & Eiserer, L. A. Role of visual imprinting in the emergence of specific filial attachment in ducklings. *Journal of Comparative and Physiological Psychology,* 1972, *81,* 399–409.

Hoffman, H. S., & Solomon, R. L. An opponent-process theory of motivation: III. Some affective dynamics in imprinting. *Learning and Motivation,* 1974, *5,* 149–164.

Hoffman, H. S., Stratton, J. W., Newby, V., & Barrett, J. E. Development of behavioral control by an imprinting stimulus. *Journal of Comparative and Physiological Psychology,* 1970, *2,* 229–236.

Jacob, F. Evolution and tinkering. *Science,* 1977, *196,* 1161–1166.

Hubel, D. H., & Wiesel, T. N. The period of susceptibility to the physiological effects of unilateral eye closure in kittens. *Journal of Physiology,* 1970, *206,* 419–436.

Jaynes, J. Imprinting: The interaction of learned and innate behavior: II. The critical period. *Journal of Comparative and Physiological Psychology,* 1957, *50,* 6–10.

Lorenz, K. Der Kumpan in der Umwelt des Vobels. *Journal of Ornithology,* 1935, *83,* 137–213.

Mason, W. A., Hill, S. D., & Thompson, C. E. Perceptual factors in the development of filial attachment. *Proceedings of the 3rd International Primatological Congress,* 1971, *3,* 125–133.

Mitchell, D. E., Freeman, R. D., Millodot, M., & Haegerstrom, G. Meridional amblyopia: Evidence for modification of the human visual system by early visual experience. *Vision Research,* 1973, *13,* 535–558.

Moore, D. J., & Shiek. Toward a theory of early infantile autism. *Psychological Review,* 1971, *78,* 451–456.

Panksepp, J., Vilberg, T., Bean, N. J., Coh, D. H., & Kastin, A. J. Reduction of distress vocalization in chicks by opiate-like peptides. *Brain Research Bulletin,* 1978, *3,* 663–667.

Rajecki, D. W. Imprinting the precocial birds: Interpretation, evidence, and evaluation. *Psychological Bulletin,* 1973, *79,* 48–58.

Ramsey, A. O., & Hess, E. H. A laboratory approach to the study of imprinting. *Wilson Bulletin*, 1954, *66*, 196–206.

Ratner, A. M., & Hoffman, H. S. Evidence for a critical period for imprinting in Khaki Campbell ducklings (anas platyrhynchos domesticus). *Animal Behavior*, 1974, *22*, 249–255.

Ratner, S. C., & Thompson, R. W. Immobility reactions (fear) of domestic fowl as a function of age and prior experience. *Animal Behavior*, 1960, *8*, 186–191.

Sackett, G. P. A neural mechanism underlying unlearned, critical period, and developmental aspects of visually controlled behavior. *Psychological Review*, 1963, *70*, 40–50.

Schaffer, H. R. The onset of fear of strangers and the incongruity hypothesis. *Journal of Child Psychology and Psychiatry*, 1966, *7*, 95–106.

Schneirla, T. C. An evolutionary and developmental theory of biphasic processes underlying approach and withdrawal. In M. R. Jones (Ed.) *Nebraska symposium on motivation*, University of Nebraska Press, 1959.

Scott, J. P. Early Experience and the Organization of Behavior. Belmont, CA: Wadsworth, 1968.

Sluckin, W., & Salzen, E. A. Imprinting and perceptual learning. *Quarterly Journal of Experimental Psychology*, 1961, *16*, 65–67.

Waller, P. F., & Waller, M. G. Some relationships between early experience and later social behavior in ducklings. *Behaviour*, 1963, *20*, 343–363.

6 Neural Insult and Critical Period Concepts

C. Robert Almli
Washington University School of Medicine

Stanley Finger
Washington University

INTRODUCTION

A critical period is a time period during which an organism is more sensitive and/or vulnerable to certain exogenous stimulus conditions than at other times in its life (Bornstein, this volume; Colombo, 1982). In this chapter, critical periods are discussed and evaluated in the context of mammalian neurobehavioral development, the effects of injuries to the central nervous system, and undernutrition. The problems associated with a strictly defined critical period concept are discussed, and the strict concept is set aside in favor of the more flexible constructs of "optimal" and "sensitive" periods.

It is shown that under conditions of circumscribed brain lesions in humans and laboratory animals, diverse behavioral outcomes appear to preclude any broad or generalizable statement about optimal periods for recovery of function following brain damage. Although early, focal brain damage may sometimes be associated with greater sparing or recovery of function than brain damage sustained later in life, the exceptions to this finding are too numerous to propose a simple rule or invariant principle. The possibility that the rapidly developing brain may be more likely to be damaged by injurious substances (e.g., lead) or affected by sub-optimal conditions (e.g., anoxia) than is the older brain also is considered. Undernutrition is examined in this context, and it is shown that the effects of undernutrition on brain and behavior are more severe when experienced during the period of rapid brain growth than later in life. This would suggest that there is a sensitive (or vulnerable) period for exposure to poor nutrition, or, the opposite case, an optimal period during which good nutrition stimulates ideal growth and development. Finally, some of the differences between diffuse brain "lesions," such as may result from undernutrition, and acute focal brain lesions are examined, and it is proposed that the potential for recovery may be a function of the magnitude of the injury and the residual growth capacity in the brain.

CONCEPTIONS AND DEFINITIONS
OF CRITICAL PERIODS

The critical period notion is not new to the biological and behavioral sciences. Stockard (1921) credited Dareste with the idea in the late 1800s (Scott, 1962), although many current formulations of the concept stem from Stockard's own work in embryology after the First World War. Stockard (1921) demonstrated that fish embryos exposed to a wide variety of inorganic chemicals could develop into "monsters," such as specimens with only one eye. He noted, however, that these effects only resulted from chemical exposure at certain times. Stockard (1921) and later Child (1941) also recognized that the tissues that were most sensitive or vulnerable to external stimulus conditions were those growing most rapidly.

Lorenz's (1935) research on imprinting in birds led to the belief that there also are critical periods for behavior. Over the years the concept has been broadened to encompass learning of motor skills in humans (McGraw, 1935), socialization in dogs (Scott, 1962), bonding in birds, foxes, and human infants (Hales, Lozoff, Sosa, & Kennel, 1977; Scott, 1962; see Myers, this volume), and human language development (Lenneberg, 1967; see Snow, this volume).

In spite of the intuitive validity of the critical period concept, it should be pointed out that the concept has also generated considerable controversy. One notable problem is that "there is scarcely a dimension of behavior to which it has not been applied" (Moltz, 1973, p. 144). A second problem has been a lack of agreement with regard to the degree to which such periods are actually "critical" (Krasten, 1975; Moltz, 1973). A third problem that has arisen is that not all researchers have used the term "critical period" in the same way. Terms such as "critical," "sensitive," "optimal," "vulnerable," and "important" have been used interchangeably by some authors and with different connotations by others. A related fourth problem is that specific criteria for determining a "critical period" have not been agreed upon. As a consequence, terms are often used without adequate experimental validation.

An issue that is generating considerable interest at the present time is the degree to which the effects of critical periods are rigid and absolute or flexible and malleable. Early research on imprinting in birds seemed to suggest that critical period effects were irreversible (Lorenz, 1935). This contention, however, failed to receive support from later imprinting studies where behavioral changes were observed after the so-called critical period ended (Salzen & Meyer, 1968). Further, studies examining language development in children (Curtiss, 1977), vision after sensory restriction (Chow & Stewart, 1972), and social isolation in monkeys (Harlow, 1965) have also shown that the effects ascribed to a critical period may be modified somewhat later in life (Bateson, 1983).

A number of attempts have been made to establish some consistency in terminology. Fox (1970), for example, distinguished between "critical" and "sensitive" periods. He defined a critical period as a period in which normal development must be "triggered," or during which a specific type of stimulation is needed for normal development. In contrast, he defined a sensitive period as a period in which the organism is extremely vulnerable to harmful stimuli. This distinction, however, is not always easy to make and some investigators have questioned whether it really provides a useful heuristic or represents merely two sides of the same coin. For example, with regard to language development, Colombo (1982) noted that a "critical" period can be defined in the sense that a child must hear language if language is to develop normally, but that one could also call the period "sensitive" in that the child is especially vulnerable to linguistic isolation at this time.

Moltz (1973) went further than Fox (1970) by attempting to develop a more complex classification system. He first distinguished between "critical" and "optimal" periods in terms of absolute and relative importance. Moltz (p. 144) viewed a critical period as "a particular period in the life history of an animal during which it must be exposed to certain stimulus conditions if these conditions are to have any influence at all on the animal's response development." An optimal period, in contrast, was viewed as one in which "a given set of stimulus conditions may exert a more profound influence on subsequent behavior if they occur during one stage of development rather than during another" (p. 144). Moltz next distinguished between contingent and non-contingent systems on the basis of whether they would still develop (non-contingent) or not develop (contingent) in the absence of the stimulus conditions being considered. His remaining distinction was between "mutable" and "immutable" — the degree to which a critical period is locked to a specific time frame.

Criteria for identifying and establishing critical periods for neurobehavioral development, in conjunction with the definitions presented by Fox (1970) and Moltz (1973), are serving to clarify the conditions under which the concept of critical period may apply. In this regard, Nash (1978) and Colombo (1982) have proposed that a critical period should be characterized by (a) an identifiable onset and termination; (b) an intrinsic maturational component; (c) an extrinsic or non-internal stimulus condition to which the organism is sensitive; and (d) an identifiable system which is affected by stimulation or its absence during the period.

Most studies of critical periods seem to show that the onset of a critical period is gradual, that there is a rise to a peak of sensitivity and that the duration of peak sensitivity can vary. Rearing animals in the dark, for example, can delay the critical period for some visual functions. Offsets of critical periods also seem to be gradual and to some extent modifiable. It appears that the presence or absence of extrinsic stimulation affects the timing of critical periods. As for the external stimulus, this is not always well-defined in behavioral studies. For example, Colombo (1982) has asked what aspect of language is essential. However, more biologically oriented research has led to definition of relatively specific stimuli in at least some instances (e.g., unit recordings after early exposure to lines in specific orientations).

Much attention also has been devoted to understanding the "intrinsic maturational component," in the context of neurobehavioral development, especially since the most rapidly growing tissues or systems seem to be those most likely to be affected by changing stimulation conditions (Scott, 1962, 1979). The perceived relation between rapid growth and susceptibility to external stimulation suggests that a critical period may be a time of enhanced neurobehavioral plasticity, related to emergent functional maturation or growth of neurobehavioral systems. This would mean that the onset of a critical period could be related to, and be signaled by, the achievement of some level of development and functional maturation, and that the critical period could end when a higher level of growth and maturation is achieved.

The notion of a critical period as a period of enhanced neurobehavioral plasticity may be exemplified by the development of binocularity of the visual system. A critical period for the development of binocularity may begin when central nervous system cells driven by each eye grow and compete for cortical synapses (Wiesel & Hubel, 1963). This critical period may end when the degree and extent of competitive synaptogenesis diminishes and stabilizes, perhaps regulated in part by the amine system (Kasamatsu & Pettigrew, 1979). The critical period for development of binocularity may take place between weeks 4 and 12 in the cat; 1 and 9 in certain monkeys; and years 1 and 3 in man. As stated by Scott (1962, p. 957):

. . . once a system become organized, whether it is the cells of the embryo that are multiplying and differentiating or the behavior patterns of a young animal that are becoming organized through learning, it becomes progressively more difficult to reorganize the system. That is, organization inhibits reorganization. Further, organization can be strongly modified only when active processes of organization are going on, and this accounts for critical periods of development.

As previously discussed, the concept of critical period has been broadly and loosely applied to a wide variety of neurobehavioral systems. However, when considering the strict definitions of critical periods proposed by Fox (1970) and Moltz (1973), and the criteria for identifying critical periods proposed by Nash (1978) and Colombo (1982), it is clear that the concept of critical periods has been over used. In the following sections, neurobehavioral development, the effects of central nervous system injury, and undernutrition are discussed and evaluated with regard to the less-absolute concepts of optimal periods (Moltz, 1973) and sensitive periods (Fox, 1970). This is not to imply that the concept of critical period does not relate to these phenomena. Rather, it is an acknowledgment that there may not be sufficient data to justify the use of a strictly defined critical period concept at the present time.

NEURAL MATURATION AND
OPTIMAL/SENSITIVE PERIODS

As noted, rapidly growing tissues are thought to be the most sensitive to external stimulation (Child, 1941). The period of most rapid growth of the mammalian central nervous system occurs prenatally and during the early postnatal period (Dobbing, 1976). At this time, neurons and glia are generated, and they migrate and aggregate. Axons and dendrites differentiate and branch, interneuronal (synaptic) connections between elements are made, and the process of myelination begins. The retrogressive processes of cell death, axon retraction, and synaptic elimination appear to contribute to the functional development and fine-tuning of the developing nervous system (Almli & Fisher, 1985; Cowan, Fawcett, O'Leary, & Stanfield, 1984; Fisher & Almli, 1984).

These growth processes peak at different times and rates both within and between neural regions. For example, neurons of some lateral brainstem areas are generated and differentiate before medial areas, and cortical neuronal generation and differentiation occur primarily after generation of brainstem areas. Further, it is becoming clear that neural growth processes may continue to be more active later in life than previously thought. Current research on natural synaptic turnover, injury induced axonal sprouting, and synaptic modification (in models of learning and memory) supports the basic idea of a relatively dynamic nervous system throughout much of the potential lifespan (Chang & Greenough, 1984; Cotman & Nieto-Sampedro, 1984; Curcio, Buell, & Coleman, 1982).

Application of the optimal period concept to issues of neural growth and development has received considerable research attention (Almli, 1984, 1985). For example, optimal periods and early experience have been studied with regard to the development of such diverse phenomena as binocularity (Wiesel & Hubel, 1963), cortical neuroanatomy (Greenough, 1976), hemispheric laterality (Denenberg Garbanati, Sherman, Yutzey, & Kaplan, 1978), and olfactory bulb physiology (Almli, Henault, Velozo, & Morgane, 1985). In these types of studies there is a consistent association between some crucial level of neural growth and maturation that allows the neural system to be influenced or modified by some external form of stimulation. However, even in these studies it has not always been possible to specify the time course of the optimal period with any degree of accuracy. The relative nature of optimal periods may be explained in part by the notion that neuroplasticity may attenuate with age, although it may never be completely lost (Cotman & Scheff, 1979; Curcio, Buell, & Coleman, 1982).

The concept of sensitive periods (Fox, 1970) in development has also received considerable research attention. It is now known that early exposure to a variety of stimulus conditions can be harmful to normal neurobehavioral development. Most noteworthy are alcohol and drugs, heavy metals such as lead, anoxia/hypoxia, irradiation, certain bacterial and viral infections, and environmental pollutants (e.g., Hicks, Cavanaugh, & O'Brien, 1962; Lenneberg, 1968). Each of these conditions has been shown to produce aberrant neural growth, and organisms appear to be exceptionally vulnerable to such conditions during certain early periods of development.

In the following sections, two related problems are addressed. The first is the relation between age at which brain damage is sustained and behavioral outcome. The evidence for, and against, defining an optimal period for sparing or recovery function following relatively circumscribed neural injury is discussed. The second is the relation between timing of exposure to undernutrition and brain and behavioral abnormality. In this context, research is evaluated to determine if there are periods of life during which the brain is especially sensitive or vulnerable to disruptive effects of exposure to undernutrition.

RECOVERY FROM ACUTE BRAIN LESIONS

The literature on early versus later focal brain lesions has been reviewed a number of times in recent years (Finger & Stein, 1982; Johnson & Almli, 1978) and has been the subject of two recent edited volumes (Almli & Finger, 1984; Finger & Almli, 1984). The possibility of differential responses to brain injuries as a function of age at the time of insult is not a new idea. Vulpian (1866) and Soltmann (1876) reported age-related differences in hemidecortication experiments on laboratory animals well over 100 years ago, and clinical investigators before the end of the nineteenth century were discussing the more transient nature of aphasia in children (Bernhardt, 1885) and the hypothesis that the functional plasticity of the brain is greatest in children (Bastian, 1898).

The experiments of Margaret Kennard (1936, 1938, 1940) on monkeys and apes of various ages were the first to attract considerable and sustained attention to the possibility that the effects of brain lesions may in part be determined by developmental status at the time of insult. During the 1930s and 1940s, Kennard (1936, 1938, 1940) showed that primates with acute motor cortex lesions sustained in infancy did not show the severe paralyses that characterized primates injured later in life. Kennard attributed this to a greater capacity for "reorganization" in the infant brain.

Kennard's publications led to a plethora of experiments attempting to ascertain whether her results would generalize to other lesion conditions, to other species, and to other tasks. The immediate result was a large number of laboratory animal experiments that seemed to support her contention that if one is to sustain brain damage, it is best to sustain it early in life. These studies examined the effects of damaging primary and secondary sensory cortical areas, such as somatosensory, auditory, and visual cortex; looked further at the effects of motor and supplementary motor zone damage; expanded findings to learning and problem solving after lesions of association cortical areas, especially prefrontal cortex; and included limbic structures such as the amygdala, hippocampus, and septum. Furthermore, these studies were conducted on a variety of laboratory animals, including monkeys, cats, rats, and dogs, and covered a broad range of dependent variables from measures of emotion and motivation to conditioning, perceptual learning, and higher order problem solving. In short, research findings obtained in controlled laboratory studies in the three decades following Kennard's initial paper led to broad acceptance of the idea that the brain is less affected by acute lesions sustained during the period of rapid brain growth than it is afterward. This contention became known as the "Kennard effect" or the "Kennard principle" (Simons & Finger, 1984), and suggested, on a superficial level at least, that there may be something like an optimal period for enhanced recovery of function following brain damage.

It is now generally acknowledged by researchers studying the effects of early and later brain lesions that the so-called "Kennard principle" may not be a principle or an invariant rule at all (Finger & Stein, 1982; Isaacson, 1975; Johnson & Almli, 1978). In fact, Kennard found that it did not hold for visual cortex lesions or on measures like placing and hopping reactions after motor cortex damage (Kennard & Fulton, 1942). By the late 1960s, papers reporting that infant-operated animals were just as impaired or debilitated as their adult-injured counterparts on some tasks were making their way into the literature in fair number. For example, no differences attributable to age at the time of insult were found on visual discriminations after posterior cortical lesions in rabbits (Murphy & Stewart, 1974), in social behavior after rats received septal lesions (Johnson, 1972), on drinking behavior following preoptic damage in rats (Almli, Golden, & McMullen, 1976), on oddity problem performance after dorsolateral prefrontal cortex ablation in monkeys (Thompson, Harlow, Blomquist, & Schiltz, 1971), or with cats tested on a delayed response task after sustaining acute, bilateral hippocampal lesions (Isaacson, Nonneman, & Schmaltz, 1968).

To at least some extent, these challenges to the Kennard principle can be attributable to methodological differences across studies (i.e., different tasks, lesion placements, etc.). There should be little doubt, however, that poor experimental designs, and perhaps strong predispositions to obtain findings consistent with those first reported by Kennard in 1936 also delayed an appreciation of the diversity of possible responses to early brain damage. The following four observations, considerations, and criticisms are pertinent in this context:

(1) In some of the earlier studies, only the infant-operated animals received brain lesions. These subjects were then compared to adult-operated cases examined at different times in other experiments, not always by the same individuals or even in the same laboratory.

(2) In very few studies were infant-operated animals compared to two important groups of adult-operated animals; one matched for age at the time of testing and the other matched for recovery period duration (see Simons & Finger, 1984). Where infants and adults were tested only at the same age, the much longer recovery period afforded the infant groups may have biased results in their favor. Where both were given matched, but short recovery periods, one could argue that age-related differences in factors such as exploration and activity levels could have affected results.

(3) Infant-operated animals were tested too soon after injury and for too short a time period to see deficits emerge in some studies. Kennard (1938) herself acknowledged that her infant-operated monkeys seemed to show increasing signs of paralyses as they matured although they never were as severely incapacitated as their adult-operated counterparts. Excellent examples of newborn rats with sensorimotor cortex ablations performing normally before Day 17 but not after this day on certain reflexive measures have been described by Hicks and D'Amato (1975). This phenomenon has also been observed by Almli (1978) in the delayed development of feeding deficits after early hypothalamic injury, and by Goldman (1974) with monkeys sustaining lesions of the dorsolateral frontal cortex "growing" into deficits on problem solving tasks more than a year after the time of insult.

(4) The size and placement of a lesion received early in life is difficult to determine from the topography of the brain months or years later since the rapidly growing brain will tend to "fill in" the area that had been ablated (Finger, Simons, & Posner, 1978). Many of the early rat studies in particular suffer from inadequate histological verification of the lesions and, even in

newer studies, questions are being raised about whether lesions in young and mature groups are really comparable in terms of size and locus.

Reports dealing with human case material show at least as much variability as the laboratory animal literature, and it is often even more difficult to draw conclusions or to generalize from clinical reports. This appears to be the case for reasons already mentioned and because clinical studies are limited by special problems of their own. One such problem is the frequent absence of autopsy material. In fact, even in some cases where histological verification of the lesion may be possible, the individuals may have died well after testing took place. In these cases, one can only guess at what the brain would have looked like if it had been examined immediately after data were collected.

Perhaps the most limiting feature of clinical studies is that the lesions sustained by infants and by older individuals are often of different types. Differences in the speed with which a lesion is evolving can markedly affect results on behavioral tests (Finger, 1978; Finger & Stein, 1982), and in a number of studies comparing the effects of brain damage in children and adults, the children are not usually suffering from strokes, missile wounds, or surgical ablations of tissue. These are the acute conditions that have led to the concept of "normative" (adult) responses to specific brain injuries.

Still, at least on the surface, the laboratory animal studies and the human case reports seem to complement each other. For example, there is a large literature showing that young children sustaining left hemispheric (language cortex) damage early in life are more likely than adults to exhibit rapid and complete or near-complete recovery (see Snow, in this volume). The findings of Milner (1974) and Penfield (Penfield & Roberts, 1959) at the Montreal Neurological Institute suggest a gradual, age-related shift to the adult response pattern. They reported that the best recovery could be seen in children under 2 years of age; that good recovery could still be observed in somewhat older children; and that the adult pattern of deficits is not yet achieved by the early teens.

One interpretation of the rapid recovery of speech from early left hemisphere lesions is that the right hemisphere can become the dominant speech hemisphere following left hemispheric injuries early in life. This hypothesis now has considerable experimental support (e.g., from sodium amytal tests) in cases where the speech areas are severely damaged on the left side. However, much has been written in recent years about the price that may be paid when speech develops in the right hemisphere following left hemisphere insult. In particular, investigators have noted that the IQ scores of such children are rarely in the normal range, that such children have trouble in school, and that functions typically attributed to the right hemisphere may themselves be affected (Alajouanine & Lhermitte, 1965; Byers & McLean, 1962; Taylor, 1984). It has been stated that these children seem able to regain what was learned but experience great difficulty learning new material. In short, the impression given is that one pays a price for the preservation of speech, perhaps because too many functions are now "crowded" into the right hemisphere (Milner, 1974). In this regard it is interesting to note that a somewhat comparable effect has now been observed after early brain damage in rats (LeVere, 1985).

The degree to which the dramatic findings involving speech can generalize across clinical syndromes is far from clear, and it may be that if the literature were searched carefully enough, just about any hypothesis about age and recovery could find support, even the contention that early brain lesions may be more deleterious than those sustained later in life (Fitzhugh & Fitzhugh, 1965; Taylor, 1984). The complexity of the situation becomes obvious when one considers that children can exhibit dramatic recovery on some tasks, while growing into deficits on others, much as was observed in monkeys by Goldman (1974). This has been seen in tests of ability of brain-damaged children to signify, without the aid of visual cues, when a tilted chair is in an upright position (which shows significant improvement with age), in contrast to the capacity to localize the source of a sound under conditions of body tilt (a task on which scores deviate from normal as development progresses) (Teuber & Rudel, 1962).

Perhaps the most striking examples of human subjects growing into deficits can be found in studies of motor development in early brain-damaged children, most notably those with parietal lobe involvement (Lenneberg, 1968). For the first few postnatal months these children do not exhibit the hemiplegias that characterize adults with lesions in this part of the brain. By the time they should be able to walk, however, signs of spasticity and abnormal reflexes can be seen, perhaps as the neural program for regulation of movement shifts from exclusively subcortical structures to involve the cortex. The clinical signs, which are barely noticeable at first, grow worse, and are accompanied by stunted bone growth on the side of the body contralateral to the lesion.

The extent to which sensory and perceptual processes may be affected by early lesions has led to some of the most interesting hypotheses in the clinical literature. Teuber and his colleagues (Rudel, Teuber, & Twitchell, 1974; Teuber, 1971; Teuber & Rudel, 1962) examined educable children with perinatal injuries resulting in cerebral palsy and noted that only 2 of 63 (3%) showed visual-field defects in contrast to 48 of 238 (20%) adults with penetrating brain wounds. Further, no children showed impaired detection of light touch (nylon filaments), diminished punctate localization, or deficits in 2-point discrimination, in contrast to the adult-injured sample where two-thirds of the individuals showed tactile threshold changes after injury. This sparing was all the more remarkable since the children still exhibited some pathological reflex and motor signs.

In contrast to these results, different findings emerged on more complex perceptual tasks, such as recognizing objects by palpation. Here, the adult-injured cases did well. However, half of the children with early brain damage showed deviant performance. In tests of route-findings, where only adults with parietal involvement performed poorly, almost all children exhibited deviant scores, regardless of the site of the damage. These observations suggested to Teuber and his co-workers that the ability to perform simple sensory tasks may be spared following early brain injuries, but that early brain damage may be even more deleterious than brain damage experienced later in life on more complex perceptual tasks.

There does not appear to be any monolithic explanation for the diversity of experimental and clinical findings pertaining to the relations among age, performance deficits, and behavioral recovery following acute brain damage. The response to brain lesions at different ages can obviously be affected by many interacting factors, among which are developmental status of remaining brain parts at the time of injury, recovery period duration, and task and demand characteristics (Finger & Stein, 1982; Johnson & Almli, 1978).

Thus, with regard to these kinds of brain injuries there do not appear to be any broad generalizations that can be made with regard to sensitive (Fox, 1970) or optimal (Moltz, 1973) periods. Whether one focuses on age-related differences in injury-induced behavioral deficits or on behavioral recovery of function as outcome measures, the results across and sometimes within studies are too diverse to allow a simple classification. At times early brain damage may be associated with enhanced recovery, but there are also many examples of remarkable recovery being achieved by humans and laboratory animals that suffered brain damage well *after* the period of rapid brain growth had ended (Finger & Stein, 1982). Because it is true that lesions of different neural areas at different developmental ages often yield different outcomes, arguments for sensitive periods for focal brain injury or optimal periods for recovery of function would have to be made on a very limited scale.

Nevertheless, it is important to recognize that these conclusions pertain to only one level of analysis (behavior), and that on anatomical, biochemical, or physiological levels the conclusions that might be reached could be quite different (see Bateson & Hinde, in this volume). Further, it is also possible that the results for behavioral recovery might be more consistent if neuro-developmental landmarks (e.g., myelination, emergence of evoked potentials) were used to classify subjects instead of chronological age, especially when different species are compared. The possibility also exists that the response to acute, focal brain damage may not serve as an adequate or appropriate model for other types of neural injury. In particular, it is necessary to ask whether a more consistent picture, and one more in keeping with the concepts of optimal and sensitive periods, may emerge under conditions of more diffuse neural insult. Studies of tetratogens, anoxias, hypoxias, irradiation, and poisonings suggest that neural damage that is relatively diffuse in nature, and/or damage that affects the growth capacity or potential of the brain, may exert its most deleterious effects when it occurs early in life in comparison to later in life (Almli & Finger, 1984; Finger & Almli, 1984). The effects of undernutrition are examined in this context for the purpose of determining whether the developing organism is more sensitive to this form of neural insult.

EFFECTS OF EARLY UNDERNUTRITION

The literature on undernutrition (malnutrition) has been reviewed many times and from a variety of perspectives (e.g., Dodge, Prensky, & Feigen, 1975; Manocha, 1972; Winick, 1976). Those studies examining the relation between the timing of periods of undernutrition and subsequent brain and behavioral development have been consistent in showing that poor diets early in life result in more marked and lasting changes than they do at later points in the lifespan. This finding has emerged with designs involving undernourished infants, and in cases where the pregnant mother's diet was deficient in one or more characteristics, thus undernourishing offspring even before birth. The susceptibility of the developing brain to nutritional insult has been confirmed in studies of protein, calorie, and protein-calorie deficiencies, as well as in cases of inadequate supplies of specific minerals (e.g., zinc). The effects of these types of undernutrition on the mature brain appear to be qualitatively different in many respects.

Gross brain changes attributable to poor early nutrition have been measured in a number of investigations. Winick (1976), for example, noted that a consistent finding in the literature is that overall brain size is reduced in children undernourished early in life, and that reduced brain size may persist even with nutritional "rehabilitation" later on. Brain size and weight reductions have also been reported in undernutrition studies using laboratory animals as subjects (Resnick, Miller, Forbes, Hall, Kemper, Bronzino, & Morgane, 1979). In fact, in one study involving rats, it was reported that limited food intake before birth can reduce total brain cell number by 15%, and that rats experiencing restricted food intake between the time of birth and weaning showed a 15–20% reduction in brain cell number. A dramatic 60% reduction in the number of brain cells was found for rats that had limited access to food both prenatally and postnatally in this study (Winick, 1976).

The trend in recent years has been to look for abnormalities in specific brain areas, rather than in the brain as a whole. Here, investigators have shown that, depending on the timing of the period of early undernutrition, some brain structures may be relatively more susceptible to abnormal development than others. In this regard, marked changes in postnatally maturing structures such as the hippocampus, cerebral cortex and cerebellum have been observed in many cases involving undernutrition during or before the time of weaning. On an even more molecular level, poor early nutrition has now been shown to affect synapse formation, dendritic arbor lengths, cell size, and a wide variety of neurotransmitter and enzyme levels in various parts of the brain (e.g., Resnick et al., 1979). Fish and Winick (1969) have suggested that structures having the most rapid cell division (e.g., cerebellum) are affected earliest and most markedly.

The effects of undernutrition on behavior appear to parallel its effect on the brain with the most marked deficits being associated with severe undernutrition, and less deviant or sometimes even normal performance levels being found on some tasks after more mild early undernutrition (Brozek, 1978; Eichenwald & Fry, 1969; Stein, Susser, Saenger, & Marolla, 1975). Delays in indices of development (e.g., eye opening, simple reflexes) and immature interactions with the mother and other offspring are well-documented (Crnic, 1980). Nutritional rehabilitation is instituted at the time of birth or at weaning in most laboratory animal studies, but even here there are numerous examples of behavioral deficits that persist well into maturity (Levine & Wiener, 1976). The dependent measures in these studies have included activity, emotional responsivity, exploration, conditioning, and higher-order problem solving. Tests of intelligence in children also show that while improved nutrition may be associated with some changes in the scores of individuals severely undernourished early in life (marasmus, kwasiorkor), control levels of achievement are rarely attained (Eichenwald & Fry, 1969; Manocha, 1972). In short, a good case can be made for the brain being vulnerable to nutritional insult at the time of its most rapid growth in that the effects of undernutrition seem much less severe and more reversible in adults.

In some respects, a more precise understanding of the importance of good early nutrition for neural and behavioral development has been hindered by a number of problems. They include a lack of knowledge about the interactions between nutrition and other environmental variables, such as the maternal response to undernourished offspring (Crnic, 1980), a limited number of long-term studies of brain-behavior relations as a function of varying time periods of malnutrition, and the use of a wide variety of experimental procedures to produce malnutrition (e.g., low protein diets, limited maternal access, reducing maternal food quantity) which renders comparisons across studies difficult. In an attempt to circumvent some of these problems, a malnutrition model was recently developed at the Worcester Foundation for Experimental Biology (Shrewsbury, MA).

The Worcester model utilizes isocaloric diets that vary in protein content. The control diet is 25% casein, the moderate undernutrition diet is 8% casein, and the severe undernutrition diet is 6% casein. Rat dams and sires are adapted to their diets for 5 weeks prior to mating and the pregnant dams are maintained on their diet throughout gestation. At birth, and again at weaning (3 weeks of age), various combinations of diet reversals are instituted selectively to study the effects of prenatal and postnatal undernutrition on the rat pups.

The results of studies using this model indicate that the effects of malnutrition on neurobehavioral development are not only related to the timing of the deficient diet (prenatal or postnatal), but also to the severity of the undernutrition (moderate or severe). Table 1 presents a comparison of the effects of prenatal and/or postnatal undernutrition (moderate = 8% casein diet, severe = 6% casein diet) on brain and body weights of rats relative to control (25% casein diet) conditions. Ages presented are birth, weaning (21 days of age), early maturity (approximately 100 days), and late maturity (approximately 200–250 days). These results were compiled from a series of unpublished and published studies (e.g., Resnick, Morgane, Hasson, & Miller, 1982).

Rats *moderately* malnourished both *pre-* and *postnatally* were born at normal body weights but displayed attenuated body growth rates through maturity. Brain growth paralleled the body weight reduction throughout development, except at late maturity when brain weights reached control levels. The effects of moderate *postnatal* undernutrition were similar to that of combined pre- and postnatal undernutrition in that postnatal undernutrition also resulted in retarded brain growth followed by a catch-up period during late maturity. Moderate *prenatal-only* undernutrition did not significantly affect body or brain weight at any age studied.

In contrast to the above findings, more *severe* undernutrition, as expected, had greater and more persistent effects on brain and body weight measures.

TABLE 1
Effects of Two Degrees of Undernutrition on Brain and Body Weights of Rats
Relative to Control Values.

	Birth		Weaning		Early maturity		Late Maturity	
	Brain	*Body*	*Brain*	*Body*	*Brain*	*Body*	*Brain*	*Body*
MODERATE UNDERNUTRITION								
PRE + POSTNATAL	N	N	↓	↓	↓	↓	N	↓
PRENATAL ONLY	N	N	N	N	N	N	N	N
POSTNATAL ONLY	N	N	↓	↓	↓	↓	N	↓
SEVERE UNDERNUTRITION								
PRE + POSTNATAL	↓	↓	↓	↓	↓	↓	↓	↓
PRENATAL ONLY	↓	↓	↓	↓	↓	N	↓	N
POSTNATAL ONLY	N	N	↓	↓	↓	↓	↓	↓

N = normal compared to control, ↓ = decreased compared to control.

Rats in the chronic prenatal + postnatal severe malnutrition condition displayed brain and body weight reductions at birth and at all ages. Likewise, *postnatal-only* severe malnutrition resulted in reduced brain and body weights at all ages (except birth). The most interesting finding, however, related to severe *prenatal-only* malnutrition. These animals displayed reduced brain and body weights at birth. However, dietary rehabilitation at birth was sufficient to produce normal body weights after the age of weaning, but this rehabilitation did not reverse the reduced brain weights.

Rats experiencing 25%, 8%, and 6% casein diets prenatally and postnatally to the time of weaning have now been tested as adults for the ability to learn a tactile discrimination and to make three reversals after reaching criterion (Bouzrara, Silva, Waksman, Finger, & Almli, 1985). The results of this study showed that the severely malnourished group performed worse than the control group both in original learning and on the reversals, and that the moderately malnourished group performed intermediate to the other two groups on these measures. These findings are consistent with what might be predicted from the brain weight data, and with results showing that the 6% animals are more severely affected than the 8% rats in physical growth, in reaching developmental milestones, and in transmitter neurochemistry, even when cross-fostered to well-nourished dams at birth (Almli & Montoya, 1982; Almli & Yang, 1983; Lundberg, Almli, Morgane, Motamedi, & Cattegno, 1983; Resnick & Morgane, 1983). The original learning data also show that normal brain weights (moderate undernutrition) do not necessarily indicate a normal brain. More detailed analyses of neural characteristics have indicated that, even in early malnourished animals with normal brain weights, alterations in neural chemical profiles, neuronal electrical activity, and dendritic arbors may be present (Almli et al., 1985; Miller & Resnick, 1980).

These and related data suggest that the effects of undernutrition are amenable to a sensitive-period analysis. The developing brain is more sensitive to undernutrition early in life than it is later on, and both physiological and behavioral measures show that the effects of early nutritional insult are especially marked if the undernutrition is severe and is not reversed during the period of rapid brain growth. Dietary rehabilitation seems most effective with moderate cases of undernutrition, especially if initiated prior to weaning, although it is not unusual to find that some brain and behavioral measures may still fall outside of the normal range later in life.

It is also possible to view these data in terms of an optimal-period time span during which certain stimulus events exert a more profound influence on subsequent growth and development. In this case, the stimulus could be defined as adequate nutrient intake, or simply a good diet during the period of rapid brain growth. In the presence of a healthy, balanced diet the nervous system will proceed to advance through a sequence of developmental stages.

CONCLUSIONS AND IMPLICATIONS

The results of the studies on relatively circumscribed or acute brain lesions show that there does not appear to be a well-defined postnatal period during which organisms display a consistent advantage for recovery of function. At this point it appears that the effects of early versus late focal lesions may be different for different lesions and tasks. In contrast, the developing brain appears to be particularly sensitive to severe undernutrition during the period of rapid brain growth, and an optimal period for adequate nutrition may be defined.

Focal neural injury, especially when sustained during periods of high neural growth rates, has been shown to alter subsequent development of neural circuitry patterns. One example involves axons projecting to structures that ordinarily would not receive them. This can occur when the normal area of termination is damaged before the growing axons reach it. In some cases it has been shown that axons that had crossed the midline en route to a structure may cross back over to end in the homologous region on the opposite (ipsilateral) side of the brain (So & Schneider, 1976). There are also instances of axons proceeding past a damaged area to a higher level that typically would be reached only after another synapse (Schneider & Jhavari, 1974). Another example relates to the programmed retraction of axons early in life, a phenomenon which is believed to be important for "fine-tuning" the nervous system (Cowan, Fawcett, O'Leary, & Stanfield, 1984). It has been shown that collaterals of axons that ordinarily would be retracted may not be retracted if the main branch of the axon is damaged early in life. This phenomenon is most apparent in cases where axons project bilaterally at birth, and then contralaterally after the infancy period. If there is early damage to one side of the brain, neurons with bilateral projections from the opposite side may retain their "immature" (bilateral) morphology. This can be observed after damage to one motor cortex (Hicks, 1975; Hicks & D'Amato, 1975) or to one optic nerve (Land & Lund, 1979) in newborn rats.

Although dramatic changes in neural circuitry like these have fostered the conviction that recovery of function may be more likely in such cases, there is little reason to suspect that such mechanisms evolved to "heal" damaged brains. In fact, an equally good case can be made for these phenomena being deleterious (Finger & Almli, 1985). For example, Schneider and Jhavari (1974) showed that hamsters with retinal projections to the "wrong" optic tectum would jump away from sunflower seeds rather than toward them, an act that would increase the probability of not finding food or even being caught by a predator that had been sighted. Also, there is reason to believe that brain-damaged children who continue to demonstrate bilateral motor movements that characterize younger children are showing these more immature responses because they have retained bilateral motor projections from one hemisphere. Whether the neural circuitry changes that follow focal injury during high neural growth rates are associated with recovery of function, abnormal function, or neutrality seem to depend on the specifics of each situation. The diverse outcomes make it difficult to integrate the research literature under the concepts of optimal or sensitive periods. Further, because focal damage is superimposed on an otherwise healthy brain it is often difficult to distinguish between real "recovery" of function and behavioral compensation.

Studies of the effects of sub-optimal environments and hazardous substances on brain structure and function suggest that the developing brain is more sensitive or vulnerable to these influences than is the mature brain. Here, the sensitive period concept may be useful not only to define behavior after some types of neural insult, but also to describe differences in vulnerability or susceptibility to neural injury in organisms of different ages.

In this regard, the consequences of diffuse neural injury are especially interesting. The developing organism does not appear to show as much recovery in this domain as it does under some conditions of focal damage. One reason is that with diffuse insult, even during periods of relatively high neural growth rates, the damage may be too extensive for significant neural reorganization to take place. Further, some conditions such as oxygen and nutritional deficiency appear to produce diffuse insult by affecting neural vitality and the growth process itself (Resnick et al., 1979; Windle, Becker, & Weil, 1944; Winick, 1976). Growth retardation during a period of normally high growth rates may result in permanent cell loss, neural stunting, and altered metabolism of surviving elements. These are conditions that are likely to be associated with reduced capacity for neural reorganization, recovery of function, and even behavioral compensation (Silva, Bouzrara, Finger, & Almli, 1984).

In conclusion, it is questionable whether a *strict* definition of the critical period concept applies well to issues of neurobehavioral development, sensitivity to neural insult, or the response to damage if it occurs. The less absolute concepts of optimal (Moltz, 1973) and sensitive (Fox, 1970) periods may be more appropriate because they are consistent with the growing appreciation of a relatively dynamic nervous system throughout life. Although the concepts of optimal and sensitive periods may represent two sides of the same coin, they are valuable because, if nothing else, they serve to specify a particular orientation toward a phenomenon. In this regard it is important to continue research efforts targeted towards specifying stimulus conditions that can facilitate or retard life-long developmental processes.

REFERENCES

Alajouanine, T., & Lhermitte, F. Q. Acquired aphasia in children. *Brain,* 1965, *88,* 653–662.
Almli, C. R. The ontogeny of feeding and drinking: Effects of early brain damage. *Neuroscience and Biobehavioral Reviews,* 1978, *2,* 281–300.

Almli, C. R. Early brain damage and time course of behavior dysfunction: Parallels with neural maturation. In S. Finger & C. R. Almli (Eds.), *Early brain damage (Vol. 2) Neurobiology and behavior.* New York: Adademic Press, 1984.

Almli, C. R. Normal sequential behavioral and physiological changes throughout the developmental arc. In D. Umphred (Ed.), *Neurological rehabilitation.* St. Louis: Mosby, 1985.

Almli, C. R., & Finger, S. (Eds.). *Early brain damage (Vol. 1) Research orientations and clinical observations.* New York: Academic Press, 1984.

Almli, C. R., & Fisher, R. S. Postnatal development of sensory influences on neurons in the ventromedial hypothalamic nucleus of the rat. *Developmental Brain Research,* 1985, *18,* 13–26.

Almli, C. R., Golden, G. T., & McMullen, N. T. Ontogeny of drinking behavior of preweanling rats with lateral preoptic damage. *Brain Research Bulletin,* 1976, *1,* 437–442.

Almli, C. R., Henault, M. A., Velozo, C. A., & Morgane, P. J. Ontogeny of electrical activity of main olfactory bulb in freely-moving normal and malnourished rats. *Developmental Brain Research,* 1985, *18,* 1–11.

Almli, C. R., & Montoya, T. *A rat model of small-for-gestation-age infants.* Paper presented at the meeting of the International Society for Developmental Psychobiology, Minneapolis, MN, 1982.

Almli, C. R., & Yang, M. I. *Analysis of sensorimotor behaviors in a rat model of small-for-gestation-age infants.* Paper presented at the meeting of the International Society for Developmental Psychobiology, Hyannis, MA, 1983.

Bastian, H. C. *A treatise on aphasia and other speech defects.* New York: D. Appleton, 1898.

Bateson, P. Sensitive periods in behavioral development. *Archives of Diseases of the Child,* 1983, *58,* 85–86.

Bernhardt, R. Veber die spastiche cercbrale paralyse im Kindersalter nebst einer Excurse uber "Aphasie bei Kindern." *Virchow's Archives für Anatomie und Physiologie,* 1885, *102.*

Bouzrara, A., Silva, M., Waksman, D., Finger, S., & Almli, C. R. Relation between the severity of early malnutrition and the effects of later frontal cortical lesions in rats. *Physiological Psychology,* 1985, *13,* 1–6.

Brozek, J. Nutrition, malnutrition and behavior. *Annual Review of Psychology,* 1978, *29,* 157–177.

Byers, R. K., & McLean, W. T. Etiology and course of certain hemiplegias with aphasia in children. *Pediatrics,* 1962, *29,* 276–383.

Chang, F.-L. F., & Greenough, W. T. Transient and enduring morphological correlates of synaptic activity and efficacy change in the rat hippocamal slice. *Brain Research,* 1984, *309,* 35–46.

Child, C. M. *Patterns and problems of development.* Chicago: University of Chicago Press, 1941.

Chow, K. L., & Stewart, D. L. Reversal of structural and functional effects of long-term visual deprivation in cats. *Experimental Neurology,* 1972, *34,* 409–433.

Colombo, J. The critical period concept: Research, methodology and theoretical issues. *Psychological Bulletin,* 1982, *91,* 260–275.

Cotman, C. W., & Nieto-Sampedro, M. Cell biology of synaptic plasticity. *Science,* 1984, *225,* 1287–1294.

Cotman, C., & Scheff, S. W. Compensatory synapse growth in aged animals after neuronal death. *Mechanisms of Aging and Development,* 1979, *9,* 103–117.

Cowan, W. M., Fawcett, J. W., O'Leary, D. D. M., & Stanfield, B. B. Regressive events in neurogenesis. *Science,* 1984, *225,* 1258–1265.

Crnic, L. S. Models of infantile malnutrition in rats: Effects upon behavior. *Developmental Psychobiology,* 1980, *13,* 615–628.

Curcio, C. P., Buell, S. J., & Coleman, P. D. Morphology of the aging central nervous system: Not all downhill: In J. A. Mortimer, F. J. Piorgollo & G. J. Maletta (Eds.), *The aging motor system.* New York: Preager Press, 1982.

Curtiss, S. *Genie: A psycholinguistic study of a modern day "wild child."* New York: Academic Press, 1977.

Denenberg, V. H., Garbanati, J., Sherman, G., Yutzey, D. A., & Kaplan, R. Infantile stimulation induces brain lateralization in rats. *Science,* 1978, *201,* 1150–1153.

Dobbing, J. Vulnerable periods in brain growth and somatic growth: In D. F. Roberts & A. M. Thompson (Eds.), *The biology of human fetal growth.* London: Taylor & Francis Press, 1976.

Dodge, P. R., Prensky, A. L., & Feigen, R. D. *Nutrition and the developing nervous system.* St. Louis: Mosby, 1975.

Eichenwald, H. F., & Fry, P. C. Nutrition and learning. *Science,* 1969, *163,* 644–648.

Finger, S. (Ed.). *Recovery from brain damage: Research and theory.* New York: Plenum, 1978.

Finger, S., & Almli, C. R. (Eds.). *Early brain damage (Vol. 2): Neurobiology and behavior.* New York: Academic Press, 1984.

Finger, S., & Almli, C. R. Brain damage and neuroplasticity: Mechanisms of recovery or development? *Brain Research Reviews,* 1985, *10,* 177–186.

Finger, S., Simons, D., & Posner, R. Anatomical, physiological and behavioral effects of neonatal sensorimotor cortex ablation in the rat. *Experimental Neurology,* 1978, *60,* 347–373.

Finger, S., & Stein, D. G. *Brain damage and recovery: Research and clinical perspectives.* New York: Academic Press, 1982.

Fisher, R. S., & Almli, C. R. Postnatal development of sensory influences on lateral hypothalamic neurons of the rat. *Developmental Brain Research,* 1984, *12,* 55–75.

Fitzhugh, K. B., & Fitzhugh, L. C. Effects of early and later onset of cerebral dysfunction upon psychological test performance. *Perceptual and Motor Skills,* 1965, *20,* 1099–1100.

Fox, R. W. Overview and critique of stages and periods in canine development. *Developmental Psychobiology,* 1970, *4,* 37–54.

Goldman, P. An alternative to developmental plasticity: Heterology of CNS structures in infants and adults: In D. G. Stein, J. J. Rosen, & N. Butters (Eds.), *Plasticity and recovery of functions in the central nervous system.* New York: Academic Press, 1974.

Greenough, W. T. Enduring brain effects of differential experience and training: In M. R. Rosenzweig & E. L. Bennett (Eds.), *Neural mechanisms of learning and memory.* Cambridge, MA: M.I.T. Press, 1976.

Hales, D. J., Lozoff, B., Sosa, R., & Kennel, J. H. Defining the limits of the maternal sensitive period. *Developmental Medicine & Child Neurology,* 1977, *19,* 454–461.

Harlow, H. F. Total isolation: Effects on Macaque monkey behavior. *Science,* 1965, *148,* 666.

Hicks, S. P. Functional adaptation after brain injury and malformation in early life in rats: In N. Ellis (Ed.), *Aberrant development in infancy.* Potomac, MD: Lawrence Erlbaum Associates, 1975.

Hicks, S. P., Cavanaugh, M. C., & O'Brien, E. D. Effects of anoxia on the developing cerebral cortex of the rat. *American Journal of Pathology,* 1962, *40,* 615–635.

Hicks, S. P., & D'Amato, C. J. Motor-sensory cortex-corticospinal system and developing locomotion and placing in rats. *American Journal of Anatomy,* 1975, *143,* 1–42.

Isaacson, R. L. The myth of recovery from early brain damage: In R. N. Ellis (Ed.), *Aberrant development in infancy.* Hillsdale, NJ: Lawrence Erlbaum Associates, 1975.

Isaacson, R. L., Nonneman, A. J., & Schmaltz, L. W. Behavioral and anatomical sequelae of damage to the infant limbic system: In R. L. Isaacson (Ed.), *The neuropsychology of development.* New York: Wiley, 1968.

Johnson, D. A. Developmental aspects of recovery of function following septal lesions in the infant rat. *Journal of Comparative and Physiological Psychology,* 1972, *78,* 331-348.

Johnson, D., & Almli, C. R. Age, brain-damage and performance: In S. Finger (Ed.), *Recovery from brain damage.* New York: Plenum, 1978.

Kasamatsu, T., & Pettigrew, J. D. Preservation of binocularity after monocular deprivation in the striate cortex of kittens treated with 6-hydroxydopamine. *Journal of Comparative Neurology,* 1979, *185,* 139-162.

Kennard, M. A. Age and other factors in motor recovery from precentral lesions in monkeys. *American Journal of Physiology,* 1936, *115,* 138-146.

Kennard, M. A. Reorganization of motor function in the cerebral cortex of monkeys deprived of motor and premotor areas in infancy. *Journal of Neurophysiology,* 1938, *1,* 477-496.

Kennard, M. A. Relation of age to motor impairment in man and in subhuman primates. *Archives of Neurology and Psychiatry,* 1940, *44,* 377-397.

Kennard, M. A., & Fulton, J. F. Age and reorganization of central nervous system. *Journal of Mount Sinai Hospital,* 1942, *9,* 594-606.

Krasten, S. D. The critical period for language and its possible bases. *Annals of the New York Academy of Science,* 1975, *263,* 211-224.

Land, P. W., & Lund, R. D. Development of the rat's uncrossed retinotectal pathway and its relationship to plasticity studies. *Science,* 1979, *205,* 698-700.

Lenneberg, E. *Biological foundations of language.* New York: Wiley, 1967.

Lenneberg, E. H. The effect of age on the outcome of central nervous system disease in children: In R. L. Isaacson (Ed.), *The neuropsychology of development.* New York: Wiley, 1968.

LeVere, T. *Recovery of function after brain damage: The qualitative consequences of lesion size.* Paper presented at the meeting of the International Neuropsychology Society, San Diego, CA, 1985.

Levine, S., & Wiener, A. A critical analysis of data on malnutrition and behavioral deficits. *Advances in Pediatrics,* 1976, *22,* 113-136.

Lorenz, K. Der Kuman in der Umwelt des Vogels; die Artgenosse als Auslosendes Moment Sozialer Verhaltungweisen. *Journal of Ornithology,* 1935, *83,* 137-213, 289-413.

Lundberg, P., Almli, C. R., Morgane, P., Motamedi, M., & Cattegno, E. Dietary rehabilitation of malnourished rats: Effects on brain lipid concentrations. *Neuroscience Abstracts,* 1983, *9,* 520.

Manocha, S. L. *Malnutrition and retarded human development.* Springfield, IL: Charles Thomas, 1972.

McGraw, R. B. *Growth: A study of Johnny and Jimmy.* New York: Appleton-Century, 1935.

Miller, M., & Resnick, O. Tryptophan availability: The importance of prepartum and postpartum dietary protein on brain indoleamine metabolism in rats. *Experimental Neurology,* 1980, *67,* 298-314.

Milner, B. Hemispheric specialization: Scope and limits: In F. O. Schmitt & F. G. Worden (Eds.), *The neurosciences: Third study program.* Cambridge, MA: M.I.T. Press, 1974.

Moltz, H. Some implications of the critical period hypothesis. *Annals of the New York Academy of Science,* 1973, *223,* 144-146.

Murphy, E. H., & Stewart, D. L. Effects of neonatal and adult striate lesions on discrimination in the rabbit. *Experimental Neurology,* 1974, *42,* 89-96.

Nash, J. *Developmental psychology: A psychobiological approach.* Englewood Cliffs, NJ: Prentice-Hall, 1978.

Penfield, W., & Roberts, L. *Speech and brain mechanisms.* Princeton, NJ: Princeton University Press, 1959.

Resnick, O., Miller, M., Forbes, W., Hall, R., Kemper, T., Bronzino, J., & Morgane, P. J. Developmental protein malnutrition: Influences on the central nervous system of the rat. *Neuroscience and Biobehavioral Reviews,* 1979, *3,* 233-246.

Resnick, O., & Morgane, P. Animal models for small-for-gestational-age (SGA) neonates and infants-at-risk (IAR). *Developmental Brain Research,* 1983, *10,* 221-225.

Resnick, O., Morgane, P. J., Hasson, R., & Miller, M. Overt and hidden forms of chronic malnutrition in the rat and their relevance to man. *Neuroscience and Biobehavioral Reviews,* 1982, *6,* 55-75.

Rudel, R. G., Teuber, H.-L., & Twitchell, T. E. Levels of impairment of sensorimotor functions in children with early brain damage. *Neuropsychologia,* 1974, *12,* 95-108.

Salzen, E., & Meyer, C. C. Reversibility of imprinting. *Journal of Comparative and Physiological Psychology,* 1968, *66,* 269-275.

Schneider, G. E., & Jhavari, S. R. Neuroanatomical correlates of spared or altered function after brain lesions in the newborn hamster: In D. G. Stein, J. J. Rosen, & N. Butters (Eds.), *Plasticity and recovery of function in the central nervous system.* New York: Academic, 1974.

Scott, J. P. Critical periods in behavioral development. *Science,* 1962, *138,* 949-958.

Scott, J. P. *Critical periods.* New York: Academic, 1979.

Silva, M., Bouzrara, A., Finger, S., & Almli, C. R. Effects of early protein undernutrition and later frontal cortex damage on habit acquisition and reversal learning in the rat. *Physiological Psychology,* 1984, *12,* 141-146.

Simons, D., & Finger, S. Some factors affecting behavior after brain damage early in life: In S. Finger & C. R. Almli (Eds.), *Early brain damage (Vol. 2) Neurobiology and behavior.* New York: Academic, 1984.

So, K. F., & Schneider, G. E. Abnormal recrossing of retinotectal projections after early lesions in Syrian hamsters: A critical-age effect. *Anatomical Records,* 1976, *184,* 535-536.

Soltmann, O. Experimentelle Studien uber die Functionen des Grosshirns der Neugeborenen. *Jarbuck für Kinderheikunde,* 1876, *9,* 106-148.

Stein, Z., Susser, M., Saenger, G., & Marolla, F. *Famine and human development: The Dutch hunger winter of 1944-1945.* New York: Oxford University Press, 1975.

Stockard, C. R. Developmental rate and structural expression: An experimental study of twins, "double monsters," and single deformities and their interaction among embryonic organs during their origins and development. *American Journal of Anatomy,* 1921, *28,* 115-275.

Taylor, H. G. Early brain injury and cognitive development: In C. R. Almli & S. Finger (Eds.), *Early brain damage (Vol. 1) Research orientations and clinical observations.* New York: Academic Press, 1984.

Teuber, H.-L. Mental retardation after early trauma to the brain: Some issues in search of facts: In C. R. Angle & E. A. Bering Jr. (Eds.), *Physical trauma as an etiological agent in mental retardation.* Bethesda, MD: N.I.H, 1971.

Teuber, H.-H., & Rudel, R. G. Behavior after cerebral lesions in children and adults. *Developmental Medicine and Child Neurology,* 1962, *4,* 3-20.

Thompson, C. I., Harlow, H. F., Blomquist, A. J., & Schiltz, K. A. Recovery of function following prefrontal lobe damage in Rhesus monkeys. *Brain Research,* 1971, *35,* 37-48.

Vulpian, A. *Lecons sur la physiologie generale et comparee du systeme nerveux.* Paris: Bailliere, 1866.

Wiesel, T. N., & Hubel, D. H. Single-cell responses in striate cortex of kittens deprived of vision in one eye. *Journal of Neurophysiology,* 1963, *26,* 1003-1017.

Windle, W. F., Becker, R. F., & Weil, A. Alterations in brain structure after asphyxiation at birth. *Journal of Neuropathology and Experimental Neurology,* 1944, *3,* 224-238.

Winick, M. *Malnutrition and brain development.* New York: Oxford University Press, 1976.

Crucial Period Effect in Psychoendocrinology: Two Syndromes, Abuse Dwarfism and Female (CVAH) Hermaphroditism

7

John Money and Charles Annecillo
*Department of Psychiatry and Behavioral Sciences
and Department of Pediatrics*
The Johns Hopkins University and Hospital

INTRODUCTION

Descartes' legacy to Western thinking was a mind and body divided, the mind allocated to religion, and the body to science, except for their tenuous conjunction in the pineal gland. When psychology became a science it adopted the Cartesian dualism, and laid claim to the mind minus the pineal. Ever since, psychology has been polarized in its relationship to the body, physiological psychology notwithstanding. Hence the juxtaposition of nature versus nurture in its various guises, heredity versus environment, biological versus psychological, organic versus psychogenic, and so on.

The polarization of nature and nurture is an intellectual strait jacket. It can be depolarized by interpolating a third term into the equation: nature + crucial period + nurture → phenotype. The phenotype may be behavioral, not only morphological. The concept of the crucial period has long been known with respect to embryonic development. Its relevance to behavioral development was formulated by European ethologists in the concept of imprinting which became popularized after World War II.

Generalization of the crucial period concept from imprint learning in animals to any aspect of human behavioral development has met with limited acceptance in psychology, as it contravenes the doctrine of unlimited behavioral modification by stimulus-response intervention and training. The example of native language has long been available, however, as an example of crucial-period development. No one has a native language at birth, only a brain preprogrammed so as to be ready to receive one. Programmed into the brain during a crucial period of development, the native language then stays there permanently, unless impaired by a brain lesion.

SYNDROME OF ABUSE DWARFISM

The nature/crucial period/nurture equation has applications beyond language to overall development staturally, intellectually, and behaviorally, as is manifest in the syndrome of abuse dwarfism (Money, 1977), also known as psychosocial dwarfism. As encountered in this syndrome, abuse means the infliction of direct bodily injury to the child resulting from burns, cuts, and blows to the body. On physical examination, observable signs of physical injury include bruises, scars, bone fractures, and/or skin lesions. Abuse means also a history of enforced isolation, usually in a closet, which can last for days or weeks or can even be extended as a regular practice for many years. There is also a history of deprivation of sleep, play, hygienic facilities, water, and food which are capriciously rationed and may be totally withheld for extended periods.

Reportedly bizarre patterns of eating and drinking prove, upon intensive investigation, to be a sequel to bizarre restrictions on the availability of food and water. Thus the chief source of food and water may be, respectively, the garbage can or the dog's feeding dish, and the toilet bowl. Though miniaturized in size, the child does not have the emaciated appearance of a child suffering gross starvation; and, in fact, may even be somewhat bloated-looking and overweight for height, with a protuberant belly.

The outcome of abuse and deprivation in the syndrome is domicile-specific impairment of statural, mental, and sociobehavioral growth during the crucial period of the juvenile years. The longer they endure, the lesser the reversibility of these impairments. They demonstrate a profound response of nature to nurture during a crucial period of development—in this case the nurture of abusive cruelty and neglect. The response is severe delay and eventual impairment of somatic, intellectual, and behavioral development of the abused child. Recovery from the effects of abuse takes place after rescue, provided the crucial period of development has not expired. An initial hospitalization for a short period of time, approximately two weeks, allows for the resumption of growth hormone secretion from the pituitary gland, and leads to the onset of catch-up statural growth. Both changes confirm the diagnosis of abuse dwarfism.

It is a singular feature of the syndrome of abuse dwarfism that it is possible to specify some, if not all, pituitary functions involved. Under conditions of abuse, some pituitary functions become dormant or hypofunctional. The secretion of growth hormone (somatotropin) fails. Pituitary ACTH (adreno-corticotropic hormone) is partially suppressed, but not so much as to be lethal. If abuse continues until the expected time of puberty, the gonadotropic hormones, LH and FSH, fail to be secreted. Thus the ovaries or testes fail to secrete their own sex hormones, and the onset of sexual maturation is delayed. All the foregoing hormonal failures are reversible upon rescue from abuse.

Before the syndrome of abuse dwarfism was first identified, it was commonly misdiagnosed as idiopathic hypopituitarism of the type that is not reversible simply by change of domicile, but requires injections of growth hormone. The definitive pair of papers differentiating the reversible from the irreversible syndrome were published from The Johns Hopkins Pediatric Endocrine Clinic eighteen years ago (Powell, Brasel, & Blizzard, 1967; Powell, Brasel, Raiti, & Blizzard, 1967). At that time, it was speculated that the chief etiologic factor might be maternal deprivation or emotional deprivation, though there was some controversy regarding nourishment deprivation.

Limits on Catch-up Growth and Development

The crucial period for statural growth extends until after puberty when the epiphyses of the bones fuse. Many abuse-dwarfism patients have shown dramatic catch-up growth following rescue. The sooner the rescue, the less the adult height can be expected to fall below the mean for the general population. Of the 50 patients on file in The Johns Hopkins Psychohormonal Research Unit, the two most severely affected (Money, Annecillo, & Hutchinson, 1985) exemplified rapid post-rescue statural catch-up growth. Following rescue at age 16, one patient, a male, had a speedy onset of puberty and gained 13 inches in three years. The other patient, a female rescued at age 9, gained 10½ inches in only one year. Nonetheless, the final adult heights were substandard at 5'4" and 4'10½" respectively. By comparison, the height of the average American adult male closely approximates 5'10" and the female 5'5".

Catch-up intellectual growth also occurs following rescue. The greatest magnitude of change, from IQ 36 to 120, occurred in a girl between the ages of 3 years, 8 months, and 13 years, 11 months. She was among a group of 23 patients (Table 1) who qualified for an investigation of IQ change among patients with various periods of consistent rescue (Money, Annecillo, & Kelley, 1983a). In this group, the initial mean IQ of 66 increased to a mean IQ of 90 which represents typically a shift from mental retardation to normal intelligence. A multiple regression analysis revealed that age and duration of rescue accounted for most of the variance in IQ change.

A comparison of IQ change relative to duration of rescue in 7 younger versus 7 older patients revealed that the younger the age at rescue the greater the gain in IQ (Table 2). Developmentally, the earlier juvenile years were cru-

TABLE 1
IQ Elevation after Rescue (N = 23)

IQ	Before Rescue	After Rescue	Increase in IQ	Age Before Rescue[a]	Age After Rescue	Increase in Age
Mean	66	90	24	7-7	12-8	5-1
SD	16	21	21	4-7	5-11	3-1

$R = 0.78; p < .005$

[a]Age in years and months.

TABLE 2
IQ Elevation after Rescue:
Younger and Older Patients

Age at Rescue[a]	Baseline IQ[b]	Followup IQ	IQ Elevation
<5-6	71 ± 21	104 ± 11	33 ± 24
>5-7	63 ± 15	78 ± 16	16 ± 7

[a]Age in years and months
[b]IQ: Mean ± Standard Deviation

cial for a greater magnitude of intellectual catch-up growth.

In a 1966 monograph, Skeels published a control-group, outcome study of a permanent and gross degree of mental retardation as a sequel to infantile institutional abuse and neglect (Skeels & Fillmore, 1937). In 1973, Dennis' monograph, *Children of the Crèche,* further demonstrated that intellectual growth was stunted and the IQ permanently reduced by as much as 50% as a sequel to uninterrupted, lifelong institutional abuse and neglect. If these institutionalized foundlings were adopted into normal family life, however, then the earlier the adoption, the sooner the resumption of normal intellectual growth, and the higher the ultimate level of adult IQ.

Other reports have given evidence for a deleterious effect of child battering and abuse on intellectual growth (Appelbaum, 1977; Brandwein, 1973; Buchanan & Oliver, 1977; Sandgrund, Gaines, & Green, 1974). The Milwaukee project (Herber & Garber, 1975) showed the deleterious effect of the neglect of developmental stimulation and the beneficial effect of early intervention in preventing developmental mental retardation.

Prior to the 1983 study of Money, Annecillo, and Kelley (1983b), there was no literature assessing the correlation between the rates of intellectual and statural catch-up growth. In this study the familiar calculation of intelligence quotient (IQ = MA/CA × 100) was paralleled with the calculation of height quotient (HQ = HA/CA × 100). Arrested and subsequent catch-up growth in stature was found to be positively correlated with arrested and subsequent catch-up growth in intelligence ($r = 0.42, p < 0.01$, Table 3).

This finding undermines the doctrine of heredity as the exclusive or chief determinant of intelligence (Eysenck, 1974; Jensen, 1969, 1973); and reinforces the critique of this doctrine as formulated, for example, by Hirsch (1975, 1981).

Sociobehavioral retardation in the syndrome of abuse dwarfism lacks a test from which to calculate a social quotient. Symptoms of maturational failure include, in addition to those related to eating and drinking (see above), enuresis, encopresis, social apathy or inertia, crying spasms, insomnia, eccentric sleeping and waking schedules associated with nocturnal privation and assault (Wolff & Money, 1973), and pain agnosia and self-injury (Money, Wolff, & Annecillo, 1972). These symptoms all occur only in the growth-retarding environment of abuse. Clinically, the social age is rated as retarded. Educationally, the academic age is retarded and special placement is needed in the early period of rescue. Psychosexual maturation is also in arrears, unless rescue has long preceded the expected age of puberty.

As in the case of statural and intellectual catch-up growth, sociobehavioral catch-up growth is related to the age and duration of rescue. The more delayed the rescue, the less the likelihood that the individual will become fully autonomous and independent socially and economically.

Dynamics of Abuse

Parents of children with the syndrome of abuse dwarfism collude as child abusers and are medical imposters regarding the symptoms of abuse. Though the mother typically initiates abuse, she cannot give a rational explanation for doing so. A study of the family dynamics in two severely affected patients (Money, Annecillo, & Hutchison, 1985) revealed the mother's history of a sexual sin expiated or atoned for symbolically by the sacrifice of the child. In

TABLE 3
Means and Correlation of IQ[a] and HQ[b] Increments
Accrued during Followup (N = 32)

Followup Status	IQ (M ± SD)	HQ (M ± SD)
Before Rescue	69 ± 17	55 ± 17
After Rescue	88 ± 18	82 ± 11
Difference	19 ± 22	27 ± 18
	r (Diff.) = 0.42; $p < 0.01$	

[a]Intelligence Quotient
[b]Height Quotient

each case the mother had been conceived illegitimately, one by incest and one by prostitution. Since the parents induce the symptoms of abuse dwarfism, the syndrome is factitious and, therefore, is characterized as Munchausen's syndrome by proxy (Money & Werlwas, 1976; Meadow, 1977, 1985). One of the self-justifications used by abusing parents is that their child instigates abuse. More fully explained, this claim may signify a failure of parent-child bonding, even from birth onward. Subsequently, it may also signify that the abused child has become addicted to abuse. The response to abuse is to stimulate more of it. The neurochemistry of this addiction may well be linked to the neurosecretion of brain endorphin which has a morphine-like effect. There is as yet no direct evidence in support of this proposition. The indirect evidence, aforementioned, is clinical, namely that abused-dwarf children exhibit signs of pain agnosia while they live under conditions of abuse. Rescued and in the hospital, they regain an aversive response to pain in about two weeks.

Whereas the theme of parental atonement and sacrifice has some etiological significance, it provides only a necessary, but not sufficient cause for the syndrome of abuse. What still is needed is an explanation of how behavior at one time forbidden and repugnant at another later time becomes endorsed and practiced. For so complete a reversal of negative into positive, Solomon (1980) formulated and tested the theory of opponent-process learning. Opponent-process is seen in action when, for example, the initial panic and terror of a novice practicing a daredevil sport gives way to the exhilaration and ecstasy of the aficionado. This conversion is undoubtedly accompanied by corresponding changes in the neurochemistries of the learning brain. Deciphering them, and their possible relationship to crucial periods of development, awaits further advances in neuroscience.

SEX DIMORPHISM OF BEHAVIOR: SHEEP AND MONKEY EXPERIMENTS

In veterinary sexology, it is experimentally easy to demonstrate a crucial period in prenatal life when steroidal sex hormones dimorphically program the brain so that subsequent mating behavior will be differentiated as either male or female. The principle involved, dubbed the "Adam and Eve principle," is that Eve takes priority over Adam. Nature's basic template is to progress without interruption from the early, sexually unimorphic stage to the differentiation of the female. The differentiation of the male requires the interruption of something added. This something is hormonal, and its source is the fetal testis. Differentiation of the male reproductive anatomy requires antimullerian hormone to suppress female development, and androgen to induce male development. Differentiation of the male brain requires only androgen. Some brain cells take up molecules of androgen and convert them to an estrogen, estradiol. The apparent paradox that a so-called female hormone has a masculinizing effect requires a revision of traditional concepts of the function of steroidal hormones and their derivatives, and a recognition that they are not sex-absolute, but sex-shared. It is the ratio of one to another that is sex different.

The crucial period for the experimental masculinization of the brain of a ewe lamb in utero (Clarke, 1977; Short & Clarke, undated) begins at day 50 of gestation and extends for the next few days. Androgen injected into the pregnant mother before day 50 (and after day 35) masculinizes the external genital anatomy, whereas after day 50 only the brain is affected. In the latter case, the lamb is born looking like a normal ewe. The effect of brain masculinization shows up half a year later, at the time of the first mating season. Although the animal at that time is producing female hormone from its own ovaries, it behaves like a ram. Anthropomorphically speaking, it impersonates a ram and is responded to as a ram by the other animals in the flock. Other rams charge at it, headlong, in mating rivalry; and ewes accept its courtship approach and allow it to mount. Brain masculinization also dictates that the animal will urinate like a ram, with the urine flow not continuous but pulsatile, and the rear legs straight, not crouched.

Like many other four-legged species, the sheep qualifies as a hormonal robot, which means that the male/female dimorphism of the mating pattern is preordained by the prenatal hormonal history. The extent to which this preordained pattern may be experimentally disrupted has not yet been investigated. In the course of ordinary ovine existence, however, it has its own autonomy, and is dependent for its activation only on the climatically regulated hormonal changes of the mating season. Then, at that climatically crucial time, the smell of the ewe in heat attracts the male to copulate.

Among primates, as compared with subprimate mammals, the male is less dependent on the nose and more on the eyes as the organs of sexuoerotic arousal and initiative. The prenatal hormonal robotic effect is also far less in evidence among primates than subprimates. The young of primates are dependent not only on their prenatal hormonal history, but also on their postnatal history of juvenile sexual rehearsal play in order to develop the full pattern of adult mating behavior. Thus, there are two crucial developmental periods with respect to male/female behavioral dimorphism. The first is prenatal, or immediately postnatal, and hormonal. The second is infantile and early juvenile, and is social in interaction with playmates. Experimentally, the developmental sequence from prenatal hormones through sociosexual rehearsal play to adult behavior has been most thoroughly investigated in rhesus monkeys.

Female rhesus monkeys whose genitals have been masculinized as a sequel to having been prenatally exposed to treatment with high-dosage testosterone injected into the mother are also masculinized in their subsequent juvenile play. More than their sisters, they engage in rough-and-tumble play, chasing and threat play, and sexual mounting play. In adolescence, however, masculinization fades. Their sexual and erotic behavior does not replicate that of normal females and also fails to replicate that of normal males (Goldfoot, personal communication, 1985).

The sexual rehearsal play of rhesus monkeys begins at around 3 months of age. It involves sexual presenting and mounting, but in a confused jumble of positioning — front, side, and rear — with boys and girls doing the same things. In the ensuing three to six months, the positioning of the female presenting on all fours, and the male mounting from the rear, becomes established. The male perfects the adult positioning of his feet, namely, grasping the legs of the female above the ankles.

Monkeys reared in isolation during the crucial period of sexual rehearsal play remain forever impaired. Later in life, even when paired with an experienced and gentle tutor, they fail to present or mount. They do not copulate, and they do not reproduce. Incomplete deprivation, by allowing as little as half an hour a day for age-mate play, reverses the impairment of complete deprivation in approximately one in three animals. They are retarded achievers, however, for they do not perfect adult positioning until 1½ or 2 years of age. Their success is, however, insufficient. As adults, they are poor breeders with a reduced birth rate (Goldfoot, 1977).

During the crucial period of sexual rehearsal play, coeducational play has a different outcome than does sex-segregated play. Monkeys allowed unrestricted play time, but only in all-male or all-female groups, engage in presenting and mounting play with one another when they become adolescent. Though normally-reared partners of the opposite sex find them sexually attractive, they cower and are scared. A normally-reared male does not mount the female even though he inspects and touches her genitalia with curiosity. A female resists the approach of a normally reared male partner, who succeeds in copulating only if he is exceptionally gentle and skilled at diminishing her fright. When back with their same-sexed friends with whom they played as juveniles, males continue to mount males, and females to mount females with a frequency unrecorded in males and females that grew up and engaged in sexual rehearsal play together as juveniles (Goldfoot & Neff, 1984; Goldfoot & Wallen, 1978; Goldfoot, Wallen, Neff, McBrair, & Goy, 1984).

FEMALE HERMAPHRODITISM WITH CONGENITAL VIRILIZING ADRENAL HYPERPLASIA (CVAH)

The Adam and Eve principle applies to human beings as it does to sheep and other animals. Whereas an embryo differentiates as female in the absence of gonadal hormone, it requires hormone secreted by the testis to differentiate as a male. In boys, at the time of birth, the level of testicular hormone is negligible. After two weeks it begins to elevate in a great surge that, after attaining the level of puberty, wanes and is spent by age 3 months (Migeon & Forest, 1980).

One speculation is that it is during this crucial period of about three months that the hormonal masculinzation of the human brain takes place. Even if this speculation is correct, it is nonetheless also correct that human beings are not hormonal robots. Hormonalization of the brain creates only a predisposition or sets a threshold for the future dimorphic differentiation of behavior under the influence of subsequent socialization—as spelled out in Money (1980).

The dual importance of both the prenatal and postnatal crucial periods in the differentiation of human behavioral dimorphism is convincingly exemplified in the matched-pair method of hermaphroditic study. Hermaphroditism, also known as intersexuality, is a form of birth defect in which the sex organs are improperly differentiated. In some syndromes of hermaphroditism, individuals concordant for prenatal history and development are discordant for their postnatal history with respect to sex announcement and rearing—one as a boy, the other as a girl. One such syndrome is the adrenogenital syndrome, also known as congenital virilizing adrenal hyperplasia (CVAH).

When CVAH occurs in a chromosomally 46,XX (female) fetus, the degree of prenatal virilization may be so extreme that the baby is born with a penis and empty scrotum externally, despite two ovaries and a uterus and tubes internally. The condition originates in a recessive genetic error which induces the adrenal cortices to secrete not their proper hormone, cortisol, but a precursor which is androgenizing. Thus, it is the fetus' own hormonal error that produces the masculinization of the external genitalia. Some affected babies are born with an extremely enlarged clitoris which lacks a urinary tube, whereas a few have a normal penis.

If a 46,XX baby with a penis is assigned as a boy, the clinical management, hormonally and surgically, is masculinizing. In adulthood, the body is typically masculine, except for lack of sperms and fertility. Without knowledge of the clinical history, no one can distinguish such a man from other normal men of his age group (Money & Daléry, 1976). He can not be singled out on account of his gender-identity/role (G-I/R), which is unremarkably masculine in accordance with the social stereotype in which, as a boy, he grew to manhood. He marries as a man, and has the heterosexual life of a man.

The person with whom this individual constitutes a matched pair is one who was assigned and habilitated, hormonally and surgically, as a girl from the neonatal period onward. At puberty she grows breasts on a normally feminized body, menstruates, and is fertile as a woman. She may have the romantic and erotic life of a heterosexual woman; or she may have fantasies and or experiences that qualify her as bisexual. In some instances, she may be a lesbian who can fall in love only with a woman.

Thirty cases of CVAH women who were born not with a penis but a greatly hypertrophied clitoris have been followed to maturity (Money & Schwartz, 1977; Money, Schwartz, & Lewis, 1984). All were assigned, reared, and habilitated as girls. In teenage, they differed from their age mates in having an undeveloped romantic and dating life. Also they were unable to talk about sex and eroticism in their own imagery or experience. Later, in their middle to late twenties, they were able to make more personal disclosures. As shown in Table 4, 11 of the 30 (37%) disclosed themselves to have had bisexual imagery and/or practice; 5 (17%) of the 11 in the group rated themselves as exclusively (N = 2) or predominantly (N = 3) lesbian. Only 12 (40%) of the 30 claimed to be exclusively heterosexual. The remaining 7 (23%) were noncommittal. These percentages were spectacularly dissimilar ($p < .001$) from those obtained from a clinical comparison or control group.

The control group was composed of 27 women with the androgen-insensitivity (A-I) syndrome (N = 15) and Rokitansky syndrome (N = 12). The two syndromes were combined because behaviorally they were indistinguishable from one another (Lewis & Money, 1983; Money & Lewis, 1983). This finding is in itself of major pertinence to the nature/crucial period/nuture issue, because in both syndromes the body morphology and hormonalization are female, the vagina is atresic, and there is no menstruation. Gonadally and chromosomally the two syndromes are divergent, namely, testicular and 46,XY in the A-I syndrome, and ovarian and 46,XX in the Rokitansky syndrome.

Table 5 compares the percentages of the present CVAH sample (with and without the seven who were too reticent to be intimately self-revelatory), with those of the control sample, and with those obtained by Kinsey in his large survey sample (Kinsey, Pomeroy, Martin, & Gebhard, 1953). The Kinsey

TABLE 4
46,XX Adrenogenital Syndrome (CVAH) Female Rearing

| | *Present Self-Rating on Erotosexual Status* | |
| | *(Imagery ± Activity)* | |
Rating	*A-G (N = 30)*	*Controls (N = 27)*[a]
Noncommittal	7 (23%)	0 (0%)
Heterosexual only	12 (40%)	25 (93%)
Bisexual	6 (20%)	2 (7%)
Homosexual only or predominantly	5 (17%)	0 (0%)
	$\chi^2 = 18.5; p < .001$[b]	

[a]Androgen-Insensitivity Syndrome (N = 15) Rokitansky Syndrome (N = 12)
[b]Omitting the noncommittal line so that N (A-G) = 23, and N (Control) = 27 and combining bisexual and homosexual ratings then Chi Square = 10.5; $p < .01$

TABLE 5
Comparison of Homoerotic Incidence in CVAH, AIS/MRKS, and Kinsey's Sample

	Kinsey's Sample	CVAH N = 30	CVAH N = 23	AIS/MRKS N = 27
Homoerotic Arousal Imagery by Age 20	15%	37%	48%	7%
Homoerotic Partner Contact by Age 20	10%	17%	22%	4%

data are old, but they have not been superseded by a more modern survey. They indicate that the CVAH percentages are unlikely to have been an artifact of sampling. The most likely explanation of these CVAH percentages, and the extremely divergent ones of the control sample, is that prenatal and or neonatal hormonal masculinization did make a difference. It masculinized not only the genitalia, but also the sexual dimorphism of the brain. Conversely, in the control sample, the corresponding hormonal demasculinization made a difference in favor of feminization.

In the CVAH group of 30 patients, the prenatal masculinization effect was not sufficient to preordain transexualism and the quest for sex reassignment in childhood or later. Whatever the degree of masculinization, it was incorporated into a gender-identity/role that in adulthood was socially recognized as acceptably feminine or as an acceptable variant thereof. The defining characteristic of those who declared themselves as predominantly or exclusively lesbian was that they could fall in love only with a woman, but not with a man. Thus it may prove to be a general rule that the crucial period of prenatal hormonal masculinization leaves its imprint on subsequent erotic life by determining the gender of the visual image of the partner with whom a pairbonded relationship of falling in love may be established.

CONCLUSIONS

In the syndromes of abuse dwarfism the equation nature + crucial period + nurture → phenotype applies to statural, intellectual, and sociobehavioral factors in development. These aspects as they apply to postnatal development are impaired in the syndrome. It is not yet known whether these impairments are preceded by a prenatal vulnerability which interacts with the postnatal influences of child abuse. Since impaired statural growth is not an expected characteristic of children subjected to abuse, it is quite possible that children who become dwarfed secondary to abuse had a prenatal factor which rendered them vulnerable to hypothalamic-pituitary malfunction under conditions of abuse.

Modern genetic theory avoids dichotomizing nature versus nurture and postulates a genetic norm of reaction which, for its proper expression, requires phyletically prescribed environmental boundaries. Child abuse imposes constriction or narrowing of the environmental boundary which, when expanded, allows for statural, intellectual and sociobehavioral catchup growth.

Sociobehavioral growth includes psychosexual development. In endocrine syndromes errors of prenatal development in combination with postnatal rearing and development can lead to alterations in adult psychosexual status.

In the syndrome of female hermaphroditism with congenital virilizing adrenal hyperplasia (CVAH) there is dual importance of both the prenatal and postnatal crucial periods in the differentiation of human behavioral dimorphism. Genetic and hormonal errors occur in association with varying degrees of virilization. The degree of virilization in a 46,XX baby can be so severe that the genitalia consist of a fully formed penis and empty scrotum. Babies born with this degree of severity of virilization have been assigned and reared male. Clinical management, hormonally and surgically, has been masculinizing. Subsequent gender-identity/role (G-I/R) has been masculine in accordance with gender of assignment and rearing. 46,XX babies with the same prenatal history assigned and reared female have developed a feminine gender-identity/role (G-I/R).

In adulthood the 46,XX CVAH individual reared male is unremarkably masculine except for lack of sperms and fertility. The same type of individual reared female may have the romantic and erotic life of a heterosexual woman, or she may have the fantasies and/or experience that qualify as bisexual. In some instances, she may be a lesbian who can fall in love only with a woman.

CVAH women provide a unique lesson on the nature + crucial period + nurture → phenotype paradigm. In these women as a group, prenatal hormonal virilization of the 46,XX brain during the crucial period for sex dimorphic brain development lowers the threshold for the possibility of postnatal development of a homosexual or bisexual G-I/R.

The periods within which psychosexual and other forms of development become stabilized may be called critical, sensitive, crucial, or whatever. The significance lies in the period being time-limited. At a specified time in development, nature and nurture interact to create a particular outcome. The timing is crucial, for the nature-nurture interaction cannot take place either earlier or later. Once it has taken place, the fate of the developmental outcome is to be more or less fixed and resistant to change.

ACKNOWLEDGMENT

This research has been supported by USPHS Grant HD00325 and Grant #83086900 from The William T. Grant Foundation.

REFERENCES

Applebaum, A. S. Developmental retardation in infants as a concomitant of physical child abuse. *Journal of Abnormal Child Psychology,* 1977, *5,* 417–423.

Brandwein, H. The battered child: A definite and significant factor in mental retardation. *Mental Retardation,* 1973, *11,* 50–51.

Buchanan, A., & Oliver, J. E. Abuse and neglect as a cause of mental retardation: A study of 140 children admitted to subnormality hospitals in Wiltshire. *British Journal of Psychiatry,* 1977, *131,* 458–467.

Clarke, I. J. The sexual behavior of prenatally androgenized ewes observed in the field. *Journal of Reproduction and Fertility,* 1977, *49,* 311–315.

Dennis, W. *Children of the Crèche.* New York: Appleton-Century-Crofts, 1973.

Eysenck, H. J. *The inequality of man.* London: Temple Smith, 1974.

Goldfoot, D. A. Sociosexual behaviors of nonhuman primates during development and maturity: Social and hormonal relationship. In A. M. Schrier (Ed.), *Behavioral primatology, advances in research and theory* (Vol. 1). Hillsdale, NJ: Erlbaum, 1977.

Goldfoot, D. A., & Neff, D. A. On measuring behavioral sex differences in social contexts. In J. M. Reinisch, L. A. Rosenblum, & S. A. Sanders (Eds.), *Masculinity/femininity: Basic perspectives.* New York: Oxford, 1984.

Goldfoot, D. A., & Wallen, K. Development of gender role behaviors in heterosexual and isosexual groups of infant rhesus monkeys. In D. J. Chivers & H. Herbert (Eds.), *Recent advances in primatology* (Vol. 1; Behavior). London: Academic Press, 1978.

Goldfoot, D. A., Wallen, K., Neff, D. A., McBrair, M. C., & Goy, R. W. Social influences upon the display of sexually dimorphic behavior in rhesus monkeys: Isosexual rearing. *Archives of Sexual Behavior,* 1984, *13,* 395–412.

Herber, R. F., & Garber, H. The Milwaukee Project: A study of the use of family intervention to prevent cultural-familial mental retardation. In J. Hellmuth (Ed.), *Exceptional infant, (Vol. 3): Assessment and Intervention.* New York: Brunner/Mazel, 1975.

Hirsch, J. Jensenism: The bankruptcy of "science" without scholarship. *United States Congressional Record,* 122: No. 73, E2671-2672; No. 74, E2693-2695; No. 75, E2703-2705, E2716-2718, E2721-2722 (originally published in *Educational Theory,* 1975, *25,* 3–27, 102.

Hirsch, J. To "Unfrock the Charlatans." *Sage Race Relations Abstracts,* 1981, *6,* 1–65.

Jensen, A. R. How much can we boost IQ and scholastic achievement? *Harvard Educational Review,* 1969, *39,* 1–123.

Jensen, A. R. *Educability and group differences.* New York: Harper and Row, 1973.

Kinsey, A. C., Pomeroy, W. B., Martin, C. E., & Gebhard, P. H. *Sexual behavior in the human female.* Philadelphia: Saunders, 1953.

Lewis, V. G., & Money, J. Gender-identity/role: G-I/R Part A: XY (androgen-insensitivity syndrome) and XX (Rokitansky syndrome) vaginal atresia compared. In L. Dennerstein & G. Burrows (Eds.), *Handbook of psychosomatic obstetrics and gynaecology.* Amsterdam-New York-London: Elsevier Biomedical Press, 1983.

Meadow, R. Munchausen syndrome by proxy—the hinterland of child abuse. *Lancet,* 1977, *ii,* 343–345.

Meadow, R. Management of Munchausen syndrome by proxy. *Archives of Disease in Childhood,* 1985, *60,* 385–393.

Migeon, C. J., & Forest, M. G. Androgens in biological fluids. In B. Rothfeld (Ed.), *Nuclear medicine in vitro.* Philadelphia: Lippincott, 1980.

Money, J. The syndrome of abuse dwarfism (psychosocial dwarfism or reversible hyposomatotropinism): Behavioral data and case report. *American Journal of Diseases of Children,* 1977, *131,* 508–513.

Money, J. *Love and love sickness: The science of sex, gender difference, and pair-bonding.* Baltimore: Johns Hopkins University Press, 1980.

Money, J., Annecillo, C., & Hutchison, J. W. Forensic and family psychiatry in abuse dwarfism: Munchausen's syndrome by proxy, atonement, and addiction to abuse. *Journal of Sex and Marital Therapy*, 1985, *11*, 30–40.

Money, J., Annecillo, C., & Kelley, J. F. Growth of intelligence: Failure and catch-up associated respectively with abuse and rescue in the syndrome of abuse dwarfism. *Psychoneuroendocrinology*, 1983, *8*, 309–319. (a)

Money, J., Annecillo, C., & Kelley, J. F. Abuse-dwarfism syndrome: After rescue, statural and intellectual catch-up growth correlate. *Journal of Clinical Child Psychology*, 1983, *12*, 279–283. (b)

Money, J., & Daléry, J. Iatrogenic homosexuality: Gender identity in seven 46,XX chromosomal females with hyperadrenocortical hermaphroditism born with a penis, three reared as boys, four reared as girls. *Journal of Homosexuality*, 1976, *1*, 357–371.

Money, J., & Lewis, V. G. Gender-identity/role: G-I/R Part B: A multiple sequential model of differentiation. In L. Dennerstein & G. Burrows (Eds.), *Handbook of psychosomatic obstetrics and gynaecology*. Amsterdam-New York-London: Elsevier Biomedical Press, 1983.

Money, J., & Schwartz, M. Dating, romantic and nonromantic friendships, and sexuality in 17 early-treated adrenogenital females, aged 16–25. In P. A. Lee, L. P. Plotnick, A. A. Kowarski & C. J. Migeon (Eds.), *Congenital adrenal hyperplasia*. Baltimore: University Park Press, 1977.

Money, J., Schwartz, M., & Lewis, V. G. Adult erotosexual status and fetal hormonal masculinization and demasculinization: 46,XX congenital virilizing adrenal hyperplasia and 46,XY androgen-insensitivity syndrome compared. *Psychoneuroendocrinology*, 1984, *9*, 405–414.

Money, J., & Werlwas, J. Folie à deux in the parents of psychosocial dwarfs: Two cases. *Bulletin of the American Academy of Psychiatry and the Law*, 1976, *4*, 351–362.

Money, J., Wolff, G., & Annecillo, C. Pain agnosia and self-injury in the syndrome of reversible somatotropin deficiency (psychosocial dwarfism). *Journal of Autism and Childhood Schizophrenia*, 1972, *2*, 127–139.

Powell, G. F., Brasel, J. A. & Blizzard, R. M. Emotional deprivation and growth retardation simulating idiopathic hypopituitarism. I. Clinical evaluation of the syndrome. *New England Journal of Medicine*, 1967, *276*, 271–1278.

Powell, G. F., Brasel, J. A., Raiti, S., & Blizzard, R. M. Emotional deprivation and growth retardation simulating idiopathic hypopituitarism. II. Endocrinologic evaluation of the syndrome. *New England Journal of Medicine*, 1967, *276*, 1279–1283.

Sandgrund, A., Gaines, R. W., & Green, A. H. Child abuse and mental retardation: A problem of cause and effect. *American Journal of Mental Deficiency*, 1974, *79*, 327–330.

Short, R. V., & Clarke, I. J. *Masculinization of the female sheep*. Distributed by R. V. Short, MRC Reproductive Biology Unit, 2 Forrest Road, Edinburgh, EHI 2QW, U.K., undated.

Skeels, H. M., & Fillmore, E. A. The mental development of children from underprivileged homes. *Journal of Genetic Psychology*, 1937, *50*, 427–439.

Solomon, R. L. The opponent-process theory of acquired motivation. *American Psychologist*, 1980, *35*, 691–712.

Wolff, G., & Money, J. Relationship between sleep and growth in patients with reversible somatotropin deficiency (psychosocial dwarfism). *Psychological Medicine*, 1973, *3*, 18–27.

III SENSITIVE PERIODS IN HUMAN PSYCHOLOGY

Section II of *Sensitive Periods in Development* illustrated behavioral and neuropsychological instances of sensitive periods. Section III is concerned almost exclusively with sensitive periods in human psychological development, and in particular with the application of sensitive periods in cognition, language, personality, bonding, and social organization. It has been argued that each sphere of inquiry gives evidence of sensitive periods; it emerges that some do, but others do not.

In Chapter 8, Catherine Tamis-LeMonda and Marc Bornstein apply the sensitive period idea in a novel, but entirely ready way to human mental development. They suggest that the growth of human cognition follows a multivariate plan that integrates over particular kinds of experience and the developmental level of the child. Certain experiences of early life—material, social, and didactic—are widely recognized to affect mature cognitive function, but a detailed developmental consideration indicates that the magnitude of their effects depends on when in the life course these several kinds of experiences are encountered. In this sense, the effects of experience on human mental development betray an interaction with developmental level, and are reasonably well conceptualized as a sensitive period. In further evaluation of the appropriateness of the sensitive period model,

Tamis-LeMonda and Bornstein assess the aptness of two common sensitive period criteria, durability and reversibility of effects. On the first, they find that the selective advantageous outcomes of early experience can endure. On the second, they question the extant body of data and conclude that deprivation-of-experience effects even early in life are remedial. Both conclusions about human mental life are compatible with the application of a sensitive period orientation, and their conclusions add force to the new significance of early experience for human learning.

Since Eric Lenneberg's renown pronouncements about a sensitive period in language learning, perhaps no activity has been so widely or readily accepted as illustrating a sensitive period in human psychology as the development of language. Yet, as Catherine Snow shows exactingly in Chapter 9, the data on language development (with only a single exception) fail to substantiate the application of the sensitive period notion. Though she is cautious to point up difficulties in evaluating claims in this area, Snow carefully analyzes diverse data sets that are relevant to the sensitive period hypothesis in language, and she concludes that each fails to substantiate implications of a sensitive period in language. Some of the arenas she examines include second-language learning (where children have been thought, however incorrectly, to possess an advantage), recovery from aphasia (where children have been thought, mostly incorrectly, to possess immunity), and the dependence of language learning on brain change (where the neurological growth that is special to childhood has been thought, almost entirely incorrectly, to betoken a special ease of language acquisition). Pace Lenneberg and general opinion, Snow's conclusions significantly enhance our understanding of language learning and seriously undermine facile application of the sensitive period concept to language acquisition.

Behavioral scientists hold widely divergent views about the origins of human personality, but among the oldest, most entrenched, and most popular in psychology is the psychoanalytic perspective. In Chapter 10, Benjamin Beit-Hallahmi recounts that both the classical Freudian and modern revisionist psychoanalytic schools of character development concur that early childhood constitutes a sensitive period (loosely though aptly applied) for personality development: Certain experiences during this time are thought to have lasting, if not irreversible, effects. In traditional psychoanalytic theory, experiences sustained through the Oedipal phase of development are believed to contribute formatively to normal or to neurotic personality traits in maturity. (Indeed, childhood experiences form the traditional basis of the psychoanalytic edifice, and immature adult acts are commonly derogated with labels of childishness like "oral.") Subsequent revisions of Freud in object-relations theory place no less emphasis on the formative experiences of childhood but have tended rather to refine the duration of sensitivity to the first 6 or 12 months of life than let it extend across the Oedipal phase.

It is most common for the notion of the sensitive period to be applied to the young, and especially to the young of infrahuman organisms; much less frequent has been any application to adult members of a species or to human beings generally. Thus, it is somewhat surprising that one of the most popular and widely recognized applications of sensitive periods has been to motherhood in humans. Specifically, Klaus and Kennel argued that mothers who experienced a prolonged contact with their newborns would later show a special affinity for their offspring. In Chapter 11, Barbara Myers evaluates the data for this claim and concludes that, however well-grounded in animal literature is infant-to-mother attachment and however humanistic may be intentions behind fostering mother-to-infant attachment, the notion of a rapid and circumscribed sensitive period for "maternal bonding" following parturition in humans is largely unsubstantiated. Combined with data that indicate clearly that the reciprocal process in humans, viz. infant attachment to mother, is both a slow and a learned phenomenon, Myers's analysis essentially removes the construct of mutual social interaction between mother and baby from the realm reserved to sensitive period phenomena.

In the final Chapter 12 of this volume, J. P. Scott substantiates his longstanding claims for the broad pertinency of the sensitive period concept by applying it to organizations of individuals. The idea of a sensitive period has been reserved, almost uniformly since its inception, to individual organs or organisms, and Scott himself has contributed original data at each of these levels. Here Scott identifies the sensitive period as a developmental and organizational process in living organisms, and so argues that, in principle and in fact, such a conceptualization permits application of the sensitive period to the formation and development of aggregates of individuals in human social and cultural groups. Scott supports this thesis with examples from dyads as well as from formal institutions. Scott also fleshes out this novel application of the sensitive period notion by developing the principles of a general theory of the sensitive period based on the development, organization, and stability of living systems.

Surprisingly, the chapters in Section III show that those aspects of human psychology most widely believed to submit to a sensitive period analysis, viz. language acquisition and mother-infant bonding, on closer inspection fail to inspire much solid support. By contrast, other areas of human psychology not usually conjured in connection with sensitive periods, viz. cognitive development, personality functioning, and social organization, seem almost naturally to embrace this approach. The counterintuitive nature of this assay is simultaneously heartening and discouraging. It is important to recognize that some basic human behaviors submit to a sensitive period conceptualization, but it is equally humbling to find that those to which we have most facilely applied this analysis fail under a close scrutiny to meet our expectations. But then it is common in science as in life for reputation to trail data.

8 Is There a "Sensitive Period" in Human Mental Development?

Catherine Tamis-LeMonda and Marc H. Bornstein
New York University

> *For any experience to have maximal effect, it is essential that it match the existing achievements of the infant.*
> —J. McV. Hunt, 1981, p. 23

INTRODUCTION

It is commonly acknowledged that variation in human cognitive achievements reflects differential experiences, especially early ones. Some researchers and theoreticians have argued that experience accounts for virtually all of the variance in developing cognitive ability, and even the staunchest geneticists admit that experience must account for a large proportion of the variance (see Eysenck & Kamin, 1981). No one asserts that human mental function is entirely endowed and uninfluenced by experience.

As a consequence, researchers and theoreticians do not ask *whether* experiences affect cognitive development, but rather *when* and *how*. Considerable progress has cumulated toward ascertaining the ways by which experiences might influence cognitive growth. Theory suggests a minimally three-term multivariate model of mental development: (1) Different experiences vary in their influence; (2) the effectiveness of different experiences differs with characteristics of the individual, notably developmental level; and (3) different experiences impact on different cognitive outcomes (Bornstein, 1986). Insofar as experiences operate selectively and select experiences tend to exert their respective influences at particular points in the life cycle, this multivariate perspective suggests that human mental development may be profitably conceptualized as a *sensitive period* phenomenon.

163

In this chapter, we explore arguments for the multivariate model of cognitive growth and develop evidence for a sensitive period in human mental development. We begin by reviewing three main classes of experience that seem to play independent roles in the intellectual development of the child. We then characterize pertinent changes in the child that occur during early ontogeny. Next, we integrate over these two domains — experience and development — as we define how the impact of specific experiences modulates with the child's developmental level. We believe that this interaction supports the application of sensitive period theory to mental life, and also that infancy and childhood constitute a special phase in ontogeny, lending greater force to this belief. We then demonstrate how different experiences affect different dimensions of cognition by illustrating some specific predictor-criterion relations. Finally, we examine how critical sensitive period effects may be in the realm of human cognition by asking how long-lasting they are and whether they are reversible. In evaluating evidence that allows us to apply the concept of a sensitive period to human mental development, we openly undertake to state the optimistic case, and we have been selective rather than exhaustive in our review of data.

EXPERIENCE AND DEVELOPMENT

Certain experiences seem to produce lasting effects in mental development. Although some effects may be explained by concurrent continuities in the child's milieu, studies of the long-term consequences of experience support a model that indicates that particular inputs can be meaningful. In addition, early experiences seem to exert more robust effects than later ones. For example, children adopted out of institutions and into intact families earlier in their lives fare better than children adopted out later (Dennis, 1976; Goldfarb, 1943; Scarr & Weinberg, 1976; Tizard & Rees, 1976), and those adopted at birth may achieve IQ scores equivalent to their adoptive siblings (Horn, Loehlin, & Willerman, 1979). Royce, Darlington, and Murray (1983) integrated over the results of a number of intervention studies and concluded that the effectiveness of experience is generally enhanced if stimulation begins as early as possible in the child's life. This interaction of experience and developmental level represents perhaps the most substantial evidence supporting application of the notion of the sensitive period to human cognitive growth.

Several classes of experience have been found to relate to cognitive development in the child. Three may be distinguished theoretically: Experience with the material environment, such as the availability, variety, and age-appropriateness of toys; social experience, including interpersonal contact and expressions of affection; and didactic experience, in which the caretaker explains, demonstrates, or introduces the milieu to the child. Of course, this is not a unique classification, nor are these categories of experience mutually exclusive. Nevertheless, this system of distinctions is emerging as theoretically meaningful in the contemporary developmental literature, and it is one that may have considerable functional as well as heuristic value (e.g., Bornstein, 1986; Hoff-Ginsberg & Shatz, 1982; Wachs & Gruen, 1982). We focus briefly on each of these experiences in anticipation of our central argument, viz. that infancy may be a sensitive period in human mental development.

Experience

Material experience.   Several characteristics of the child's physical environment have been posited to affect the development of cognition either concurrently or predictively. These effects may be direct, as by exposure learning, or they may be indirect, fostering neurological development or stimulating exploration, both of which in turn eventuate in cognitive advance.

First, simple availability of materials in the home seems to be an important factor. Availability of toys, for example, correlates with Bayley Scale performance (Riksen-Walraven, 1974) and with Griffiths Infant Scale scores (Ainsworth & Bell, 1974). Second is the variety of stimulants found in the child's environment. Variety correlates with Bayley Scale scores (Riksen-Walraven, 1974; Yarrow, Rubenstein, & Pedersen, 1975) and with object permanence, exploratory behavior, and problem solving (Yarrow et al., 1975). Gottfried and Gottfried (1984) found that the "variety of stimulation" subscale of the HOME assessed at 15 months consistently and pervasively predicted 18- and 24-month Bayley, 24-month recognition memory, and 30-, 36-, and 42-month McCarthy performance (McCarthy, 1972); likewise, Siegel (1984) reported that children who had lower variety scores on the HOME at 12 months were delayed in expressive language at 3 years and on the McCarthy at 5 years. Third is contingent responsivity. Specifically, the extent to which aspects of the inanimate environment change as a result of the child's actions has been found to relate to Bayley Scale scores and to levels of goal directedness and exploratory behavior at 5 months (Yarrow et al., 1975) and to Bayley Scale scores at 5 and at 11 months (Riksen-Walraven, 1974).

The physical arrangement of the home constitutes a related and reportedly important factor. Physical restrictions, such as barriers and playpens, apparently inhibit exploration, and thus may indirectly hinder cognitive development. The importance of exploratory floor freedom has been documented across a range of populations to relate to Gesell and to Griffiths performance

(Ainsworth, 1977; Ainsworth & Bell, 1974; Beckwith, Cohen, Kopp, Parmalee, & Marcy, 1976) and to object permanence, foresight and causality, and Binet Scale scores (Wachs, 1978, 1979) in infancy as well as to 4-year IQ scores (Barnard, Bee, & Hammond, 1984). In a longitudinal study of environmental restriction, Tulkin and Covitz (1975) obtained a negative correlation between the time 10-month-olds spent in a playpen and their PPVT scores at 6 years.

Social experience. Research indicates that concurrent and predictive relations also obtain between certain social experiences, such as the amount of interpersonal contact a child receives in terms of being held, rocked, or touched, and the child's intellectual achievements. Specifically, contact during infancy has been found to relate concurrently to infants' performance on the Gesell (Casler, 1965), Bayley (Coates & Lewis, 1984; Lagerspetz, Nygard, & Strondvik, 1971; Solkoff, Sumner, Weintraub, & Blase, 1969), Griffiths (Brossard & Decarie, 1971), and Brazelton tests (Solkoff & Matuzsak, 1975), to infants' object permanence and spatial abilities (Goldberg, 1972, 1977), to their recognition memory (Rose, 1980), and to their verbal proficiency and play sophistication (Vibbert & Bornstein, 1986), and it has been found to relate predictively from 6 months to 36-month Binet score (Farran, Ramey, & Campbell, 1977).

In parallel with the effects of the physical environment, social stimulation that is contingent on infants' actions relates concurrently and predictively to a number of cognitive measures. Hunt and his colleagues (1976) conducted an intervention program in which caretakers at a Tehran orphanage were trained to respond to infant boredom, interest, and distress. When later compared with American infants from professional households, the Iranian infants demonstrated earlier achievement of object permanence, foresight, imitation, and causality. In addition, contingent social responsiveness has been related concurrently to habituation rate in the first 6 months (Lewis & Goldberg, 1969; Tamis-LeMonda & Bornstein, 1986) and predictively from the first three-quarters of infancy to communicative competence at 12 months (Bell & Ainsworth, 1972; Bornstein, 1986), exploratory skill at 12 months (Riksen-Walraven, 1978), WPPSI scores at 4 years (Bornstein, 1986), and WISC-R and Block design scores at 6 years (Coates & Lewis, 1984).

Reciprocally, parents' behaviors that restrict, interrupt, or punish a child's actions consistently impact adversely on cognitive outcome. In one example longitudinal study, Nelson (1973) found that 13-month maternal intrusive or command-oriented behaviors negatively predicted children's vocabulary size at 20 months. Other studies have demonstrated predictive relations between "avoidance of restriction and punishment" on the HOME inventory scale in the second year of life and language development at 3 years (Elardo, Bradley,

& Caldwell, 1977) and Stanford Binet scores at 3-4 years (Barnard et al., 1984; Bradley & Caldwell, 1980).

Didactic experience. Parents mediate between their child and the external world by presenting, showing, demonstrating, interpreting, and the like. Specifically, in such mediated learning experiences, the adult negotiates sources of stimulation for the child, selecting, framing, and feeding back environmental experiences so as to engender in the child appropriate learning sets and knowledge. These are important didactic experiences for the child.

A number of researchers have uncovered generally consistent and positive relations between parental didactics and early cognitive development. For example, mothers' encouraging their infants to attend to particular aspects of the environment relates concurrently to infants' visual and tactual exploration at both 2 and 5 months and relates predictively to visual exploration from 2 to 5 months (Tamis-LeMonda & Bornstein, 1986). In addition, didactic experiences at 2 months predict aspects of infants' habituation at 5-months (Bornstein & Tamis-LeMonda, 1986). Bornstein (1985) found that mothers who more frequently encouraged their 4-month-olds to attend to properties, objects, and events in the environment had infants who scored higher on the Bayley Scale and possessed larger productive vocabularies at 12 months and who later scored higher on the WPPSI at 4 years. Vibbert and Bornstein (1986) found that the same maternal activities were concurrently associated with 13-month-olds' sophistication in language and play. Olson, Bayles, and Bates (1986) demonstrated relations between didactic verbal stimulation at 24 months and children's PPVT scores at 6 years of age. Adults' deictic utterances (in which the target referent is already the focus of the child's attention) consistently predict advanced language performance in the child (Newport, Gleitman, & Gleitman, 1977; Shatz, 1978; Tomasello & Mannle, 1985).

In a similar vein, intervention and modeling studies report performance advantages for experimental over control infants for elicited versus spontaneous play. That is, children's play following modeling sequences is more complex (O'Connel & Bretherton, 1984), more effective (Lockman & McHale, 1985), and more advanced (DeLoache & Plaetzer, 1985) than the level infants achieve when they play on their own. Likewise, training mothers to focus their infants' attention enhances subsequent infant exploratory competence (Belsky, Goode, & Most, 1980) and habituation (Riksen-Walraven, 1978). Smith, Adamson, and Bakeman (1986) found that mothers who more often exhibited attention-focusing strategies and joint object play with their 15-month-olds had children with larger vocabularies at 18 months.

Various aspects of maternal "communicative style" have also been associated with children's cognitive competence (predominantly language development). Nelson (1973) found that mothers who were object oriented, question asking, and linguistically concise at 13 months had children with larger working vocabularies at 20 months. Likewise, Furrow, Nelson, and Benedict (1979) found that maternal imperatives, yes-no questions, and noun/pronoun ratios related positively to growth in child language. Even more specifically, mothers' expansions of their children's attempts at specific words or phrases have been shown to relate to the growth of auxiliaries (Newport et al., 1977) and of MLU (Barnes, Gutfreund, Satterly, & Wells, 1983) in child speech. Expansions that change one item of the child's statement or replace utterances with a *wh* form (e.g., "You want what?") positively predict utterance length (Brown, 1958; Moerk, 1972; Nelson, Denninger, Kaplan, & Bonvillian, 1979). Additionally, mothers' own language expansions predict children's speech advances (Cross, 1978).

In the everyday life of the child, material and social or social and didactic experiences are often naturally confounded. Studies that partial among associations between these particular experiences and cognitive growth tend to support the independent association of each, leading to the conclusion that material, social, and didactic experiences make significant and perhaps independent contributions to the cognitive development of the child. For example, Vibbert and Bornstein (1986) found that maternal social and didactic interactions accounted for independent proportions of variance in their 13-month-olds' verbal competence.

Development

Simply to integrate over material, social, and didactic experiences tempts us to conclude that they alone or together function to enhance the growth of cognition in children. However, experience is not effective independent of the child; rather the impact of different experiences is inevitably modulated by the developmental level of the child. During ontogeny, children traverse courses of motor and mental change whose plateaus and transitions help to determine how different types of experience affect cognitive growth. To illustrate with an obvious but nonetheless telling example, the child's achieving locomotion can be seen to alter dramatically the effects of different classes of experience. Concretely, floor freedom will have little meaning to the neonate but doubtlessly assumes increasing significance around 8 months in parallel with the child's developing motor capabilities. Similarly, deixis is unlikely to affect the preverbal child the way it does the verbal child.

In overview, we have distinguished three kinds of experience and demonstrated that each affects cognitive growth in the child. We have also pointed out that since the child is developing over time experiences cannot be regarded as simple "main effects" in an implicit univariate way, but rather as factors in a model that includes development and hence stresses the importance of experiences interacting with children's developmental level.

SENSITIVE PERIODS IN
HUMAN MENTAL DEVELOPMENT:
THE INTERACTION OF EXPERIENCE AND
DEVELOPMENTAL LEVEL

In this section, we explore systematically the ways in which particular experiences vary in effectiveness as a function of the child's development. To evaluate the interaction of experience and developmental level, we might want to compare the effects of two experiences that are equally available to the child but at different developmental times. To elaborate the example introduced in the foregoing section, floor freedom is ineffective in the neonatal period though it seems to become increasingly important in later infancy. By contrast, maternal touch may be influential in the neonatal period, but may be less important thereafter. Comparing the two experiences leads to the conclusion that experience interacts with developmental level, and that the nature of the interaction can be specified.

Little extant research conforms to so simple but ideal a design. Nevertheless, comparisons across several studies help to illustrate how the effects of particular experiences are limited to specific periods of development. The interaction of experiences with developmental level has been frequently, if indirectly, suggested in theory (e.g., Kagan, 1976, 1979; McCall, 1981; Wohlwill, 1973), but few researchers have explored the empirical validity of specific interactions. We argue that validity and suggest that the interaction of different kinds of experience with developmental level supports the utility of a sensitive period perspective in human mental development. To support this view, we capitulate over the effectiveness of material, social, and didactic experiences.

The extent to which environmental stimulation actually "matches" the child's development level consistently relates to cognitive achievement. A series of studies conducted by Bradley and Caldwell (1976a, 1976b, 1980) uncovered relations between the age-appropriateness of play materials children had available to them at 6, 12, and 24 months and their 36- and 54-month Binet scores; likewise, a series of studies with preterm and fullterm infants conducted by Siegel (1981, 1982, 1984) found that stimulation that appropriately matched 12-month-olds' competences predicted their 18- and 24-months Bayley scores, 24-, 36-, and 48-month Reynell scores, and 5-year McCarthy IQ scores (McCarthy, 1972). And, as we have noted already, concurrent and predictive relations between floor freedom and cognitive performance only appear at around 8 months (Ainsworth & Bell, 1974; Beckwith et al., 1976; Tulkin & Covitz, 1975), clearly matched to children's emerging locomotor capabilities.

Effectiveness of the social environment is likewise developmentally dependent. Kinesthetic stimulation seems to exert primary influence during the first 6 months of life; afterward, such contact has been found to be unrelated or even negatively related to cognitive development. Goldberg (1972, 1977) observed that infants whose mothers stimulated them kinesthetically at 6 months performed in more advanced ways on tasks involving spatial abilities at 6 months and in object permanence at both 6 and 12 months, whereas maternal kinesthetic stimulation at 9 and at 12 months related negatively to task performance.

The effectiveness of specific types of contingent experience seems also to be age-specific. Beckwith and her colleagues (1976) explored relations between dimensions of maternal responsivity and infant sensorimotor development; at 3 months only responses to infant distress predicted 9-month sensorimotor performance, whereas at 8 months only responses to non-distress were associated with later performance. Similarly, Tamis-LeMonda and Bornstein (1986) found that maternal responsivity to infant distress at 2 months predicted infants' visual and tactual exploration at 5 months, whereas responsivity to infant non-distress over the same time period had no effect. Coates and Lewis's (1984) detailed analysis of concurrent and predictive relations among eight dimensions of maternal responsivity for child cognitive performance found that proximal responsivity to distress and tactile responsivity were the only measures that related concurrently to 3-month Bayley performance, proximal responsivity to distress was the only variable that predicted 6-year reading achievement, and overall distress responsivity was the only measure that predicted 6-year mathematics achievement performance. By contrast, Wachs (1984) failed to find any relation between adult response to distress and children's sensorimotor development during the second year of life; however, adult responses to infants' vocalizations were among the most salient environmental predictors of sensorimotor development through the same period.

Linguistic experience seems to exert equally clear time-specific effects; indeed, the interaction of developmental level and experience helps to account for many seeming empirical inconsistencies. Consider two conflicting studies. Furrow et al. (1979) analyzed predictive associations between linguistic input to children who were all at the one-word stage, at approximately 18 months, and language function 9 months later. Newport et al. (1977) analyzed a somewhat overlapping set of input-output relations in an age-heterogeneous group of children 12- to 27-months-old. Furrow and co-workers found that a greater number of maternal variables related to language development than did Newport and coworkers. Specifically, Furrow et al. found that maternal speech predicted several basic measures of child language competence (e.g., MLU, noun phrases, and verbs per utterance), whereas Newport et al. found that maternal speech predicted none of these measures. In cases where models of development are structured from empirical results the failure to attend to age differences may lead to strongly opposing views. In the cited contrast, Newport et al. proposed a nativist view of language growth in which universal properties of verbal proficiency are innately specified, whereas Furrow et al. concluded that universal structures of child language related to properties of maternal speech.

Didactics also seem to influence cognitive growth in age-specific ways. In a longitudinal study, Bornstein (1985) found that mothers' encouraging their infants to attend to properties, objects, and events in the environment at 4 months predicted children's long-term cognitive accomplishments better than did analogous maternal prompting at 12 months. Similarly, O'Connel and Bretherton (1984) found that maternal aid in exploratory and combinatorial play enhanced 20-month-olds' play competence, whereas maternal guidance of pretense play did not benefit children. By contrast, 28-month-olds were aided by symbolic directions, and ignored maternal suggestions relevant to lower play levels. Children must achieve different levels of ability before they are able to advantage themselves of different types of didactics. Experience beyond that threshold seems to be ineffective.

Even different types of didactics apparently have age-specific impacts. For example, physically encouraging an infant to attend to some aspect of the environment seems to facilitate cognitive development during the first year more efficiently than does verbally encouraging the infant (Belsky et al., 1980; Tamis-LeMonda & Bornstein, 1986). Also different subcomponents of didactics may be more or less effective. Shatz (1982) found that maternal gesturing to 19-month-olds related positively to comprehension, whereas the same deictic strategy was unrelated to comprehension in older children.

It is important to pursue *why* such age-related interactions might obtain. Consider the following examples. Interpersonal stimulation provides the newborn with direct experience during the developmental period when such contact seems to be primary; later, the same stimulation may actually inhibit the exercise of newly developing exploratory skills, and thereby circumscribe the child's experiences detrimentally. Similarly, to the extent that direct physical contact engages infant attention it may also enhance the infant's opportunities to acquire information (Korner, 1971, 1972; Yarrow et al., 1975). Alternatively, early physical contact may serve to establish a secure social relationship between infant and mother that promotes the child's exploration and, in turn, competence (Matas, Arend, & Sroufe, 1978). Likewise, maternal responsivity to infant distress seems to be effective in the first year and maternal responsivity to infants' other non-distress activities afterward, perhaps on account of the changing communicative value of distress and non-distress signals during early development. Frets and cries represent young infants' primary means of communication, and responsiveness to them should be salient during the first months of life, whereas other positive modes of vocal communication later supersede and responding to them in turn gains significance.

Generally speaking, adults' mediating their infants' intellectual experiences is more effective early in life, after which the child's own cognitive, linguistic, and exploratory abilities take over and adult mediation reciprocally declines. Thus, the value of particular didactics declines from 4 to 12 months (Bornstein, 1985). Carew (1980) provides a particularly clear illustration. She studied 12- to 36-month-old toddlers longitudinally, and across this time frame found a clear shift from the "parent as a source of intellectual experiences" to the "child as source of intellectual experiences" as the stronger predictor of children's 3-year Stanford Binet scores. Carew observed that caregivers' structuring language mastery experiences (e.g., by reading books or naming objects) early in their children's lives supplied the foundation as well as the impetus for self-direction in children's own intellectually rewarding experiences. After infancy, children's self-initiated play predicted their IQ; moreover, children's own ability to structure their intellectual experiences at 30 months reflected their earlier interactions, especially those that had focused on understanding and learning about the world.

In overview, experiences vary in their optimal developmental timing, and that timing is partly determined by unfolding perceptual, motor, and cognitive abilities of the child. It may be interesting to note as well that individual variation along dimensions other than developmental stage can be expected to contribute to the effectiveness of given experiences. For example, the phenomenology of individuals at the same developmental level but with different temperaments may condition them to integrate different experiences differently (Bornstein, Gaughran, & Homel, 1986). As a consequence, assessing whether a particular experience alone affects cognitive development is meaningless if characteristics of the individual, most notably developmental level, are omitted from consideration.

A MULTIVARIATE VIEW
OF EARLY INTELLECTUAL GROWTH

Dimensions of experience interact with developmental level to predict cognitive development in the child. In this section, we necessarily complicate this story by introducing specificity in a third variable, namely outcome.

Intelligence is multidimensional (Gardner, 1984; Guilford, 1967, 1979). It is improbable, therefore, that specific experiences at specific developmental times relate to *all* components of mature cognition. Rather, it is to be expected that interactions of experience and developmental level will have specific outcomes. In order to assess exact sensitive period relations properly, therefore, it is necessary to assess multiple outcomes for controlled predictor-by-developmental level contrasts.

A series of intervention studies conducted by Hunt and his colleagues

(1976) demonstrates the phenomenon of predictor-criterion specificity. Successive cohorts of orphaned infants were placed in different stimulation programs ranging from enhanced inanimate auditory/visual input to trained enrichment. Dependent measures, taken at different points of development, were based on the ordinal scales of Užgiris and Hunt (1975) and demonstrated several intervention-by-outcome interactions. As an example, comparisons between an audio-visual stimulation group and a group of infants receiving untutored human enrichment showed the groups to be matched on vocal imitation and spontaneous naming but the first to be delayed on aspects of object permanence.

Unfortunately, few studies distinguish among components of the dependent measure and even fewer directly address issues of differential prediction. One exception is a short-term longitudinal study conducted by Riksen-Walraven (1978). She implemented two types of training programs for mothers of 9-month-old infants. One group (randomly assigned) received instructions on the importance of sensory stimulation for infants (primarily visual stimulation, such as encouraging the child's attention to objects in the environment). The second group was given instructions on the importance of responding contingently to their infants' signals. Otherwise treatments between the groups were comparable. Two major outcomes, habituation and exploratory competence, were assessed in all infants 3 months later. Mothers trained on responsivity had infants who demonstrated higher levels of exploratory competence, whereas mothers trained on sensory stimulation had infants who habituated more efficiently. The significance of this study extends beyond the experimental effects obtained from intervention; the results demonstrate how particular environmental experiences influence particular outcomes.

Predictor-criterion specificity may exist even within what appears to be a single behavioral domain. Tamis-LeMonda and Bornstein (1986) partitioned maternal encouraging of infant attention into "dyadic" (a mother's focusing her infant's attention on herself) versus "extradyadic" (a mother's focusing her infant's attention on properties, objects, or events in the environment). Two- and 5-month-olds whose mothers were predominantly dyadic looked at their mothers more at both ages; infants whose mothers were predominantly extradyadic visually explored and tactually manipulated objects more at both ages. Similarly, specific linguistic experiences relate to specific dimensions of language development. Nelson (1977) conducted two sets of language intervention sessions, the first designed to promote question forms, the second to promote verb forms. The outcome of these manipulations was the selective increase in children's question production by the first group and verb use by the second group.

An experience-by-developmental level interaction, or sensitive period, seems to obtain in human mental development. Additionally, specific experiences applied at specific times appear to affect specific dimensions of cognition. We now turn to explore whether cognitive effects produced during sensitive periods are reversible and whether they are long-lasting.

CRITERIA OF SENSITIVE PERIODS IN HUMAN MENTAL DEVELOPMENT

How enduring are cognitive effects produced during sensitive periods? Are such effects reversible? Traditional "critical period" models have maintained, on these two criteria, that the effects of experience on development are long-lasting and, perhaps, irreversible.

Duration of Effects

Sources of information on the duration criterion tend to derive from naturalistic observations of mothers and their children and from intervention studies. Research in this area necessitates distinguishing the durations "short-term" from "long-lasting." Additionally, our understanding of the durability of effects will reflect the types of experiences being considered; for example, both touching and didactic stimulation may be maximally effective during limited periods of development, although their impacts may endure for unequal amounts of time. Nevertheless, research suggests that certain early experiences have long-term implications for cognitive development.

Much of the research we cited in the early portions of this chapter demonstrates that stimulation in infancy may endure a remarkably long time, with many effects spanning periods of years. However, conclusions regarding predictive relations between specific experiences of early life and later cognitive outcomes must be tempered by the argument that general consistency in the environment during development might maintain an effect. When experience is shown to influence cognitive performance, but the experience is also stable, it is unclear whether the critical influence of the experience was exerted when it first occurred with lasting effect or whether the experience has had continuing influence. As an example, Olson, Bates, and Bayles (1984) used path analysis to explore the influence of select maternal behaviors at 6, 13, and 24 months for infants' 24-month Bayley and PPVT performance. They found relations between 6-month maternal stimulation and 24-month infant performance, but also showed that these effects reflected continuity in maternal activity over time, over and above any unique contribution of early maternal behavior. Similarly, a number of studies have revealed attenuation of early effects when the contributions of later ones are partialled (Bradley & Caldwell, 1980; Gottfried & Gottfried, 1984). But, still other cases show clearly that early effects may make unique contributions to later development on their own; Bornstein (1985), for example, demonstrated relations between maternal didactic activities at 4 months and children's intelligence at 4 years, partialling from their association continuing maternal didactics. Thus, particular early experiences may predict later cognitive performance uniquely or indirectly.

Intervention studies also support long-term impact of early experiences. Intervention programs traditionally last for only limited time periods, and so the enduring effects they produce escape the continuous support critique. The durability of interventions depends on the definition of this temporal criterion. Gray, Ramsey, and Klaus's (1983) analysis of intervention in a group of disadvantaged children illustrates the not uncommon temporal patterning of effects. They found that early and relatively large increases in IQ soon leveled off and then declined when intervention was discontinued, although differences between control and treatment groups endured for years after intervention had ceased. Unfortunately, it is often difficult to compare across intervention studies since they vary so much in timing and in types of treatment. Beller's (1983) study of economically disadvantaged 4-year-olds demonstrated that no preschool, 1-year, and 2-year preschool intervention programs produced variable results, leading to the conclusion that no firm generalizations regarding intervention should be drawn based on only short periods of input. By contrast, Palmer (1983) clearly demonstrated that 45 hours of intervention at age 2 or 3 years produced gains in intelligence test scores that endured for more than a decade. The discrepancy between these two studies may be attributable to any number of variables: For example, in Beller's study the teacher-child ratio was 1:15, whereas in Palmer's the ratio was 1:1.

Despite many conditionals, Lazar (1983) reviewed 11 independent intervention studies and concluded that preschool programs typically increase standard intelligence test scores significantly even over 3- to 4-year periods following program termination and that preschool program graduates are less likely to be placed in special education or remedial classes, are more likely to meet school requirements, and are more likely to graduate from high school than are controls.

Reversibility of Effects

Early studies that found critical period effects to be irreversible derived from both natural and controlled manipulations of deprivation in animals. However, many of these studies were experimentally flawed, and where follow-up assessments have been made returns to normal levels of performance have been noted (e.g., Clarke & Clarke, 1976; Novak & Harlow, 1975). Moreover, the duration and severity of animal studies were often draconian; it may be that normal development requires only minimal stimulation, and the failure to meet this minimal threshold results in irreversible effects, but stimulation above a minimal threshold will not produce unalterable consequences.

Human data on the reversibility question tend to derive from cases of institutionalization. Here the notion is that early deprivation of stimulation would have irreversible consequences for cognitive development. However, among such populations there exists an acute dearth of information about alternative original causes of eventual retardation, and considerable research refutes a notion of irreversibility. A number of institutional studies demonstrate spontaneous improvements in IQ over time even within institutional situations. The Clarkes (1953) posit spontaneous delayed recovery from early adversity, whereas Tizard and Rees (1976) attribute reversals in cognitive retardation to varied experiences and increased frequency in verbal input at later ages. Case studies of human deprivation and recovery further limit any strong critical period claim. Both Davis (1947) and Koluchova (1972, 1976) reported about children reared in extreme isolation until 6 or 7 years of age who when assessed postpubertally gave IQ scores in the normal range. Likewise, many studies document improved development among early disadvantaged but adopted populations (Dennis, 1976; Scarr & Weinberg, 1976) and reinforce the notion of reversibility of early deprivation (Kagan, 1976, 1979).

If early experiences were determinative, positive and negative fluctuations in intelligence over the life course would be unlikely. However, large variations in individual IQ have been documented (McCall et al., 1973). Indeed, the Fels study found that some children varied over a range of 28 IQ points between 2½ and 17 years of age. Children who move from one social class to another also fluctuate in reading and mathematics performance depending on the direction of social change (Fogelman & Goldstein, 1976). In summing across this variety of findings, Clarke and Clarke (1976, p. 268) concluded that "it appears that there is virtually no psychosocial adversity to which some children have not been subjected, yet later recovered, granted a radical change in circumstances." Data like these militate against the criterion of irreversibility that underpins a strong critical period hypothesis in human mental development.

Before dismissing the strong form of the sensitive period hypothesis, it is useful to distinguish "behavioral recovery" from "neurological recovery." The celebrated case of Genie is illuminating in this regard (Curtiss, 1977). This young girl was deprived of normal linguistic input until about age 13; nevertheless, she eventually learned to communicate. However, close inspection of Genie's abilities, through dichotic listening tasks for example, demonstrated that Genie had language localized in the right hemisphere (even though she was right handed). When assessing sensitive period effects, therefore, it is necessary to take into account enormously intricate and powerful mechanisms at work in adaptation; for example, behavioral compensation may mask permanent underlying neurological alterations.

CONCLUSIONS

Is there a "sensitive period" in human mental development? If an experience-by-developmental level interaction can be taken to define a sensitive period, then the answer is *Yes*. The same experiences before, during, and after sensitive periods particularly in early life appear to yield different effects on human cognitive development.

This application of the sensitive-period concept is not so distinctive or unusual. In fact, recognition of sensitive periods in mental life may be in evidence in intuitive everyday exchanges between caretakers and their children. Parents commonly shift their activities with children over time in ways that match their children's developing abilities. Some well-known examples are increases in semantic and syntactic complexity, as well as shifts from physical stimulation to conversation and mutual role sharing (Papoušek, Papoušek, & Bornstein, 1985). These adjustments may stem from parents' sensitivity to their children's development, or they may be called for by children's changing levels of competence. Their implication is clear: The suitability and predictive efficacy of different kinds of cognitive experience for differential developmental levels — sensitive periods, in effect — is an acknowledged and long recognized fact of cognitive development.

ACKNOWLEDGMENTS

C.T.-L. was supported by a Helbein Scholarship and a University Fellowship from New York University. M.H.B. was supported by a research grant (HD20559) and by a Research Career Development Award (HD00521) from the National Institute of Child Health and Human Development and by a grant from the Center of Developmental Education and Research, Japan. This chapter was written during M.H.B.'s tenure as Visiting Professor at the Faculty of Education of the University of Tokyo. We thank M. Tress for assistance in preparation of the manuscript.

REFERENCES

Ainsworth, M. D. S. Infant development and mother-infant interaction among Ganda and American families. In P. Liederman, S. Tulkin, & A. Rosenfeld (Eds.), *Culture and infancy*. New York: Academic Press, 1977.

Ainsworth, M. D. S., & Bell, S. M. Mother-infant interaction and the development of competence. In K. J. Connolly & J. S. Bruner (Eds.), *The growth of competence*. New York: Academic Press, 1974.

Barnard, K. E., Bee, H. L., & Hammond, M. A. Home environment and cognitive development in a healthy, low-risk sample: The Seattle Study. In A. W. Gottfried (Ed.), *Home environment and early cognitive development*. Orlando, FL: Academic Press, 1984.

Barnes, S., Guttfreund, M., Satterly, D. & Wells, G. Characteristics of adult speech which predict children's language development. *Journal of Child Language*, 1983, *10*, 65-84.

Beckwith, L., Cohen, S., Kopp, C., Parmelee, A., & Marcy, T. Caregiver-infant interaction and early cognitive development in preterm infants. *Child Development*, 1976, *47*, 579-587.

Bell, S. M., & Ainsworth, M. D. S. Infant crying and maternal responsiveness. *Child Development*, 1972, *43*, 1171-1190.

Beller, E. K. The Philadelphia Study: The impact of preschool on intellectual and socioemotional development. In The Consortium for Longitudinal Studies, *As the twig is bent: Lasting effects of preschool programs*. Hillsdale, NJ: Erlbaum Associates, 1983.

Belsky, J., Goode, M. K., & Most, R. K. Maternal stimulation and infant exploratory competence: Cross-sectional, correlational, and experimental analyses. *Child Development*, 1980, *51*, 1163-1178.

Bornstein, M. H. How infant and mother jointly contribute to developing cognitive competence in the child. *Proceedings of the National Academy of Sciences*, 1985, *82*, 7470-7473.

Bornstein, M. H. *Social and didactic caretaking: Toward a multivariate model of interactive experiences that contribute to early mental development in the child*. Unpublished manuscript, New York University, 1986.

Bornstein, M. H., Gaughran, J., & Homel, P. Infant temperament: Theory, tradition, critique, and new assessments. In C. Izard & P. B. Read (Eds.), *Measurement of emotions in infants and children* (Vol. 2). New York: Cambridge University Press, 1986.

Bornstein, M. H., & Tamis-LeMonda, C. *Origins of cognitive skills in infants*. Poster presented at the International Conference on Infancy Studies, Los Angeles, 1986.

Bradley, R., & Caldwell, B. Early home environment and changes in mental test performance in children from 6-36 months. *Developmental Psychology*, 1976, *12*, 93-97. (a)

Bradley, R., & Caldwell, B. The relation of infants' home environment to mental test performance at 54 months: A follow up study. *Child Development*, 1976, *47*, 1172-1174. (b)

Bradley, R. H., & Caldwell, B. M. Competence and IQ among males and females. *Child Development*, 1980, *51*, 1140-1148.

Brossard, M., & Decarie, T. The effects of 3 kinds of perceptual-social stimulation on the development of institutionalized infants. *Early Child Development and Care*, 1971, *1*, 111-130.

Brown, R. How shall a thing be called? *Psychological Review*, 1958, *65*, 14-21.

Carew, J. V. Experience and the development of intelligence in young children at home and in day care. *Monographs of the Society for Research in Child Development*, 1980, Serial No. 187.

Casler, L. The effects of extra tactile stimulation on a group of institutionalized infants. *Genetic Psychology Monographs*, 1965, *71*, 137-175.

Clarke, A. D. B., & Clarke, A. M. How constant is the IQ? *Lancet*, 1953, *2*, 877-880.

Clarke, A. M., & Clarke, A. D. B. *Early experience: Myth and evidence*. New York: The Free Press, 1976.

Coates, D. L., & Lewis, M. Early mother-infant interaction and cognitive status as predictors of school performance and cognitive behavior in six-year olds. *Child Development*, 1984, *55*, 1219-1230.

Cross, T. Mothers' speech and its association with rate of linguistic development in young children. In N. Waterson & C. Snow (Eds.), *The development of communication*. New York: Wiley, 1978.

Curtiss, S. *Genie: A psycholinguistic study of a modern-day "wild child."* New York: Academic Press, 1977.

Davis, K. Final note on a case of extreme isolation. *American Journal of Sociology,* 1947, *52,* 432–437.

DeLoache, J. S., & Plaetzer, B. Tea for two: Joint mother-child symbolic play. In J. S. DeLoache & B. Rogoff (Chairs), *Collaborative cognition: Parents as guides in cognitive development.* Symposium conducted at the meeting of the Society for Research in Child Development, Toronto, Canada, 1985.

Dennis, W. Children of the creche: Conclusions and implications. In A. M. Clarke & A. D. B. Clarke (Eds.), *Early experience: Myth and evidence.* New York: The Free Press, 1976.

Elardo, R., Bradley, R. H., & Caldwell, B. M. A. A longitudinal study of the relation of infants' home environments to language development at age three. *Child Development,* 1977, *48,* 595–603.

Eysenck, H. J., & Kamin, L. *Intelligence: The battle for the mind.* London: Pan Books, 1981.

Farran, D., Ramey, C., & Campbell, F. *Social interactions of mothers and young children.* Paper presented to the Society of Research in Child Development, New Orleans, 1977.

Fogelman, K., & Goldstein, H. Social factors associated with changes in educational attainment between 7 and 11 years of age. *Educational Studies,* 1976, *2,* 95–109.

Furrow, D., Nelson, K., & Benedict, H. Mothers' speech to children and syntactic development: Some simple relationships. *Journal of Child Language,* 1979, *6,* 423–442.

Gardner, H. *Frames of mind: The theory of multiple intelligences.* New York: Basic Books, 1984.

Goldberg, S. Infant care and growth in urban Zambia. *Human Development,* 1972, *15,* 77–89.

Goldberg, S. Social competence in infancy: A model of parent-infant interaction. *Merrill-Palmer Quarterly,* 1977, *23,* 163–178.

Goldfarb, W. The effects of early institutional care on adolescent personality. *Journal of Experimental Education,* 1943, *12,* 106–29.

Gottfried, A. W., & Gottfried, A. E. Children of middle-SES families. In A. W. Gottfried (Ed.), *Home environment and early cognitive development.* Orlando, FL: Acadmic Press, 1984.

Gray, S. W., Ramsey, B. K., & Klaus, R. A. The early training project 1962-1980. In The Consortium for Longitudinal Studies, *As the twig is bent: Lasting effects of preschool programs.* Hillsdale, NJ: Erlbaum Associates, 1983.

Guilford, J. P. *The nature of human intelligence.* New York: McGraw-Hill, 1967.

Guilford, J. P. Intelligence isn't what it used to be: What to do about it. *Journal of Research and Development in Education,* 1979, *12,* 33–44.

Hoff-Ginsberg, E., & Shatz, M. Linguistic input and the child's acquisition of language. *Psychological Bulletin,* 1982, *92,* 3–26.

Horn, J. M., Loehlin, J. C., & Willerman, L. Intellectual resemblance among adoptive and biological relatives: The Texas Adoption Project. *Behavior Genetics,* 1979, *9,* 177–207.

Hunt, J. M., Modahessi, K. Ghodssi, M., & Akiyama, M. The psychological development of orphanage-reared infants: Interventions with outcomes. *Genetic Psychology Monographs,* 1976, *94,* 177–226.

Kagan, J. Resilience and continuity in psychological development. In A. M. Clarke & A. D. B. Clarke (Eds.), *Early experience: Myth and evidence.* New York: The Free Press, 1976.

Kagan, J. Family experience and the child's development. *American Psychologist,* 1979, *34,* 886–891.

Koluchova, J. Severe deprivation in twins: A case study. *Journal of Child Psychology and Psychiatry,* 1972, *13,* 107–114.

Koluchova, J. A report on the further development of twins after severe and prolonged deprivation. In A. M. Clarke & A. D. B. Clarke (Eds.), *Early experience: Myth and evidence.* New York: The Free Press, 1976.

Korner, A. Individual differences at birth: Implications for early experience and later development. *American Journal of Orthopsychiatry,* 1971, *41,* 608–619.

Korner, A. State as variable, as obstacle, and as mediator of stimulation in infant research. *Merrill-Palmer Quarterly,* 1972, *18,* 77–94.

Lagerspetz, K., Nygard, M., & Strondvik, C. The effects of training in crawling on the motor and mental development of infants. *Scandinavian Journal of Psychology,* 1971, *12,* 192–197.

Lazar, I. Discussion and implication of the findings. In The Consortium for Longitudinal Studies, *As the twig is bent: Lasting effects of preschool programs.* Hillsdale, NJ: Lawrence Erlbaum Associates, 1983.

Lewis, M., & Goldberg, S. Perceptual-cognitive development in infancy: A generalized expectancy model as a function of the mother-infant interaction. *Merrill-Palmer Quarterly,* 1969, *15,* 82–100.

Lockman, J. J., & McHale, J. P. *Infant and maternal exploration of objects.* Paper presented at the meetings of the Society for Research in Child Development, 1985.

Matas, L., Arend, R., & Sroufe, L. A. Continuity of adaptation in the second year: The relationship between quality of attachment and later competence. *Child Development,* 1978, *49,* 547–556.

McCall, R. B. Early predictors of later IQ: The search continues. *Intelligence,* 1981, *5,* 141–147.

McCall, R. B., Appelbaum, M., & Hogarty, P. S. Developmental changes in mental performance. *Monographs of the Society for Research in Child Development,* 1973, *42* (3, Whole No. 171).

McCarthy, D. *McCarthy scales of children's abilities.* New York: Psychological Corporation, 1972.

Moerk, E. L. Principles of interaction in language learning. *Merrill–Palmer Quarterly,* 1972, *18,* 229–257.

Nelson, K. Structure and strategy in learning to talk. *Monographs of the Society for Research in Child Development,* 1973, *38* (1-2, Serial No. 149).

Nelson, K. E. Facilitating children's syntax acquisition. *Developmental Psychology,* 1977, *13,* 101–107.

Nelson, K. E., Denninger, M., Kaplan, B., & Bonvillian, J. D. *Varied angles on how children progress in syntax.* Paper presented at the meeting of the Society for Research in Child Development, San Francisco, 1979.

Newport, E. L., Gleitman, H., & Gleitman, L. R. Mother, I'd rather do it myself: Some effects and noneffects of maternal speech style. In C. Snow & C. A. Ferguson (Eds.), *Talking to children: Language input and acquisition.* Cambridge: Cambridge University Press, 1977.

Novak, M. A., & Harlow, H. F. Social recovery of monkeys isolated for the first year of life: I. Rehabilitation and therapy. *Developmental Psychology,* 1975, *11,* 453–465.

O'Connel, B., & Bretherton, I. Toddlers play alone and with mother: The role of maternal guidance. In I. Bretherton (Ed.), *Symbolic play.* Orlando FL: Academic Press, 1984.

Olson, S. L., Bates, J. E., & Bayles, K. Mother-infant interaction and the development of individual differences in children's cognitive competence. *Developmental Psychology,* 1984, *20,* 166–179.

Olson, S. L., Bayles, K., & Bates, J. E. *Predicting competence at 6 from mother-infant interactions.* Paper presented at the International Conference of Infancy Studies, Los Angeles, 1986.

Palmer, F. H. The Harlem Study: Effects by type of training, age of training, and social class. In The Consortium for Longitudinal Studies, *As the twig is bent: Lasting effects of preschool programs.* Hillsdale, NJ: Lawrence Erlbaum Associates, 1983.

Papoušek, M., Papoušek, H., & Bornstein, M. H. The naturalistic vocal environment of young infants: On the significance of homogeneity and variability in parental speech. In T. M. Field & N. Fox (Eds.), *Social perception in infants.* Norwood, NJ: Ablex, 1985.

Riksen-Walraven, J. *Infant development, environmental variables and social class.* Unpublished paper, 1974.

Riksen-Walraven, J. M. Effects of caregiver behavior on habituation rate and self-efficacy in infants. *International Journal of Behavioral Development,* 1978, *1,* 105–130.

Rose, S. Enhancing visual recognition memory in pre-term infants. *Developmental Psychology,* 1980, *16,* 85–92.

Royce, J. M., Darlington, R. B., & Murray, H. W. Pooled analyses: Findings across studies. In The Consortium for Longitudinal Studies, *As the twig is bent: Lasting effects of preschool programs.* Hillsdale, NJ: Lawrence Erlbaum Associates, 1983.

Scarr, S., & Weinberg, R. A. IQ test performance of black children adopted by white families. *American Psychologist,* 1976, *31,* 726–739.

Shatz, M. The relationship between cognitive processes and the development of communicative skills. In C. B. Keasey (Ed.), *Nebraska symposium on motivation* (Vol. 25). Lincoln, NB: University of Nebraska Press, 1978.

Shatz, M. On mechanisms of language acquisition: Can features of the communicative environment account for development? In L. Gleitman & E. Wanner (Eds.), *Language acquisition: The state of the art.* New York: Cambridge University Press, 1982.

Siegel, L. S. Infant tests as predictors of cognitive and language development at two years. *Child Development,* 1981, *52,* 545–557.

Siegel, L. S. Early cognitive and environmental correlates of language development at 4 years. *International Journal of Behavioral Development,* 1982, *5,* 433–444.

Siegel, L. S. Home environmental influences on cognitive development in preterm and full-term children during the first 5 years. In A. W. Gottfried (Ed.), *Home environmental and early cognitive development.* Orlando, FL: Academic Press, 1984.

Smith, C. B., Adamson, L. B., & Bakeman, R. *Interactional predictors of early language.* Paper presented at the International Conference on Infancy Studies, Los Angeles, 1986.

Solkoff, N., & Matuzsak, D. Tactile stimulation and behavioral development among low birthweight infants. *Child Psychiatry and Human Development,* 1975, *6,* 33–37.

Solkoff, N., Sumner, Y., Weintraub, D., & Blase, B. Effects of handling on the subsequent development of premature infants. *Developmental Psychology,* 1969, *1,* 765–768.

Tamis-LeMonda, C., & Bornstein, M. H. *Two kinds of maternal responsivity in relation to infant exploration and information processing.* Paper presented at the Jean Piaget Society, Philadelphia, 1986.

Tizard, B., & Rees, J. A comparison of the effects of adoption, restoration to the natural mother, and continued institutionalization on the cognitive development of four-year old children. In A. M. Clarke & A. D. B. Clarke (Eds.), *Early experience: Myth and evidence.* New York: The Free Press, 1976.

Tomasello, M., & Mannle, S. Pragmatics of sibling speech to one-year-olds. *Child Development,* 1985, *56,* 911–917.

Tulkin, S. & Covitz, F. *Mother-infant interaction and intellectual functioning at age 6.* Paper presented at the Biennial Meeting of the Society for Research in Child Development, Denver, 1975.

Užgiris, I. C., & Hunt, J. McV. *Assessment in infancy: Ordinal scales of psychological development.* Urbana, IL: University Illinois Press, 1975.

Vibbert, M., & Bornstein, M. H. *Maternal social and didactic interactions and their 13-month-olds' language and play.* Unpublished manuscript, New York University, 1986.

Wachs, T. D. The relationship of infants' physical environment to their Binet performance at 2½ years. *International Journal of Behavioral Development,* 1978, *1,* 51–65.

Wachs, T. D. Proximal experience and early cognitive—intellectual development: The physical environment. *Merrill-Palmer Quarterly,* 1979, *25,* 3–41.

Wachs, T. D. Proximal experience and early cognitive-intellectual development: The social environment. In A. W. Gottfried (Ed.), *Home environment and early cognitive development.* Orlando, FL: Academic Press, 1984.

Wachs, T. D., & Gruen, G. E. *Early experience and human development.* New York: Plenum Press, 1982.

Wohlwill, J. F. The concept of experience: S or R? *Human Development,* 1973, *16,* 90–107.

Yarrow, L. J., Rubenstein, J., & Pederson, F. *Infant and environment.* New York: Wiley, 1975.

9 Relevance of the Notion of a Critical Period to Language Acquisition

Catherine Snow
Harvard University Graduate School of Education

INTRODUCTION

The notion that there is a critical period for language development is a widely accepted one. The woman-in-the-street is convinced that her children can learn a foreign language more quickly, easily, and well than she or her husband, and if pressed would attribute these age differences to the adult's lack of "flexibility" in learning new rules, new sounds, and new ways of thinking. Introductory psychology textbooks present a version of the same idea phrased more specifically in terms of neuropsychology, or biological limits on learning,

> There is an important and familiar problem we have ignored thus far — language learning is very much easier in children than in adults. This and related facts are often regarded as evidence that there is a *critical period* for language learning. This period is thought to extend from roughly three months to puberty. According to the hypothesis, some characteristics of the brain change as the critical period draws to its close so that later language learning (both of the first language and of later ones) becomes more difficult. (Gleitman, 1981, p. 403)

> Several phenomena suggest that there is a *critical period* for language learning in humans, just as there is for the development of bird song in certain sparrows. Evidence comes from studies of isolated children, of second-language learning, and of recovery from aphasia. (ibid., p. 411)

In fact, though, despite the seeming simplicity of the claims made by the woman-in-the-street or the introductory text, the hypothesis that there exists a critical period for language acquisition turns out to be a very complex one, involving many ancillary claims. Accordingly, it is an extremely complicated matter to evaluate evidence marshalled in favor of this hypothesis, since it is rarely absolutely clear which version of the hypothesis with which set of ancillary claims is being evaluated.

In this chapter I attempt to assess the evidence relevant to the hypothesis that a critical period for language learning exists. In order to determine what evidence might be relevant, I first present alternate formulations of the critical period hypothesis, and the specific claims associated with them. I then present and evaluate the following kinds of available evidence: data on the speed and nature of language acquisition outside the normal childhood period, whether in monolinguals or in multilinguals: data on the reversibility of the learning that occurs during the hypothesized critical period, both of speech sound perception and of phonological production: and data on physiological differences in brain processes for late versus early learned languages. The goal is to go beyond a simple acceptance or rejection of the critical period hypothesis for language learning, to a formulation of it that is sufficiently differentiated to make clear what data are relevant and where more data are needed in evaluating the hypothesis.

THE CRITICAL PERIOD
IN THEORIES OF LANGUAGE DEVELOPMENT

Formulations of the Critical Period Hypothesis

Many different formulations of the critical period hypothesis can be distinguished.[1] Perhaps it is useful here to formulate a strong version, before going on to consider specific less sweeping claims and evidence against which to test these various claims. In common with critical period hypotheses (CPH) for other domains of development, the strongest formulation of the CPH for language involves the following claims:

(1) That there is a period during which the organism is particularly responsive to environmental input of a particular sort (in this case, input consisting of environmental language).

(2) That the same amount and kind of input that during the critical period

---

[1] Within the field of language development, the term "critical period" has been used almost exclusively, although it has sensibly been suggested (Oyama, 1979) that "sensitive period" would be more accurate, a suggestion honored in the title of this book. The terms "critical period" and "CPH" will, however, be used in this chapter in accordance with the conventions of the language field.

supports language development is ineffective outside the critical period in producing the same learning.

(3) That the learning that occurs during the critical period is stable and irreversible by subsequent non-sensitive period learning.

(4) That the existence and timing of the critical period is controlled by biological maturation; for language, the relevant dimensions of maturation have been variously hypothesized to be myelination (Scovel, 1981), hemispheric specialization (Lenneberg, 1967), and early maturing neuronal circuits (Walsh & Diller, 1981).

(5) That, since it is biologically controlled, the critical period and its consequences for learning during and after the relevant period of maturation are universal within the species.

Some more specific ancillary claims about language development that can be derived from the above general claims include the following:

(1) Outside the critical period, language acquisition stops. This claim has two versions: (a) First language acquisition must be complete within the critical period; thus, for example, retardates whose acquisition is very slow will simply stop at whatever point they have reached when the critical period ends. (b) Second language acquisition after the critical period is impossible; this claim is clearly too strong, and has not been seriously made.

(2) Outside the critical period, language acquisition slows down. Thus, second language learning after the end of the critical period is predicted to be slower than first language acquisition or than second language acquisition during the critical period.

(3) Outside the critical period, language acquisition occurs but never to fully native-like levels. Incomplete acquisition may be claimed to be true for the entire linguistic system, or to be restricted to components of it. It is, for example, widely accepted as regards pronunciation in foreign languages acquired after the critical period, though less widely accepted for other domains (e.g., syntax or the lexicon).

(4) Outside the critical period, language acquisition is a different process, not a natural "triggering" of innate language structures, but a process guided more by conscious application of learning strategies, and one that requires formal training. Krashen (1980) has lexified this claim, reserving in his writings the term "acquisition" for natural language development such as young children engage in, and "learning" for the more formal and conscious process presumed to be typical of adult learners. I do not endorse this distinction in terms nor the conceptual distinction it alludes to, since in fact both first and second language acquisition at both earlier and later ages seem to combine unconscious with more intentional learning processes (Snow, 1986). Accord-

ingly, acquisition and development are used interchangeably in this chapter. The hypothesis that there are qualitative differences in the process of language learning during and after the critical period remains open to testing, however.

(5) A different version of the claim that noncritical period language learning is qualitatively different involves the hypothesis that it occurs in a different part of the brain from critical period language learning. Although we recognize that for most right-handed adults language is primarily localized in the left hemisphere, it has been hypothesized that later learned languages are more likely to be bilaterally represented. Differences in brain localization would, of course, imply differences in processing of earlier and later learned languages.

(6) Finally, a very weak version of the critical period hypothesis for language restricts it to first language acquisition, claiming that a first language must be learned during the critical period, but making no claims about the speed and or quality of subsequent language learning. This claim actually proposes a model much like that well attested for sensitive periods in visual system development: that during the sensitive period experience (in that case of seeing binocularly, in this case of learning language) has an organizing effect on the brain that subsequently renders it fully capable of supporting further functioning of a similar sort (see Hirsch & Tieman, this volume). In contrast, most versions of the critical period hypothesis proffered and discussed within the language literature emphasize the control of learning by brain maturation, not the control of brain maturation by learning.

When is the Critical Period for Language?

So far, I have not specified exactly what age range is included in the critical period for language development. In fact, a major source of ambiguity in interpreting data as relevant to the critical period hypothesis is that the temporal limits of the proposed period have often been specified either from behavioral data or from data on parameters of brain maturation, whereas a rigorous formulation of the CPH requires that data from both sources converge on the delimitation of a single period of sensitivity.

Lenneberg's (1967) classic formulation of the CPH for language development derived data from both behavior and biology. His interpretation of findings from a variety of research fields led him to argue that the critical period for language starts at about 1 year of age and ends at puberty, when most parameters of brain maturation have achieved adult levels. Lenneberg proposed that hemispheric specialization, or cerebral dominance, was fully established by puberty, though still malleable before, and that the greater equipotentiality of the brain (associated with its not yet having achieved adult levels on the various parameters of growth) before puberty accounted for the prepubertal child's greater capacities to learn a first language, to recover language after brain trauma leading to aphasia, and to learn foreign languages. (The basis for these empirical claims will be reviewed in later sections.) Lenneberg's formulation was widely accepted (e.g., Krashen, 1975; Scovel, 1969; Seliger, 1978), and even led to hypotheses that the inability to develop a native-like accent in a foreign language after puberty was somehow evolutionarily desirable, since it prevented breeding males from "passing" in nonnative groups (Hill, 1972). (The value to the group of this constraint on passing is perhaps arguable; its value to the breeding male seems, however, negative. On Hill's own argument, males who could pass as natives of several groups would have bred more widely and transmitted their "foreign-accent genes" more successfully than males who suffered from the critical period-induced constraint.)

Lenneberg's timing of the critical period depended heavily on his interpretation of evidence suggesting that cerebral dominance is malleable until puberty. Subsequent reanalyses of data Lenneberg reviewed (Krashen, 1973), as well as analyses of results from more recently introduced techniques for assessing hemispheric specialization, have led to the now widely accepted conclusion that dominance and left hemisphere specialization for the type of sequential processing crucial to language are present at birth. These data are supported by demonstrations showing anatomical differences between right and left hemispheres as early as 18 weeks of fetal life, with relevant structures in the left hemisphere already larger (see Kinsbourne, 1981, and Whitaker, Bub, & Leventer, 1981, for reviews). Thus, the convergence between the biological and the behavioral data on which Lenneberg's argument rested vanishes, if it is maintained that hemispheric specialization is the crucial biological process determining the timing of the critical period. It is, of course, still possible that plasticity is characteristic of the period of brain growth, but these data suggest that plasticity cannot be linked to a growing specialization of the left hemisphere for language functions.

Furthermore, other aspects of brain maturation may be relevant to establishing a critical period. Scovel (1981) argues that myelination may be the crucial factor. Although there is evidence that myelination continues over the first decade of life, there do not seem to be good data connecting deficiencies in myelination to deficiencies in language acquisition, premature myelination to an early end to acquisition, or any other aspect of language learning or language use to any part of the myelination process.[2] In other words, the proposal rests on pure speculation.

---

[2]As John Locke has pointed out to me (personal communication), unmyelinated fibers are, furthermore, perfectly capable of functioning, only somewhat noisier and faster to fatigue than myelinated fibers. Information about what percentage of the adult level of myelination is needed for adult-like performance is, likewise, unavailable (Locke, 1983).

Lenneberg's (1967) linking hemispheric specialization to brain maturation rested on his presumption that brain maturation was essentially unidimensional, that a single growth curve characterized change for all the different important variables of cerebral maturation. Whitaker et al. (1981) have reviewed the evidence showing that this view is incorrect — that significant differences in growth patterns characterize different cerebral regions, and even different cortical layers within regions. Despite the differences among different regions and layers, however, Whitaker et al. argue convincingly that none of the brain growth data are easily related to parameters of language development, simply because all growth variables have reached close to their adult values by age 5. In other words, relying on brain growth as the biological process that times the critical period would predict a critical period ending at about 5; this is not an age at which any sharp discontinuities in language acquisition can be observed, however.

A further hypothesized dimension of brain maturation that may be relevant to a critical period is intrahemispheric specialization (Scovel, 1981). As the differential localization of lesions leading to Broca versus Wernicke aphasias clearly demonstrates, there is considerable specialization of function at different sites within one cerebral hemisphere. The degree to which the intrahemispheric specialization is malleable, and the age limits on its malleability, are unknown. Obler, Albert, Goodglass, and Benson (1978) found that Broca aphasics (anterior lesions) were, on average, 12 years younger than Wernicke aphasics (posterior lesions). This age difference may suggest some intrahemispheric shifting or increasing specialization of functions continuing on through middle age. Such findings are indeed intriguing, but hardly relevant to any serious formulation of the CPH, since the behavioral data to be explained typically show shifts in middle childhood, not late middle age!

The classic formulation of the critical period for language places its end at puberty, and much of the research directed to testing the CPH therefore includes pubertal children as a critical test case. In reviewing the literature relevant to the CPH, it is important to remember that the end-point of the critical period is as much a matter at empirical issue as is the very existence of the critical period. Neither the physiological nor the behavioral data currently available give a clear basis for identifying the onset or offset of the critical period. However, most researchers whose work is reviewed here assumed that puberty marks the end of the critical period for language acquisition.[3]

---

[3]While popular belief in the claims of the CPH have been emphasized here, Jean Berko Gleason has pointed out (personal communication) that the CPH also conflicts with some commonly held beliefs. The CPH predicts that late maturers (i.e., boys) will have a longer period of plasticity, and thus be better language learners. In fact, the generally held view is that girls are better learners, both of first and of later languages.

Evidence for a Critical Period in Language

What kind of evidence could be used to test the critical period hypothesis? Ideally, we would like to find evidence for an irreversible change in the process, speed, ease, and/or product of language acquisition associated with a change in some relevant parameter of brain growth or function, equivalent perhaps to the evidence that post-hatching exposure to estrogens in the male zebra finch controls the development of the song nuclei in the brain (Gurney & Koniski, 1981), and thereby makes possible the learning of species-specific songs. In the absence of any clear cut demonstration of this sort, though, we must look to weaker sources of evidence:

(1) Evidence for changes in acquisition, either speed, process, product, or all three, that are demonstrably *not* the result of changes in environmental factors. Evidence that such changes are irreversible would strengthen them as support for the CPH.

(2) Evidence for major changes in components of brain growth or development that are demonstrably relevant to language. If (1) and (2) also converge in timing, support for the CPH for language development would be quite strong.

In the following sections, three basic sets of data relevant to the CPH are reviewed: first, data about the course of language learning that occurs later than the "normal" period for primary language acquisition; second, data about the reversibility of learning, specifically of speech perception and speech articulation, that has occurred during primary language acquisition; and, third, data about the localization in the brain of earlier versus later learned languages. These three sets constitute, not all the kinds of data that are potentially relevant to the CPH, but rather all that are available. In the final section, the conclusions that can at this point be drawn about the critical period hypothesis are outlined.

Acquisition Outside the Normal Period

The kind of evidence most widely available and most often cited in support of the CPH for language derives from situations where language is learned past childhood, beyond the period when first language acquisition normally occurs. Circumstances that necessitate language acquisition after early childhood include (a) loss of language through brain injury and the subsequent need to relearn it, (b) cases where, because of deafness or severe neglect or other unusual circumstances, children do not have the opportunity to learn language at the normal time, and (c), most frequently, second language acquisition. For each of these cases, it is possible to ask the question whether post-childhood acquisition is as fast, as effortless, as successful, and similar in process, to normal first language acquisition. For each case, it is also crucial to remember, though, that circumstances in addition to age differentiate the post-childhood language learner from the normally developing child. Aphasics are relearning language with a damaged brain. Wolf children very likely have physiological, cognitive, and emotional consequences of the early experience that prevented their learning language, and may have suffered from organic or cognitive deficits prior to their isolation. Hearing-impaired children are typically not learning their first language (ASL) from their parents, since their hearing parents are unlikely to know it. And second language learners approach the second language with knowledge of a first language (which may cause interference as well as provide some help in analyzing the new language) and typically in a very different social situation from that of the first language learner.

Recovery from aphasia.   One of the situations that gives rise to the need for language acquisition outside the normal period and context of language development is occasioned by brain trauma, usually to the left hemisphere which is the principal site for language in most right-handed individuals. Depending on the amount and locus of damage, left hemisphere trauma may result in aphasia, or the reduction of the language faculty. A major stimulus to Lenneberg's formulation of the CPH in 1967 was the conclusion by Basser (1962), based on a number of clinical observations, that traumas which in adults produce severe and lasting aphasic symptoms were, if incurred in childhood, followed by transitory and less severe loss of language. It was proposed that children's recovery from such symptoms indicated the potential of young right hemispheres to learn language, a potential which is presumably lost by the end of childhood, such that adults can no longer relearn language after an aphasia-inducing injury. However, more recent reviews of the sequelae to brain trauma indicate that children are as impaired as adults following injuries of similar severity and locus (Robinson, 1981). Even children who appear to have recovered fully from head trauma show persistent word finding difficulties (Gilbert, Mitchell, Brown, & Chow, 1985). Studies of children's language acquisition after left hemispherectomies very early in life have found considerable learning but also permanent linguistic deficits (Dennis, 1979, 1980; Dennis & Kohn, 1975; Dennis & Whitaker, 1976, 1977), suggesting that even the very young child's right-hemispheric potential for acquisition is not equivalent to that of the left hemisphere.

Indeed, other types of evidence on the development of functions associated differentially with the left and right hemispheres now converge on the conclusion that differential functioning of the hemispheres is present from birth. Evidence from behavioral studies suggests that hand preference is identifiable in infants of a few months of age (Caplan & Kinsbourne, 1976) and that dichotic ear preference is well established early in childhood (Kinsbourne & Hiscock, 1977; Woods, 1984), perhaps as early as 3 to 4 months (Best, Hoffman, & Glanville, 1982). These behavioral indices are supported by physiological evidence of hemispheric differences in evoked potential in infancy (Molfese, Freeman, & Palermo, 1975) and from anatomical findings of left/right hemisphere asymmetries in neonates (Wada, Clarke, & Hamm, 1975). Thus, the Lennebergian notion that language lateralization is a maturational phenomenon related to the plasticity of the infant brain must be rejected (Kinsbourne, 1975). The cortical hemispheres seem to be well differentiated very early in life in terms of their preferred information-processing modes; what develops is evidently the ability to recruit the most efficient and appropriate mode of analysis, and thus hemisphere, in solving the problems the environment sets.

The fact of congenital hemispheric specialization does not obviate, however, the possibility of greater plasticity in the younger than the older brain. Such plasticity may, for example, derive from the development of intrahemispheric (rather than interhemispheric) specialization. As early as 1942, Guttman argued that the young left hemisphere was less specialized than the mature left hemisphere, basing his conclusion on the observation that all aphasics under 14 years of age show the same symptoms and patterns of recovery, regardless of the site of the injury. Differentiated aphasias (e.g., Broca's versus Wernicke's) were not found in patients younger than 14. Whatever the value of Guttman's claim, evidence for plasticity in the developing human brain is incontrovertible; for example, hemidecorticated infants develop close to normal language capacities whether the hemispherectomy is left or right — a result that could never be expected after hemispherectomy in adulthood (Mehler, Morton, & Jusczyk, 1984). However, such plasticity is demonstrated in childhood only after structural damage, and extrapolations to the intact brain are hard to make (Kinsbourne, 1981).

"Wolf" children.   Children who are excluded from normal human contact and caretaking naturally fail to learn language. Do such children, if restored to normal social settings and perhaps provided with remediation, learn language normally later in life? The most famous cases include Victor, the Wild Boy of Aveyron (Lane, 1977), and Genie, a 20th century American child discovered at age 13 (Curtiss, 1977). Neither of these children learned to speak normally, though both made some progress in communication, in word learning, and in sign language, and Victor developed considerable skills with reading, as well as writing and oral comprehension. Unfortunately, it is impossible to determine whether these children, and others with similar though less well documented histories, were of normal intelligence and language-learning capacity prior to their isolation. Their failure to learn at an advanced age may simply be a reflection of some organic incapacity to ac-

quire language. One case, of Isabelle (Davis, 1947, cited in Brown, 1958), the 6-year-old daughter of an isolated deaf mute, showed recovery to normal language skills and IQ within 2 years after remediation was started, suggesting that deficits in language experience before 6 years of age may not be irreversible in normal children.

In the case of Genie, the explanation of preisolation cognitive deficits seems somewhat unlikely. The small amount of evidence available about her early months suggests that she was born with normal capacities and that her early development was normal. Furthermore, elaborate testing after her discovery revealed that Genie showed very poor left-hemisphere functioning, although she often scored suprisingly well on tasks of right-hemisphere functioning. The language that Genie learned was quite similar in the pattern of deficits to that acquired by left-hemispherectomized children, i.e., much stronger in vocabulary and in comprehension than in syntax or in production, leading Curtiss (1977) to conclude that Genie's left hemisphere was nonfunctional. It is possible, then, that the unavailability to Genie of linguistic stimuli throughout her childhood was responsible for the atrophy of left hemisphere functioning, and resultant inability to acquire language normally. However, it is also possible that Genie, like a small percentage of normal adults, would have had language localized in the right hemisphere even with a normal childhood (Kinsbourne, 1981).

Non-native language acquisition.   By far the most voluminous source of data on language learning outside the normal period derives from studies of second language acquisition. As with recovery from aphasia, the contrast of interest compares childhood second language learners to adults. The popularly accepted view of this contrast suggests that children learn second languages quickly, automatically, effortlessly, and to a level indistinguishable from that of native speakers, whereas adults even with the help of specially designed materials and trained teachers learn slowly, with great effort, and imperfectly. Such a picture is, of course, precisely consonant with the predictions of the CPH.

Research results fail to confirm this picture, however. Second language learning appears, upon more careful examination, to be slow, effortful, and often less than perfectly successful for younger as well as older learners. In fact, speed of second language acquisition seems in general to be positively correlated with age. For most domains of acquisition studied, older learners acquire more in the same amount of time than younger learners (e.g., Asher & Price, 1967; Ekstrand, 1976; Fathman, 1975; Snow & Hoefnagel-Hohle, 1978; Stevens, 1984; see Krashen, Long, & Scarcella, 1982; and McLaughlin, 1984, for reviews.) The one exception to this generalization is pronunciation (see the following).

Of course, it is not the case that age is the only factor of influence in speed of second language learning. It is well documented that such factors as amount of exposure, quality of language exposure, motivation to learn, desire to identify with the second-language group, tolerance for the psychological stress associated with functioning in two cultural settings, and language aptitude play important roles as well. It is, thus, possible that these factors all make acquisition easier for older learners and mask the maturationally determined superiority of younger learners. For the populations studied so far, though, this explanation could not be correct. All the additional factors would, in fact, work in favor of the younger learners, who nonetheless end up learning more slowly. Consider the 51 English speakers aged 3 to 60 learning Dutch in Holland, who were studied by Snow and Hoefnagel-Hohle (1978, 1982). The children were all in school, receiving a minimum of 30 hours a week of Dutch input, while the adults were typically working at home or in an environment where English was frequently used even by native Dutch speakers. The children were seeking the majority of their social contacts among Dutch speakers who had little control of English, whereas the adults' contacts were either with compatriots or with Dutch adults who preferred to use English. Although motivation was not systematically assessed, the children's school success depended on their Dutch learning, whereas the adults' professional functioning could be accomplished in English. The children's acquisition was supported by activities they engaged in daily at school, and by much direct interaction with teachers, whereas the adults had access to at most an hour a week of instruction (see Burling, 1981, and Cochrane, 1977, for similar reports). Thus, on all factors that might be thought to explain differences in speed of acquisition, the adults actually would be expected to be at a disadvantage, yet they learned faster during the early stages of acquisition. Thus it seems incontrovertible that older learners are faster at learning second languages than younger learners – an unsurprising conclusion unless one assumes a priori that language is different from other complex learning tasks human beings face.

An alternative way of looking at age differences, suggested by the findings on pronunciation, is to consider ultimate attainment rather than speed of acquisition. Here, even for domains outside phonology, the data accord better with the predictions of the CPH. Paradoxically, given their early head starts, older learners' ultimate level of attainment is likely to be lower than younger learners'. After more than 3-5 years of exposure to the second language, learners who had started learning in childhood have been shown to perform better on sentence comprehension through white noise (Oyama, 1976), syntactic correctness in writing (Patkowski, 1980), and grammaticality judgements (Johnson, 1986). With respect to the predictions of the CPH, it is particularly important to consider the curve of the decline with age. The only good data on this come from Johnson, since the other studies tended to compare only "older" to "younger" learners, split wherever the current version of the CPH suggests. Johnson found a linear decline with age after 7, but no difference between natives and pre 7-year-old learners (when one outlier was excluded). She points out that within-group variability increases with age, as overall performance declines, and it is clear from her tables that the best 17- to 39-year-old learners were as good as the best 11- to 15-year-old learners and as the worst 8-10 learners, but that the worst older learners were much worse. Furthermore, the onset of decline in the Johnson study (age 7-8) does not match the age in the other studies cited above that differentiates native-like from nonnative-like achievement (13-15), nor does it coincide with any particularly salient change in brain functioning.

While the results of these few studies of ultimate attainment are interesting, they all have some limitations and leave many questions unanswered. First, the language skills tested are, except for pronunciation, fairly remote from normal language use. Patkowski's task was perhaps the most ecologically valid (learners' written essays were rated for syntactic correctness by native speakers), though the effects of schooling may have enhanced the performance of younger learners on a task like writing. Metalinguistic judgements are known to show greater individual variation even in monolingual populations than sound production or comprehension skills. The degree of bilingualism of the subjects (known to affect performance in tasks requiring lexical access) was not controlled. It is likely (though not necessarily the case) that younger learners of the second language were ultimately *less* proficient in their first language, and thus perhaps able to perform better in tasks such as Oyama's. Finally, the existence of late learners who can achieve native-like levels of proficiency in a second language needs to be accounted for. Perhaps further study of such gifted language learners will reveal whether they count as evidence against the CPH, or whether their acquisition of the second language is somehow quite different from that of young children.

Pronunciation of the second language is a domain in which the pattern of older learners' temporary superiority in the acquisition of vocabulary, syntax, morphology, and fluency is broken. Some studies report that older learners' accents in the second language are poorer than those of younger learners, while others report no difference or even transient advantages for older learners. These inconsistencies may be explainable as a function of how far into the acquisition period the accent is assessed. Studies of the very early stages of acquisition suggest differences favoring older learners (e.g., Snow & Hoefnagel-Hohle, 1978; Politzer & Weiss, 1969; Winitz, 1981), whereas measures taken somewhat later in the acquisition period show no differences (Snow & Hoefnagel-Hohle, 1977). Assessments of accent very long after initial acquisition typically find that correctness of accent is negatively related to age at first exposure to the second language, suggesting that younger learners are more likely eventually to lose their accents than older learners (Asher & Garcia, 1969; Oyama, 1976; Tahta, Wood, & Lowenthal, 1981). This finding is intriguing because it suggests that full acquisition of the phonology of a language occurs over a period of several years, not just during the first two or three years that are typically considered sufficient for complete learning (see Lieberman, 1985, for similar findings on first language articulation, and Flege & Eefting, 1985, for first language speech perception).

Of greatest relevance to the topic of this chapter, the facts of the age differences in second language learning cannot be easily matched to any predictions from a biologically based critical period. First, the age differences found are statistical, not absolute. Some young learners retain their accents, and some older learners lose theirs totally, suggesting that a categorical change in brain state is an unlikely explanation. Second, the degree of success of adults in acquiring a good second language accent can be increased greatly with training in, for example, programs that enforce a period of listening without speaking (Neufeld, 1978). Third, the patterns of decline in native-like pronunciation with age of first exposure to the second language documented by Oyama (1976, see above) is a gradual, linear decline, not a decline characterized by an abrupt change of rate such as the critical period would predict. Fourth, the age differences that occur emerge only after a couple of years of second language learning. It is hard to relate such slow-to-emerge differences in learning to any parameter of brain growth or development.

Thus, language acquisition in childhood seems not to outstrip second language learning in adulthood, nor necessarily to be more complete. Is it perhaps different in process? Although rather little evidence is available, all that can be mustered suggests that child and adult second language learners are very similar to one another in terms of the errors they make, the strategies they use, and the order of acquisition they follow (Cook, 1973; Ervin-Tripp, 1976; Snow & Hoefnagel-Hohle, 1978; Snow, Smith, & Hoefnagel-Hohle, 1980).

Studies of age differences in second language acquisition do not support the notion of a childhood period during which language learning is relatively fast, effortless, and successful, nor during which it is different in process from adult language learning. It is primarily in the domain of pronunciation that the age differences found even go in the right direction to accord with such a hypothesis, and there the details of the differences found cannot be related to any existent information about biological factors in development.

Deaf children's acquisition of sign.   If severe hearing impairments prevent children born to normally hearing parents from being able to process the parental language, such children may spend the first several years of their lives able to engage in little or no language learning. Only at entry to school would such children (on the assumption their parents have not learned a sign

language to use in communicating with them) typically start to receive significant amounts of exposure to a sign language. These children, then, constitute
another natural experiment in the acquisition of language beyond the normal
period. As is typically the case with such natural experiments, many of the
data one would like to have are unavailable, and only tentative conclusions
can be drawn.

Studies of the knowledge of American Sign Language (ASL) by hearing-
impaired adults who use it as their first and dominant language have compared groups that vary on two dimensions: the age of their first exposure to
ASL, and the degree of nativeness of their ASL models. All the subjects were
at the time of testing dominant ASL users, but they varied in the degree to
which they controlled the complex morphology of ASL. For movement
verbs, for example, hand shape is a morphological marker of the moving
class, and the path, direction and manner of movement are all marked in specific ways drawn from a small number of possibilities. Furthermore, there
are rules for combining the various morphemes that sometimes obscure their
separability. Newport (1984; see also Newport, 1981; Supalla, 1982) found
that age of first exposure to ASL (birth, for those whose parents were deaf
themselves, age 4-6, or after age 12) was highly related to how well adult signers produced and comprehended this morphological system. Late learners
were much more likely to use unanalyzed or 'frozen' signs: they constitute errors very different from those made by the youngest learners as children.
These results accord well with those from Woodward (1973), who also found
that certain rules of ASL were learned only by those who had acquired the
language before age 6.

Furthermore, Newport (1981, 1984) argues that native signers end up with
much the same system whether or not their primary models were native signers. Thus, even those deaf children learning ASL from late-learning parents,
whose language is characterized by much frozen, unanalyzed morphology,
acquire fully productive morphological systems. Newport interprets these
findings in the context of a hypothesis about how pidgin languages become
creoles — that the acquisition of a language by a child, even a language which
is impoverished of natural language characteristics in its presentation, results
in a restructuring such that what is learned is more "natural" and "language
like" than the input (Bickerton, 1981). For some reason, the restructuring
that Newport describes for ASL adds far more morphological richness than
is ever added to spoken Creoles. Spoken Creoles typically have rather reduced morphologies, characterized neither by elaborate inflectional options
nor by classification systems nor by very rich sets of derivational rules.

It is not clear, though, that one can interpret the restructuring of either basic ASL or of a spoken pidgin into a richer, more natural Creole as an effect
that occurs only when the system is filtered through the mind of a very young
learner. Sankoff (1979) denies that creolization of Tok Pisin in Papua New

Guinea is occurring in the domains that "native speakers" have the most influence on, and Woolford (1983) argues that social factors, such as the expansion of the domains in which the language is used from purely domestic to government, politics, economics, and other more abstract matters, are a more important source of development in Creoles. Furthermore, the nature and quality of the input presented to the young learner is different from that available to the older learner, in a pidgin as in a standard language; it may be that preschool learners, because the topics they discuss with parents are simpler, more concrete, and more interpretable with the help of the nonlinguistic structure than most pidgin utterances. Newport and Bickerton would argue that such could not be the case—that the input from pidgin speakers could not display the morphological contrasts to be learned, since the pidgin speaker/signer does not use them. However, it is known that ASL, like other natural human languages, is subject to regular variability explainable by sociolinguistic principles. Furthermore, even Newport's late learners displayed considerable control of the morphological system. Although poorer than natives in use of the system, they were certainly not totally ignorant of it. Until first-generation signers' actual input to second-generation ASL learners is analyzed, the possibility remains open that their limited knowledge of the morphological system is displayed quite fully and consistently in this interactive setting. Understanding the source of the age differences Newport reports must, likewise, await studies of the nature of the language learning situation in which 4-6- and post-12-year-olds learn ASL.

Summary.   Age differences in the speed of second language acquisition during the early stages of acquisition seem quite generally to favor older learners. Paradoxically, though, the ultimate level of language knowledge attained is often higher for younger learners. Although this fact has been taken as support for the notion of a critical period, in my opinion it is insufficient basis for such a conclusion for a number of reasons: (a) even in the oldest group of learners, some do achieve native-like levels (b) in the younger groups, some typically do not, (c) the contexts of learning all militate against success for the older groups, and (d) a correlation between age at which achievement declines and parameters of brain growth or functioning cannot be supported. One case of first language acquisition to normal levels after age 6 has been reported, and much evidence suggests that brain injury produces some lasting deficits even in very young children, though the interhemispheric plasticity of the infant brain is clearly greater than that of the mature brain. Thus, the picture derived from a variety of cases of language acquisition outside the normal early childhood period is that it is remarkably fast, though perhaps somewhat more likely to stop before native-like proficiency is achieved, for reasons which are not clear but are difficult to attribute to biology.

Reversibility of Acquisition

A second broad set of data relevant to the critical period hypothesis for language development addresses the issue of reversibility. Once certain learning has occurred, as during first language acquisition, it may be irreversible (as, for example, a first language accent when speaking a second language suggests that some aspects of pronunciation are irreversible). Evidence that some aspects of language are learned irreversibly during a certain period would lend support to the notion of a critical period.

Data about the reversibility of early learning come from three major sources: studies of foreign accents; studies of dialect shifts at different points in childhood; and studies of auditory discrimination of phonemic distinctions not in one's native language.

Foreign accents.   As noted above, during the earliest stages of second language acquisition, younger learners may acquire second language pronunciation more slowly than older learners, but with increasing length of the acquisition period, younger learners show an increasing advantage. The same data speak to a slightly different question: is it possible for learners to lose all trace of their native language when pronouncing a second language? If so, is this possible at any age, or only at young ages?

Typically, second language learners retain some accent; the positive value of such a distinctive marker of "nonnativeness" has been widely discussed (e.g., Flege, 1985; Snow, 1983). But a few lose their accents completely, to the extent that they may be mistaken for native speakers both in casual conversation and when pronouncing difficult second language items in isolation (Neufeld, 1978). Furthermore, Neufeld demonstrated that after being exposed to 9 hours of silent ear training, followed by 9 hours of producing whispered, then vocalized imitations, of Japanese and of Chinese, half of the subjects (native speakers of English with no knowlege of Chinese or Japanese) could imitate utterances up to 16 syllables in length well enough to be judged as native speakers by native speakers. The success rate was not perfect, nor did the learning induced extend beyond imitation. Nonetheless these subjects evidently attained considerable control over the segmental and intonational features of foreign languages. These findings suggest that the generally poor achievements of adult foreign language learners in pronunciation reflect ill-designed teaching programs (which require talking too early in the learning process) and/or some active maintenance of the foreign accent. However, it remains unclear from Neufeld's reports how general the ability to achieve very good second language pronunciation is, and whether this ability can be displayed in more natural language use situations. It is worth noting that adults can show discrimination of certain nonnative contrasts under some testing conditions, but still not be able to discriminate under conditions that approximate normal language processing (Werker & Tees, 1984; Werker & Logan, 1985). The situation for pronunciation may be similar; subjects with perfect pronunciation in an imitation condition may show an accent if they actually have to formulate utterances themselves, and meet the additional processing demands associated with lexical access and syntactic planning.

Native dialect.   A process analogous to learning the correct accent in a foreign language occurs when families move across dialect boundaries. How long does it take before children or adults lose their original dialects and come to sound like natives of their adopted region, if they ever do?

Two studies directly relevant to the issue of dialect shift both deal with rather subtle aspects of pronunciation. It seems obvious (though it has not, to my knowledge, been documented) that grosser aspects of dialect (*y'all* for plural you, lexical items, *ain't,* etc.) are adopted by newcomers of all ages. Payne (1980) analysed the vowels of three groups of children: local born with local born parents; local born with out-of-state parents; out-of-state born with out-of-state parents. She found that the regularly conditioned vowel phonemes — those that were highly predictable across the lexicon — were acquired by all the children who had exposure to the dialect in question. Another much less predictable pattern of vowel alternations, which was characterized by several unmotivated exceptions (i.e., one needed to represent the pattern lexically rather than phonetically) was learned only by children with locally born parents. Evidently, the underlying representations of words that governed correct production of the vowels in question were laid down early and were not reversed by exposure to the alternate system. Deser (personal communication), on the other hand, has found that older adolescents can show more extreme dialect features than their younger siblings, suggesting some restructuring of dialect during adolescence; this finding confirms the hypothesis that adolescents are in fact responsible for much of the language change that occurs over time. It seems, then, that many details of pronunciation learned early in life are mutable, but that new learning is unlikely if it requires introducing distinctions that are unmotivated, thus requiring the revision of old lexical representations.

Speech perception.   It has often been suggested that the difficulty in acquiring a perfect accent in a second language, or perfect control of a later learned dialect, resides not in the articulation process, but in the perceptual process. It is impossible to pronounce perfectly a pair of phonemes that, in perception, one merges. To those of us who grew up learning that merry, marry, and Mary all contained the same vowel, making a consistent distinction in adulthood is hard, not because we cannot produce all three vowels, but because we do not know which we are producing at any given time or because correct selection under the pressures of fluent speech is too demanding. Similarly, the Japanese or Chinese speaker who hears no differences between *r* and *l* can hardly be expected to avoid productions like "cindalella" or "Lonald Leagan."

Evidence in support of perceptual control of accent comes from the analysis by Snow and Hoefnagel-Hohle (1979) of the interrelation among various second language skills attained by their English-speaking subjects learning Dutch. During the first 6 months of acquisition, auditory discrimination and pronunciation were uncorrelated, but by 9 to 12 months after first exposure to Dutch, the subjects with the best pronunciation also discriminated Dutch phonemic contrasts not made in English with the fewest errors. These results suggest that, in the long run, skill at speech perception was a limiting factor in correctness of pronunciation.

What do we know, then, about the development of speech perception abilities? Although older second language learners typically have difficulty discriminating sounds not distinguished in their native language, these problems are as large or larger for younger learners. Snow and Hoefnagel-Hohle (1978) found that auditory discrimination showed age differences similar to those for syntax or lexicon in natural second language learners, and Winitz (1981, 1985) found adults and adolescent English speakers were superior to 8-year-olds in hearing tone and obstruent distinctions used in Chinese. Thus, age differences in speech perception do not explain age differences in pronunciation very easily.

Is there any evidence for irreversibility of the distinctions made in one's native tongue? The classic study by Eimas, Siqueland, Jusczyk, and Vigorito (1971) provided evidence that infants as young as 1 month can discriminate a phonemic category with precisely the same boundaries as adults, and later work demonstrated this capacity in infants so young that explanations based on experience were rendered extremely unlikely. Definitive evidence that such perceptual abilities are independent of experience came from testing infants on contrasts not found in the language of their communities; it turns out that, for example, Canadian 6-month-olds are almost as good at hearing the difference between retroflex and dental initial stops, and between a voiceless aspirated versus a breathy voiced initial stop, as are adult native speakers of Hindi, a language in which these distinctions are phonemic (Werker, Gilbert, Humphrey, & Tees, 1981). In contrast, English 4-year-olds were quite incapable of making this discrimination (Werker & Tees, 1983). Later research by Werker and Tees (1984) narrowed the decline in the ability to make discriminations unsupported by one's linguistic environment to the period between 8 and 10 months; infants aged 10-12 months performed as poorly as did 4-year-olds on non-English contrasts. A longitudinal replication confirmed that the same infants who at 7 months had heard the contrast between the Hindi retroflex and dental stops were unable to do so by 10-12 months. In addition, another non-English contrast (Salish velar versus uvular initial un-voiced glottalized stops) which had been discriminated earlier was at 9 months heard by only half the children. These results present a remarkable picture of very early experiential effects on language; at 9 months of age, most children have not yet produced their first words, and they typically comprehend only a few, routinized utterances. Yet somehow they have dis-covered which set of phonetic contrasts in their native language signal mean-ingful distinctions and must be attended to.

How reversible is the decline in speech perception documented by Werker and her colleagues? Can training or exposure in childhood or adulthood to the nonnative contrast produce recovery of the abilities lost at 10 months of age? Too little evidence is available to answer these questions. It would, for example, be instructive to use the perceptual discrimination paradigm with various groups of seemingly perfect adult bilinguals who had acquired their second language at various ages, as well as with adult speakers who have switched dominance from their first to a second language. Do the first lan-guage contrasts stay perceptible even after the first language is no longer sup-ported by the environmental language? Do early bilinguals develop two com-plete sets of contrasts, or some merging of the two separate language systems?

The small amount of evidence available concerning reversibility comes from a study by Werker and Tees (1983; Tees & Werker, 1984) using the two Hindi contrasts discussed earlier: a distinction of place (retroflex versus den-tal unaspirated unvoiced initial stops) and a distinction of voicing (voiceless aspirated versus breathy voiced initial stops). Werker and Tees found that even untrained subjects 8 years of age and older were more likely to make one of these contrasts, the voicing distinction that is more common across the world's languages, though no age gradient was found for the place distinc-tion. Furthermore, a very few (8-11) training trials improved adults' perform-ance slightly but significantly on the voicing distinction, but had no effect on the place distinction. Further training studies showed that 9 out of 10 subjects could learn the voicing contrast within 50 training trials, whereas only 6 of 14 learned the place of articulation contrast within 300 trials. Furthermore, all nine of the subjects who learned the voicing contrast within 50 trials retained it for 30-40 days with no additional environmental support, whereas only two of the six who learned the place contrast retained it.

The relative ease of the voicing contrast was confirmed in further work with adults who were studying Hindi. Within a week of starting their study, essentially all the students had mastered this distinction. In comparison, the place distinction was learned by English speakers who had studied Hindi for at least 5 years, but not by those with only 1 year's study. Importantly, though, adult English speakers who had heard significant amounts of spoken Hindi only in early childhood could make the difficult retroflex-dental distinction after only a week of classroom study in Hindi (and may have been able with no such classroom experience, had they been tested earlier). However, in another study Werker (1986) found that the early experience supported the distinction only if it included exposure to that specific distinction: Multilingual adults were not better than monolinguals on contrasts not included in any of their languages.

These findings confirm those of MacKain, Best, and Strange (1981) that adult Japanese speakers master the perceptual distinction between *r* and *l* only with intensive training in English. Both the Japanese learners of English and the English learners of Hindi were often found to be able to pronounce the distinction in question better than their perceptual abilities would have predicted.

The results from the speech perception literature suggest, then, that the first year of life constitutes a sensitive period for *loss* (not learning) of perceptual capacities to distinguish certain phonetic contrasts. The availability in the environment of speakers who make a distinction during this period somehow operates to protect the infant against the otherwise natural loss of the distinction. We do not know how much exposure to the distinction during the second half of the first year of life is necessary to prevent the loss, nor if there is a gradual or a sharp decline in the effectiveness of relevant input in restoring the discrimination ability. It is clear from the work of Werker and her colleagues, and of MacKain and her colleagues, that the loss is reversible, but in some cases (place of articulation distinctions seem particularly difficult) considerable training in adulthood is needed to reverse the discrimination failure.

Summary. The evidence from research in three domains of language learning — learning to hear consonant contrasts not in one's native language, learning to produce vowel contrasts not in one's native dialect, and learning to produce both segmental and intonational features of another language — converges on the conclusion that the first year of life constitutes a sensitive period for the operation of environmental stimuli in organizing perception and related production systems. However, it must also be pointed out that the organization attained by 1 year of age is reversible, with training, even in adulthood; some aspects of that organization may be relatively easy to reorganize, whereas others are relatively recalcitrant. Nonetheless, attaining the ability to hear all the perceptual contrasts and to produce an authentic, native-like pronunciation of a foreign language seems, from the evidence presented, to be within the reach of most adults. The vulnerability of the perception/phonological production system to organization by the environment during the first year of life stands in sharp contrast to all the other domains of language — lexicon, syntax, morphology, conversational fluency, comprehension — that are not subject to strong environmental effects during the early years of life, nor resistant to learning in later years.

Late Learned Languages and Brain Localization

Some support for the notion that brain maturation interacts with language learning capacity would be offered by the finding that earlier and later learned languages were localized in different places in the brain. Patterns of breakdown and recovery in polyglot aphasics confirm this possibility, since in a significant minority of the cases the aphasic's different languages are differently affected (Albert & Obler, 1978; Paradis, 1977). Brain stimulation of multilinguals also suggest that somewhat different, though overlapping, sites control naming in the two languages (see Ojemann, 1983, and Whitaker et al., 1981, for reviews). The test case, though, involves comparison of localization of second languages acquired by early (before 5 years of age) versus late (after 5 years of age) bilinguals, who are however all equally proficient in a second language. More specifically, it could be predicted that early-acquired second languages are localized in ways indistinguishable from first languages, whereas late acquired second languages are more likely to be bilaterally represented.

Although considerable support for this hypothesis can be found, from studies using a variety of techniques for determining localization (e.g., evoked potential, used by Genesee, Hamers, Lambert, Mononen, Seitz, & Stark 1978; dichotic listening, used by Gordon, 1980; concurrent verbal-manual tasks to assess interference during speech production, used by Sussman, Franklin, & Simon, 1982, and by Hynd, Teeter, & Stewart, 1980; and tachistoscopic presentation of stimuli to right versus left visual fields, used by Vaid, 1984, and Vaid & Lambert, 1979), the interpretation of the findings remains open. First, some studies find left hemisphere superiority for later bilinguals as great as for monolinguals (Soares, 1982, 1984; Soares & Grosjean, 1981; Vaid, 1984). Second, the results in general suggest only somewhat more bilateral involvement for processing later learned languages, not complete localization in the right hemisphere. Third, the right hemisphere involvement is highly task and materials dependent — as if the effect depends somehow on the subject's strategy for processing the language task presented. One difference between early and later language learning is the primacy of visual representation in learning and analysis. Individuals who learn a language before age 5 probably speak it for a few years before learning to read it. Lexical representations must, therefore, be primarily phonetic/acoustic in nature. A language learned later in life will typically be read as soon as it is spoken. Thus, many lexical items stored by the early bilingual primarily as sequential-phonetic representations may be stored visually (holistically) as well as phonetically by the late bilingual. The late bilingual would, thus, have more options for processing these words. A couple of possibilities for testing this hypothesis present themselves, e.g., comparing early and late bilinguals' processing of uncommon, literary, or scientific words, which are more likely to have been learned by both groups through reading, or testing late bilinguals who acquired a spoken language with a different orthography from their native language without learning to read it.

It seems, then, that the fact that late learned languages may be processed somewhat differently from early learned languages may not relate to any aspect of brain maturation, but rather to psychological characteristics of the learner and demands of the learning task at different ages. This set of findings does not, thus, lend any support to a notion of a sensitive period for language acquisition, after which the nature of the learning is qualitatively different because of changes in the brain.

A related set of findings derives from studies of localization in congenitally deaf adults. Results from studies of evoked potentials suggest that the absence of early auditory experience contributes to a reorganization of the brain, such that cortical areas responsive to auditory stimulation in hearing subjects are responsive to visual stimulation in the deaf (Neville, Schmidt, & Kutas, 1983). Deaf adults also show more right hemisphere involvement in reading than do hearing adults (Neville, 1985). These differences in brain organization are not apparent for adventitiously deaf adults whose hearing loss occurred after age 4 (Neville, 1985). Obviously, it would be of considerable importance to determine precisely how much and over how long a period early auditory experience is ncessary to maintain the patterns of cortical involvement typical of hearing adults, in order to discover the limits on the period during which brain organization occurs. Here we see, though, an example suggesting that the functions the brain is exercised for control aspects of brain-development, rather than parameters of brain growth controlling the development of functions.

CONCLUSIONS

The classic formulations of the CPH for language acquisition emerge out of claims about children's superiority for second language acquisition and for recovery from aphasia, associated with hypothesized changes in parameters of brain growth and functioning. The available literature actually supports the much more circumscribed view that there is a period of extreme sensitivity to environmental, linguistic stimulation between 8 and 10 months of age and limited to the domain of speech perception. Further evidence that the first year of life may represent a sensitive period emerges from studies of dialect shift and from studies of children with severe brain damage, including hemidecortications, who show relatively (though not completely) normal development if the damage is sustained very early. In contrast, no discontinuities in acquisition or in recovery of language functions at 5-6 years of age (the time when brain growth is essentially completed) nor at 10-12 years of age (at puberty) have been well documented. Discontinuities in the acquisition of ASL might constitute a basis for identifying 5-6 years as the end of sensitive period for acquiring morphological productivity, but much more data are needed before such a claim could be accepted uncritically, and cases such as that of Isabelle, who learned language after age 6, constitute important counter evidence.

In contrast to the predictions of the CPH, perhaps the most striking aspect of the data is the degree to which older children and adults reveal their potential for fast, natural, and successful language learning. Myths about the difficulty and non-naturalness of language acquisition for post-pubertal children have influenced educational policy and expectations for achievement held by both foreign language teachers and by clinicians treating patients with brain trauma. It is time such myths were re-examined in the light of data: They tell us quite unequivocally that the 20-year-old, who by anyone's estimate is beyond the period of brain growth, equipotentiality, or plasticity, is ceteris paribus a better language learner than the 3-year-old or the 6-year-old. It is time for researchers to start searching for explanations—in cognitive and social spheres—for the facts as they are, rather than continuing to search for biological explanations of unproven claims. It is also time for defenders of the CPH to offer plausible hypotheses about the biological factors they believe can explain age differences in behavior, rather than taking behavioral data as a basis for extrapolating to biological processes.

ACKNOWLEDGMENTS

I would like to thank John Locke, Jean Berko Gleason, and Janet Werker, who all gave me helpful comments and suggestions on this paper, as well as Marc Bornstein, whose editorial prerogative was productively exercised on an early version. Needless to say, none of these people necessarily agree with my position in general or in particular. The Netherlands Organization for Scientific Research (Z.W.O.) funded my research on age differences in second language acquisition, and the Spencer Foundation and the Office for Educational Research and Improvement through the Center for Language Education and Research (CLEAR) are supporting current related work.

REFERENCES

Albert, M., & Obler, L. *The bilingual brain—Neuropsychological and neurolinguistic aspects of bilingualism.* New York: Academic Press, 1978.

Asher, J., & Garcia. The optimal age to learn a foreign language. *Modern Language Journal,* 1969, *53,* 334–341.

Asher, J., & Price, B. The learning strategy of the total physical response: Some age differences. *Child Development,* 1967, *38,* 1219–1227.

Basser, L. S. Hemiplegia of early onset and the faculty of speech with special reference to the effects of hemispherectomy. *Brain*, 1962, *85*, 427–460.

Best, C., Hoffman, H., & Glanville, B. Development of infant ear asymmetries for speech. *Perception & Psychophysics*, 1982, *31*, 75–85.

Bickerton, D. *The roots of language*. Ann Arbor, MI: Karoma Publishers, 1981.

Brown, R. *Words and things*. New York: The Free Press, 1958.

Burling, R. Social constraints on adult language learning. In H. Winitz (Ed.), *Native language and foreign language acquisition*. New York: New York Academy of Sciences, 1981.

Caplan, P. J., & Kinsbourne, M. Baby drops the rattle: Asymmetry of duration of grasp by infants. *Child Development*, 1976, *47*, 532–534.

Cochrane, R. *The acquisition of /r/ and /l/ by Japanese children and adults learning English as a second language*. Unpublished Ph.D. thesis, University of Connecticut, 1977.

Cook, V. J. The comparison of language development in native children and foreign adults. *International Review of Applied Linguistics*, 1973, *11*, 13–28.

Curtiss, S. *Genie: A psycholinguistic study of a modern-day 'wild child.'* New York: Academic Press, 1977.

Davis, K. Final note on a case of extreme isolation. *American Journal of Sociology*, 1947, *52*, 432–37.

Dennis, M. Correlates of syntactic comprehension in hemidecorticate infantile hemiplegics: Hemispheric asymmetry for language strategy? *Brain and Language*, 1979, *6*, 153–169.

Dennis, M. Capacity and strategy for syntactic comprehension after left and right hemidecortication. *Brain and Language*, 1980, *7*, 287–317.

Dennis, M., & Kohn, B. Comprehension of syntax in infantile hemiplegics after cerebral hemidecortication: left-hemisphere superiority. *Brain and Language*, 1975, *2*, 472–482.

Dennis, M., & Whitaker, H. A. Language acquisition following hemidecortication: Linguistic superiority of the left over the right hemisphere. *Brain and Language*, 1976, *3*, 404–433.

Dennis, M., & Whitaker, H. A. Hemisphere equipotentiality and language acquisition. In S. J. Segalowitz, & F. A. Gruber (Eds.), *Language development and neurological theory*. New York: Academic Press, 1977.

Eimas, P., Siqueland, E., Jusczyk, P., & Vigorito, J. Speech perception in infants. *Science*, 1971, *171*, 303–306.

Ekstrand, L. Age and length of residence as variables related to the adjustment of migrant children, with special reference to second language learning. In G. Nickel (Ed.), *Proceedings of the Fourth International Congress of Applied Psycholinguistics* (Vol. 3), Stuttgart: Hochschulverlag, 1976.

Ervin-Tripp, S. Is second language learning like the first? *TESOL Quarterly*, 1976, *8*, 111–127.

Fathman, A. The relationship between age and second language learning productive ability. *Language Learning*, 1975, *25*, 245–253.

Flege, J. E. The production and perception of foreign language speech sounds. In H. Winitz (Ed.), *Human communication and its disorders, I*. Norwood: Ablex, 1985.

Flege, J. E., & Eefting, W. Z. Effects of age and linguistic experience on the production and perception of stop consonants. *Journal of the Acoustical Society of America*, 1985, submitted.

Genesee, F., Hamers, J., Lambert, W., Mononen, L., Seitz, M., & Stark, R. Language processing in bilinguals. *Brain and language*, 1978, *5*, 1–12.

Gilbert, J., Mitchell, G., Brown, L., & Chow, P. *Long term linguistic consequences of traumatic head injury in childhood and adolescence*. Paper presented at Boston University Child Language Conference, 1985.

Gleitman, H. *Psychology*. New York: Norton, 1981.

Gordon, H. Cerebral organization in bilinguals: 1. lateralization. *Brain and Language*, 1980, *9*, 225–268.

Gurney, M., & Konishi, M. Hormone-induced sexual differentiation of brain and behavior in zebra finches. *Science,* 1980, *208,* 1380–1383.

Hill, J. On the evolutionary foundations of language. *American Anthropologist,* 1972, *74.*

Hynd, G., Teeter, A., & Stewart, A. Acculturation and the lateralization of speech in the bilingual native American. *International Journal of Neuroscience,* 1980, *11,* 1–7.

Johnson, J. *The critical period and second language acquisition: Any connection?* Master's thesis, University of Illinois at Urbana-Champaign, 1986.

Kinsbourne, M. The ontogeny of cerebral dominance. In D. Aaronson, & R. W. Rieber (Eds.), *Developmental psycholinguistics and communication disorders.* New York: New York Academy of Sciences, 1975.

Kinsbourne, M. Neuropsychological aspects of bilingualism. In H. Winitz (Ed.), *Native language and foreign language acquisition.* New York: New York Academy of Sciences, 1981.

Kinsbourne, M., & Hiscock, M. Does cerebral dominance develop? In S. Segalowitz, & F. Gruber (Eds.), *Language development and neurological theory.* New York: Academic Press, 1977.

Krashen, S. Lateralization, language learning, and the critical period: Some new evidence. *Language Learning,* 1973, *23,* 63–74.

Krashen, S. The critical period for language acquisition and its possible bases. In D. Aaronson, & R. W. Rieber (Eds.), *Developmental psycholinguistics and communication disorders.* New York: New York Academy of Sciences, 1975.

Krashen, S. The input hypothesis. In J. Alatis (Ed.), *Current issues in bilingual education.* Washington, D.C.: Georgetown University Press, 1980.

Krashen, S., Long, M., & Scarcella, R. Age, rate, and eventual attainment in second language acquisition. In S. Krashen, R. Scarcella, & M. Long (Eds.), *Child-adult differences in second language acquisition.* Rowley, MA: Newbury House, 1982.

Lane, H. *The wild boy of Aveyron.* New York: Basic Books, 1977.

Lenneberg, E. *Biological foundations of language.* New York: Wiley, 1967.

Lieberman, P. On the evolution of human syntactic ability: Its preadaptive bases, motor control, and speech. *Journal of Human Evolution,* 1985, *14,* 657–668.

Locke, J. *Phonological acquisition and change.* New York: Academic Press, 1983.

MacKain, K. Best, C., & Strange, W. Categorical perception of English /r/ and /l/ by Japanese bilinguals. *Applied Psycholinguistics,* 1981, *2,* 323–330.

McLaughlin, B. *Second-language acquisition in childhood: Volume 2. School-age children.* Hillsdale: Lawrence Erlbaum Associates, 1984.

Mehler, J., Morton, J., & Jusczyk, P. On reducing language to biology. *Cognitive Neuropsychology,* 1984, *1,* 83–116.

Molfese, D. L., Freeman, R. B., & Palermo, D. S. The ontogeny of brain lateralization for speech and non-speech stimuli. *Brain and Language,* 1975, *2,* 356–358.

Neville, H. Effects of early sensory and language experience on the development of the human brain. In J. Mehler (Ed.), *Neonate and infant cognition.* Hillsdale, NJ: Lawrence Erlbaum Associates, 1985.

Neville, H., Schmidt, A., & Kutas, M. Altered visual-evoked potentials in congenitally deaf adults. *Brain Research,* 1983, *266,* 127–132.

Neufeld, G. On the acquisition of prosodic and articulatory features in adult second language learning. *Canadian Modern Language Review,* 1978, *34.*

Newport, E. Constraints on structure: Evidence from American Sign Language and language learning. In W. A. Collins (Ed.), *Aspects of the development of competence.* Minnesota Symposium on Child Psychology, Vol. 14, Hillsdale, NJ: Lawrence Erlbaum Associates, 1981.

Newport, E. Constraints on learning: Studies in the acquisition of American Sign Language. *Papers and Reports on Child Language Development,* 1984, *23,* 1–22.

Obler, L., Albert, M., Goodglass, H., & Benson, D. Aphasia type and aging. *Brain and Language,* 1978, *6,* 318–327.

Ojemann, G. Brain organization for language from the perspective of electrical stimulation mapping. *The Behavioral and Brain Sciences,* 1983, *6,* 189–206.

Oyama, S. A sensitive period for the acquisition of a non-native phonological system. *Journal of Psycholinguistic Research,* 1976, *5,* 261–285.

Oyama, S. The concept of the sensitive period in developmental studies. *Merrill-Palmer Quarterly,* 1979, *25,* 83–102.

Paradis, M. Bilingualism and aphasia. In H. A. Whitaker, & H. Whitaker (Eds.), *Studies in neurolinguistics* (Vol. 3). New York: Academic Press, 1977.

Patkowski, M. The sensitive period for the acquisition of syntax in a second language. *Language Learning,* 1980, *30,* 449–472.

Payne, A. Factors controlling the acquisition of the Philadelphia dialect by out-of-state children. In W. Labov (Ed.), *Locating language in time and space.* New York: Academic Press, 1980.

Politzer, R., & Weiss, L. Developmental aspects of auditory discrimination, echo response, and recall. *The Modern Language Journal,* 1969, *53,* 75–85.

Robinson, R. O. Equal recovery in child and adult brain? *Developmental Medicine and Child Neurology,* 1981, *23,* 379–382.

Sankoff, G. The genesis of a language. In K. C. Hill (Ed.), *The genesis of language.* Ann Arbor, MI: Karoma Publishers, 1979.

Scovel, T. Foreign accents, language acquisition, and cerebral dominance. *Language Learning,* 1969, *19,* 245–253.

Scovel, T. The recognition of foreign accents. In J.-G. Savard and L. Laforge (Eds.), *Proceedings of the 5th Congress of the International Association of Applied Linguistics.* Quebec: University of Laval Press, 1981.

Seliger, H. Implications of a multiple critical periods hypothesis for second language learning. In *Second language acquisition research.* New York: Academic Press, 1978.

Snow, C. E. Age differences in second language acquisition: Research findings and folk psychology. In K. Bailey, M. Long, & S. Peck (Eds.), *Second language acquisition studies.* Rowley, MA: Newbury House, 1983.

Snow, C. E. Beyond conversation: Second language learners' acquisition of description and explanation. In J. Lantolf & A. Labarca (Eds.), *Research in second language learning: Focus on the classroom.* Norwood, NJ: Ablex, 1986.

Snow, C., & Hoefnagal-Hohle, M. Age differences in the pronunciation of foreign sounds. *Language and Speech,* 1977, *20,* 357–365.

Snow, C., & Hoefnagal-Hohle, M. The critical period for language acquisition: Evidence from second language learning. *Child Development,* 1978, *49,* 1114–1128.

Snow, C., & Hoefnagal-Hohle, M. Individual differences in second language ability: A factor-analytic study. *Language and Speech,* 1979, *22,* 151–162.

Snow, C., & Hoefnagal-Hohle, M. The linguistic environment of school-age second language learners. *Language Learning,* 1982, *32,* 411–430.

Snow, C., Smith, N. S., & Hoefnagal-Hohle, M. The acquisition of some Dutch morphological rules. *Journal of Child Language,* 1980, *7,* 539–553.

Soares, C. Converging evidence for left hemisphere language lateralization in bilinguals, *Neuropsychologia,* 1982, *20,* 653–659.

Soares, C. Left hemisphere language lateralization in bilinguals: Use of the concurrent activities paradigm. *Brain and Language,* 1984, *23,* 86–96.

Soares, C., & Grosjean, F. Left hemisphere language lateralization in bilinguals and monolinguals. *Perception and Psychophysics,* 1981, *29,* 599–604.

Stevens, F. *Strategies for second language acquisition.* Montreal: Eden Press, 1984.

Supalla, T. *Structure and acquisition of verbs of motion and location in American sign language.* Ph.D. thesis, University of California at San Diego, 1982.

Sussman, H., Franklin, P., & Simon, T. Bilingual speech: Bilateral control? *Brain and Language*, 1982, *15*, 125–142.

Tahta, S., Wood, M., & Lowenthal, K. Foreign accents: Factors relating to transfer of accent from the first language to the second language. *Language and Speech*, 1981, *24*, 265–272.

Tees, R., & Werker, J. Perceptual flexibility: Maintenance or recovery of the ability to discriminate non-native speech sounds. *Canadian Journal of Psychology*, 1984, *38*, 579–590.

Vaid, J. Visual, phonetic and semantic processing in early and late bilinguals. In M. Paradis, & Y. Lebrun (Eds.), *Early bilingualism and child development*. Lisse: Swets and Zeitlinger, 1984.

Vaid, J., & Lambert, W. Differential cerebral involvement in the cognitive functioning of bilinguals. *Brain and Language*, 1979, *8*, 92–110.

Wada, J., Clarke, R., & Hamm, A. Cerebral hemispheric asymmetry in humans: Cortical speech zones in 100 adult and 100 infant brains. *Archives of Neurology*, 1975, *32*, 239–246.

Walsh, T., & Diller, K. Neurolinguistic considerations on the optimum age for second language learning. In K. Diller (Ed.), *Individual differences and universals in language learning aptitude*. Rowley, MA: Newbury House, 1981.

Werker, J. The effect of multilingualism on phonetic perceptual flexibility. *Applied Psycholinguistics*, 1986, *7*, 141–155.

Werker, J., Gilbert, J., Humphrey, K., & Tees, R. Developmental aspects of cross-language speech perception. *Child Development*, 1981, *52*, 349–355.

Werker, J., & Logan, J. S. Cross-language evidence for three factors in speech perception. *Perception & Psychophysics*, 1985, *37*, 35–44.

Werker, J., & Tees, R. Cross language speech perception: Evidence for perceptual reorganization during the first year of life. *Infant Behavior and Development*, 1984, *7*, 49–63.

Werker, J., & Tees, R. Developmental changes across childhood in the perception of non-native speech sounds. *Canadian Journal of Psychology*, 1983, *37*, 278–286.

Werker, J., & Tees, R. Phonemic and phonetic factors in adult cross-language speech perception. *Journal of the Acoustical Society of America*, 1984, *75*, 1866–1878.

Whitaker, H., Bub, D., & Leventer, S. Neurolinguistic aspects of language acquisition and bilingualism. In H. Winitz (Ed.), *Native language and foreign language acquisition*. New York: New York Academy of the Sciences, 1981.

Winitz, H. Input considerations in the comprehension of first and second language. In H. Winitz (Ed.), *Native language and foreign language acquisition*. New York: New York Academy of Sciences, 1981.

Winitz, H. *Discrimination of Mandarin Chinese sounds and tones*. Address, New York Academy of Sciences, 14 January 1985.

Woods, B. T. Dichotic listening ear preference after childhood cerebral lesions. *Neuropsychologia*, 1984, *22* (3), 303–310.

Woodward, J. C. Inter-rule implication in American sign language. *Sign Language Studies*, 1973, *3*, 47–56.

Woolford, E. Introduction: The social context of creolization. In E. Woolford, & W. Washabaugh (Eds.), *The social context of creolization*. Ann Arbor, MI: Karoma Publishers, 1983.

10 Critical Periods in Psychoanalytic Theories of Personality Development

Benjamin Beit-Hallahmi
University of Haifa

INTRODUCTION

Psychoanalytic theories of personality have invoked the idea of critical periods in development in more than one way. Winson (1985, p. 162) describes the critical period as ". . . a sensitive period within a specific domain. Beyond this period the ability to learn within the domain ceases and whatever has been learned constitutes the basis for future behavior." Although the concept of a critical period is never mentioned in psychoanalytic writings, the idea is very clearly expressed in most psychoanalytic writings on personality development, from those originally in Sigmund Freud himself to more recent and less Freudian works.

In considering possible critical periods in personality development, the psychoanalytic tradition of theorizing merits consideration for two reasons. First, despite its origins outside of academic psychology and its ambivalent status today, psychoanalysis remains a powerful and attractive theory in personality studies, as evidenced by thousands of books and articles appearing every year. Second, psychoanalysis represents a tradition in which discussion of critical periods, however referred to, has been a major topic.

Psychoanalytic views of personality development have become so much a part of our culture that in numerous everyday conversations, people are prone to explain adult behavior and adult uniqueness in personality on the basis of early childhood experiences. "How do you account for the fact that Joe, in the face of so much adversity in his life so far, has managed to keep up such an optimistic, positive spirit? This has to do, undoubtedly, with some positive early experiences in his childhood, especially in the way he was

211

treated by his parents." As Anna Freud noted in 1954, the lay public got wind of the psychoanalytic emphasis on the early critical period, but in the form of the mistaken notion that only the mother's early behavior is crucial for the child's development. And she responded: "To put the blame for the infantile neurosis on the mother's shortcoming in the oral phase is no more than a facile and misleading generalization" (p. 11).

Psychoanalytic theories rely on impressionistic "clinical" observations to collect data, which may appear to be unreliable, but the influence of those theories is totally unrelated to their basis in collected data. Even researchers who start from a nonpsychoanalytic point of view often conclude with psychoanalytic findings. Thus, Greenspan and Greenspan (1985) recently rediscovered what all psychoanalytic schools have maintained all along: that the first four years of life are the critical period for personality development.

Psychoanalysis, the theory originating with Freud and developed and transformed by countless disciples, is marked by three conceptual starting points, or biases. It is biological, developmental, and learning-oriented. It is biological because it starts by stating certain biological givens and limitations. It is developmental because it sees behavior in the context of time changes. It is learning-oriented because it emphasizes that consistencies in behavior are best explained by earlier experiences of interaction between biological givens and environmental pressures.

When Hartmann (1939) proposed the idea of a "conflict-free ego sphere" in which the functions of perception, thinking, and motor development operate, he referred also to ". . . the struggle with instinctual drives, with love objects, with the superego . . ." (p. 7). The latter sphere is exactly where the process of personality development, according to psychoanalytic theory, takes place. The issue of critical period learning in psychoanalysis is not one of all or none occurrence — the question is not whether learning takes place or not, because there is always some kind of learning. The question is the quality and quantity of learned responses. The result of experiences during the critical period may be optimal, average, marginal, or pathological behavior.

The basic idea of the critical period, with learning so powerful that it cannot be reversed by later experiences, is a biological idea, which is at the basis of Freud's theoretical edifice of psychoanalysis. There has been a profound change in the psychoanalytic conception of critical periods in development over the past two generations, as part of a thorough revision of Freud's ideas. Discussing these historical changes is one way of introducing the most recent version of psychoanalytic personality theory, with which most developmental psychologists are totally unfamiliar.

In this chapter I overview and contrast two psychoanalytic approaches to discussing critical periods in personality development. The first is the classical tradition, based on the well-known structural model of id, ego, and superego, and on the assumption of innate instincts. The second approach, object relations theory, which is the most important development of the past fifty years in psychoanalysis, leaves behind the structural-instinctual view, to focus on interpersonal relations in early life. Following the review of the two approaches, I return to the question of the unique fascination of psychoanalysis as a developmental theory.

THE CLASSICAL VIEW: FREUD AND OTHERS

The importance of early childhood in the development of personality is considered to be one of the building blocks of psychoanalytic theory, together with the ideas of unconscious mechanism in behavior and the transformation of basic instinctual energies. The well-known Freudian assumption is that early childhood is the critical period for learning both functional and dysfunctional habitual behaviors. Moreover, while the whole period of early childhood, until the age of 6, is a critical period, it is experience in the Oedipal stage, between the ages of approximately 3 and 6 years, that is most crucial in determining normal and abnormal behaviors. All psychoanalytic theorists assume a biologically predetermined maturation of ego-apparatuses, which is the basis for all psychological development.

The classical Freudian conception of the ideal or optimal learning situation during the critical period has been one of balance between satisfaction and frustration for the child. Without frustration, the ego will not develop; without satisfaction, it will be smothered.

The stages of psychosexual development, the readiness of the organism to learn at this early stage, and the critical periods involved are universal and biologically determined. What is learned during the critical period of early childhood are ways of handling internal instincts and external reality, known in psychoanalysis as "ego defenses." It is these ego defenses that form unique personality behavioral styles. Over- or underlearning certain defenses will lead to less than optimal personality structure and functioning. Freud's (1926/1959, p. 241) phrasing of this early condition was: "A feebleness of the ego of this sort is to be found in all of us in childhood; and that is why the experiences of the earliest years of childhood are of such greater importance for later life."

Freud (1964, p. 184) expressed the importance of early childhood in normal and abnormal personality development as follows: "It seems that neuroses are acquired only in early childhood (up to the age of six), even though their symptoms may not make their appearance till much later . . . . In every case the later neurotic illness links up with the prelude in childhood." And in discussing one of his famous cases, the Wolfman, Freud (1918/1955, p. 99), wrote that ". . . every neurosis in an adult is built upon a neurosis which has occurred in his childhood. . . ." As quoted by Jones (1955, p. 443), Freud said on November 17, 1909, "We expect it would turn out that the severe neuroses all have their prototypes in childhood life, so that we should find the kernels of the later neuroses in the disturbances of development in childhood."

From Freud's writings then it becomes clear that on many occasions he regarded the Oedipal phase of development as the critical period of personality development, which determines whether later development will be "normal" or "neurotic," while the whole of early childhood, from birth to age 6, was considered the critical period for the formation of personality. As Freud (1926/1959, pp. 245–246) wrote, "It has been found to be characteristic of a normal individual that he learns to master his Oedipus complex, whereas the neurotic subject remains involved in it."

Freud (1925/1959) explained why the Oedipal stage becomes the critical period for the development of sexual identity, since sexual identity is formed from the contribution of genetics, environment, and relations with parents. During the Oedipal stage the child is optimally ready to formulate a sexual identity, and thus whatever happens during those years is crucial.

For Freud, all of childhood is a critical period, because of the greater fluidity of behavior, and every psychological stage is a critical period for the learning of specific behaviors. During the oral period the child will learn to deal with oral impulses. During the anal stage he will deal with anal impulses, and the ego will learn to integrate those with earlier ones. During the phallic-Oedipal period the issue is basic genital identity, and this is why it becomes the critical period par excellence. While the whole of childhood is a rehearsal for adulthood, the Oedipal stage is the final dress rehearsal.

Freud's (1919/1955) classical paper, "A Child is Being Beaten," expresses clearly the idea that perversion and neuroses results from an "unresolved Oedipus complex," that is faulty learning during the critical period of ages 3-6. Nagera (1966, p. 57), representing the traditional instinctual-structural approach, echoes that ". . . the 'phallic-oedipal' phase is in fact an essential turning point in human development."

The classical Freudian assumptions about personality development are exemplified by Fenichel (1945), who analyzes every instance of adult behavior, normal or neurotic, through its having been learned at a particular time in childhood. Every piece of adult behavior is translated back to a related infantile stage of development. Behavior is "oral," "anal," or "phallic."

According to Balint (1957), it is the sexual objects of infancy that remain the sexual objects of adolescence and adulthood, though in disguised and perverted forms. The reason Freud determined the sensitive period to be age 3-5, the Oedipal period, was that examining the psychological processes at an earlier age was too difficult and uncertain.

CURRENT THEORETICAL CONCEPTIONS

When Margaret S. Mahler died, she was described in an obituary (Bird, 1985, p. 23) as ". . . a children's psychiatrist who developed the thesis that the first three years of life represented the critical period in the development of a person's character . . . ." Mahler herself described her major theoretical thesis as follows:

> We refer to the psychological birth of the individual as the *separation-individuation process:* the establishment of a sense of separateness from, and relation to, a world of reality, particularly with regard to the experiences of *one's own body* and to the principal representative of the world as the infant experiences it, the *primary love object.* Like any intrapsychic process, this one reverberates throughout the life cycle. It is never finished; it remains always active; new phases of the life cycle see new derivatives of the earliest processes still at work. But the principal psychological achievements of this process take place in the period from about the fourth or fifth month to the thirtieth or thirty-sixth month, a period we refer to as the *separation-individuation phase* (Mahler, Pine, & Bergman, 1975, p. 3).

Mahler (1963, p. 307) defined her own starting point in looking at object-relations by basing it on a psychological-biological observation: "the fact that a lifelong, albeit diminishing, emotional dependence on the mother is a universal truth of human existence. The biological unpreparedness of the human infant to maintain his life separately conditions that species-specific prolonged phase which has been designated 'the mother-infant symbiosis'." According to Mahler, crucial events for eventual personality development take place during the first year of life, and even during the first 6 months of life. Mahler's work represents one contemporary version of new ideas in psychoanalysis about early personality development.

There has been an historical change in the definition of the critical period in personality development within the framework of classical psychoanalysis. This momentous change, strangely enough (or not so strangely) has remained largely unknown to most academic and developmental psychologists. As a result of this historical change, the critical period in personality development has been moved earlier, from age 3-6 years to birth-2 years.

Over this time, theoretical debates and theoretical changes have hinged on the following two questions. First, when is the critical period? Second, what is learned during this period? The original answer to the first question, provided by Freud, was age 3-6. The original answer to the second question was the handling of instincts. Later answers moved the critical period back to age birth-2, and changed the answer to the second question to "object relations" or "the self."

Explaining why such dramatic changes have taken place over the past two generations of psychoanalytic theory and practice is beyond the scope of this chapter. Suffice it to say that psychoanalysts themselves regard theoretical change as stemming from observations, i.e., the old theory no longer fitted the new data. (Data here are always clinical observations and judgment. Outside observers may want to point to historical changes in Western urban societies, i.e., London, New York, Chicago, and Los Angeles, where most psychoanalytic work has been based.)

The classical theory stated that what the child learned during the critical period was a way of handling instincts, whereas the latest modern version states that the child learns attitudes toward the self and others. The more recent theoretical formulations, to use the classical terms, choose to place the critical period in pre-Oedipal or pre-genital stages. This focus immediately reduces the importance of genital sexual drives, assumed by Freud to be crucial in the shaping of personality, and increases the importance of interpersonal behavior.

According to object relations theory, what is learned during the critical period of infancy is a way of relating to objects (i.e., other people) and of imagining these others internally. The debate, so to speak, between the traditional Freudian approach and the more recent views is whether the crucial sensitive period is in the Oedipal stage of personality development, i.e., age 3-5, or in the pre-Oedipal stage, age birth-3. At this point it seems that there is no longer a debate, and there is consensus in the field that the earlier stage is the crucial one.

The new emphasis on pre-genital stages of personality development has even led to a new pre-genital conception of the origins of hysteria, the "classical neurosis of classical psychoanalysis." While Freud emphasized the connection between hysterical behaviors and the Oedipal stage, newer conceptions now distinguish between oral hysterics, whose personality is dominated by behavior patterns learned during the oral stage, and phallic hysterics, whose characteristics were learned during the phallic-Oedipal stage (Chodoff, 1974).

According to Freud's original terminology, the historical change among theorists has been from the emphasis on the phallic-Oedipal period (3-6 years) to the oral stage (birth-1). The historical sea change has been a movement for focusing attention not on the Oedipal stage (3-6 years) and "Oedipal neurosis," but to earlier years, and to other, more serious kinds of psychopathology, namely borderline and psychotic conditions. Within classical psychoanalysis, the change is tied to the names of Melanie Klein, W. R. D. Fairbairn, D. W. Winnicott, Michael Balint, and others, who formed the "British school of object relations."

It was Melanie Klein (1948) who claimed for the first time that crucial processes for personality development take place during the first few months of life. Klein (1948), Fairbairn (1952), and Guntrip (1968) focused on object relations and object representations during the first two years of life. Kernberg (1975, 1976) followed in their footsteps and suggested an emphasis on the internal representations of self and others. In the latest American versions of object-relations theory, the concept of self, only rarely mentioned in classical psychoanalysis, plays a central role.

As Ryan and Bell (1984, p. 209) put it, the assumption in modern object relations theory is that "The quality of this representational world then becomes the mental template for the development of all future psychic structures and, thus, for the basic structure of a person's character." Object relations theory rejects the classical notions of innate instincts and the id-ego-superego personality structure. It assumes no instincts except object-seeking. The basic assumption in object relations theory, as opposed to classical instinctual structural psychoanalysis, is that the crucial determinant of personality consistencies, whether normal or pathological, is the relations between self and others, real or imagined by the self. Object relations theory agrees with classical instinctual structural theory on the importance of early childhood. As Ryan and Bell observed (1984, p. 210), "The explicit or implicit suggestion in much of this work is that object-relations patterns are set down in early childhood, become consolidated through late childhood and adolescence, and remain relatively fixed throughout adult life as the transference paradigms of character. Adult functioning, whether normal, neurotic, or psychotic, is assumed to be dependent on the maturity of one's object relations, that is, on the relatively stable level one has achieved along the developmental continuum."

In the more recent versions of psychoanalytic personality theories, the critical period is one during which the child is preverbal and essentially passive. As Langman and Kaplan (1978, p. 362) observed, "The preverbal child is said to experience a variety of tension states, but is most limited in its capacity to relieve these tensions through action or thought. With the exception of some reflexes and simple sensori-motor schematas, the child is ill equipped to organize experience, much less master or change events."

Erikson (1963) could also be numbered among object-relations theorists who conceive of the critical period as coming much earlier. His model of the eight stages of personality development is clearly intended to convey the impression that the first one, basic trust versus basic mistrust at age birth-1, is a critical period in personality development.

CONCLUSIONS

Psychoanalysis, starting from a biological orientation to personality development, initially regarded the first five years of life as a sensitive period, emphasizing especially the Oedipal stage in years 3-5. Later theorists paid more attention to earlier stages. Current conceptions view the first year of life as the crucial period for the development of enduring personality structures (see Table 1).

All psychoanalytic theorists agree that personality development is organized through predetermined stages, with continuities from earlier to later ones. All theorists in the psychoanalytic tradition also agree that personality structures formed during critical periods in early childhood are almost irreversible, short of successful psychotherapy, which is not easy to achieve. Implied already in Freud's writings there is a great deal of pessimism, which has even been construed as nihilism, regarding the possibilities of a real change in personality during the adult years. One might say that over the years theoretical pessimism has been growing, as the critical period for the learning of basic personality style has moved to earlier and earlier ages.

The mere notion of personality implies the assumption of consistency over time and situations. So the question is not one of reversibility, but one of stability in behavior. Psychoanalytic approaches assume that structures acquired during the critical period of childhood will endure, and the results of early learning will be irreversible because no similar learning experience is likely to occur later on in life.

In all versions of psychoanalytic theory, from Freud to Kohut (see Kohut, 1971), parents play a central role and are really the most important factors in events during the critical period. The mother, of course, holds dominance in the child's emotional world. "When we distill some of the main points of psychoanalytic self-theorists, we see that maternal empathy is to healthy development of the self as early cognitive stimulation is to later intelligence or calcium intake to skeletal growth" (Langman & Kaplan, 1978, pp. 361–362).

If we want to explain the success and the attraction of psychoanalytic theories of personality, despite their speculative nature and their reliance on pri-

TABLE 1
Critical Periods in Personality Development

Theorist	Critical Period	Critical Period Content
Freud, Fenichel, Nagera	(age birth-6)/Oedipal stage, age 3-6	Handling libidinal impulses/sexual identity
Klein	birth-12 months	Handling libidinal impulses
Fairbairn, Winnicott	birth-24 months	Object-relations
Mahler	4-36 months	Separation-individuation
Erikson	birth-12 months/14-22 years (??)	Basic trust-basic mistrust/Identity-Identity diffusion
Kernberg, Kohut	birth-24 months	Attitudes toward the self

vate experiences, one major factor emerges from the preceding discussion. Psychoanalytic theories of personality follow an essentially biological rationale. The notion of a sensitive period, during which enduring patterns of behavior may be learned, is intrinsically attractive, since it fits our knowledge about the development of behavior.

Nobody will argue with the assumption that the organism is most open to influence during childhood, and that the impact of early learning will be long-lasting. We all agree with the notion that what is sensitive during critical periods is the central nervous system, and we have much anatomical evidence to support that thesis. In an attempt to integrate recent findings in neuroscience with psychoanalysis, Winson (1985, p. 162) states: "Recent research has found that a broader critical period exists in the organization of sensory perception and learning in young mammals, including young children. The critical period coincides with the time period during which the neocortex develops anatomically, and it may be related to this development."

The critical period in personality development, according to psychoanalysis, parallels exactly the period of highest brain growth. The newborn brain weighs 330 grams. By age 2 years it reaches 1,000 grams, by age 7 years, 1,250 grams, that is 90% of the adult weight, achieved at age 14 years. Winson (1985, p. 220) hypothesizes that what is unique about the critical period in personality development (which may extend until adolescence) is that impressions ". . . are integrated into the unconscious during off-line processing in REM sleep. . . . REM sleep processing continues throughout life, but it is the early impressions, those acquired during the critical period, that are the basis for the interpretations of many later events. Above and beyond this there is normal learning, which grows throughout life."

Psychoanalysis is a theory that does not easily lead to good measurement or good prediction, but is nevertheless immensely attractive to a large number of psychologists. The reason for this attraction must have something to do with the basic biological rationale of the theory, as shown above. This discussion of critical periods in psychoanalysis has demonstrated again its essentially biological starting point, which makes its developmental theory intuitively attractive and plausible. Psychoanalysis, even when it is most speculative, is anchored in a biological model, or a biological analogue, which we find intuitively attractive and persuasive.

Psychoanalysis draws our attention to a universal sequence of psychological development, which becomes a basic epistemological ordering of the world and of individual personality, culture, and humanity. The universal experience of the human infants includes a developing awareness of three realms, always in the following order: first, knowledge of one's body and its experienced needs. Second, awareness of the existence of another. Third, knowledge of relations between ourselves and others. All further experiences must be based on these early experiences and reactions, acquired in that order. All further experiences will be assimilated into that order. The existence of such a universal sequence cannot be challenged, and here lies the attraction of psychoanalysis for those wanting to understand not only human personality, but also human society and culture.

ACKNOWLEDGMENTS

Preparation of this chapter was supported by the Social Science Research Committee, University of Haifa. The chapter was completed while the author was a visiting scholar at the Department of Psychology, New York University. The friendly support of James Uleman is hereby gratefully acknowledged.

REFERENCES

Bird, D. Dr. Margaret S. Mahler, 88; studied child development. *The New York Times,* October 3, 1985, p. 23.

Balint, M. *Problems of human pleasure and behaviour.* New York: Liveright, 1957.

Chodoff, P. The diagnosis of hysteria: An overview. *The American Journal of Psychiatry,* 1974, *31,* 1073–1078.

Erikson, E. H. *Childhood and society.* New York: W. W. Norton, 1963.

Fairbairn, W. R. D. *An object relations theory of personality.* New York: Basic Books, 1952.

Fenichel, O. *The psychoanalytic theory of neurosis.* New York: W. W. Norton, 1945.

Freud, S. From the history of an infantile neurosis. In *The standard edition of the complete psychological works of Sigmund Freud* (Vol. 17). London: Hogarth, 1955. (Originally published 1918.)

Freud, S. A child is being beaten. In *The standard edition of the complete psychological works of Sigmund Freud* (Vol. 17). London: Hogarth, 1955. (Originally published 1919.)

Freud, S. Inhibitions, symptoms, and anxiety. In *The standard edition of the complete psychological works of Sigmund Freud* (Vol. 20). London: Hogarth, 1959. (Originally published 1925.)

Freud, S. The question of lay analysis. In *The standard edition of the complete psychological works of Sigmund Freud* (Vol. 20). London: Hogarth, 1959. (Originally published 1926.)

Freud, S. An outline of psychoanalysis. In *The standard edition of the complete psychological works of Sigmund Freud* (Vol. 23). London: Hogarth, 1964.

Greenspan, S., & Greenspan, N. T. *First feelings.* New York: Viking, 1985.

Guntrip, H. *Schizoid phenomena, object relations and the self.* New York: International Universities, 1968.

Hartmann, H. *Ego psychology and the problem of adaptation.* New York: International Universities, 1939.

Jones, E. *The life and work of Sigmund Freud* (Vol. 2). New York: Basic, 1955

Kernberg, O. *Borderline conditions and pathological narcissism.* New York: Jason Aronson, 1975.

Kernberg, O. *Object relations and clinical psychoanalysis.* New York: Jason Aronson, 1976.

Klein, M. *Contributions to psychoanalysis.* London: Hogarth, 1948.

Kohut, H. *The analysis of the self.* New York: International Universities, 1971.

Langman, L., & Kaplan L. V. The crises of self and state under late capitalism: A critical perspective. *International Journal of Law and Psychiatry,* 1978, *1,* 343-374.

Mahler, M. S. Thoughts about development and individuation. *The psychoanalytic study of the child,* 1963, *18,* 307-324.

Mahler, M. S., Pine, F., & Bergman, A. *The psychological birth of the human infant: Symbiosis and individuation.* New York: Basic, 1975.

Nagera, H. *Early childhood disturbances, the infantike neurosis, and the adulthood disturbances.* New York: International Universities, 1966.

Ryan, E. R., & Bell, M. D. Changes in object relations from psychosis to recovery. *Journal of Abnormal Psychology,* 1984, *93,* 209-215.

Winson, J. *Brain and psyche: The biology of the unconscious.* Garden City, NY: Anchor, 1985.

11 Mother-Infant Bonding as a Critical Period

Barbara J. Myers
Virginia Commonwealth University

INTRODUCTION

In recent years, the issue of what happens to mothers and infants in the period immediately following birth has received attention both from researchers and from new and prospective parents. Hospitals traditionally separated the mother and infant just after birth and for much of their hospital stay, caring for the infant in the nursery and for the mother in the maternity ward. Pediatricians Klaus and Kennell (1976, 1982) and their associates made strong claims that separation of mother and infant may disrupt the formation of a maternal bond to the infant and that the first minutes and hours after birth are the most crucial to the formation of this bond. Proponents of early contact suggested that just after birth the mother and infant should lie together in a warm and private place, joined when possible by the father. Such early contact, Klaus and Kennell suggested, facilitates the formation of a warm, loving bond between the parents and their newborn. When mother and infant are separated, this bond is said to form more slowly, or perhaps not at all. Klaus and Kennell's claim was never an extreme one of early contact being the sole factor in human maternal behavior, yet their work became the focal point for research and discussion concerning mother-infant bonding.

Their analysis of the effects of early tactile contact on "mother-infant bonding" was not accepted uncritically. Criticisms were leveled concerning the validity of measures, the reseach methodology, and the strength of the data presented. Despite these theoretical and empirical concerns, bonding has become a household word, popularized by the mass media and accepted with enthusiasm by expectant parents. A number of studies have tested the hypothesis, with both positive and negative results. I review these studies in an effort to clarify the theoretical underpinnings and untangle the empirical findings that are now available. In the end of this review I indicate (along with Lamb, 1982, and Morgan, 1981) that the evidence does not support the hypothesis that a sensitive period for human social bonding exists. Many disagree with this conclusion and find that the available evidence points compellingly toward accepting, or at least further exploring, the bonding hypothesis. This chapter contributes toward evaluating this interesting and important question.

DEFINING BONDING AND ATTACHMENT

A first point of confusion in research in this field has been the unfortunate melding together of the concepts of bonding and attachment. The term *bonding* is used to describe a rapidly occurring process that transpires immediately after birth in which the mother forms an affectionate attachment to her infant: The direction is mother-to-infant. Bonding is thought to be facilitated by early contact between the mother and newborn that involves skin-to-skin touching, mutual visual regard, and suckling (Klaus & Kennell, 1976, 1982). Bowlby (1969) originally spoke of *attachment* as the emotional bond between an infant and caretaker that the child displays through proximity-seeking behaviors of crying, sucking, calling, following, watching, and protest at separation. An ethologist, Bowlby believed that these behaviors served to keep the child close to an adult and thus safe from predators or neglect. Ainsworth, Blehar, Waters, and Wall (1978) have spearheaded empirical work on attachment, defining it as a unique relationship between two people that is specific to them and endures over distance and time. Attachment behaviors shown by the older infant, such as separation distress and stranger anxiety, are not shown until the infant nears 1 year. Thus, the construct of attachment has been defined primarily in the direction of infant-to-mother (or significant other). It develops gradually over a period of months.

Although both bonding and attachment develop through dyadic interchange (both mother and baby are active participants), the two terms are distinct and should not be used interchangeably. *Bonding* is the very early mother-to-infant affection; *attachment* is the slowly developing infant-to-mother affection. Much of the bonding literature uses the terms *bonding* and *attachment* as though the two were identical, though this use is imprecise and incorrect.

EFFECTS OF MOTHER-INFANT
CONTACT AND SEPARATION

The Klaus and Kennell Work

The guilding problem of the research in mother-infant contact is whether traditional hospital practices damage the mother-infant bond. One longitudinal study conducted by Klaus, Kennell, and their associates examined this question in detail, following a small set of families from birth to 5 years (Kennell et al., 1974; Klaus et al., 1972; Ringler, Kennell, Jarvella, Navojosky, & Klaus, 1975; Ringler, Trause, Klaus, & Kennell, 1978). These widely cited studies have been most influential, despite a variety of methodological problems. Klaus and associates reported superior maternal bonding and child development persisting for several years in families afforded early mother-infant contact. Thus, this series of studies are presented in detail.

Klaus et al. (1972) compared two groups of 14 lower class, primarily black mothers of full-term healthy infants. The groups were matched for age, social class, marital status, race, medication, and infants' birthweight, and the mothers were randomly assigned to the control or experimental group. The control group had contact with their babies that was routine at the time in American hospitals: a glance at the baby just after the birth, a short visit at 6 to 12 hours for identification, and then 20- to 30-minute visits for feeding every 4 hours during the day. Mothers in the extended-contact group, in contrast, were given their babies for 1 hour of skin-to-skin contact under a warming panel within the first 2 hours after birth. They also had their babies with them for 5 extra hours on each of the next 3 days of life. Thus the experimental manipulation involved both early and extended contact.

At 1 month, the mothers returned to the hospital for interviews and blind observations. The extended-contact mothers showed certain behavioral differences. They were more likely to stand and watch during their babies' physical exams, and they showed more soothing behavior when their babies cried during the exam. Also, the extended-contact mothers reported picking the baby up more when it cried and not wanting to leave the baby. The researchers evaluated this as evidence of stronger mother-infant bonding.

All mothers were also videotaped as they fed their infants at this 1-month visit. Each second of the first 10 minutes of the feeding was analyzed for caregiving and attachment behaviors. Groups did not differ on any of the unspecified caregiving behaviors, but did differ on two of the four "attachment" behaviors: Extended-contact mothers spent more time in the *en face* position (looking at the baby's face, with eyes aligned in the same plane) and more time in fondling, though they spent no more time holding the infants close or in looking at them.

At 1 year a new set of investigators, blind to group status, examined the mothers and infants (Kennell et al., 1974). The sample at this point was cut in half, although no mention is made of what happened to the rest of the sample. A great quantity of data were collected in these visits using time-lapse films, checklists, and continuous narrative recording during seven separate situations: an interview, a physical exam of the infant, a separation episode, picture taking, free play, a Bayley exam, and a feeding. Only four differences emerged, which again were interpreted as indicating more "attachment" in the experimental group of mothers: Upon returning to work more extended-contact mothers reported missing their infants; they spent more time standing near the table when their infants were being examined; and they spent more time soothing and kissing their infants when they cried. The extended-contact babies themselves scored an average of 5 points higher on the Bayley exam (a mean of 98 vs. a mean of 93, $p < .05$).

At the 1-year visit, then, there were four measures that discriminated the two groups, but there was a far larger body of data that showed no differences. Specifically, none of the mother-infant interactions during the Bayley exam, the interview, the picture taking, or the free play showed differences. The observations during the feeding and separation episodes were not examined due to unexplained "differing motor development of the infants." The behaviors in all these analyses are not listed, nor are the number of behaviors included, so it is not possible to determine the probability that the four significant differences occurred by chance.

At 2 years, the linguistic behavior of the mothers while speaking to the children was compared (9 extra-contact; 10 controls) (Ringler, Kennell, Jarvella, Navojosky, & Klaus, 1975). At the 1-year visit it had been noted that the extended-contact mothers' speech differed in one respect: They used fewer statements than the control mothers. It is difficult to assign meaning to this finding, especially since it was the only one of many linguistic measures that distinguished the groups. It is not clear how many language variables were involved. At the 2-year visit, the group differed on the following linguistic behaviors: The extended-contact mothers used fewer content words, asked more questions, expressed fewer commands, and used more words per proposition than did the control-group mothers. The experimenters interpreted these differences as indicating a style of speech that is greater in variety and elaboration. It is not clear from the report what other linguistic factors were tested for differences, so it is again difficult to determine to what extent the reported differences might have occurred by chance.

When the children were 5, the same sample of 19 again returned with their mothers and was administered tests of intelligence (Stanford-Binet) and language (Assessment of Children's Language Comprehension and Northwest Syntax), and the mothers were administered the WAIS IQ (Ringler, Trause, Klaus, & Kennell, 1978). There were no significant differences on any of the tests between the mean scores of the extra-contact and the control children. There were also no differences between the groups on maternal IQ. Dimensions of mothers' speech to their 2-year-olds were compared with the children's intellectual and linguistic performance at 5, and an interesting pattern emerged. None of the correlations was significant in the group as a whole, nor were any significant for the control children. However, among the early-contact pairs, several dimensions of maternal speech (number of adjectives, words per proposition) were correlated with children's performance (receptive abilities, IQ). In this group, mothers' IQ was also significantly related to their children's IQ ($r = .78$, $p < .01$), although this was not the case for the control pairs. The *lack* of mother-child correlation in IQ for the control pairs is puzzling and unusual, for a mother-child IQ relation normally occurs. Unfortunately, neither the r values nor the raw scores are provided. Thus a relation between mothers' speech when the children were 2 and the children's intellectual and language performance at 5 occurred only among mother-child pairs who experienced extra contact in the early postpartum period. The researchers suggest that the extra postpartum contact increased the degree of association between mothers' and children's behavior by expanding on such early behaviors as looking *en face*.

Critique of Klaus and Kennell's Work

This set of studies does not adequately consider the statistical error of performing a great many univariate tests of mean difference. It is often difficult to tell how many tests were performed so that the likelihood of chance findings can be assessed. The practice of gathering a surplus of data and then examining all of it to see what variables distinguish the groups (as may be inferred from the 1-year observation) is a technique that capitalizes on chance findings. This technique is perhaps defensible in exploratory research, but then the researcher must take special care in delineating the likelihood of chance findings.

Another problem concerns the validity of the dependent measures used, and specifically the relation of these measures to the feelings of affection and bonding that maternal-infant contact is suggested to bring about. Ross (1980) points out the problem of interpreting the finding that extra-contact mothers spend more time near the examining table during pediatric examination, at both 1 month and 1 year. The researchers interpret this result as indicating more positive maternal feeling, although Ross suggests it could also indicate overprotectiveness. An alternate interpretation is that the early experience of having doctors and nurses witness a mother holding her baby skin-to-skin helps her to overcome any shyness or reticence she might have about showing her feelings in the presence of medical personnel. Thus she might more readily assert herself and play a strong role with her child in the presence of a physician — as manifest by staying near during the exam. While this interpretation might be seen as a positive effect, it has nothing to do with bonding. Similarly, the maternal language variables measured by Ringler et al. (1975) bear little relation to maternal affection (for example, number of content words). Another variable was created by pooling the responses concerning picking up the crying baby with feelings about going out. Neither of these questions yielded a significant difference when taken alone, but they distinguish the groups when artificially combined. While it is common and accepted practice to planfully combine individual test items into a composite score in order to increase the reliability of a measure, it is not acceptable to do this combining in a post hoc way. There is no evidence that there was an a priori plan to create a scale including these two particular measures. The two questions tap such different behaviors that it is hard to picture what underlying trait is being measured by their combination. In addition, the meaning of these responses is not directly interpretable: The practice of picking up a crying baby or letting the baby cry for a while is probably more determined by cultural beliefs than by degree of affection, and feeling worried when away from a baby could as easily be engendered by insecurity as it could be by affection.

Further Studies Supporting the Bonding Hypothesis

A much-cited investigation of bonding is a longitudinal study of a middle-class Swedish sample (de Chateau & Wiberg, 1977a, 1977b; de Chateau, 1980a, 1980b). de Chateau's manipulation consisted of 15-minutes skin-to-skin contact and suckling, beginning 10-15 minutes after delivery, for 22 early-contact primiparous mothers and routine treatment for 20 primiparous control mothers. After this period, mothers were treated identically for the remainder of their 6- to 8-day hospital stay. Behavioral measures were taken at 36 hours, 1 year, and 3 years postpartum by observers blind to group membership. Although a number of significant differences emerged, these must be considered again in relation to the very large number of variables measured. The differences found were sometimes *fewer* than would be expected by chance. At 36 hours, one relevant difference appeared: The experimental group mother held their babies more during a 25-minute observation period. Two other differences are reported, but their significance is less clear: The experimental-group mothers sat up more, and the control-group mothers leaned on an elbow more. These three differences were the only effects found in 35 items observed, and the effects were found only for the mothers of boys. No "negative" effects were reported, i.e., effects favoring the control group (except for the elbow-leaning just mentioned).

At 3 months, a home observation and interview were conducted. The experimental-group infants were found to smile more and cry less than the control-group infants, and the experimental-group mothers were found to look *en face* more, kiss the babies more, and clean them *less* than control-group mothers. Again, these differences were found only for the boy infants. A total of 61 different behavioral items were scored, and *t*-tests were performed on these using 6 sets of paired comparisons for each behavior sampled. This resulted in a total of 366 *t*-tests, in which 16 differences of $p <$ .05 were found. de Chateau acknowledged that chance findings are a possibility, but stated that the observed differences are "more pronounced than can be expected by chance only" (de Chateau & Wiberg, 1977b, p. 150). Actually, 18 significant differences would be expected at a $p < .05$ level.

At 1 year after delivery, measures included a pediatric exam, an interview, the Gesell test, the Vineland Social Maturity Scale, a test of maternal personality, breast-feeding reports, and review of a diary which the mother kept of the child's habits (de Chateau, 1980b). An observation of mother's behavior took place during the pediatric examination. Of 26 behaviors recorded, three distinguished the two groups: Experimental-group mothers held the babies in close contact more, touched and caressed more, and used more "positive talking" (the *p*-values of these differences are not provided). The experimental-group infants showed superior performance on all five subtests of the Gesell Developmental Test (although reports of the significance of the mean differences are not provided). The magnitude of the differences is small, with two differences being less than 1 week, two less than 2 weeks, and one, gross motor, being 3.3 weeks superiority for the experimental group. No differences were found for the Vineland Social Maturity Scale, the maternal personality measure, or the mother's diary record of sleeping and eating habits of the babies.

The maternal interview at 1 year revealed a number of group differences. The meaning of these differences, however, is difficult to interpret. Specifically, the experimental-group mothers reported a longer duration of breast feeding (for boys but not girls), a lower incidence of returning to outside employment, a higher incidence of letting the baby sleep in a room alone, a lower incidence of early bladder training, and that fathers were *less* active in helping to care for the infant. Although de Chateau interprets all these differences as indicating a superior mother-infant relationship for the experimental group, this conclusion is not clearly justified. It is not evident, for example, that moving the baby to a room alone, having a less involved father, and delaying a return to work are necessarily positive findings.

At 3 years again, a great many variables were measured, including an observation of mother-child play with a doll house, observation of the child, interview with the mother, interview with the father, hormonal studies, and a Denver Developmental Screening Test. Three differences were found: The experimental-group mothers were less likely than controls to report retrospectively that the time they had spent with their babies after delivery was insufficient (20% vs. 60%); the experimental-group families had had more subsequent children (9 vs. 4); and the experimental-group mothers judged that their children had achieved two-word utterances sooner (no measures of child language were actually taken). It is not clear what questions or how many questions were asked the mothers that resulted in these three findings.

A second study favoring the bonding hypothesis was one carried out in Guatemala (Hales, Lozoff, Sosa, & Kennell, 1977). This study varied the timing of early contact and made a single observation at 36 hours. Sixty low-income urban women in Guatemala City who had routine vaginal deliveries and no medication, anesthesia, or sedatives, were included. All the babies were full term and healthy. The mothers were randomly assigned to three groups. The 20 early-contact mothers lay skin-to-skin with the infants under a heat panel for 45 minutes shortly after delivery. A second group of 20 mothers in the delayed-contact condition were separated from their infants at birth but had the same 45 minutes of private skin-to-skin contact 12 hours *after* birth. The control group of 20 mothers were separated from their infants at birth and first saw their wrapped infants at 12 hours when the nurse brought the babies to their mothers' beds. Babies in each group remained with their mothers during the day, and all were breast fed. The only treatment variables that differentiated the groups, therefore, were whether they had skin-to-skin contact and whether that occurred at birth or 12 hours later.

At 36 hours, an observer blind to group membership found that mothers having early contact with their infants showed significantly more affectionate behavior, defined as the sum of ratings of looking at the baby, *en face* looking, talking to baby, fondling, kissing, and smiling, than did either the delayed-contact or the control group. When these affectionate behaviors were taken individually, only *en face* showed a significant difference among the groups. (Again the problem of artificially combined scores looms over this procedure.) The delayed-contact mothers showed an intermediate amount of affectionate behavior, falling between the early-contact and the control groups. There were no group differences in caretaking activities or in proximity-maintaining behavior. This study found ordered differences in affectionate behavior: The early-contact mothers showed the most, then the delayed-contact mothers, and the control mothers showed the least.

A carefully done Canadian study finds support for the hypothesis that early contact facilitates maternal bonding, and also provides evidence that rooming-in further facilitates affectionate behavior (Kontos, 1978). Middle-class, healthy primiparous mothers chose whether they wanted rooming-in or not and then were randomly assigned to either an early-contact or a routine-contact group. Thus four groups of 12 mothers were created, with rooming-in a self-selected variable and early contact a randomly assigned variable. At 1 and 3 months, the mothers and infants were observed at home for 10 minutes, and the observer checked the frequency of 19 maternal behaviors. A summary "attachment score" was devised by adding together the 15 behavioral items judged to indicate "attachment." These behaviors were chosen to concentrate on the amount of attention, bodily contact, and stimulation provided the infant. While some maternal behaviors meet these criteria (smile, hold close, kiss), some behaviors bear little relation to bonding (for example, hold on shoulder, change position, play with toy, play without toy, walk or stand with infant). Nevertheless, there were strong main effects for both the early-contact and the rooming-in conditions, at both the 1-month and the 3-month observation periods. The same observer was present at all births and therefore not blind to group membership, although reliability checks made on 25% of the sample revealed no observer bias.

One final study also lends support to the bonding hypothesis. Peterson and Mehl (1978) examined 46 middle- or upper class white families, whose delivery experience divided them into three groups: natural childbirth in the hospital, natural childbirth at home, and childbirth under anesthesia in the hospital. The three conditions were self-selected, except when complications forced more medical intervention than the parents desired. Mothers and fathers were interviewed prenatally, the first week after delivery, and 1, 2, 4, and 6 months postpartum. From these interviews, mothers were assigned a birth experience score (reflecting how positive they felt the experience was), a disappointment score (reflecting how closely the delivery resembled what the mother had planned), and an "attachment" score (based on her feelings of closeness, involvement, and confidence with the baby). Factors concerning the delivery, such as amount of maternal-infant separation and length of labor, were used to predict the "attachment" score. For the entire sample of 46, the most significant variable predicting attachment was the amount of maternal-infant separation during the first 72 postpartum hours. In looking separately at the three groups of mothers, however, separation was not the most important factor for any of them. For the two natural-childbirth groups, the birth experience was the most important, and for the anesthesia group, the disappointment factor was most predictive of attachment: the more disappointed, the less attached. The separation factor entered the regression equations much later, when at all, in each of the three groups. Thus, the initial finding of separation being the most important factor may be a statistical artifact that is not descriptive of any of the groups.

Early Contact and Breast Feeding

One of the claims made by proponents of bonding is that early contact promotes the frequency and the duration of breast feeding (Klaus & Kennell,

1976; Sosa, Kennell, Klaus, & Urrutia, 1976; Winters, 1973). To explore the question of whether early contact influences nursing, three separate but identical studies involving a total of 160 poor, urban women from two hospitals in Guatemala City were conducted (Sosa et al., 1976). In all three studies, randomly selected control groups of women were separated from their infants immediately after delivery and first received their infants at either 12 or 24 hours after delivery (depending on the usual waiting period in the hospital involved). Those in the experimental groups were given their infants on the delivery table, and were then moved to a private room where they spent 45 minutes in skin-to-skin contact with their babies and were encouraged to breast feed. All the babies were kept in the nursery thereafter except for feeding times.

By 12 months, a longer period of breast feeding was evident for the early-contact mothers in two of the studies, whereas the third study found longer nursing for the control group. In all three groups, the early-contact infants suffered fewer infections.

Three other studies found that extra contact in the neonatal period correlated with more and longer breast feeding. In a small study, Winters (1973) compared six mothers who began nursing shortly after birth with six mothers who did not have contact with their infants until 16 hours after birth. All the mothers originally intended to breast feed and none stopped because of physical problems. When checked 2 months later, all six of the mothers with early contact were still nursing their infants, but only one of the six in the late-contact group was still nursing her infant.

In a larger study, two groups of 100 Brazilian women who delivered normal full-term infants were compared for success in breast feeding (Sousa et al., 1974). The experimental group nursed their infants just after delivery, and the infant stayed with the mother in her room. In that group, a nurse worked with the mothers to stimulate and encourage breast feeding. The control group had the routine hospital contact, consisting of a glimpse at birth, then feedings every 3 hours for 30 minutes starting at 12 to 14 hours after birth. At 2 months, 77% of the early-contact mothers were still nursing, in contrast to 27% of the controls. More than early contact is compared here on account of the rooming-in, special nurse, and urgings to continue breast feeding.

The final study concerning the effects of early contact on nursing is that of de Chateau (1980a), already discussed. The prolongation of nursing in his sample was found for boy infants only.

In summary, there is some evidence to suggest that early contact contributes to a higher incidence and longer duration of breast feedings, although the findings are not consistent. Important to this discussion, however, is the point that no study has demonstrated that mothers who breast feed rather than bottle feed or who breast feed for longer periods of time are actually more successfully "bonded" to their infants. All the above studies imply that breast feeding is both an index and an outcome of bonding. There are mothers all over the world, though, who breast feed their babies and who show a full range of degrees of affection for their infants; the same can no doubt be said for bottle-feeding mothers. The choice of type of feeding depends on cultural values, social and economic conditions in the family, and personal preference. It may be that if nursing is started on the delivery table it is more likely to succeed. Early contact and early nursing may, as some of the data suggest, contribute to a longer duration of breast feeding, but even these data are contradictory. Certainly many women begin nursing several days postpartum and continue successfully as well. None of this, however, means that breast feeding is an index of bonding, nor is there conclusive evidence that breast feeding facilitates maternal bonding.

Early Contact and Child Abuse

Mother-infant separation has been implicated in child abuse because of the assumption that bonding is established in the first few hours or days and that an initial failure to form an appropriate mother-infant bond is the root cause of child abuse or neglect. These two beliefs were supported by initial findings that reports of child abuse are disproportionately high among infants who are born prematurely and who spend long periods separated from their parents in a neonatal nursery. These findings come primarily from retrospective follow-up investigations into child abuse files to find how many battered and neglected children were premature or suffered other neonatal complications. These studies commonly find that a larger than expected proportion of abused and neglected children had been separated from their mothers at birth on account of low birthweight or neonatal medical complications (Elmer & Gregg, 1967; Fomufod, Sinkford, & Luoy, 1975; Klein & Stern, 1971; Lynch & Roberts, 1977).

The problem in drawing the conclusion that early separation is the cause of the later abuse from these studies is that there is no attempt to assess the quality of the mother-infant bond during early infancy. Later abuse is taken as evidence that a bond had never formed in infancy or that it had broken down. This post hoc explanation is an easy one to draw, but as Egeland and Vaughn (1981) point out, there is no evidence in these retrospective studies that a bonding problem initially existed or that such potential bonding problems are the cause of later abuse and neglect.

One important study experimentally assigned families to different contact conditions at birth and followed them for subsequent parenting failure (O'Connor, Vietze, Sherrod, Sandler, & Altemeier, 1980). The random assignment to groups qualifies this project as an experimental study, thus making it methodologically stronger than the above reports. Infants born in a hospital serving low-income families were assigned over a 9-month period either to rooming-in ($n = 143$) or to routine ($n = 158$) postpartum contact. There was no early contact for either group. Control mothers first held their babies at about 12 hours postpartum and rooming-in mothers at 7 to 21 hours. Control mothers had their babies at feeding times only (about 2 hours per day) while rooming-in mothers averaged 11½ hours contact per day.

Outcome data concerning abuse and neglect were obtained from hospital and state records when the infants averaged 17 months of age. Evidence of abuse or neglect was found in 10 control and 2 rooming-in families ($p < .05$). Since the rooming-in and control families were comparable at time of delivery (mother's age, infant birthweight, married/single status, black/white ratio, mother's education, welfare status, employment), it seems likely that the rooming-in was related to the lower incidence of parenting failure. Note that this study did not include a condition of *early* contact, but rather of *extended* contact. The researchers caution that, besides the extended contact in the rooming-in condition, these mothers also were able to have almost unlimited visits by the baby's father or grandmother; control mothers did not receive this privilege. The treatment effect may, then, have been one of solidifying the family unit with resultant benefit to the mother's parenting. This confound cannot be separated from mother-infant contact effects.

Abuse is not a probable outcome for a child just because of early separation. To give an accurate picture of the probability of abuse after separation, prospective (rather than retrospective) studies are required. One such study (Egeland & Vaughn, 1981) kept longitudinal data on a sample of 267 lower income women in Minneapolis from the time of their pregnancy through 9 months after delivery. Two groups of mothers were selected from this sample for comparison, the 33 women who provided the best quality care and the 32 women who abused, neglected, or in some way mistreated their infants. Comparing these "best" and "worst" cases, there were no differences between the groups in events thought to be related to bonding. Specifically, there were no differences in number of premature births, delivery complications, medical problems requiring mother-infant separation, or number of infants born with physical anomalies. Not only were the best and worst groups indistinguishable from each other, they were indistinguishable from the larger sample of 267 as well.

It is necessary to weigh carefully how seriously to take findings of "no difference." A finding of "no difference" can never establish absolutely that a difference does not exist. This is true alone on logical grounds, but is underlined because if a study is poorly conducted it is easy to obtain a no-difference finding. If measures are unreliable, the treatment is too weak, or the groupings are produced by ambiguous criteria, a finding of no difference is more a commentary on the research method than on the hypothesis being tested.

It is clear, then, that the Egeland and Vaughn study cannot establish with certainty that postnatal events are unrelated to abuse. In this case, this uncertainty does not come from a poorly executed study, however. Their results are to be taken seriously, for the study demonstrated that at least for this large sample abuse groups were not different on sensibly chosen postnatal indices. The authors suggest that rather than accepting the simple conclusion that abuse is "caused by" a lack of bonding that is "caused by" early separation, researchers should search more closely for multiple causes of abuse. These causes might include personality defects in the parents, social isolation, parents' abuse as children, marital stress, economic stress ascribable to unemployment, a cultural acceptance of severe punishment or a host of other factors.

STUDIES FAILING TO SUPPORT
THE BONDING HYPOTHESIS

The possibility that early contact enhances, and separation harms, mother-infant interaction was picked up by the mass media and has been accepted enthusiastically as truth and amplified beyond its original boundaries by a growing number of people. Hospitals, normally slow to change medical policies, moved toward promoting early contact of mother and infant and involvement by the father: The last 10 years have witnessed a welcomed "humanizing" of the birth experience. A review of the available evidence concerning bonding has convinced many, however, that conclusions have been too hastily drawn and that strong opinions they have generated have gone beyond the data. This assessment could be reached solely on the basis of criticisms of the studies that purport to find a relation between early contact and later maternal behavior and attitudes. The case is made even more strongly by examining studies that fail to obtain such a relation.

Direct Failures to Replicate

A Denver study with careful procedural and methodological controls failed to find differences between extra-contact and control mothers (Svedja, Campos, & Emde, 1980). Thirty primiparous lower-middle-class mothers with healthy, full-term babies were randomly assigned to two infant contact groups. Extra-contact mothers received their infants on the delivery table for 15-minute skin-to-skin contact, and then had an extra 45 minutes of private contact in their rooms. Extra-contact mothers also received their babies every 4 hours for feeding, but for each feeding had 90 minutes rather than the usual 30 minutes. Control mothers saw and briefly held their wrapped infants in the delivery room, and then had the babies for feeding every 4 hours for 30 minutes. In order to eliminate procedural confounds, only one mother at a time was present on the unit, and spot checks were made on the amount of time nurses spent with study mothers. Additionally, roommates of extra-contact mothers also were given 90-minute feeds to eliminate a feeling of "specialness" in extra-contact mothers. The observers were blind to group membership and were trained to a high interobserver reliability. All mothers and infants were videotaped about 36 hours after delivery during a 10-minute interaction and a 15-minute breast-feeding episode. Observers scored the videotapes for 28 discrete response measures. Results showed that *none* of the 28 behaviors differed between the two groups, nor were any group differences found when the 28 measures were pooled into four general response categories. This study came close to replicating the original Klaus and Kennell protocol, except that important methodological considerations were more closely controlled, yet no differences were found. These results call into question the notion that early or extended contact necessarily affects maternal behavior.

Another carefully conducted study was a close replication of the Klaus and Kennell design, but again had primarily negative results (Taylor, Taylor, Campbell, Maloni, & Dickey, 1979). Women in labor were randomly assigned to extra-contact or control groups. The women were matched with regard to demographic, obstetric, and early neonatal variables. The extra-contact mothers had 50 minutes of holding their infants in the recovery room; this was the only treatment that was different from control mothers. At 2 days and 1 month, interaction during a feeding was assessed, and at 1 month the Klaus and Kennell attachment questions were asked (response to crying and how they felt when they had to go out). Records were also kept of how much time the mother chose to have her baby with her in a modified rooming-in situation. At both measurement periods, mothers were also asked to respond to the Neonatal Perception Inventory (NPI), which is a measure of a mother's perception of her baby compared with an average baby of the same age with respect to crying, feeding, spitting up, sleeping, elimination, and predictability of eating and sleeping patterns. The researchers hypothesized that extra-contact mothers would be superior on all these measures. However, the results showed that extra contact had no demonstrable effect on the attachment questions at 1 month, on the amount of time the mother chose to spend with the infant in the hospital, or on the mother's perception of her infant (NPI) at 2 days or 1 month. Extra contact was associated with better quality interaction during feeding, but only for mother-male infant pairs.

It was also hypothesized that the extra-contact mothers would rate their infants in a more positive direction in terms of their temperament at 8 months than would control mothers. Specifically, extra-contact mothers were expected to rate their infants as more positive in mood, more regular, less intense, and more adaptable (Campbell, Maloni, & Taylor, 1979). However, there were no contact group differences for any of these temperament categories. Similarly, when infants were classified as "difficult," "easy," or "intermediate," there was no effect of early treatment.

A third major study was conducted by a research team in North Carolina (Siegel, Bauman, Schaefer, Saunders, & Ingram, 1980). Theirs was a longitudinal experimental study involving 321 low-income mothers and infants and examining the effects of two treatments: early and extended contact, and home visits by a health care paraprofessional. Women in their third trimester were randomly assigned to four treatment groups: (1) both early and extended contact and home visits by a paraprofessional infant case worker; (2) early and extended hospital contact only; (3) home visits only; and (4) routine hospital care and no home visits. Home visit workers were carefully recruited and given 200 hours of preservice training as well as continuous supervision throughout the project. The workers first visited the mother in the hospital and then made nine home visits during the first 3 months of the infant's life. The early- and extended-contact intervention (which closely resembles the Klaus and Kennell intervention) comprised at least 45 minutes of mother-infant contact during the first 3 hours after delivery ("early contact") and at least 5 additional hours each day during the hospital stay ("extended contact"). Mothers without the extra contact had the traditional brief contact after birth and about 2½ hours of feeding time each day.

The researchers hypothesized that the extra contact between the mother and her infant and the home support visits would positively influence maternal attachment and also reduce child abuse and neglect. They also hypothesized that both interventions would affect health care utilization, as measured by more reliable well-baby health care visits and fewer emergency room visits and hospitalizations.

Data were collected by interview during the last trimester of pregnancy and by interviews and observations in the home when the infants were 4 and 12 months of age, and from hospital, health, and welfare records. All data collectors were blind to contact group membership. Attachment ratings were created from factor analyses of two groups of data from the home visits: a 92-item Attachment Inventory and a 30-item behavioral list of mother attachment behaviors. Both scales were completed by two home observers after watching the mother bathing, dressing, feeding, and playing with the infant. The factor analysis produced three factors at 4 months: acceptance of infant, interaction/stimulation, and consoling of crying infant. At 12 months, the acceptance and interaction/stimulation factors emerged again, but the consoling factor was replaced by a factor indicating the infant's positive versus negative behavior.

This study's methodology has been explained at some length to make the point that it was a well-planned and ambitious undertaking that required a large investment in trainers, home workers, and data collectors and a sophisticated data analysis plan. The results, however, indicated that the two interventions were far less important in explaining variance in the groups than were the maternal background variables of race, marital status, parity, education, age, and verbal test score. Data were analyzed by multiple regression analysis in which the background variables and the intervention variables were used to predict the attachment factor scores explained above. The home visits were not significant predictors of any of the factors. Early and extended contact added 2.5% to the amount of variance explained in two of the three factors at 4 months, and added 3.2% to one factor at 12 months. As Siegel et al. (1980, p. 188) note, "Each of these relationships are statistically significant, but the amount of contributed variance is small and the relatively limited impacts at 4 months were even less noteworthy at 12 months." The interventions were also found to be unrelated to child abuse/neglect and health care utilization.

In overview, this was a true experimental study in which the effects of two interventions, early and extended contact and home visits, were tested on a large sample of low-income mothers. Early and extended contact explained a significant but very modest (2-3%) amount of variance in maternal attachment scores at 4 and 12 months and was unrelated to abuse/neglect and health care usage. The home visits were unrelated to any of the dependent measures. The researchers suggest (p. 189) that in spite of "some enhancement of maternal attachment . . . it appears that programs other than early and extended contact and home visitation must be developed to produce substantial influences on attachment, reports of abuse and neglect, and health care utilization."

Early Contact and Later Infant Attachment

Several studies have sought to test whether the effects of early contact or separation might extend to the later attachment of infants to others. The assumption is that disrupted bonding behavior of the mother, brought on by separation, might lead to a breakdown of the complex behavioral synchrony that is involved in the infant's formation of an attachment to the mother. Twenty-four 12- to 19-month-old infants who had suffered prolonged separation in an intensive care unit due to prematurity or serious illness just after birth were tested in the Ainsworth Strange Situation, the standard procedure for measuring the quality of infant attachment. Despite this lengthy separation from their parents after birth, these infants were comparable in their patterns of attachment to groups previously studied who were not separated at birth (Rode, Chang, Fisch, & Sroufe, 1981). The researchers suggest that, rather than connecting interaction patterns to events occurring soon after birth, the quality of a mother-infant relationship is a product of the entire history of their interaction.

In a similar study, Hock, Coady, and Cordero (1973) also compared Strange Situation behavior of 31 premature infants with that of 30 fullterms when both groups were about 11 months past term age. The premature group had averaged 1500 grams at birth and were in the hospital an average of 40 days past birth in contrast to 3- to 4-day hospital stay for the full-term group. As in the Rode et al. study, no differences in attachment were found between groups.

A German study varied both the timing of contact (early or delayed) and the amount of contact during the hospital stay (every 4 hours for feeding or modified rooming-in) (Grossmann, Grossmann, Huber, & Wartner, 1981) and studied infants' attachment a year later. For the 54 middle-class families in this study, however, there was again no connection between either early or extended contact and the babies' attachment to their mothers at 12 months.

As a final note, the Taylor study described earlier which replicated the Klaus and Kennell design followed up their babies with the Ainsworth attachment rating (Ottaviano, Campbell, & Taylor, 1979). The 25 infants with extra contact were no more likely to be classified as securely attached to their mothers than were the routine contact babies.

The lack of connection in these four studies between postpartum experience and infants' attachment to mother at 1 year underscores the point made at the outset: Bonding and attachment are two different things. They are different by definition, and the results of the above studies suggest that early contact, which is purported to influence maternal bonding, does not show an effect on later infant attachment.

Early Effects That Later Disappear

According to the hypothesis that early contact leads to stronger maternal bonding, the early behavioral differences shown by mothers permitted early contact might be expected to increase and grow. An early pattern of synchronous interaction should be started which would have a "fanning out" effect, leading to later patterns of optimal parenting for the mother and superior functioning in the child. Longitudinal reports by both the Klaus and Kennell group (Ringler et al., 1978) and de Chateau (1980a) would attest to this, for both find superiorities in extra-contact mother-child pairs at older ages (5 and 3 years, respectively).

Not all investigators report such long-lasting effects, however. Even some studies which find favorable outcomes in the early postpartum days find that in ensuing weeks or months these differences disappear. One such study is the West German investigation introduced earlier, in which four groups of mothers provided all combinations of early contact, extra contact, and routine conditions (Grossmann, Grossmann, Huber, & Wartner, 1981). Besides the 12-month attachment testing sequence already described, videotaped recordings of feedings were made on days 2 or 3, 4 or 5, and 7, 8, or 9 of the hospital stay (Grossmann, Thane, & Grossmann, 1981). Observers blind to group membership scored skin contacts which were considered either caretaking touches or "tender" touches. Early contact had a significant effect on both the frequency and the duration of tender touches of the mothers on the first two recording periods (up to 5 days), but this effect did not endure into the final recording period (7 to 9 days). Oddly, this effect was also restricted to those mothers who reported the pregnancy as being planned. Early contact has no significant effect on mothers with unplanned pregnancies. Mothers with extended contact (5 hours of rooming-in each day) showed neither early nor enduring effects. Rather, they showed *less* tender touch than mothers without the extended contact, a tendency significant only in the last of the three recording periods, and only for mothers with planned pregnancies. The authors conclude that "we have to face the possibility that under stable living conditions a single event, even as powerful as early contact, may yield to the regularity of other influences throughout the first year on the mother-child relationship" (Grossmann et al., 1981, p. 168).

A final study gives perhaps the strongest case for the "washing out" of early effects of extra contact. Leiderman (1981) headed a well-designed longitudinal effort that compared three groups of children from birth up to a period of 5 to 8 years (see early reports of this research in Leiderman & Seashore, 1975; Leifer, Leiderman, Barnett, & Williams, 1972; Seashore, Leifer, Barnett, & Leiderman, 1973). They obtained an abundance of data through interviews, observations, and questionnaires in the hospital and at home at staggered intervals of every few months from birth up to 2 years. Finally, 24 of the original 72 families were located and interviewed when the children were 5 to 8 years old. The three infant groups included a group of 24 full-term infants and two groups of pre-term infants. The mothers of preterms were randomly assigned to a routine separation condition (20 mothers) of no physical contact until the baby left the intensive care nursery (3 to 12 weeks) or to a contact group (22 mothers) who were permitted to enter the nursery and touch, change, feed, and handle their infants throughout the duration of the hospital stay. All the families were intact and middle class.

Initial differences in maternal commitment and self-confidence were apparent at 1 week after discharge but disappeared by 1 month post-discharge. Initial behavioral differences in ventral-ventral contact disappeared by 1 year post-discharge. By 21 months, *all* differences in maternal behavior among the three groups disappeared, except that mothers of preterms touched and attended to their children *more* than mothers of fullterms, and the separated mothers seemed especially attentive. Both of these findings seem to favor the separated or pre-term group, contrary to the bonding prediction. No other maternal behaviors were differentiated either as a result of the separation or by prematurity.

At 21 months the infants were also given the Bayley exam. A multiple regression analysis revealed that none of the early variables — treatment group, early maternal attitudes, early maternal behaviors, or family SES — predicted the motor score on the Bayley. On the mental scale, higher SES infants performed better, and girls outscored boys. None of the treatment group variables — prematurity, separation/contact, or birthweight — predicted mental test performance. On maternal attitude and behavior variables, infants whose mothers felt closer to them and held them more closely (which might be interpreted as indicating stronger bonding) did *less* well on the mental test.

In the 5- to 8-year postdischarge interview, coders blind to group membership discerned no outstanding differences among the groups. This lack of difference emerged among groups whose postnatal experience was quite dramatically different.

Leiderman concludes that family variables (such as SES and parity) and later postpartum experiences are more powerful than immediate postpartum experiences in accounting for infant performance as well as for maternal performance. "Events prior to and following the initial birth contact of the mother with her infant in our studies play a larger role in determination of maternal behavior and infant development than do the events immediately following parturition" (Leiderman, 1978, p. 55).

CONCLUSIONS

Reviewing the evidence presented thus far, it is difficult to find support that the postpartum period is in any way critical for human mother-infant affectional bonding. There are too many weaknesses in the "positive" studies and too many negative findings in other studies to suggest that maternal-infant contact just after birth is central to the mother's affection for her infant. Leiderman and Seashore (1975) suggest that the postpartum period is simply a time of high saliency and arousal in which learning can take place rapidly. Subsequent events in the family's life, though, take on their own saliency, and the first days after birth become ancient history.

While it may be that other mammals become aware of their offspring only at the time of birth, and thus have the need for a quick bonding such as is seen in sheep and goats, human mothers think about their babies for months before they are born. The preparation for the baby's arrival further focuses the parents' attention and feelings as they attend childbirth classes, select nursery furnishings, prepare a layette, and are offered the advice and support of family and friends. When the day (or night) of the birth finally arrives, there is already a well-laid foundation of feelings and expectations. At that point, events surrounding the birth experience and for the next few days surely form a special saliency for the parents. These events may be among the most special experiences of the parents' whole lives, and good or bad, the stories and the feelings will be recounted for years to come. These events do not, however, constitute a critical period such as occurs in embryological development or in the rapidly cemented bond between a sheep and a lamb. Life will change, the baby will change, parenting will change, and the events surrounding the first days' experience will fade in importance.

What is gained and lost by claiming that early contact is essential for mother-infant bonding to take place? A strong gain is a recognition of the need for families to have a family-centered personal experience around the birth of their baby. Parents have been advocating such a supportive and humanistic atmosphere for some time, not because of a critical period, but because the harsh sterility and rules of traditional hospitals interfered with the very special event of the birth of their child. If hospital management heeded warnings for a critical period for mother-infant bonding where they ignored parents' requests, then the outcome may be a positive one for new families, regardless of whether the appeal was enforced on a theoretically sound basis.

Two negative consequences for claiming that evidence supports the notion of a critical period for bonding complement this positive consequence. First, as the term *bonding* is popularized in magazines and other media, parents who are not permitted early contact — either for medical reasons or on account of hospital policy — may feel deprived of the opportunity to become fully attached to their child. Indeed, mothers have been overheard to recommend a certain hospital which "lets you have bonding," while a competing hospital "does not offer bonding." This simplistic idea of the necessary conditions for the complex human behavior of love for a child is supported by media coverage which presents bonding as an all-or-nothing, one-chance event. The result is parents who feel needlessly cheated.

The first problem probably applies mostly to well-educated, middle-class families who are aware of medical trends and anxious to do everything possible to be good parents. The problem for deprived mothers differs. There is, second, the possibility that "bonding" will be seen by social planners as another in the long list of quick and inexpensive cures to the problems of poverty and parenting failure. If poverty level parents are viewed as less successful at raising healthy, intelligent, secure children, perhaps "bonding" will offer an inexpensive solution. But no short-term intervention, like an extra hour of contact after birth, can be expected to counteract the long-term effects of poverty. Though early contact may aid in the formation of an affectional tie, and perhaps even more so for an economically deprived mother than for an advantaged one, it should not be seen as an easy cure-all, for its effects are slight and short-lived.

No one comes away from the studies on parenting disorders suggesting that early contact is trivial and should be abandoned. The humanizing changes seen in American birthing traditions in the last 15 years — prepared childbirth, drug-free deliveries, fathers' presence, early contact, rooming-in, increased support for breast feeding — have been a blessing to millions of new families. These changes are beneficial whether "bonding" is a phenomenon of scientific validity or not. Kennell and Klaus are owed a debt of gratitude for their contribution in drawing attention to the importance of making childbirth a natural, family affair rather than a stark medical event. Although some modest and beneficial effects of early or extended contact have been shown for certain populations, on balance the available research does not support the notion of a sensitive period for mother-infant bonding.

ACKNOWLEDGMENTS

This chapter revises material which originally appeared in two articles published in *Developmental Review:* Myers, B. J. Mother-infant bonding: The status of this critical-period hypothesis. *Developmental Review,* 1984, *4,* 240–274, and Myers, B. J. Mother-infant bonding: Rejoinder to Kennell and Klaus. *Developmental Review,* 1984, *4,* 283–288.

REFERENCES

Ainsworth, M. S., Blehar, M. C., Waters, E., & Wall, S. *Patterns of attachment: A psychological study of the strange situation.* Hillsdale, NJ: Erlbaum, 1978.

Bowlby, J. *Attachment* (Vol. 1). New York: Basic Books, 1969.

Campbell, S. B. G., Maloni, J., & Taylor, P. Early contact and maternal perceptions of infant temperament. In P. M. Taylor (Chair), *Early contact and rooming-in: Effects on bonding and attachment.* Symposium presented at the meeting of the Society for Research in Child Development, San Francisco, March 1979.

de Chateau, P. Early postpartum contact and later attitudes. *International Journal of Behavioral Development,* 1980, *3,* 273–286. (a)

de Chateau, P. Parent-neonate interaction and its long-term effects. In E. G. Simmel (Ed.), *Early experiences and early behavior: Implications for social development.* New York: Academic Press, 1980. (b)

de Chateau, P., & Wiberg, B. Long-term effect on mother-infant behavior of extra contact during the first hour postpartum: I. First observation at 36 hours. *Acta Paediatrica Scandinavica,* 1977, *66,* 137–144. (a)

de Chateau, P., & Wiberg, B. Long-term effect on mother-infant behavior of extra contact during the first hour postpatum: II. A follow-up at three months. *Acta Paediatrica Scandinavica,* 1977, *66,* 145–151. (b)

Egeland, B., & Vaughn, B. Failure of "bond formation" as a cause of abuse, neglect, and maltreatment. *American Journal of Orthopsychiatry,* 1981, *51,* 78–84.

Elmer, E., & Gregg, G. S. Developmental characteristics of abused children, *Pediatrics,* 1967, *40,* 596–602.

Fomufod, A., Sinkford, S., & Louy, V. Mother-child separation at birth. A contributing factor in child-abuse. *Lancet,* 1975, *2,* 549–550.

Grossmann, K. E., Grossmann, K., Huber, F., & Wartner U. German children's behavior towards their mothers at 12 months and their fathers at 18 months in Ainsworth Strange Situation. *International Journal of Behavioral Development,* 1981, *4,* 157–181.

Grossmann, K., Thane, K., & Grossmann, K. E. Maternal tactual contact of the newborn after various postpartum conditions of mother-infant contact. *Developmental Psychology,* 1981, *17,* 158–169.

Hales, D. J., Lozoff, B., Sosa, R., & Kennell, J. Defining the limits of the maternal sensitive period. *Developmental Medicine and Child Neurology,* 1977, *19,* 454–461.

Hock, E., Coady, S., & Cordero, L. *Patterns of attachment to mothers of one-year-old infants: A comparative study of full-term infants and prematurely born infants who were hospitalized throughout the neonatal period.* Paper presented at the biennial meeting of the Society for Research in Child Development, Philadelphia, March, 1973.

Kennell, J. H., Jerauld, R., Wolfe, H., Chesler, D., Kreger, N., McAlpine, W., Steffa, M., & Klaus, M. Maternal behavior one year after early and extended post-partum contact. *Develomental Medicine and Child Neurology,* 1974, *16,* 172–179.

Kennell, J. H., & Klaus, M. H. Mother-infant bonding: Weighing the evidence. *Developmental Review,* 1984, *4,* 275–282.

Klaus, M. H., Jerauld, R., Kreger, N. C., McAlpine, W., Steffa, M., & Kennell, J. H. Maternal attachment: Importance of the first postpartum days. *New England Journal of Medicine,* 1972, *286,* 460–463.

Klaus, M. H., & Kennell, J. H. *Maternal-infant bonding.* St. Louis, MO: Mosby, 1976.

Klaus, M. H., & Kennell, J. H. *Parent-infant bonding,* St. Louis, MO: Mosby, 1982.

Klein, M., & Stern, L. Low birth weight and the battered child syndrome. *Journal of Diseases of the Child,* 1971, *122,* 15–18.

Kontos, D. A study of the effects of extended mother-infant contact on maternal behavior at one and three months. *Birth and the Family Journal,* 1978, *5,* 133–140.

Lamb, M. E. Early contact and maternal-infant bonding: One decade later. *Pediatrics,* 1982, *70,* 763–768.

Leiderman, P. The critical period hypothesis revisited: Mother to infant social bonding in the neonatal period. In F. Horowitz (Ed.), *Early developmental hazards: Predictors and precautions.* AAAS Selected Symposia Series. Boulder, CO: Westview, 1978.

Leiderman, P. H. Human mother to infant social bonding: Is there a sensitive phase? In K. Immelmann & G. Barlow et al. (Ed.), *Behavioral development.* New York: Cambridge University Press, 1981.

Leiderman, P., & Seashore, M. J. Mother-infant neonatal separation: Some delayed consequences. In Ciba Foundation Symposium 33, *Parent-infant interaction.* Amsterdam: Elsevier, 1975.

Leifer, A. D., Leiderman, P. H., Barnett, C. R., & Williams, J. A. Effects of mother-infant separation on maternal attachment behavior. *Child Development,* 1972, *43,* 1203–1218.

Lynch, M., & Roberts, J. Predicting child abuse: Signs of bonding failure in the maternity hospital. *British Medical Journal,* 1977, *1,* 624–626.

Morgan, L. J. Methodological review of research on mother-infant bonding. In B. W. Camp (Ed.), *Advances in behavioral pediatrics* (Vol. 2). Greenwich, CT: JAI, 1981.

O'Connor, S., Vietze, P. M., Sherrod, K. B., Sandler, H. M., & Altemeier, W. A. Reduced incidence of parenting inadequacy following rooming-in. *Pediatrics,* 1980, *66,* 176–182.

Ottaviano, C., Campbell, S., & Taylor, P. *Early contact and infant-mother attachment at one year.* Paper presented at the biennial meeting of the Society for Research in Child Development, San Francisco, March 1979.

Peterson, G. H., & Mehl, L. E. Some determinants of maternal attachment. *American Journal of Psychiatry,* 1978, *135,* 1168–1173.

Ringler, N. M., Kennell, J. H., Jarvella, R., Navojosky, B. J., & Klaus, M. H. Mother-to-child speech at 2 years: Effects of early postnatal contact. *Journal of Pediatrics,* 1975, *85,* 141–144.

Ringler, N. M., Trause, M. A., Klaus, M., & Kennell, J. The effects of extra post-partum contact and maternal speech patterns on children's IQ's, speech and language comprehension at five. *Child Development,* 1978, *49,* 862–865.

Rode, S. E., Chang, P., Fisch, R. O., & Sroufe, L. A. Attachment patterns of infants separated at birth. *Developmental Psychology,* 1981, *17,* 188–191.

Ross, G. S. Parental responses to infants in intensive care: The separation issues reevaluated. *Clinics in Perinatology,* 1980, *7,* 47–60.

Seashore, M. J., Leifer, A. D., Barnett, C. R., & Leiderman, P. H. The effects of denial of early mother-infant interaction on maternal self-confidence. *Journal of Personality and Social Psychology,* 1973, *26,* 369–378.

Siegel, E., Bauman, K. E., Schaefer, E. S., Saunders, M. M., & Ingram, D. D. Hospital and home support during infancy: Impact on maternal attachment, child abuse and neglect, and health care utilization. *Pediatrics,* 1980, *66,* 183–190.

Sosa, R., Kennell, J., Klaus, M., & Urrutia, J. The effect of early mother-infant contact on breast feeding, infection and growth. In Ciba Foundation Symposium 45, *Breast feeding and the mother.* Amsterdam: Associated Scientific Publishers, 1976.

Sousa, P. L. R., Barros, F. C., Gazalle, R. V., Begeres, R. M., Pinheiro, G. N., Menezes, S. T., & Arruda, L. A. *Attachment and lactation.* Paper presented at the Fifteenth International Congress of Pediatrics, Buenos Aires, 1974.

Svedja, M. J., Campos, J. J., & Emde, R. N. Mother-infant "bonding": Failure to generalize. *Child Development,* 1980, *51,* 775–779.

Taylor, P. M., Taylor, F. H., Campbell, S. B. G., Maloni, J., & Dickey, D. Effects of extra contact on early maternal attitudes, perceptions, and behaviors. In P. M. Taylor (Chair), *Early contact and rooming-in: Effects on bonding and attachment.* Symposium presented at the meeting of the Society for Research in Child Development, San Francisco, March 1979.

Winters, M. The relationship of time of initial feeding to success of breastfeeding. Unpublished master's thesis, University of Washington, Seattle, 1973. Reported in Klaus, M. H., & Kennell, J. H. *Maternal-infant bonding.* St. Louis: Mosby, 1976.

12 Critical Periods in Processes of Social Organization

J. P. Scott
Bowling Green State University
and *Tufts University*

INTRODUCTION

In any discussion of critical periods it is important to distinguish between the theory and the phenomenon. The *theory* (Scott, 1986) deals with developmental processes in the organization of living systems on whatever level of organization the theory may be applied. The *phenomenon* was first established on the level of embryonic development in the classical work of Stockard (1907, 1921) who discovered in experimental studies on fish embryos that development of form could be distorted at particular periods in development and, more importantly, that the nature of the disturbance depended not on the nature of the modifying agent but on the time at which its action took place. Since that time the phenomenon has been abundantly confirmed for the embryonic developmental processes of a variety of organisms including man (Moore, 1982).

Similar phenomena have been described for a great number of other developmental processes (Scott, 1962, 1978). One of the earliest discoveries of critical periods in behavioral development was that observed by Lorenz (1935) on imprinting in birds (see Hoffman, in this volume). This phenomenon was later extended to a variety of other species and to other behavioral processes (Scott, 1962). The phenomenon has also been established with respect to the development of binocular vision and the hormonal modification of the development of the brain see (Hirsch & Tieman, and Money & Annecillo, this volume). Of special importance to humans is the potential critical period for language development (Lenneberg, 1967; Snow, this volume).

Complementary to the phenomena of critical periods, the theory is an explanation of these phenomena. Like any other theory that is usable, it must

247

be subject to experimental testing, and the empirical work appears in hundreds of papers and experiments. Here, it is important to remember that if a particular experiment seems to invalidate a particular theory of critical periods, it does not follow that the phenomenon is invalidated, only that its explanation is incorrect. In such a case, a new hypothesis should be developed. Therefore, it is always important first to establish the existence of critical period phenomena by careful observation and description before testing hypotheses regarding them. Otherwise, experimenting with the nature of supposed organizational change processes involved in a presumptive critical period is likely to be futile.

THE GENERAL THEORY OF CRITICAL PERIODS

I have developed a general theory of critical periods in earlier papers (Scott, 1979; Scott, Stewart, & DeGhett, 1974), but have stated it in its most complete form in a chapter entitled "Critical Periods in Organizational Processes" (Scott, 1986). This theory explains the organization of living systems and depends on certain characteristics of those systems. One of these is the tendency of living systems to become increasingly organized (that is, to be *negentropic*). A second is the tendency of living systems to become increasingly stable as they become increasingly organized. Verification of the theory therefore depends on the description and measurement of organizational processes.

A fundamental dimension of the development of organization is time. Organizational processes go forward in time, not backward. Living organization may be disrupted or disorganized, but it is very seldom deorganized. This leads to a general principle of organization: *no re-organization without de-organization.* I have previously stated this as *no re-organization without disorganization* in order to emphasize the disastrous consequences of disorganization and because this is the most common form of disruption of organization. However, a more general statement includes the term *de-organization* which can cover both milder forms of loss of organization as well as more drastic ones. Living systems often become disorganized, one of the examples being injury or death to individual organisms. In general, the more highly organized an organism is, the more limited are its powers of deorganization. Even in such organisms, however, it is possible to reserve a portion of un-organized or partially organized material. Examples are the capacities for wound repair and the continual growth of mucous epithelium in the intestinal lining even in such complex organisms as mammals.

The theory of critical periods is further based on the observed phenomenon that organizational processes may proceed at different rates at different times in development. For example, growth processes go on very rapidly in the early history of an embryo and become almost non-existent at adulthood. This represents one of the most common situations: a very rapid ongoing process early in development which thereafter may cease entirely. Among other processes such as attachment, a common phenomenon is an early period of rapid organization followed by a declining rate that stabilizes at a very low level (see Myers, this volume).

Here we must distinguish between *developmental processes* that result in changes in organization that become stable and permanent, and *maintenance processes* that produce temporary effects and usually continue throughout the life of an organism. Such maintenance processes do not show the phenomenon of critical periods.

In its most concise form, the theory of critical periods states that the time when a developmental organization process is proceeding most rapidly is the time during which it is most easily modified. Before the process begins nothing can be modified, and after it ceases the possibility of change is also absent. How such modifications of an organizational process are achieved depends on the nature of the process itself. It is also possible that, through experimental or accidental intervention, an organizational process may start earlier or continue longer than is the usual case. This means that there are two important objectives in critical period research. The first is to establish the time periods during which the organizational process proceeds most rapidly. The second and equally fundamental objective is to discover the nature of the organizational process itself.

In short, the theory of critical periods applies to the development of organization at any level of systems organization. The theory depends on the nature of the organizational processes involved, and consequently its use at any particular level will vary. At any level, the theory has enormous practical importance, as understanding it makes it possible to avoid maladaptive organization and promote adaptive organization. In previous papers I have emphasized critical periods with respect to the development of primary social relationships (attachment and primary socialization). Here I extend the concept to the level of human cultural organization. Since phenomena on this level are rarely subject to experimental manipulation, I rely chiefly on theoretical reasoning as applied to the best observational and descriptive information that we now have, in order, first, to lay the basis for future experimental testing and, second, to point out situations in which it is now possible to apply the theory to practical affairs.

CRITICAL PERIODS IN HUMAN SOCIAL INTERACTION

The organization of human groups and institutions involves many phenomena, none of which are entirely independent of each other, but the basic one is interaction between the constituent entities of such systems, namely individual organisms. Such interaction is largely behavioral rather than biochemical (as it usually is on the physiological level of organization), although physiological and biochemical interactions are also involved in behavior. Among humans, one of the chief kinds of interaction is verbal communication, although non-verbal communication is also important. I now state several self-evident propositions that apply to human social interaction.

PROPOSITION 1

The time during which a human group first becomes organized is a critical period. During this time the potential organization can be easily modified. Such a period may vary in length, but seldom lasts more than a year.

PROPOSITION 2

Any long-lasting human group must reward its members for participation. Rewards can take many forms, but I deal here only with direct satisfaction of needs. Many human groups utilize such simple rewards as food and drink, and anyone who wishes to work with human interactions should not neglect these, simple as they are. Beyond this, the theory of social needs (Scott, 1971) states that each individual will need to express behavior related to each motivational-emotional system in amounts regulated by the strength of external and internal stimulation, previous experience, and genetic variation. There are 10 major systems as listed in Table 1. Most of these are expressed in dyadic relationships and may serve as rewards in such social systems. Of major importance to larger groups is the need, often unrecognized, for *allelomimetic* behavior; such behavior is defined as doing what the other individuals in the group do with some degree of mutual imitation. Another obvious need is that for communication itself, which involves allelomimetic behavior as well as exchange of information.

PROPOSITION 3

Feedback is essential for any well-functioning social organization. This proposition is based on the general principle that in any living system the entities involved interact with two-way causation. Any group or institution that does not provide feedback tends to be unrewarding. Also, such a group loses one of the principal advantages of group interactions through language, namely group problem solving (Lieberman, 1984).

PROPOSITION 4

The organization of any living system, including social systems, tends to become increasingly stable with time. Eventually a system approaches a

TABLE 1
Theory of Social Needs

Behavior	Definition and/or Example	Need
A. Primitive and general needs:		
Investigative Behavior	Looking, touching, tasting, etc.	Exploration, satisfaction of curiosity
Ingestive Behavior	Eating, drinking, breathing	Food, water, nourishment oxygen
Shelter-seeking Behavior	Finding shelter from cold, moisture, heat	For comfortable environment
Defensive Behavior	Defense against injury by another animal of same or other species	To respond to prevent injury
Sexual behavior	Behavior that facilitates fertilization	For sexual gratification and reproduction
B. Advanced and specialized needs:		
Caregiving Behavior	Care, protection, feeding of offspring or species mates	To care for self and others
Care-soliciting Behavior	Distress signals, often by infants	Variety of basic needs: hunger, relief from pain, danger, etc.
Agonistic Behavior	Behavior adaptive in conflict between species mates	To express anger, fear, behaviorally and verbally
Allelomimetic Behavior	Two or more persons doing same thing with some degree of mutual imitation	For continual social contact and similar behavior
Eliminative Behavior	Defecation, urination	For relief of bowels, bladder

With the exception of that for eliminative behavior, all these needs may, in one form or another, serve as rewards for participation in groups.

state of complete stability. Therefore, the period preceding the achievement of a steady state is a critical one for determining the nature of the organization of the group.

PROPOSITION 5

Any human social organization must lose its constituent entities or members. Inevitably membership loss occurs through death, but also for a variety of other causes. Therefore such an organization must replace its members through recruitment. Loss results in special critical periods as follows: First, the loss of a key member may disorganize the group, creating the necessity for reorganization, which is of course a critical period. If a stable organization is desirable or desired, the system should be organized in such a way that the organization will not be seriously disrupted by such losses. This has always been a serious problem with respect to political organization, where primitive organization was almost always centered around a single individual who might be a king or other sort of autocrat. History is replete with examples of the disruption and disorganization following the death of kings. Second, if an individual is recruited to the organization, either as a replacement or an addition, the addition of a new person may also disrupt organization as the previous members attempt to readjust. A mutual process of organization goes on between the old members and the new ones, resulting in a critical period for both on the level of individual conduct organization. Most primitive tribal groups and many modern social groups conduct initiation ceremonies whose functions are to mitigate the disruption of the group and also to inform the new initiate how his or her behavior should be organized with respect to the rest of the group. Especially in the case of males, such ceremonies frequently involve some form of punishment directed toward the initiate, presumably intended to release some of the resentment produced by the entrance of the new member and also to show the initiate what may happen if he does not adjust to the group. Similarly, there should be a critical period in nuclear family organization following the arrival of a new baby, and many cultures exhibit a ceremonial form of initiation for the newcomer, often including some form of violence such as circumcision or ducking the infant in cold water (Landauer & Whiting, 1964).

PROPOSITION 6

Human social groups organized on a formal basis become unusually stable. Stability occurs because of the lasting and invariant nature of the verbal rules involved, especially if the rules are written. Therefore, the period during which such rules are established is a major critical period for the organization of that group.

PROPOSITION 7

Because verbal rules are so stable, it is important to build into the system a process for changing them when necessity arises. In our culture, formally-organized groups usually have some form of amendment process that meets this need.

PROPOSITION 8

Unlike organization on the physiological level, human social organizations can either rapidly stabilize or continue to develop. The choice depends on the basis of the organization involved. If it is desirable to have a developing organization, it is important to build into the formal organization of the group a process for continual growth and development. This again implies a critical period in the organization of such a group. This principle is particularly important in the organization of dyadic relationships such as those in mating or marriage. Such a relationship can become richer and more rewarding if its organizational basis does not become entirely stable. The time of establishing such an organization is thus a critical one, even though the maintenance of a developmental process implies partial avoidance of a critical period.

PROPOSITION 9

In any culture, the origination of new institutions will tend to follow the model of organization of pre-existing institutions. This will occur partly because of economy of effort (it is easier to follow an old model than to create a new one) and partly because it is easier to attract members to something that is familiar and readily understandable. If a totally new form of organization is created deliberately, it is likely to be unsuccessful unless there is an overwhelming need for the rewards it can give its members.

STABILITY VERSUS CHANGE IN HUMAN SOCIAL SYSTEMS

There are four principal change processes in human social systems. The first of these is *biological evolution,* whose speed is related to the number of possible generations per unit of time, size of the discrete populations involved, rates of mutational variation, and nature and degree of processes producing differential survival (natural selection). Analysis of present-day human populations leads to the conclusion that overall population changes should be very slow but that current conditions of extensive migration, increases in survival rates, and maintenance of or increases in mutation rates should lead to increases in genetic variation both in individual genes and, more importantly, in the gene combinations that are the basis of expressed variation (see Scott, in Scott & Fuller, 1965). In short, genetic variation among human individuals is increasing. Relative to other organisms, these changes are slow because of the long human generation time, but they are nevertheless inevitable.

The second change process is that of *behavioral development.* Like all developmental processes, that of behavior is not pre-formed, but becomes organized progressively as a result of interactions among systems at all levels: genetic, physiological, organismic, social, and ecological (Scott, 1968). Because of this interaction, the resulting organization is unique for each individual; that is, the result is again to produce change and variation among individuals. All individual organization is inevitably destroyed by death and cannot persist beyond the life of the person concerned; thus, the developmental process is an integral part of cultural evolution.

The third process, and a very important one in human societies, is that of *cultural evolution.* Historically, human cultural change has been very rapid, as its major change processes do not depend on biological evolution, but on changes in the transmission of verbal and non-verbal information from one generation to the next. Since learned information cannot be biologically transmitted, and since the process of learning is an internal, integrative, and selective one, and since the cumulative store of information to which an individual in a given generation has access differs from that in the last, change is inevitable. While cultural evolution is not as rigidly governed by generation time as biological evolution is, cultural change is nevertheless strongly influenced by the ability of successive generations to accept change.

Finally, there is *ecoevolution,* or ecosystems change, which to some extent takes place independently of biological evolution. For example, human social systems have modified ecosystems grossly through agricultural and industrial revolutions and have themselves been changed as a result of the feedback from such changes.

Because of all these processes, each operating on a different time scale, *change in human social systems is inevitable,* a conclusion that is abundantly supported by the historical evidence. The degree to which such changes have and can be brought about by conscious and purposeful action provides another set of problems, and this is where the theory of critical periods achieves special importance. If there are times when the development of organization of human social systems proceeds more rapidly, the general theory of critical periods should apply.

As pointed out earlier, there is a general tendency for all living systems to stabilize their organization. This principle has been well established in non-human social systems, even in such simple ones as the dominance hierarchy of hens. Guhl termed this phenomenon "social inertia" and demonstrated experimentally that such systems function more efficiently when stable than when they are constantly disrupted (Guhl & Allee, 1944). The same principle should operate unconsciously in human social systems. In addition, the fact that human social systems are organized in part through verbal language and associated verbally-transmitted information contributes an additional process leading towards stability. Once uttered, words are no longer part of the living process, and undergo no further change. Words are themselves organized into symbolic systems that lose their function if disrupted. Useful verbal systems persist, and can endure for very long periods, especially if written. The writings of religious leaders have persisted for thousands of years, and we still teach some of the geometric principles developed by Pythagoras.

Because forming a verbal utterance is an organization process, the time preceding that utterance is a critical period, a fact well known to creative writers and scientists, although not usually expressed in these terms.

APPLICATION OF CRITICAL PERIOD
THEORY TO HUMAN SOCIAL ORGANIZATION

In this section, I discuss critical periods in the organization of three levels of human social systems: dyadic relationships, small groups, and institutions.

Dyadic Relationships

In order for any social system to develop, the individuals involved (the potential entities of the system) must remain in contact long enough for organizational processes to take place, and thereafter must remain in contact in order to maintain the system. In a dyadic relationship, the attachment process is essential for maintaining contact. Findings concerning the process of social attachment in mammals, including man, indicate that the process proceeds very rapidly at an early time in development that is a critical period for the formation of primary social relationships (see Hoffman & Meyer, in this volume). The infant will become attached to whatever individual or individuals are perceived at that time. In humans, because of family institutional organization, these are usually close biological relatives but may include nonrelated caretakers or any other persons who remain in contact for sufficiently long periods of time (Scott, 1963).

Although the physiological basis of the attachment process is still unknown, the following facts have been established:

(1) The process is an internal one, not dependent on external stimulation. All that is necessary is that the infant become aware of (perceive) the potential object of attachment. It follows that social attachment to some individual or individuals is inevitable.

(2) Active social interaction speeds the process of attachment, probably by increasing perception (if the infant does not notice the stranger, there is no perception) and also by producing emotional arousal.

(3) Emotional arousal will intensify the process, irrespective of the nature of the emotion. It has not been established that the arousal of noxious emotions will speed up the process, but it is known that such emotions will not inhibit it. Abused children still become attached to their abusing parents.

(4) Once an attachment is formed, separation will produce distress, an intense, prolonged, and subjectively painful emotion. It has been suggested by Panksepp (e.g., Panksepp et al., 1983) that this emotion is related to the function of brain opioids.

(5) The capacity for social attachment does not cease entirely after the early critical period, but tapers off and is maintained at a relatively low level

throughout life. Thus an adult can still form attachments, but these usually take much longer to develop than in infancy. This means that prolonged contact must be maintained in some way. Such contact is often produced by human institutional organization: familial, educational, religious, economic, and even political.

(6) It is possible that intense emotional stimulation speeds attachment in adults as well as in children. Thus one would predict that the intense pleasure produced by sexual interaction would facilitate rapid attachment.

So far I have discussed a largely unconscious, internal, and involuntary organizational process that results in maintenance of contact. The organization of the behavioral interaction between the entities composing the system (in this case a dyad) is largely produced by another set of processes: learning, problem-solving or cognition, and habit formation. The operation of these processes in social interaction is best known through studies of dyadic dominance-subordination relationships in non-human animals. When two individuals meet for the first time, they may show a great variety of behaviors, including agonistic ones. If the last, they are likely to fight or contest, ending with one individual winning and the other losing. When they meet again, the individuals repeat their behavior, but eventually reduce it to symbolic threat and avoidance reactions that become established firmly through habit formation. Obviously, the early part of this process is a critical one for determining both the nature of the behavior that may be developed in the relationship and the way it becomes organized.

In respect to the sorts of behavior that are found in dyadic relationships, I have already mentioned sexual and agonistic examples. To these may be added caregiving and soliciting, usually organized into care-dependency relationships that may involve caregiving on the part of only one member of the dyad (as in the parent-infant relationships) or, in other cases, mutual care. Then there is the allelomimetic relationship, in which the members of the pair imitate each other, and which may be differentiated into a leader-follower relationship. Any human dyadic relationship usually involves two or more of such behavioral relationships, which may be organized independently or may be integrated (see Table 1 for a list of possibilities.)

We may conclude that the early part of the formation of dyadic relationships is a critical one for establishing the nature of such a relationship. To be more specific, the early period is crucial in the following ways:

(1) The relationship must be organized in such ways that sufficient contact time is available to permit the attachment process to take place. For example, if two adults choose to live together in the same house or apartment, attach-

ment is almost certain to develop, whether the individuals are of the same or opposite genders. The quality of the relationship will differ, but the attachment process (which is basically independent of sex) will take place. Another example is courtship behavior, where two individuals repeatedly meet for a variety of excuses — entertainment, dining, etc. One can also predict that if two individuals meet only rarely at long intervals, the essential process of attachment will either not take place or be only minimally effective. Still another example is that of a dyadic attachment formed as a result of a shared task. This can be voluntary, or it may be part of a formal work situation. In the latter case, the choice of a work situation that involves individuals with whom one might wish to become attached is very important: the attachment will take place automatically whether one wishes it or not.

(2) The process of attachment will be speeded by a shared emotional experience. I have already mentioned sexual emotion, but there are other possibilities, such as the fear associated with a natural disaster. Such experiences are not always under voluntary control, but the early part of the attachment process is nevertheless critical.

(3) Other organizational processes show similar critical periods. Of these one of the most basic is that of learning; there is an inevitable tendency to reduce repeated interactions to fixed habits, with the result that the dyad functions smoothly and relatively effortlessly. If the habit is established too quickly it may take a poorly adaptive or even maladaptive form. In any case, it will become more and more difficult to modify later.

(4) Among human dyads, the habit of verbal communication is a prominent part of a developed relationship. Therefore it is critical, in the early stages of such a relationship, to make sure that such habits are formed in desirable ways; i.e., so that communication on important matters as well as trivial ones will take place. Also, the process of communication has the best possibility of remaining in part unorganized so that the relationship may continue to develop. This may determine the difference between a shallow and barren relationship and a deep and enriched one.

Small Informal Groups

A group of this sort can be conceptualized as a system in which each entity forms a reciprocal relationship with every other entity, the whole forming a network that is equivalent to Moreno's (1934) sociogram. The simplest organization would be one in which all dyadic relationships are alike. But if, as Moreno realized, this is not the case, then the organization becomes more complex. It follows that the total organization of a group is not the sum of the dyadic relationships involved, but forms a unique combination that is not entirely predictable from its constituent parts. Also, humans are capable of forming relationships including three or more individuals, contributing to further complexity.

In our culture, such groups are usually formed to undertake some activity that it is either unsatisfactory or impossible for a dyad. The activity may be entertainment, as in a bridge club or discussion group, or it may be initiated to undertake some more serious task. If the latter, there is usually a tendency to institutionalize the group, a process that I discuss below.

For the informal group, the first meeting is always a critical one. The organizer must do advance work to ensure that the persons involved understand the purpose of the group and are motivated to meet its goals. The first meeting must be a rewarding one for as many of the group members as possible; otherwise there will be no second meeting. Also, the members need to know how they will function in the group. This is often best accomplished through discussion leading to the assumption of responsibility and its division among the members. If these basic functions are established during the critical first meeting, there will probably be a second successful gathering with increasing stability in each successive session.

All of these considerations apply to more formal groups as well; for example, good teachers always make good use of the first meeting of a class, consciously or unconsciously applying the theory of critical periods in order to achieve desirable organization rapidly. But formal institutionalized organization has certain unique features as well as those held in common with informal groups.

Institutions

A small informal group is likely to fall apart if one or more members leave it. Consequently, new groups often attempt to institutionalize themselves, thus ensuring greater stability. An institution is a peculiarly human form of organization that has certain general characteristics that depend on spoken or written language:

(1) Precise and often rigidly prescribed forms of interaction between the members, usually conceptualized as social roles or stereotypes.
(2) Methods for filling vacant roles.
(3) Methods for expansion.
(4) Some broadly defined purpose or purposes, not necessarily realistic in nature.

There is a tendency for new institutions to adopt a form of organization that is characteristic of one of the predominant institutions of the culture, probably because it is easier to follow an old model than it is to devise a new one (see Proposition 9 above). In the culture of the United States, for example, there are three ancient institutional models: those of family, religion, and government, to which may be added two somewhat newer ones, the educational and the economic or industrial model that is the dominant contemporary institution.

The numerous benevolent societies in our culture exemplify institutions formed on the family model. The members are often called brothers and sisters and, since the Christian religion also was institutionalized on a family model, such organizations often prescribe certain kinds of moralistic behavior and objectives, and their meetings feature certain ceremonies and ritualistic activities. The basic functions of such organizations are also those of a family: mutual support and stability. Consequently, they constitute a valuable form of social support and a useful adjunct to the biological family of a member.

Another common form of institutionalized organization in our culture is the political one. In such an organization, there is a constitution and by-laws, usually modelled after those of the United States Government and setting forth the governing officers, dues, and methods of amendment. Among latter-day institutions, there is a tendency to substitute an economic or commercial form of organization for the political one. In this form of organization, all power is delegated to a board of directors that becomes a self-perpetuating (and often self-serving) body whose members elect the officers who do the actual administrative work of the organization. One can find examples of both models of organization among contemporary scientific societies, some of which follow the model of a political democracy and others the model of a closed corporation.

The merits of various forms of organization can be argued endlessly, but certain objective criteria can be applied. First, the strength of an organization of whatever nature depends on the degree of member participation, and the form of organization can either encourage or discourage such participation. Second, the efficiency of an organization as well as the emotional satisfaction of its members depends on two-way interaction or feedback; this also can be limited or facilitated by formal organization.

Whatever the form of institutionalization, the time of setting up the written form of organization is a critical one. The person or persons who write the constitution and by-laws can easily set the tone and direction of all future activities of a society. Once these have been adopted and put into practice, they become increasingly difficult to change.

Are there other critical periods in the lives of institutions? As Thurman Arnold (1937) once observed, institutions rarely ever die, a tribute to their enormous stability. If an institution runs well and smoothly, there are no critical periods after its inception. But if it runs badly enough the members may rebel, forcing a reorganization and hence another critical period. Similarly, a period of rapid growth and expansion may make possible some degree of organizational change and bring on a secondary critical period.

The time of inception of a new institution, during which it first becomes organized, is its *primary critical period.* If its organization is disrupted in some way, a *secondary critical period* may occur, secondary because it involves a modification of the original organization. If an institution's organization is completely disrupted, the institution no longer exists, possibly but not necessarily leaving room for the formation of a completely new institution with a concommitant primary critical period.

All three levels of human social organization exhibit the critical period phenomenon as a relatively brief time early in the formation of each kind of social system when organization proceeds rapidly before becoming stable. During this time, the nature of the organization can be easily modified. The power of an individual consciously to determine the nature of the future organization is inversely proportional to the size of the group, but is never absolute, as other individuals with varying degrees of autonomy are always involved.

The effects of conscious action during critical periods are also inversely proportional to the size of the group, but, if changes in organization can be achieved in larger groups, more people are affected and the effects may persist over long periods of time. Dyadic relationships and small groups are always formed within the larger system of an institution. If an institution can be changed, it may affect all dyads and groups within it. Further, dyads, informal groups, and institutions differ in longevity. A dyad can persist, at the most, only as long as both individuals live, but an institution persists generation after generation unless its organization is totally destroyed. Consequently, the phenomenon of institutional change and the possible existence of critical periods in its organization provides a practical problem of major importance.

CRITICAL PERIODS IN
AMERICAN INSTITUTIONS OF HIGHER EDUCATION

In the following section I briefly outline how the theory of critical periods can be usefully applied to understanding and, to some extent, manipulating one sort of institution that has special interest for academic scientists. In so doing I refer back to the propositions stated on earlier pages.

American colleges and universities have their historical roots in the medieval colleges of Oxford and Cambridge, the first of which were founded in the 13th century. Originally, English colleges were all-male institutions for the training of priests and clerics. The time of inception of each must have been a critical period for determining its organization (Proposition 1). Each was established by some wealthy and notable person, perhaps a member of the clerical hierarchy or the nobility or both. They were organized on the pattern of monasteries, each with an authoritarian father figure who was supposed to have complete control over the students and teachers under him. While authority has gradually weakened, a considerable portion of this religious organization still remains; the head of Lincoln College at Oxford, founded in 1429 by the Bishop of Lincoln, is still known as "The Rector" (see Proposition 4 on stability).

Eventually, such independent foundations banded together in a loose confederation called a university which was able to perform certain functions that would have been impossible for the smaller units. The first sign of such organization was the appointment of a Chancellor whose primary function was not educational but legal, that of keeping civil order. Only much later were University Councils established and still later such all-university institutions as a library, museums, and scientific laboratories. The educational functions of the University remained in the colleges, typically organized with a Head of some sort, Fellows, Scholars, and Commoners. Unlike the tight monolithic organization of American universities, the identity and independence of the individual colleges still remains, again illustrating the principle of stability.

The first colleges to be established in what is now the United States — Harvard, Yale, William and Mary, and the like — were private foundations that largely followed the English model. But they were different in one important respect. They were not founded in one or two university towns but in geographically widely separate communities. Because of actions taken in the critical period of inception, they never had the opportunity to form confederations. Some of them expanded into large universities, but only as outgrowths of the original institutions.

Much later, the states that were created after the Revolution, and especially those that were added after the original 13, began to establish state colleges and universities over and above the numerous private denominational foundations that sprang up. In accordance with the United States Constitution, the state universities were free from religious ties but still followed the older model of organization with its authoritarian head but with the addition of a supervisory body that was supposed to represent the public interest but protect the university from direct political control. Usually all authority was legally vested in a Board of Trustees or similar body which was responsible for the operation and financing of the institution. Thus, in accordance with Proposition 9, most of these universities were organized along similar lines.

Since, as a practical matter, a Board of Trustees could not operate a university, the usual solution was for the Board to delegate its power to a President who was supposed to run the institution with complete authority over the teachers and students, much as in the medieval model. Unless the president was unusually perceptive and intelligent, such an authoritarian regime tended to violate Proposition 2, the necessity for feedback in a well-running system. It was an ideal set-up for a petty tyrant, but up until fairly recent times the potential damage was usually limited by the doctrine of "in loco parentis;" i.e., that the president and faculty should act as parents to the students entrusted to their care. As with the biological parents of the day, it was assumed that the university administrators and faculty had complete legal authority over the students, who were supposed to submit to them. One of the results was a lot of childish behavior on the part of the students, who frequently rebelled.

An institution organized in this way operated fairly well as long as the president and those to whom he delegated his authority were sensible and kindly people. Conversely, such organization always provided an opportunity for the abuse of power, and any American college or university can find examples of such abuses in its history.

From the viewpoint of critical periods, the time at which a new college or university is founded is a critical one, for at that time the basis for future organization is laid down, soon to become set as firmly as in concrete, in accordance with the principle of stability. For example, when the legislature of the state of Oregon passed the enabling act to found the University of Oregon at Eugene in 1872, they vested university governance in the faculty, a unique feature among American universities and one that avoids many of the difficulties inherent in authoritarian control. By contrast, the act establishing Bowling Green State University in Ohio in 1910 gave no power to the faculty except that of awarding honorary degrees, an arrangement that eventually led to major conflicts between the president on one hand and the faculty and students on the other. The conflict was settled when the trustees delegated some of their power to the faculty in the form of a Faculty Charter, but not until an active riot took place. This was an example of a secondary critical period, involving extensive reorganization.

As always happens in an institution in which one individual wields a great deal of power, the time of change from one president to another produces a secondary critical period resulting from the disorganization and possible reorganization that occurs at that time (Proposition 5). In addition, a new president often tries to reorganize the system. In a well-established and stable institution this usually has little effect except to emotionally disturb the faculty members who, as entities in a well-organized system, resist any change that may affect them. So the new president usually accomplishes little except to replace or to rename the officials immediately responsible to him. If the president happens to know anything about the organization of systems, the president can mold the administration into one that facilitates the basic functions of a university, namely the discovery and transmission of knowledge. If the president does not, and few university administrators have had any formal training in the techniques of administration (or any qualifications other than a lust for power), the president may eventually poison most interactions within the system.

Similarly, in any university organized as an authoritarian hierarchy, the replacement of a dean or department head also may bring on a critical period resulting from disorganization and reorganization in that part of the institution. In most cases, the principal way that one can utilize critical period theory is through involvement in the choice of a new head. Also, it may be desirable, in a well-running institution, to avoid a critical period by minimizing disorganization. One simple way to produce this ameliorative effect is to award all entities in the system, individuals or combinations of individuals, a part in the choice of the new head, thus initiating favorable interaction before disruption can occur.

Another sort of critical period may occur in an academic institution when it has the opportunity to take on a new function, as when a new college is authorized, or graduate work is installed for the first time. At such a period, organization to carry out the new function must be set up. Since the system is not yet functioning, considerable freedom can be exercised, although academics, like all other humans, tend to cling to old models of organization rather than to innovate or create (Proposition 9).

Finally, a critical period can be brought about by rebellions such as those that occurred in university bodies in the 1960s and early 1970s, producing widespread disorganization and even violence. The result was mainly negative, but far-reaching. Most universities and colleges abandoned the family model of institutional organization and began to treat students as adults with (almost) full rights of citizenship. As might have been expected from Proposition 9, many universities then tended to adopt the dominant model of institutional organization in the culture, the economic one, and began analogizing students with industrial products, research with marketable items, and evaluating both in terms of the money they brought in. As a reaction, many faculties have organized themselves on the model of labor unions in order to protect themselves against economic exploitation.

With all their cultural limitations, including systemic stability, universities and colleges act as agents of change. Through their general function of the discovery and transmission of knowledge, they transmit new information to each generation of students. But since students rarely achieve positions of power before 15 or 20 years have passed, the results may come slowly. For example, William James, who was a professor at Harvard in 1910, put forward his idea of a "Peace Army" as a means of preventing war. Among the students at that institution at that time was Franklin Roosevelt. Whether or not he listened to James, one of the creations of his Presidency some 20 years later was the Civilian Conservation Corps, modeled very closely along the lines of James's proposal. Its effect was less than James had hoped, but the idea arose again during the Presidency of another Harvard graduate, J. F. Kennedy, as the Peace Corps.

Such long-range changes would have little to do with the concept of critical periods were it not for the fact that undergraduate students themselves often go through a critical period of intellectual development while at college. Away from family and friends, young people often undergo considerable emotional disorganization as a result of separation and intellectual disorganization as a result of encountering ideas new to them and disturbing to their established beliefs. Students may react in many ways. Some close their minds and so protect themselves against disorganization and reorganization; others may reorganize their beliefs in new creative fashions, not necessarily what they have been told. Teachers can and should take advantage of this critical period, the major time when they have an opportunity to set the stage for future institutional change and (what one hopes may be) progress.

Again, the results may be slow, simply because of the time lag until students achieve positions of power. Also, the speed of change in other institutions and the larger social system that includes them will depend on the degree of consensus among faculty members and the number of students that are exposed to a specific new idea. Thus, with one or two percent of the population attending college, it took nearly 100 years after the Civil War before the black population of the United States achieved substantial gains in civil rights in the 1960s, and parallel gains in economic rights are still to be made.

Irrespective of race and ethnicity, the problems of poverty and violence in our culture demand solution. We know the answer, but it involves a major change in our cultural mores, emphasizing as they do the doctrine of competition which leads to the belief that both these problems and their solutions are rooted in individual action. Our culture still clings to the Horatio Alger stereotype of the climb from rags to riches: that anyone can accomplish such success if he wishes, neglecting the fact that competition inherently determines that some indviduals must lose.

We need to introduce a new ethic, that of full employment in well-paid, constructive and congenial activity, a solution that would not only eliminate poverty but would greatly reduce crime and violence. A person fully employed in congenial work has no time for crime, is forming habits of peaceful and constructive behavior, and, if adequately paid, has little to gain and much to lose from crime (Scott, 1977).

Such a cultural change will not be easy to bring about, even employing the critical period technique, because the very persons who have the most opportunity to initiate such a change are those who best fit the individual effort, rags-to-riches stereotype and have no personal reasons for bringing about change. It is not likely to happen in less than a generation, and even then may eventuate only during some critical period such as may be brought about by a major breakdown in the economic system. While this is now less likely to happen than it was in 1929, because of the buffering devices instituted at that time, it could still happen, and it is essential that a substantial proportion of people be ready to take appropriate action.

CONCLUSIONS

The general theory of critical periods applies to any living system, no matter what the level of organization, provided only that the organizational process or processes concerned proceed more rapidly during certain time periods. At any level, this is usually early in the organization process. Consequently, critical period research must concentrate on two basic problems: identification and description of the organizational process or processes involved, and measurement of the speed and timing of the processes. Negatively, if an organizational process continues at a constant or nearly constant rate, there can be no critical period.

The technique of modifying the outcome of an organizational process depends on its nature. Very different means must be employed to manipulate a growth process from those required to alter a process of social organization, but this does not necessitate a change in the basic concepts of the general theory.

One of these is the principle that reorganization (that is, attempting to reinstate the phenomena of a critical period) is impossible without de-organization. Second, as they become organized, all living systems become increasingly stable and resistant to de-organization. Once a system has reached a stable state it is extremely difficult to modify its organization in any fundamental way. The principal options are then reduced to either working within the system, extending it, or deliberately attempting to disorganize it, as is the case of political revolutions. The last option is always dangerous. Whether or not the revolutionaries use violence deliberately, social disorganization is itself a major cause of harmful violence (Scott, 1975).

One of the most serious problems of social organization is how to bring about desirable social change without violence and in a peaceful and constructive manner. Utilizing critical period theory, one possibility is to watch for spontaneous or naturally-occurring cases of de-organization. The ultimate example of this sort is death, a phenomenon that does occur regularly on the organismic level. The organization of the dead person is totally destroyed, and since the behavior of an infant is organized anew and partially independently from that of the preceding generation, change in social organization is inevitable. As noted above, the death of an individual, particularly if the person holds a key position in the organization, will disrupt organization on the social level, producing a secondary critical period that can be utilized.

Further, a social system can be studied from the viewpoint of discovering institutions that may be vulnerable to change. In our culture, one such institution is that of education. Like other institutions its own organization tends to be stable, but in performing its basic function of transferring information from one generation to the next it acts as a change agent by selective transmission, even if this is confined only to adding new information.

The last is a major function of higher institutions of learning, that of research and discovery. This is not a critical period phenomenon, but the time of attendance at a college or university is often a critical period for individual students for whom the experience is de-organizing. Consciously or unconsciously, competent teachers may have major effects on their students during this period of reorganization. Earlier critical periods in the educational process may also be readily identified; for example, the time of first attendance in school, and the critical period for language learning. Further, many young people make crucial career decisions during adolescence.

Comparing critical period phenomena on the physiological level with those on the level of social organization, it is obvious that knowledge of critical periods in the development of an embryo is chiefly useful in avoiding harm to the organism; we still do not know how to use them to make a better baby. On the other hand, critical periods in the development of a social relationship or of a larger social system may be used to motivate that organization in a variety of directions that may be more or less useful and adaptive. Here are problems that are amenable to research, such as how to foresee the effects of changes in a complex system, and methods of increasing the rate of social change. We know that technological changes in a culture often proceed very rapidly, but changes in social organization tend to be slow and resistant to change.

Then, there is the problem of relations among critical periods on different levels of organization. In the past, biologists have been primarily interested in critical periods in the embryonic development of organisms. Events at this time may have extensive effects on the behavior of an organism and so influence what happens in critical periods of behavioral development. A developmental accident during a critical period of brain formation may render a child unable to respond adequately during the critical period of language learning.

Ethologists and comparative psychologists have been principally interested in the critical period for primary social attachment and species identification. Often such research has concentrated on the individual, neglecting the fact that attachment is a two-way process leading to the formation of dyadic and other more extensive social relationships. The period is not only critical for the individual but also for organization on the social level. Its manipulation has extraordinarily wide significance. It should be possible to rear children in such ways that they become attached and socialized not only to a few special individuals, but to the entire human race.

Finally, we should not forget the principle of feedback. Organizational processes on lower levels not only affect those on higher levels, but those on higher levels can modify those on lower ones. Social organization on the cultural and institutional levels can reduce the chances for deformities produced during critical periods of organ formation and increase the chances for mutually beneficial social attachment. And although institutional and cultural organizations tend to resist change, in common with all living systems, the phenomena and general theory of critical periods offer opportunities to pace and to direct such changes.

REFERENCES

Arnold, T. W. *The folklore of capitalism*. New Haven: Yale University Press, 1937.

Guhl, A. M., & Allee, W. C. Some measureable effects of social organization in chickens. *Physiological Zoology*, 1944, *17*, 320–347.

Landauer, T. K., & Whiting, J. W. M. Infantile stimulation and adult stature of human males. *American Anthropologist*, 1964, *66*, 1007–1028.

Lenneberg, E. H. *Biological foundations of language*. New York: Wiley, 1967.

Lieberman, P. *The biology and evolution of language*. Cambridge: Harvard University Press, 1984.

Lorenz, K. Der Kumpan in der Umwelt des Vogels. *Journal für Ornithologie*, 1935, *83*, 137–214, 289–413.

Moore, K. L. *The developing human: Clinically oriented embryology*. Philadelphia: Saunders, 1982.

Moreno, J. L. *Who shall survive: Foundations of sociometry, group psychotherapy, and psychodrama*. New York: Beacon House, 1934.

Panksepp, J., Conner, R. L., Forster, P. K., Bishop, P., & Scott, J. P. Opioid effects on social behavior of kennel dogs. *Journal of Applied Ethology*, 1983, *10*, 63–74.

Scott, J. P. Critical periods in behavioral development. *Science*, 1962, *138*, 949–958.

Scott, J. P. The process of primary socialization in canine and human infants. *Child Development Monographs*, 1963, *28*, 1–47.

Scott, J. P. *Early experience and the organization of behavior*. Belmont, CA: Wadsworth, 1968.

Scott, J. P. The biological basis of social behavior. In J. P. Scott & S. F. Scott, (Eds.) *Social control and social change*. Chicago: University of Chicago Press, 1971.

Scott, J. P. Violence and the disaggregated society. *Aggressive Behavior*, 1975, *1*, 235–260.

Scott, J. P. Agonistic behavior: function and dysfunction in social conflict. *Journal of Social Issues*, 1977, *33*, 9–21.

Scott, J. P. (Ed.) Critical periods in organizational processes. In F. Falkner & J. M. Tanner (Eds.), *Human growth* (Vol. 1, 2nd ed.). New York: Plenum, 1986.

Scott, J. P. Critical periods in organizational processes. In F. Falkner & J. M. Tanner (Eds.) *Human growth (Vol. 3)*. New York: Plenum, 1979.

Scott, J. P. *Critical periods in organizational processes*. Unpublished manuscript, Bowling Green State University, 1986.

Scott, J. P., & Fuller, J. L. *Genetics and the social behavior of the dog.* Chicago: University of Chicago Press, 1965.

Scott, J. P., Stewart, J. M., & DeGhett, V. J. Critical periods in the organization of systems. *Developmental Psychobiology,* 1974, *7,* 487–513.

Stockard, C. R. The artificial production of a single median cyclopean eye in the fish embryo by means of seawater solutions of magnesium chloride. *Archiv für Entwicklungsmechanik,* 1907, *23,* 249.

Stockard, C. R. Developmental rate and structural expression. *American Journal of Anatomy,* 1921, *28,* 115–277.

Biographical Notes

C. ROBERT ALMLI is Associate Professor of Anatomy and Neurobiology, Preventive Medicine, Psychology, Neural Science, and Occupational Therapy at Washington University School of Medicine, St. Louis, Missouri. He received his doctorate at Michigan State University and has been a faculty member at Ohio University and the University of Illinois, and a Research Scientist at the Worcester Foundation for Experimental Biology. He serves on the Editorial Boards of *Developmental Psychobiology, Brain Research Bulletin,* and *Neuroscience and Biobehavioral Reviews.* Almli and S. Finger are coauthors of *Early Brain Damage: Vol. 1 Research Orientations and Clinical Observations* and *Vol. 2 Neurobiology and Behavior.* His scientific publications have centered on the development of sensorimotor integration, effects of early brain damage in humans and other animals, and developmental neurobiology.

CHARLES ANNECILLO received his predoctoral training in Maryland and obtained a Sc.D. from The Johns Hopkins University in 1982. He is a Postdoctoral Clinical Research Fellow in Medical Psychology in the Psychohormonal Research Unit at The Johns Hopkins University and Hospital. He has coauthored several papers with John Money on the syndrome of abuse dwarfism. Most recently he and Money conducted an investigation into the psychodynamics of this unique psychophysiological disorder.

PATRICK BATESON is Professor of Ethology and Director of the Sub-Department of Animal Behaviour at the University of Cambridge. He obtained his B.A. and Ph.D. at Cambridge and then spent two years as a

Harkness Fellow at Stanford University Medical Center. He coedits the series *Perspectives in Ethology,* coedited *Growing Points in Ethology,* edited *Mate Choice,* and recently coauthored *Measuring Behaviour.* His principal research interest is in the development of behavior.

BENJAMIN BEIT-HALLAHMI is Associate Professor of Psychology at the University of Haifa. He received his B.A. from the Hebrew University, Jerusalem, and his M.A. and Ph.D. from Michigan State University. He has been affiliated with the University of Michigan, the University of Pennsylvania, the Hebrew University, and Columbia University, among other institutions. His interests encompass personality theory, the psychology of religion, and the history of psychology. He has edited *Research in Religious Behavior* and coauthored *The Social Psychology of Religion, Twenty Years Later: Kibbutz Children Grow Up,* and *The Kibbutz Bibliography.*

ELLIOTT M. BLASS is a Professor of Psychology and Psychiatry at The Johns Hopkins University. After receiving his Ph.D. from the University of Virginia, Blass spent two years as Postdoctoral Fellow at The University of Pennsylvania. Blass has been a consulting editor for the *Journal of Comparative and Physiological Psychology, Behavioral Neurosciences, Developmental Psychobiology* and *Appetite.* Blass' developmental research has focused on early ingestive mechanisms, brain reward mechanisms, early and prenatal learning. He has been a John Simon Guggenheim Memorial Fellow and a Fulbright-Hayes Research Professor at the Hebrew University of Jerusalem.

MARC H. BORNSTEIN is Professor of Psychology and Human Development at New York University. He received a B.A. from Columbia College and the M.S. and Ph.D. from Yale University. Bornstein was awarded the C. S. Ford Cross-Cultural Research Award from the Human Relations Area Files and the B. R. McCandles Young Scientist Award from the American Psychological Association; he was also a J. S. Guggenheim Foundation Fellow. Bornstein has been Visiting Scientist at the Max-Planck-Institute for Psychiatry in Munich, Visiting Fellow at University College London, Professeur Invité at the Laboratoire de Psychologie Expérimentale in Paris, Child Clinical Fellow at the Institute for Behavior Therapy in New York, and Visiting Professor at the University of Tokyo. Bornstein is coauthor of *Development in Infancy* (with M. E. Lamb); he is editor of *The Crosscurrents in Contemporary Psychology Series,* including *Psychological Development from Infancy* (with W. Kessen), *Comparative Methods in Psychology, Psychology and Its Allied Disciplines* (Vols. 1–3); and he is coeditor of *Developmental Psychology* (with M. E. Lamb). Bornstein has contributed over 100 papers in the areas of human experimental, methodological, comparative, developmental, cross-cultural, and aesthetic psychology.

STANLEY FINGER is Professor of Psychology at Washington University in St. Louis and is also on the school's Neural Science Faculty. He received his B.A. from Hunter College (C.U.N.Y.) and M.A. and Ph.D. from Indiana University. He has published over 50 articles in scientific journals, most dealing with recovery from brain damage. His edited books include *Recovery from Brain Damage* and with C. Robert Almli *Early Brain Damage*. He is also author of a monograph, *Brain Damage and Recovery: Research and Clinical Perspectives* with Donald G. Stein.

ROBERT A. HINDE is Royal Society Research Professor at the University of Cambridge and Honorary Director of the Medical Research Council Unit on the Development and Integration of Behaviour. He received Bachelors degrees from Cambridge and London Universities and the D.Phil. degree from Oxford. He has worked at the Madingley laboratory throughout his postdoctoral career. He is author of *Animal Behaviour*. His current research interests are concerned with the development of social behavior in children.

HELMUT V.B. HIRSCH is Professor of Biological Sciences at the State University of New York at Albany. He received his A.B. from the University of Chicago and his Ph.D. from Stanford University. Hirsch then did two years of postdoctoral work at Johns Hopkins University. He has been a consulting editor for *Developmental Psychobiology* and is currently on the editorial board of the *Journal of Visual Neuroscience*. He studies the effects of early experience on the development of the mammalian visual system.

HOWARD S. HOFFMAN is Professor of Psychology at Bryn Mawr College. He received his undergraduate degree from the New School for Social Research, his Master's degree from Brooklyn College, and his Ph.D. from the University of Connecticut. His scientific publications have centered on the issues of speech perception, aversive controls, imprinting and social attachments, and on the modification of elicited reflexes.

JOHN MONEY received his predoctoral education in New Zealand and obtained a Ph.D. from Harvard University in 1952. He is Professor of Medical Psychology and Pediatrics and director of the Psychohormonal Research Unit at The Johns Hopkins University and Hospital. He has published extensively in both sexology and psychoendocrinology. His most recent book is *The Destroying Angel: Sex, Fitness, and Food in the Legacy of Degeneracy Theory, Graham Crackers, Kellogg's Corn Flakes, and American Health*

History. Others of Money's books include *Man and Woman, Boy and Girl, Love and Love Sickness, Handbook of Sexology,* and *Lovemaps: Clinical Concepts of Sexual/Erotic Health & Pathology, Paraphilia, and Gender Transposition in Childhood, Adolescence, & Maturity.* His next book collects his theoretical writings in sexology and sexosophy.

BARBARA J. MYERS is Assistant Professor of Psychology at Virginia Commonwealth University. She received an A.B. from Earlham College, a M.S. in human development from the University of Maryland, and the Ph.D. in developmental psychology from Temple University. Myers studies social development across the lifespan concentrating on grandmother-mother-child interchanges and how illness affects development in premature infants.

JOHN PAUL SCOTT first became interested in critical periods as an outcome of his Ph.D. dissertation on developmental genetics of the guinea pig at the University of Chicago. Since then he has done extensive research on the development of social behavior in sheep, mice, and dogs. He is author of *Early Experience and the Organization of Behavior,* coauthor with John L. Fuller of *Genetics and the Social Behavior of the Dog,* and editor of *Critical Periods.* He is past-president of the International Society for Developmental Psychobiology, the Behavior Genetics Association, and the International Society for Research on Aggression. Currently Scott is Regents Professor Emeritus of Psychology at Bowling Green State University and a Visiting Scholar at Tufts University.

CATHERINE E. SNOW is Associate Professor at The Harvard Graduate School of Education. She received her doctorate in psychology from McGill University and subsequently worked in the Institute for General Linguistics at the University of Amsterdam, where she conducted research on age differences in second language learning. She has published extensively on social-interactive factors affecting first language acquisition, cultural differences in parent-child interaction, emergent literacy, factors affecting school literacy skills, and second language acquisition. She edits *Applied Psycholinguistics* and codirects the Child Language Data Exchange System.

CATHERINE TAMIS-LeMONDA is a doctoral candidate at New York University where she received her B.A. Her interests center on mother-infant interaction and infant cognitive development, especially visual perception, habituation, recognition memory, and play and language development during the second year of life. Tamis-LeMonda has received various honorary awards and is currently a Helbein scholar and NYU fellow.

SUZANNAH BLISS TIEMAN is a Research Associate and Adjunct Associate Professor at the State University of New York at Albany. She received her A.B. from Cornell University and her Ph.D. from Stanford University. Tieman then spent three postdoctoral years at the University of California, San Francisco. Her publications have focussed on the transfer of information between the left and right halves of the brain and the role of experience in the development of the mammalian visual system.

Author Index

Subject Index